A Boy's Civil War Story

Charles Nagel

Fig. 1: Charles Nagel

A Boy's Civil War Story — Charles Nagel

Originally published in 1935 by Eden Publishing House, St Louis, Mo. USA. (Gemeinfrei).

This edition edited and with added notes and illustrations from Wikipedia and other sources

© 2017 Stephen A. Engelking (Editor)

ISBN: 978-1-9998691-8-2

PREFACE

This is the simple account of a boy's actual experiences. It makes no pretense to literary merit, and is published for private circulation.

C.N.

Editor's Preface

I was shown a copy of this book by my lawyer friend Jamie Elick of Bellville and it immediately appealed to me because of the considerable content relating to my ancestors and the area of Cat Spring and Millheim where they originally settled.

A small group of interested persons have been sharing the task of republishing relevant material, the forgotten treasures of Texas history. We go by the name of *The Millheim Literary Circle* and have already uncovered a number of interesting works and brought them to print again.

So it was decided to republish this book and Jamie was kind enough to lend me his copy of the original as a starting point. This particular copy in his possession has been personalized by the author himself for his friend Francis G. Lange dated May 27 1937. Lange has written a note underneath the dedication:

> "Mr. Charles Nagel (loaned me $200 (paid back) in Graduate School. He was Secretary of Commerce during Taff Administration. He gave me this copy about his boyhood in Texas."

Many of the references to persons or events will probably not be clear to the reader of today so I have added footnotes to the original text as way of explanation. These are mostly biographical information which I have generally gleaned from the online encyclopedia Wikipedia unless otherwise stated. I apologize in advance if I have sometimes provided information obvious to the informed reader but many may not be familiar with this part of history and may appreciate the additional historical data. I have also taken the liberty of adding some relevant illustrations as the original work contained no pictures of the characters or places mentioned. Of course space forbids that I would include all the endless information available in Wikipedia and other online sources but the reader is encouraged to follow up in more detail any items which are of particular interest.

I hope the reader will enjoy this extremely well written book as I have done and hopefully learn something about the origins of the German-Texans as well as the biography of this most interesting and highly educated character.

Stephen Engelking.

Table of Contents

INTRODUCTION	15
EARLY YOUTH IN THE FIRST SETTLEMENT	19
MILLHEIM —THE GERMAN SETTLEMENT	51
THE OLD HOME IN GERMANY	69
OUR NEW HOME IN MILLHEIM	83
HOME LIFE	95
MAETZE'S SCHOOL	109
PLAY AND WORK AT HOME	127
SPORTS ALL OUR OWN	161
THE LIFE OF OLDER PEOPLE	191
THE SHADOW OF THE WAR	205
WE LEAVE HOME	225
MONTEREY	261
WE GO TO SEA	287
THE FINISH	319
APPENDIX	339
Alphabetical Index	441
Picture References	459
Further Reading	467

List of Illustrations

Fig. 1: Charles Nagel 3
Fig. 2: Razor Back Hog (Feral Pig) 20
Fig. 3: Wild Turkey(Meleagris gallopavo) 21
Fig. 4: Male Pantanal Jaguar 25
Fig. 5: Florida Water Moccasin Agkistrodon piscivorus conanti 26
Fig. 6: Western diamondback rattlesnake (Crotalus atrox), responsible for the majority of venomous snakebites in North America, coiled in defensive posture with rattle erection. 27
Fig. 7: Young Hare" (German: Feldhase) Albrecht Dürer 1502. 28
Fig. 8: Sam Houston, circa 1850 32
Fig. 9: American Alligator (A. mississippiensis) 42
Fig. 10: Pink variety flower clusters on a Dogwood Tree 50
Fig. 11: The Nagel House Today 80
Fig. 12: Unter den Linden, around 1900 197
Fig. 13: Berlin University in 1850 198
Fig. 14: Robert Gould Shaw Memorial, Boston 214
Fig. 15: Charles Sealsfield 1864 228
Fig. 16: Cerro de la Silla (Saddle Mountain) near Monterey today 257
Fig. 17: Emperor Maximiliano around 1864 258
Fig. 18: Zachary Taylor 261
Fig. 19: Edmund J. Davis (1827-1883) 277
Fig. 20: Ulysses S. Grant 278
Fig. 21: The Blücher Memorial in Berlin, Unter den Linden 292
Fig. 22: Swordfish (Xiphias gladius) 294

Fig. 23: Menticirrhus americanus (Kingfish) 295

Fig. 24: A statue of Gambrinus with a goat at the Falstaff brewery in New Orleans 296

Fig. 25: Tartuffe 336

Fig. 26: Unfinished cathedral, 1856 with 15th-century crane on south tower. 342

Fig. 27: Bayard Taylor 343

Fig. 28: Photograph of Johann Strauss II by Fritz Luckhardt 346

Fig. 29: Thousands of gravestones are crammed into the Old Jewish Cemetery in Prague. 348

Fig. 30: The Old New Synagogue in Prague 349

Fig. 31: Gardekürassier etwa 1830 351

Fig. 32: Polish uhlans from the Army of the Duchy of Warsaw 1807–1815 January Suchodolski painting 353

Fig. 33: Isaac I. Hayes portrait by Mathew B. Brady, circa 1860-1875 362

Fig. 34: Euphrosyne Parepa-Rosa 372

Fig. 35: Ben DeBar as Falstaff 373

Fig. 36: Henry Hitchcock 377

Fig. 37: Thomas McIntyre Cooley 379

Fig. 38: Rudolf Virchow 385

Fig. 39: Franz von Lenbach Self-portrait (1903) 387

Fig. 40: Adolph Wagner 388

Fig. 41: James Coolidge Carter 389

Fig. 42: Frederick III, German Emperor 395

Fig. 43: The Marriage of Victoria, Princess Royal and Prince Frederick William of Prussia, 25 January 1858, by John Phillip. 396

Fig. 44: Albert Niemann 399

Fig. 45: Oscar Wilde - Photograph taken in 1882 by Napoleon Sarony — 408

Fig. 46: Self portrait by Keppler — 409

Fig. 47: Carl Schurz is Don Quixote in this cartoon by Thomas Nast from Harper's Weekly of April 6, 1872 — 410

Fig. 48: Rutherford B. Hayes — 412

Fig. 49: Columbia wearing a warship bearing the words "World Power" as her "Easter bonnet", cover of Puck (April 6, 1901) — 413

Fig. 50: The Chair of John Stuart Mill - currently in the editor's custody — 422

Fig. 51: Anders Zorn's Portrait of William Howard Taft — 428

INTRODUCTION

After some hesitation I have taken courage to write of my boyhood. Perhaps I should make some excuse, as we sing and speak upon invitation—a salutary restraint upon prospective bores.

My reason, however slender for others, is rather persuasive to me. It must appeal to any one fortunate enough to have a family, and wise enough to cherish an intimate relation with younger generations. It is urged by my children—not without generous encouragement by my wife. There are five children, now ranging from forty-seven to thirty in age. Each has at some stage in her or his life exacted from me a kind of promise to put down in black and white the story of my early experiences, which I have from time to time related to them for their entertainment. True, they were quite young then—too young to know how difficult it is to write about one's self—to give personal experiences in an impersonal way. Neither were they old enough to have their wish reflect a safe judgment, except in so far as a child's intuition may be a better guide than an adult's criticism. A proper sense of values is a rare quality. But it is most essential when, as Mark Twain says, a "book is intended mainly for the entertainment of boys and girls," with the hope that "it will not be shunned by men and women on that account."

By this time these children are reinforced, in a manner quite irresistible to an old man. There are six grandchildren. Even now I see the oldest one, supported by the anticipating countenances of the others, with her wistful expression, half hoping, half pleading, wondering whether she can induce grandfather to abandon his patronizing nonsense, and get him started on some of his real stories that she knows he has stored away in his head, and of which she has heard only remote echoes from her mother.

There are still others—chiefly friends of advanced years—who feel a natural tolerance for the disposition of old age to reminisce. Their encouragement is the more persuasive because their own active lives have left something to tell. As they withdraw from the scenes of conflict, their sympathy with the child's world becomes the more trustworthy. Finally, I lean upon the counsel of other well-wishers and tempters, kindly listeners of all ages, of whose sincerity of purpose I can make no question.

I am well aware that every life has its phases of interest. But inasmuch as they can not all be written, there may be the more reason for choosing a life here or there which exemplifies the peculiar conditions of a particular time or environment. Perhaps I may assume this role. My early youth, it is true, was just a part of a common experience under perhaps unique conditions. But during the Civil War[a] I was thrust into a turmoil of trials and even dangers that in the hands of a facile writer might well take on the form of romance and fiction. This circumstance encourages me to accept the part of an amateur's task. I do not boast of challenges issued by me. I can only recount how in the course of my young life it fell to me to accept a few. I was merely a victim or subject of circumstances, for the creation of which I could by no stretch of imagination claim remotest credit.

a The American Civil War was an internal conflict fought in the United States (U.S.) from 1861 to 1865. The Union (i.e., The United States) faced secessionists in eleven Southern states grouped together as the Confederate States of America. The Union won the war, which remains the bloodiest in U.S. history.

I have in mind that to my friends the experiences of the Civil War constitute the chief interest. But to give the proper setting, I must try to picture the life of the little colony of which our family was a part—in the far South before the Civil War. To do this I must give some account of how these people came as immigrants to this country; the conditions under which they settled; and, finally, the ordeals of the war, with all its consequences to us. A distinguished general once listened to my story with that kindly interest which older men are wont to extend to each other. I had listened to him with the same interest, no doubt with better reason. But having written his own story he suddenly turned upon me to say that if I did not write mine, I ought to be shot. He added that every military action of the Civil War had been described in one form or another; but that nowhere had any one given an adequate picture of the Union civilian of the Civil War in the South, particularly not when that civilian was a German immigrant with scarcely time enough to have been naturalized. The dear General quite impressed me with his sincerity and with my responsibility. Since then the Great War has consigned all such experiences to relative obscurity. It seems almost presumptuous to speak of the joys and trials and final escape of a mere boy, when since then thousands upon thousands were mowed down in mass destruction.

Even so there may be some truth in what he said. In any event, my tacit promise to my children will have been kept, and I shall know that if by this time my story proves more attractive to their children than it continues to be to them, the greater will be my satisfaction and the deeper their pleasure.

Substantially everything I shall tell relates to a time when I was under fifteen years of age. Many years and many experiences, good and bad, sweet and sad, have served to blur detail of this or that situation. In the main, however, my recollection is very clear of what befell me. Some of the things that were part of current gossip, or were even accepted as true, I shall use with care, because maturer judgment may consign them to the region of extravagance or fiction.

After writing my story I came upon quite an extensive correspondence, mostly letters from my parents to relatives abroad, covering the period in question, and earlier and later years. There are also some of my own letters. I find it unnecessary in any essential to correct the impressions which I have sought to relate. Indeed, I am amazed at the confirmation which these letters provide. The explanation is perhaps a simple one. In calling to mind those early days, I find that I see everything in the shape of pictures. Only father's straitened financial condition after the war saved me from the hazardous ambition to become an artist, as the desire to become an actor was abruptly cured by seeing one performance of Hamlet by Booth. The impulse must have been strong. Every detail of scenes—men, women and children, the animal world, forest and prairie stand out in clear relief. If I could now command an artist's pencil or brush, this attempt at reproduction might take a more happy shape. As it is, I must have only the one care, to have imagination properly restrained by essential fact.

A Boy's Civil War Story

EARLY YOUTH IN THE FIRST SETTLEMENT

I was born August 9, 1849. Until I was six years old we lived on a small and rather secluded farm in Colorado County, Texas, at a point called Saint Bernardo (named after a river which was noted chiefly for an abundance of water when it was not needed and none at all when it was). The house stood less than a mile back from the stream, half hidden among trees, mostly black jack oaks[a]. Our view was limited, because to the south we were cut off from the great stretch of prairie to the Gulf of Mexico by an arm of modest forest—the home of rabbits (cotton tail), squirrel and wild turkey, and even razorback hogs[b]. Our outlook beyond the picket fence was upon neglected

---

a *Quercus marilandica* (blackjack oak) is a small oak, one of the red oak group *Quercus sect. Lobatae*. It is native to the eastern and central United States, from Long Island to Florida, west as far as Texas, Oklahoma, and Nebraska. There are reports of a few isolated populations in southern Michigan, but these appear to represent introductions.

b Razorback and wild hog are American colloquialisms, loosely applied to any type of feral domestic pig, wild boar or hybrid in North America.

grounds, with the gnarled roots of trees exposed, and open pasture beyond where cattle grazed, always grouped to the artist's taste, and horse and mule were sometimes

Fig. 2: Razor Back Hog (Feral Pig)

"staked" to feed. Then upon a pond which to us was a lake, favorite resting place for wild geese and ducks during their wanderings north and south. Beyond that, the Saint Bernardo with its banks of clean white sand, set off by picturesque cottonwood trees, arranged as it were to tempt the skill of a modern etcher. A ride of but fifteen minutes left all this behind, to bring us out upon the endless prairie, with a tree only here and there to accentuate the space; and with cattle of varied ownership, in haphazard artistic groupings to test the owner's eye.

It was for us to keep a lookout upon our wandering animals. The annual round-up was determined largely by the direction which members of the herds were known to have taken; and although we did not think or speak in learned terms, we knew that cattle like people are given to

EARLY YOUTH IN THE FIRST SETTLEMENT

Fig. 3: Wild Turkey(Meleagris gallopavo)

travel in company or in solitude—to be as it were individualists or socialists.

Of this early life my memory is necessarily vague, although certain experiences that serve to mark its character stand out in strong relief. No canvas by Shreyer[a]—not

---

a   Adolf Schreyer (July 9, 1828 Frankfurt-am-Main–July 29, 1899 Kronberg im Taunus) was a German painter, associated with the Düs-

even his great picture of horses tearing panic-stricken before the approaching flames—can ever give me the vivid impression of the sudden descent upon us at our gates of a band of wild horses—mustangs, we called them. In broad daylight they came down upon us, in a mad rush as though formed for attack. I simply gaped in silent wonder as they reared and ran in a circle under the hanging branches and amid threatening roots, neighing their call to the wild. But our elders told us that these mustangs were trying to lure our horses to join them in their life of freedom. We may wonder why the conquest was not reversed then and there, as was done in time when the horse was given its true value. But not then, when rumor had it that my father had bought his first horse for a pair of trousers, and his first cow for a pair of shoes; and surely father was never known to get the best of a bargain. For he, a graduate in medicine at the University of Berlin, had come with the true pioneer's dream, and unpreparedness. Health and freedom were to be found in the conquest of plain and forest, and medicine was to be avoided rather than used. As the sequence will show, chills and fever in which Texas seemed to specialize, aided by other more serious ailments, soon dispelled that dream. The incessant appeal of sufferers who had learned of father's training, by degrees pointed the way back into his profession. Incidentally, it is more than likely that the farmer's life was not quite what it had been supposed to be; and that sliding back into the chosen avocation afforded a welcome solution to a more and more perplexing problem.[a]

But the appearance of mustangs at our gate was no more

   seldorf school of painting.
a Charles Nagel's father, Hermann Nagel was born in Pritzwalk in 1820. His father had been a miller. Hermann Nagel studied Medicine in Halle, Würzburg and Berlin. He was a liberal thinker and married the daughter of a pastor

than the high point of a common experience. It marked the life of freedom and hardship. I feel that I heard the wolves at night; although proper tribute to my ability to sleep tells me that probably I heard them in my dreams; and they now appear so real, because in those days of my boyhood I saw and sometimes chased them. Not that I ever captured one. But the air of early Texas would prompt even a boy to try to lasso anything from a wolf in the open to an alligator on shore; with the surprising revelation that one is as agile to escape the noose, as the other is to catch it in his jaws. Perhaps I really did not hear the wild turkeys; but who will say that I did not, when a hunter would go out an hour before supper to bring in the next day's feast. To this day I can not hear the call of wild geese or ducks on their weary journey North or South without bringing back the deep blue sky or the starry heavens of amazing clearness and beauty; without seeing again the long wedge-shaped lines of travelers, and listening to the quaint quack of command which allows the leader, having borne the brunt of the movement, to fall back for a lighter task, and sending forward to the point of honor another who has had the chance to save his strength. Animals know and depend upon leadership as men do. Even a cow adorned with a bell will assume the walk of conscious distinction. These flocks of thousands of ducks and geese descending upon the pond not more than a quarter of a mile away, anticipating the manners that prevail during the luncheon hour in modern restaurants, created a racket and din that might not arouse an army, but before which any attempt at ordinary speech would yield in despair. It is no doubt true that I did not really catch the largest fish that was ever caught, but while I have since then seen a whale or two, none has ever impressed me with its enormous proportions like the first thirty pound catfish that I saw hauled to the bank. And as for snakes, the unattractive brutes in the

Zoo look like fake imitations compared to my youthful impressions.

But I must be fair and not leave the menagerie of my memory incomplete. I have never seen a bear out of captivity, in all my travels from Texas to Alaska, although they were then said to live in our immediate vicinity. Their tracks left no doubt; and as one of father's letters shows, he came upon them a mile from the house. This, however, disturbed no one but father's horse, his favorite dog who was intimidated the first time in his life, and the neighbors who wasted much time in a vain effort to locate the intruders. Panthers[a], too, we heard of but never saw. Where is the boy who would not hear them by night when he was told by grown people that they were there? Indeed, had not father returned late one night to tell us how his trusted horse

had refused to pass along the road under an overhanging tree, and how upon being punished with spur and whip it had in its despair lunged into the forest and had by a long circuit come back to the road to plunge and run as if possessed? And had we not been told that the following morning a panther had been shot in that tree? What more does a boy want to have him see and hear things in the forest? Under such surroundings every boy is forever dreaming of the challenges of the enemies in the forest; and I was no exception. Day dreams were safe enough. But my real terror was nightmares in the shape of hand to

---

a It is not clear here what is meant by "Panther". Possibly this is the Jagurundi or eyra cat which is a small wild cat native to southern North America and South America. Alternatively it could be the Jaguar (Panthera onca) which is a big cat, a feline in the Panthera genus, and is the only extant Panthera species native to the Americas. The jaguar is the third-largest feline after the tiger and the lion, and the largest in the Americas.

hand fights with Indians, of whom I had not seen so much as a specimen. Worse still, I would imagine myself tied hand and foot with a panther slowly creeping upon me, with all the malice of a cat playing with a mouse. This

Fig. 4: Male Pantanal Jaguar

form of torture pursued me until I took my first ocean voyage, when for many years seasickness provided a common, although a no more welcome substitute. Worse still was the terror when I dreamed that I had studied medicine, and sat in despair by the bedside of a patient, wondering how I should write a prescription when I knew neither Latin nor Greek.

I am glad to be able to say that I never shot a deer. I did shoot at one, and felt so relieved at missing him that I half suspected myself of having done it on purpose. Today I would boast of it. Is there an animal more appealing to human sympathy? So clean, so graceful and so agile, with eyes forever haunting him who has the courage to look into them after the blow has been struck. Deer abounded

Fig. 5: Florida Water Moccasin Agkistrodon piscivorus conanti

in large herds; but while some were shot, somehow the custom of destructive sport, the mere desire to kill never prevailed among us. Perhaps we did the more cruel thing, to bring them up as pets, only to have them finally regain their wanted liberty and to fall the easier prey to some ruthless hunter.

Then there were the squirrel, cunning and graceful, constant warning to hungry boys not to eat more than is good for them; the rabbit, cute and appealing; the coon, prowling in the high grass near the stream's banks; and the opossum, playing that he was dead, or hanging by his tail to prove that he was not—both symbolic of the South; and the skunk, which gave our imported dog Murf his first touch of real pioneer life, and which I would be glad to forget, but can not because of a Sunday suit sacrificed to my first encounter with him. The snake family was well represented. Of the poisonous class there was a variety of

Fig. 6: Western diamondback rattlesnake (Crotalus atrox), responsible for the majority of venomous snakebites in North America, coiled defensive posture with rattle erection.

rattlesnakes, the moccasin[a] and the copperhead. The innocent embraced everything from the striped grass snakes to the huge black snake. The scorpion made his home under the bark of dead trees or fence rails; and the tarantula was a recognized terror to old and young. The razorback, virtually in a native state; the wild turkey[b], whose stiff and lanky legs seem to help him to make time; the prairie chicken and partridge everywhere, although their sudden break almost from under one's feet was startling even to the initiated. The ever present but not popular blackbird, the swallows, Spring's cheering messenger, the mocking

a   Agkistrodon piscivorus is a venomous snake, a species of pit viper, found in the southeastern United States. Common names include variants on water moccasin, swamp moccasin, black moccasin, cottonmouth, gapper, or simply viper.
b   The Wild Turkey (Meleagris gallopavo) is an upland ground bird native to North America and is the heaviest member of the diverse Galliformes.

Fig. 7: Young Hare" (German: Feldhase) Albrecht Dürer 1502.

bird, ever true to his mimicry, tireless court jester in the animal world; the "Kardinal" (red bird) always regal, with a grip of his beak that his captor will remember; the lighthearted larks invading the fields in endless flocks and filling during the mating season the air with song. The owl, bent on mischief when boys are asleep; the crow, a thief, but not of things for which a boy would care; the hawk, arch-enemy of chickens, large and small, making them scuttle for safety as they saw the shadow of the circling menace play upon the ground. Such scenes roused the sense of championship for the innocent and helpless in every boy's heart. No picture was more gladdening to him than to see outraged birds, small as sparrows, scolding and sputtering, lighting upon and pecking at the wicked intruder as he was making his escape. For such should be the fate of all enemies of peaceful homes. About the distinction in taste between hawk and man we never philosophized any more than did the chickens. They ran in fear from one and for help to the other — with no difference in the final result. But I must not forget the buzzard, as repellant nearby as he is graceful in his effortless swing under the vast skies of Texas. Nor the bat, gruesome and mysterious, but fascinating in his dexterous and tireless chase after every object thrown at him. And the pigeon or dove (Taube we called them) whose selection as the symbol of peace even a child would understand. And finally the humming-bird; so tiny and so neat; with colors so varied and so brilliant, darting from flower to flower, to find a blossom with its fragrance untouched, to press his beak deep into it, hanging there as if suspended in the air, until he had exhausted the flower, or had his fill, and darted off out of our world. We never knew where he came from or where he went, lived or nested; and with all our efforts we never caught one. I read now that this tiny bird travels hundreds and hundreds of miles between seasons.

As I watch my grandchildren at play even in the open during vacation, I wonder whether any one can catch the charm of the forest with its unfathomable mysteries — a note more eloquent than language itself; or the feeling of peace and dignity in the prairie's endless expanse, suggesting the eternity that the starry heavens proclaim, unless he has been the unconscious recipient of their impress, while mood and character are responsive and flexible. Can school or training ever supply the intuitive appreciation of an animal's natural grace so native and so true that every movement spells joy, or have Durer's famous drawing of the rabbit win instant approval without knowing why?

English was to us a foreign tongue. We knew most of our animal friends and enemies by their German names. We therefore knew least of those that were peculiar to our country. About them even our parents had to learn with us, and could tell us little. For these we used the American names; and in a fashion their characteristics bridged the way to keener interest in our own country.

Such was the wild life which formed the setting to our primitive home on the border of the forest that looked out upon the great prairie. But this setting gave no idea of the character of that home, which was the simple effort to transplant the advantages and customs of an old civilization into this nook of the wilds; and from that basis to conquer by combining the comforts of the old with the freedom of the new world. How the house was built I do not know. I revisited the spot for the first time in 1909, forty-three years after I had last seen it, and found not a sign of habitation, although the black jack trees seemed to stand in their old integrity. However, I do remember the general condition of the home. There was an old double log house reenforced with clay, and without windows. There was the usual passage between the two doors opening into the two rooms, if they may be so dignified. Father and mother seem to have depended upon this house in a measure while they were building their real home; and this was unexpectedly delayed because father had been cheated out of some money and did not know how to provide the window panes. Even defalcations did not run over two figures then. Later we used the house for storing

EARLY YOUTH IN THE FIRST SETTLEMENT

corn on one side and as shelter for horses on the other. It had probably in its time been occupied by "white trash"; and even bore a hint of housing for slaves, in days when slavery was more common in that section than it had now come to be among the newcomers. From it opened out the customary cornfield, just beyond the very rare, but rather complete vegetable garden, all surrounded with the old-fashioned and picturesque zigzag rail fence, which has played so unique a part in the romance of our political history. No one in our little community ever appealed to his rail splitting skill for promotion. But every one of us, even those who took their lessons by watching others, learned enough to appreciate later in life the speech of Lincoln when accepting the compliment for having split a particular rail carried into the convention hall by his friends, he deprecatingly added that "I might have split a better rail than that." In any event, our fence withstood all ordinary attacks; always excepting the enterprising and resourceful American hog which, lured by the novel attractions of real corn, vegetables and melon, seemed to be able to circumvent all the obstacles presented by German precaution and thoroughness.

Of the family home proper I have only a dim remembrance. The walls were made of clay and straw and gravel, probably of the adobe character, with porches, no doubt to protect the walls rather than the inmates from wind and weather. Perhaps two bed rooms and a common sitting and dining room, with a fireplace large enough to take the common hickory or oak logs, of which we had an abundance; and, finally, a board lean-to kitchen. Contrary to modern custom trees had been cut only to make room for the house; so that we had perfect shade. The well under the trees from which we drew our water supply looked cool and fresh in its natural setting. Altogether, the little

Fig. 8: Sam Houston, circa 1850

place in its neatness and simple order seemed to defy its setting, and even today would stand comparison with many a farm that bears the mark of decay rather than progress.

Maids there were none. How my mother met her task I can not imagine. There were two children besides myself; my brother Paul, two years younger than I; and my sister Helene (Elly we called her), a baby when we left the place, about 1855, after my parents had lived there for eight years. But now and then there was a man to help out. Father's time was gradually being absorbed by his profession, making his rounds on horseback, covering a circuit of say ten miles or more in either direction. Mother—again I say how she did it is a mystery to me—in addition to the common household duties, took care of the vegetable garden, aided by such help as we might from time to time secure, or the children could give; and, incidentally, prepared the prescriptions written by father. Fortunately for her and no doubt unfortunately for the patients, medicines were at that time still comparatively scarce. Under these conditions, men who were employed to manage the small acreage in cultivation, helped out in the house where they could. We were so to speak a cooperative society in the most generous sense. Of these men I remember one in particular, a man of education and refinement, who as so many others had probably escaped from the turmoil of 1848 in Germany[a], and had come to make his fortune with nought to rely upon but his hands, his courage and his mind. To me and even to the younger children he gave some of his spare time; and on one occasion, as I clearly recollect and have reason to recall, he rescued Paul and me from imminent danger. It was a sultry day, and we were playing on the bare ground under the shingle roof of the porch. Near us lay our black dog, and we were moving closer to him, fascinated by beautiful white foam that was flowing from his mouth. Suddenly we were picked up by a strong arm and thrown into the sitting room. The door was slammed to; we heard a shot, and were told what I understand better now, that one of our pets had to be killed because he was mad. Soon after this man left us. He walked off with all his possessions tied in a bandanna handkerchief, fastened to a hickory stick carried over his shoulder. We never heard of him again until some years after, during the Civil War, father and I, despairing of our efforts to make our escape into Mexico, stumbled upon

a The immigrants coming over at this time were referred to as the 'forty-eighters'.

him; and I at least for the second time owed my protection from impending danger to him. But that is another story. Horses we had only two at that time. One the rather impressive grey, used only by father in making his professional circuit. I really remember him chiefly because of what we were told about the capers he cut at the time of his meeting with the bears, and his good sense in refusing to go under the leaning tree with the panther all set to pounce upon him. Such experiences soon taught us to have greater respect for the judgment of a horse than for our own. For illustration, we knew that a horse and certainly a mule may be trusted to scent with absolute certainty the danger of a bog; and while a fool may punish an animal for refusing to go upon unsafe bottom, the horse will never permit him to suffer the penalty which he has earned. The other was in every respect a horse of a different color. A roan of advanced years named "Sam" by us — no doubt the expression of warmest patriotism. If we were still strangers to Uncle Sam, we all knew and loved Sam Houston[a]. Sam was the ideal horse for youthful equestrian experiments. He was too old to feel any temptation to throw off terrified boys, and his pace was gentle enough to arouse the envy of a family rocking chair. Nevertheless, my first attempt to sit this horse was not free from anxiety. Bareback riding, or a saddle without stirrups presents demands upon a boy's ability to balance, and to hold on

---

a Samuel "Sam" Houston (March 2, 1793–July 26, 1863) was an American politician and soldier, best known for his role in bringing Texas into the United States as a constituent state. His victory at the Battle of San Jacinto secured the independence of Texas from Mexico in one of the shortest decisive battles in modern history. He was also the only governor within a future Confederate state to oppose secession (which led to the outbreak of the American Civil War) and to refuse an oath of allegiance to the Confederacy, a decision that led to his removal from office by the Texas secession convention.

with the knees, that even the gentlest intention of old Sam would not necessarily meet; at least not in the boy's mind. However, my experiences in falling off were reserved for the peculiar satisfaction of a small mule, who in my opinion must have received his early impressions in Indian and Mexican camps, and his later training as a trick performer in a circus. He taught me that "eternal vigilance is the price of liberty" long before I suspected the universality of that rule's application, or heard of the period in our history when that slogan inspired the people, or this later period when it is so sadly neglected. No, Sam lives in my kindly remembrance, even though he threatened to lie down with me in the Saint Bernardo, on one of the few occasions when it did not need water and had it; and even though his gentle pace forever deprived me of the ability to enjoy the trot of a true saddle horse.

But our ever loyal and indeed only pet was "Murf" — no doubt of the bull dog species. I can not quite make myself believe that he was brought from the other side. Money was scarce, and in those days a sea voyage of say eight weeks was complicated enough without the care of a pet dog. Nevertheless, that is my impression, enforced by father's great love for dogs, the fact that this species was not native to a country that had barely emerged from Mexican supremacy, and because father speaks of him in describing his early encounter with the three bears. Whatever the truth may be, there was "Murf" — a dog whose story would be more fascinating than mine, provided an apt hand could be found to write it. He was father's unfailing companion, accompanying him on all his short rides, and on many of his long ones. His last trip was ten miles — nothing unusual. Father had to remain away over night. Murf (known far beyond our child's world, and the pet everywhere), was given a pillow to sleep upon, which he gratefully accepted, and laid his weary head upon it; no doubt to dream of his many conflicts and conquests, but never to wake again. My memory of him covers only a few years, and with the exception of some thrilling incidents, rests with the comforting impression of the name which he had made for himself for loyalty and courage. I wonder how often our best impulses may be traced to such early and humble influences. By mutual consent he was the accepted guardian of the household, old and young, for it was he who detected and dealt with snakes before we children could stumble upon them. If, owing to weakness in our rail fences, intruders found their way into cornfield or vegetable garden, Murf was trusted to discover and to expel the invaders. Our vegetable garden had peculiar attractions for hogs, as somehow the more or less wild razorback had been supplanted by or had grown into a more sleek and prosperous looking species. It may have been a question of food as it is in other walks of life. At this distance of time I quite sympathize with these hogs for their good taste, and for their resource in finding ways and means to satisfy it. At the time I confess I had no patience with any kind of competition in the enjoyment of water melon, sugar corn, etc., for which small country boys have the traditional sweet tooth. In this conflict for the good things of this world Murf was our friend; and what small loss we may have suffered by inroads upon our preserves, was more than made up by the excitement which Murf provided in carrying out his accepted part. No Shepherd dog ever steered a flock of sheep with more skill and, if you please, with more thoughtful care, than Murf showed in urging a pack of hogs to leave the forbidden premises. So much at least was true in the beginning of the movement. But it must be remembered that while patience may be a predominating trait of a Shepherd dog, it is at best only an acquired and not altogether dependable attribute of a bull dog. It is likewise true that there is something about an offending hog that is much more apt to excite one's ire than is an innocent sheep. Whatever the explanation, Murf's efforts at persuasion never quite won out without the aid of more or less radical measures. Inasmuch as Murf did not know the hog's port of entry, he instinctively (perhaps to get the proper credit) drove the offenders in the direction of the house, the one point which the hogs were least anxious to reach. The process was sometimes brief and sometimes long, but by hook or crook the procession always found its way towards the house, where the hogs were mercifully let out of the enclosure. As is customary on greater occasions, this procession was never unannounced; nor could there be any doubt as to the identity of the hero of the occasion. A squeal of despair would at once herald Murf's loss of patience and resort to more drastic measures, and warn of the approach of the procession of terrified victims. In one respect the process was ever the same. The number of hogs might vary, as might the sizes and colors. But with unfailing custom Murf always had some hog by the ear, leading it as a warning example, while terror held the rest in line until the exit was made. One occasion, however, proved the exception. Later in life I was taught that all simple rules have bewildering exceptions. There was no one present to open the gates to freedom for the captured culprits. Murf had them corralled; he demanded their expulsion, and there was no way of escape. It was a sultry day—enough to make a saint feel contrary. All the doors of the house were wide open, and so were the windows of French design from sill to top. My uncle Louis was there, down with chills and fever, hearing the racket no doubt, but not caring one rap whether school kept or not. "Chills and Fever" was then the unchallenged passport to Texas recognition. I suspect that as applicants for naturalization are now asked whether they have read the Constitution, those of the Texas variety were usually put to the quite obvious proof that they had felt the effects of chills and fever for several seasons. Nor am I sure that the result of the inquiry would be more conclusive in one case than in the other. However, Uncle Louis was now being initiated, or, if you prefer, acclimated. He had moved a lounge close to the outer opening of the sitting room, just opposite the main door. He was reclining with that utter loss of all ambition that nothing can compass like chills and fever. His helplessness, however, was no greater than the despair of the hogs; and the leadership of despair is not monopolized by sheep. Even a hog may take a desperate chance, unmindful of consequences. Thus it was that, led by one bewildered bristling, squealing hog, the whole pack in wild confusion and uproar, broke for the open door, rushed madly across the room, scrambling over my suffering uncle on the lounge, and achieved their freedom from further pursuit by escape through the French window into the open. Murf retired with the sense of duty well performed. Uncle Louis ever after insisted that he had stumbled upon an unfailing cure for chills and fever — much better than quinine or desperate experiments with the extracts of bitter peach kernels — and the hogs became much more wary about entering our garden patch. Indeed, I am strongly inclined to credit even a hog with greater power of reflection and reason than we generally attribute to him, as the following incident will go to show.

We found that the hogs no longer entered our patch in large numbers; but that the visits were usually made by the younger and smaller ones — a few at a time. We found also as did Murf, that while we might surprise these marauders in our patch, we could never catch them. Murf had the burden of detecting them, but was denied the joy of escorting them by the ear to the point of egress. It was a case of all work and no play for Murf, and in a sense perhaps also for us. So we set watches to discover the secret. We found that a few of the smaller pigs had some means of surreptitious entry and escape, and like all great inventions, the trick was simple. Our fences at the corner where the rails crossed each other always rested on some foundation, to keep the lower rail from lying on the bare ground and rotting. Of course, care had to be taken to leave no space that would permit marauders to crawl under the lower rail. This condition had been met, but without guarding against a more subtle danger. The foundation upon which the corners of the fence rested were usually logs. In one instance a very large hollow and rather crooked log had been used. Not to raise the fence too high, this log had been sunk, leaving one hollow end in the enclosure and the other in the open. Some of the smaller hogs had made the discovery and were using this tunnel as their way into and out of the forbidden garden. A mere remedy was easy; but entertainments were scarce, and so we provided them for ourselves when we could. The plan was as simple as had been the pig's use of the hollow log. With some pains and much aid we shifted the log, so that the elbow of the crook rested within the field and the two ends opened outside of it. That part was simple enough; but we were now less interested in saving our garden patch than we were to gloat over the pigs' surprise. Our labor was rewarded beyond all expectations, although patience was the price of our pleasure. The pig had no known schedule for his appearance. Accordingly our meals were cut short, and all plans abandoned to make sure of a perfect view of the pigs' performance. The hours were long and the sun was hot, but the first day's watch brought its reward to two small boys lying in wait, hiding as best they could. Along came a solitary pig, his twisted tail wiggling a little to give token of the self-satisfaction that only a pig can feel. Even his snout and little eyes gave token of inward contentment. Here was the discoverer of the deep secret, known perhaps to a few other pigs, most of them happily too big to share the advantage; but to no one else. Neither dog nor man could suspect the ingenuity of this simple device, laid by man in his ignorance and used by a pig in his wisdom. On he came; written all over him visions of water melon and sugar corn, coveted prize of interfering boys; and the sense of absolute security against capture even in the improbable event of detection. There was the log, and there the well known opening. Just a half unconscious look seemed to suggest a slight change in the lay of the log, and the earth about it seemed to be a little disturbed. But what of that? The water melon and sugar corn were almost in view; and really the hollow log had been placed more conveniently than it had been before; only another proof of how fate rewards the vigilant, and how man in his ignorance serves the ever observing pig. The die was cast. The pig made his entry, and two boys in hiding nearly burst their hickory shirt collars to restrain their mirth. The pig emerged. Water melons and suger corn there were none; something had happened. He could actually hear the other pigs root in the brush nearby —a search for grub which his fortune had taught him to despise. He reflected; the twisted tail stood ready; this was no time for trifling; a problem had to be solved; a situation had to be met. Well, clearly, this had been an accident. There were the water melons and the sugar corn all prepared for the joy of a pig; and here was the hollow log—gateway to the feast. Doubt yielding to judgment, and with just a faint sign of hesitation, the pig turned to make his second entry. But, as if to find some escape from the fate of accident, he advanced upon the other end of the log. He could not fail this time; water melon and sugar corn were not to escape him as easily as that. He entered. Progress seemed to be somewhat slow, as if the culprit sought to delay the fate of the awful final decision. At last he emerged. You may say that pigs have no expression of countenance, but no boys that have had a chance to observe them under such conditions will ever admit the charge. He looked it only for one moment. He gave only one grunt. But no diplomat, seeing all his well laid schemes go up in smoke has ever looked more crestfallen; no candidate defeated on the point of triumph ever gave a sign more eloquent. After that the pig behaved better than either. True, the world was a delusion and a snare, but he bore no resentment. He walked back to his companions, looking as much as possible like any other pig; he resumed his rooting among the shrubs; and pulled down the curtain upon a performance, in which two boys had played only a minor part, and to which they had been the sole audience; because they had not dared to take with them Murf, the chief inspirer of the play, whose resentful eagerness would have brought it to an untimely end.

Such little incidents filled our lives at home. No doubt there were many more similar ones; but my memory does not go back with enough clearness to have me attempt to picture them. To be taken away from home on expeditions was at that early stage so rare a treat that I think I can recall every one of them. I remember sitting on the bank of a stream or lake holding the line in an effort to catch fish under father's guidance. I can not imagine fish enjoying a greater state of security than they did under our combined efforts. We relied upon the old combination of pole, line, hook, cork and bait; good enough in skillful hands, provided there are fish. But inasmuch as a good-sized alligator was in clear view just before us, the chance for catching fish was not immediate. Father's knowledge of alligators

Fig. 9: American Alligator (A. mississippiensis)

was probably not greater than his experience as a fisherman. The line was left in the water, and father held me close with his eye on the alligator, perhaps suspecting the brute of the purpose to sweep me into the water by a lash of his tail. The session was adjourned, with the satisfactory result that I got no fish and the alligator did not get me. Nevertheless, my imagination was fired for other occasions when I saw real alligators. On one of them we camped not far from Eagle Lake, which I pictured as a great pond filled with alligators and barely water enough to cover them. I credited them with the most terrifying roar, indicative of their reputed savagery, until I was told the next morning that I had been listening to the croaking of bull frogs, which in spite of the uproarious noise had probably left the alligators to rest in sweet repose.

That was probably my first camping experience. What boy

can ever forget it? Miles away from home, the horses staked out or hobbled; no tents, but a great fire of dry wood—sometimes for warmth, always for cooking. What boy that ever got his teeth into a piece of fresh beef toasted over wood fire coals, or potatoes baked in wood ashes, can ever permit even the last word of a metropolitan restaurant to efface that first taste? Take a boy who has rolled himself up in his blanket to sleep under the great deep sky, searching for this or that star that has been named to him, and yielding all too readily to the friendly nod of the dipper. How can he ever again feel just that awe of the vastness of the heavens; or sense the first faint suggestion of a belief in eternity? What more could Tolstoi let his hero feel as he lay upon the battlefield, approaching as he thought transition into future life? What more could Kant say when he based the infinite upon our inability to fathom the beginning and the end?

But even camping trips have their variety. One other that I remember before we left for our new home, we had on the banks of the Saint Bernardo. It was a good many miles south, where even in the severest drought the springs provided large pools of fresh water sometimes of great depth. Every kind of fish indigenous to that country was to be found there. We suspected that in spite of the depth alligators did not shun them but found shallow places to their taste; and we knew that because of the unfailing supply of water large herds of roaming cattle could always be found within reasonable distance. Many were the tales about these pools that filled small boys' minds. There was the young man who was bitten by a tarantula, and who, under the influence of the maddening poison, had mounted his horse without saddle or bridle, to race over endless prairies. So much no doubt was true. But the young man recovered and returned; and the ride had to end somewhere, preferably with some miraculous cure. Even a doctor's children lean to miracles. So our young minds, no doubt aided by elderly suggestion, just landed horse and man in the cooling depths of the Saint Bernardo, to the comforting terror of all our enemies within them, and with an extravagant belief in the curative properties of pure water. More authentic was the account of the newly arrived owner, who in an effort to teach his young horse to swim, managed to handle the halter in such fashion as to keep the nose of the horse under water long enough to drown him. This was one of the many prices which we boys in our wisdom charged to experience. And quite reliable was the story of the finish of the rider who undertook to break in a particularly obstreperous young horse. The art of riding a broncho was still in its infancy among us, and therefore the preparations then were elaborate enough to start an ordinary circus now. The plan was this. The horse was to be headed for the prairie, stretching for ten or more miles without a tree. The rider once safely in the saddle, was to be flanked on either side by riders on trustworthy horses. All was arranged for a dead run ahead, and exhaustion was relied upon as the guaranty of ultimate safety. All worked according to program. Without bucking or remonstrance of any kind to the surprise of every one, the three riders swept forward. No three musketeers ever looked more sure of their goal. On they went mile after mile, scattering unsuspecting cattle to the right and left, until they and the horizon were lost to vision in clouds of dust. And then the possibilities of the situation began to dawn upon them. They tugged and fought to change their course. But of no avail; the young horse acted as though he also had had a plan in mind from the start. Nearer and nearer was their approach. The banks of the great pool were actually in sight, and the speed of the mad brute seemed to accelerate. There was no option. It was a case of every man for himself. The two trusted guardians pulled in their willing mounts. But the untamed animal never faltering, with its rider sitting his saddle true to form, went over the bank and disappeared from view, only to rise, gasping for breath, struggling desperately, and gradually swimming to reach the sand beach on the other side. Again the cure was had. This time no doubt the coolness of water worked the charm. Both horse and master had enough; the horse was subdued, and the rider had received a new impression of how fresh horses ought or might be broken in fresh water.

To camp on the banks of such a pool was joy enough. To this day I have as clear a vision of the tales I heard as of the things I really saw. During the afternoon after school we caught some of the ordinary but good fish—probably perch and sunfish and the like, although when they resembled fish found abroad we called them by German names. But for the big fish—the clear water catfish—the lines had to be laid for the night. This we did, on one of our camping trips using strong lines with generous bait. In the morning we had our triumph. A catfish weighing thirty pounds, they said, not content with one bait had taken all three. It was never settled who caught that fish, but it is recorded that bringing him in was one of the earliest Texas efforts at cooperation.

The true sport was still to come. Murf made his last great fight, and this time with a raccoon—no mean antagonist. How it started I do not remember; probably in the high grass on the bank where coons like to hunt. The first I saw were Murf and coon in close embrace in the midst of the pool, supposed to be twenty feet deep. I did think of alligators, because I had heard that they preferred dogs. But barring that, I could have no fear for Murf, who had never been defeated by anything short of a skunk. Our confidence in him was unshakeable. I accepted now that there could be but one outcome. For observation we were not given much chance; for most of the fighting seemed to be had under water. Up they would come, apparently for air, still in that close embrace, and down they would go as if to touch bottom. We could give no help; they were too far out; and Murf might have resented that as a reflection upon his sportsmanship. At last, after a long suspense they came up again. Murf apparently felt no concern, and with a look out of one eye that I defy any human to imitate or to describe, he seemed to say to me, "Don't worry; this is easy"; and having thus set me at ease, down they went again, no noise or fuss, just business. This time they remained under water alarmingly long. Then we saw bubbles, a commotion on the surface, a paw reaching out—it was Murf's—then the nose, and finally the whole dear dog swimming with unruffled determination to our side of the pool. He returned alone—no need to say anything, for who could doubt the outcome so eloquently announced by a speechless dog.

I was then about six years old. I should say it was in 1855. Brother Paul, baby Helene and I comprised about all our child life. Amusement centered largely upon the domesticated animals; and wider interest embraced the wild life of forest and prairie. With a sense of the child's ingratitude, I confess that I can recall every animal that contributed to my pleasure; but have only the vaguest remembrance of the cows or even the chickens that gave me sustenance; barring perhaps a recollection of a rooster's stilted and impudent strut across the ground. We lived far apart; there was neither school nor church, and, indeed, but little chance for communication or association of any kind.

A settlement ten miles away was more promising for collective efforts, and father's practice drew him more and more that way. Millheim[a], in Austin County, no doubt derived from Muehlheim in Germany as it was originally named, and then half Anglicized perhaps to avoid the inevitable and somewhat embarrassing Muleheim; perhaps Americanized without even so much provocation. So we were to desert the region of the Colorado river where we had at least bathed—alligator or no alligator—and go nearer the Brazos river, where we were still to find our adventures. One fine morning the wagons were loaded with our furniture, I perched on the top of one amidst chairs and table and lounge. On we went, eastward ho! farewell to old home, moving along the country road. There was the old gate dividing the neatly kept place from the neglected outside with bare roots of old trees sprawling all over the ground; here the mustangs had made their charge, like a last challenge to our invasion. There was the garden where the big black snake had settled himself in our basket to enjoy the sun, while we were gathering peas and radishes and tomatoes, to carry home. There was the old fence that sometimes kept out the pigs, always with the support of Murf. There was the tree where the owl sat blind in the sunlight, but responding to a shot only by casting feathers right and left and perching one limb higher. There was the puddle of water with frogs splashing in and big black snakes sliding in at our approach. There was the big pond in which we could see the water

a   Millheim was established eight miles south of Bellville in central Austin County about 1845, when a mill was constructed on Clear Creek, a tributary of Mill Creek. The founders of the community were German immigrants who moved southeast through Mill Creek Valley from settlements in the vicinity of Cat Spring. The town received its name in the 1850s at a meeting held in the Engelking and Noltke general store. (https://tshaonline.org/handbook/online/articles/hlm70. Accessed May 22 2017.

from the house when it was not hidden by wild geese and ducks. There was the Saint Bernardo where old Sam had threatened to lie down with me on one of the few days when it held water in embarrassing quantity. All according to rule and custom as it had always been. But father's white horse was gone; trusted old Sam was dead; and Murf had found his last sleep on a friendly pillow far away from home. We were moving beyond our known world. The old home was fading away. We children did not even know whether it would be cared for or neglected. I was six years old, about to start life all over again. There was the first farm. I knew the owner's name. And as other homes were passed I wondered whether they had children; most grown people had. Father and mother probably knew, but they were riding in front, and I could not hear what they said.

Then came the weary ride on a country road until we reached Catspring[a], five miles away. We had heard of it;

a   Cat Spring was founded by immigrants from Oldenburg and Westphalia in 1834 and named for a nearby spring where a puma was killed by one of the German immigrants. The community was the location of Texas' first agricultural society, and was the site of a station on the Missouri-Kansas-Texas Railroad established in the 1890s. The community began to decline after World War II. The families of Marcus Amsler, Ludwig Anton Sigmund von Roeder and Robert J. and Louis Kleberg settled in 1834 where Cat Spring now is. The reports these families senmt to their former homes caused others to follow. (The German Settlers of Millheim (Texas) before the Civil War Author(s): Adalbert Regenbrecht Source: The Southwestern Historical Quarterly, Vol. 20, No. 1 (Jul., 1916), pp. 28-34 Published by: Texas State Historical Association Stable URL: http://www.jstor.org/stable/30234693 Accessed: 22-05-2017 13:39 UTC). Adalbert Regenbrecht writes in this article: "We went in a sailing vessel to New Orleans and arrived there in January, 1856. Thence we went in a steamboat to Galveston, thence in another steamboat to Houston, thence in an ambulance drawn by mules to the farm of said farmer. In April I moved to Millheim,

even knew that there was a storekeeper, quaint old character, with the suggestive name of Soder; a hunchback whose bills his customers were beginning to scrutinize with more and more care. But of that more anon. And still there were a few settlers whose names we had heard, and about whom all else was left to a child's fancy. But people were friendly; still scarce enough to make sure of a kindly greeting to all comers. On we went. There was the last place, not entirely strange—another successful owner, Amslin. How smart it looked under the shade trees. And there lived the daughter, whose fame rested secure in the heart of every boy, for of her it was said that she broke the horses that her brothers were afraid to ride, and in those days ladies used only side saddles. Where is the boy whose fancy would not be aroused by such heroic legend, who later on having had the privilege to ride for five, I say five, miles by the side of this heroine, would still later not be happy to read romance about fair ladies, even if he is over eighty years of age?

After that all was new and strange. The farms were more closely dotted, but none suggested so much as an echo of past account. At last we crossed another stream of sand, called creek, to remind that in case of heavy rain it would go over the banks, and named Constant to perpetuate an otherwise unheralded reputation. We pulled up the steep incline, amid blossoming dogwood[a], Spanish oak with its

where I boarded with E. G. Maetze and lateri with Dr. H. Nagel."

a   Cornus florida (flowering dogwood) is a species of flowering plant in the family Cornaceae native to eastern North America and northern Mexico. An endemic population once spanned from southernmost coastal Maine south to northern Florida and west to the Mississippi River. The tree is commonly planted as an ornamental in residential and public areas because of its showy bracts and interesting bark structure.

picturesque drooping moss, pecan and hickory tree; and there at the very top of a hill we stopped at a new adobe house, the last home of my Texas childhood.

Fig. 10: Pink variety flower clusters on a Dogwood Tree

MILLHEIM — THE GERMAN SETTLEMENT

In a way there was nothing peculiar about this settlement in Austin County—named after the man who had helped pave the way for Houston's fame. But how different it seemed from the conditions we had left. There most of the neighbors seemed to be far away. True, Reichardt was nearby; farmer and stock raiser on a small scale. Also, Uncle Louis Litzman (mother's brother), a farmer in still more modest fashion, one too upon whose aid we could always count, as he could upon ours. Perhaps one or two more, comparative strangers. There was Himly whose name is like an echo, associated with books and like serious things. For aught we knew some may have been poets. Certainly imagination had had its part to prompt men and women to embark upon this Texas venture. And then fifteen miles away, Uncle Dittmar (husband of my mother's sister). He was a dear man, children loved him in spite of his fierce beard. People spoke of his beautiful tenor voice, which he no doubt had a better chance to exercise in those wilds than his profession of surveyor. He had cleared some ground in a remote forest of black jack oaks, where the squatter's title was perhaps more respected than any surveyor's certificate that he might give or receive. In most of these homes there were large families of children, but they had scarcely entered into our young lives.

It was very different in Millheim. Kloss, our neighbor in plain view, came from Rostock, near the Baltic. His neat home nestled among large trees. The abundance of flowers marked the foreigner, as his barn and his thriving field of grain and corn did the man of honest toil and fair training. He had had a city man's trade or profession; but the pioneer's ambition carried him over the top. Even the entrance to his barn was impressive. It had an arch over the gate. I should still feel that it must have been very high but for the memory of our neighbor's accident. His favorite horse ran away with one of the sons (our age). It came tearing past our house, and report said that finding the gate closed, the horse stopped so abruptly that the rider was not only unseated, but rose in the air over the arch and landed in the barnyard. All this was grist to our mill at the time. Relations with the neighbor's boys were rather strained at the moment. There had been a fight, two against two, about a rabbit in the hollow of a tree. The rabbit had escaped, and the fight had been a draw. Anything as humiliating to the enemy as being thrown by his own horse over the arch of the gate into a barnyard among cattle, hogs, and chickens, had a very soothing influence upon our lacerated nerves.

Most influential in our midst was Ernst Gustav Maetze[a], a

a   Maetze, Ernst Gustav (1817–1891). Ernst Gustav Maetze, teacher and legislator, was born in Glogan, Silesia, on September 20, 1817. He graduated from the University of Breslau (now Wroc_aw, Poland) with a degree in Protestant theology, but he preached only one sermon before he became headmaster of the intermediate school at Bernstadt in Silesia. He participated in the German revolutionary movement of 1848 and in the early 1850s immigrated to Texas, where he first taught at a private school at Millheim, Austin County. Shortly afterwards Maetze founded the first public school in Millheim and subsequently taught there for twenty-seven years. In the election of 1888, about ten years after his retirement as a teacher, Maetze won election to the Texas Senate from District Twelve. He served as a member of twelve committees in the Twenty-first and Twenty-second legislatures and chaired the Committee on Rules. He was president pro tem of the Senate when he

graduate of Breslau, I believe; one of the many who had barely made the border after the revolution of 1848, and who was now to be our teacher, giving impressions and inspiration far beyond our youthful appreciation. His home, too, was almost hidden by trees. Shrubs and flowers greeted one at the front gate, and living chiefly by his profession, his garden was more important than his farm. It appears that Maetze had gone to New Ulm, and was working for a farmer when Engelking[a] met him and induced him to come to Millheim as a tutor for his children—thus laying the foundation for what came to be our common school. If not a trained, he was a born teacher.

Next came Engelking, a graduate of Bonn, at law, I think, who now dispensed justice by giving fair measure in calicoes, ropes, molasses, coffee, etc., to the customers of his country store. Again the farm was an incident to his main business. He was married to a von Roeder[b], member of a family of nobility, some of whom had come early enough

died at his home in Millheim on October 12, 1891. (Handbook of Texas Online, Rudolph L. Biesele, "Maetze, Ernst Gustav," accessed May 22, 2017, http://www.tshaonline.org/handbook/online/articles/fma11. Uploaded on June 15, 2010. Modified on April 27, 2016. Published by the Texas State Historical Association. Accessed May22, 2017)

a   Ferdinand Friedrich Engelking (SB24/B!)was the editor's 2nd great grandfather, born in Schlüsselburg 20 February 1810, Died Millheim 15 August 1895. More information can be found in: "The Engelking Letters - A Collection of Letters Written by or Pertaining to Ferdinand Friedrich Engelking 1810- 1885" Translated and Edited from the German by Flora von Roeder ISBN 9781481059992. The Engelking family continues to hold regular reunions in Millheim to this day.

b   Ottilie Elisabeth Caroline Louise von Roeder (SB24/B)was the editor's 2nd great grandmother. Born 20 November 1823 died Millheim 9 February 1905. She was the daughter of Lt. Anton Ludwig Sigismund von Roeder (SB24/B) who had been the Lord of the Manor of Hoym in Westfalia in Prussia.

in the '30's to take part in the fight for Texas independence. Their house was exceptionally large, but not too large for the size of their family.

Another member of the Roeder family was married to Kleberg[a], a few miles beyond; the man of massive head, somewhat small stature and indomitable will. He, I think, was justice of the peace or notary public, but since law suits and legal forms were still spared our happy colony, we were wont to profit by his unofficial wisdom; and wonder at his daughter's beautiful name—Valeska.

Next to him, Trenckmann[b], proud proprietor of a grain mill, and the customary farm. A descendant[c] is now the

a   Robert Justus Kleberg (September 10, 1803 – October 30, 1888), christened Johan Christian Justus Robert Kleberg, was a German Texan from Herstelle, Westphalia, then part of the Kingdom of Prussia. He was a veteran of the Battle of San Jacinto and the brother of Louis Kleberg. He arrived in Texas in 1836 with his wife Philippine Sophie Rosalie "Rosa" von Roeder, who was a child of the at one-time aristocratic von Roeder family, which was allied with the wealthy and aristocratic Sack family of Nordrhein Westphalia. Robert and Rosa had eleven children, seven of whom lived to adulthood; Clara, Johanna, Caroline, Rudolph, Marcellus, and Robert, Jr. He is the namesake of Kleberg County, Texas. His sons also achieved success. Rudolph Kleberg (1847-1924) became a United States congressman, Marcellus Kleberg (1849-1913) studied law and served as city attorney for Galveston, Texas, and the youngest Kleberg son, Robert Justus Kleberg, Jr. (1853-1932) managed the King Ranch and later married Alice Gertrudis King, the youngest daughter of cattle baron, Captain Richard King.
b   Andreas Friedrich Trenckmann. He was the son of the master carpenter and farmer Johann Gottfried Trenckmann (1782-1837) and Anna Elisabeth Schneider (1781-1816), both from Wefensleben. Trenckmann married Johanna Jokusch.
c   William Andreas Trenckmann (born 23. August 1859 in Millheim , Austin County , died 22. March 1935 in Austin) was an American publisher and democratic deputy in the Texas House of Representatives. Trenckmann, son of the German immigrants Andreas

proprietor and editor of "Das Wochenblatt" published in Austin, Texas.

Farther away beyond "Dead Man's Creek," among others lived several branches of the Langhammer family, respected by all but at that time scarcely known to children[a].

Dead Man's Creek stood fully as ominous in our imagination as its name was unique. It was not a creek at all, but a trickling stream running through a marsh, with here and there a bog, which gave horse or mule a chance to prove his superior intelligence or instinct. Most points in a new country are associated with some story, either half true or the mere product of fancy. Dead Man's Creek had several, as so uncommon a name would suggest. That a man had been killed there no boy could doubt, but the incident was too remote to challenge our interest — perhaps Indians had done it. More authentic was the tale of the two men who had tried to quench their thirst at this stream. The first one lay down flat on the ground, but rested his arm on what he took to be the remnant of a tree. When the second one had got down, he suddenly jumped to his feet with the exclamation, "Gee, that is an alligator you have been rest-

---

Friedrich Trenckmann and Johanna Trenckmann, born Jokusch, visited the school in Millheim. There Ernst G. Matzen was his teacher. From 1876 to 1879 Trenckmann studied at the Texas A & M University . Subsequently he taught as a teacher in Frelsburg, Shelby and then became head of the Bellville School. On April 20, 1886, he married Mathilde Miller. He published the German-language weekly newspaper Wochenblatt. (Editor's translation of article from German Wikipedia).

[a] Many member of the Langhammer family are also related to the editor. At the time Nagel is writing, Marie Langhammer (SB29/6!) 24 November 1831 – 2 January 1925, for example. Some married into the Klebergs, Engelkings and Ploegers. The Silver Book of the family Sack lists some 11 Langhammers today.

ing on." "Is it?" was the answer, "I thought I heard something snore." We thought that a great story, and wondered at the inexperience of grown men. Finally there was the rumor that one family living on this creek insisted that there was no difference between chicken and snake meat, and we fancied that they were always eager to try it on people to convince them. We of course felt sure that this family was on the lookout for small boys as easiest victims, and Dead Man's Creek was one place at which we never tarried about meal time. Indeed, our minds were not quite at ease on the subject as it was. Before hearing of the story, we had taken a meal at one of these homes, and afterwards some one had said something about the whiteness and tenderness of snake meat. We suspected that we might have stood the ordeal once, but if so were the more resolved never to be caught again. Our imagination was so wrought upon that eels were regarded as little better than snakes; and for years frog legs had a narrow escape from the same judgment.

Immediately north was Hagemann, fair model for a picture of a prophet. He made a living for his family on his farm, raised very fine horses, and during the Civil War employed his training by making Rhine wine out of tomatoes,—a product which was unquestionably alluring to the eye, and was reluctantly admitted to be bearable to a starved taste.

In the other direction across the creek was Constant, who was said to be an actor by profession. He certainly seemed out of place off the stage. It is said that he planned to make Mill Creek navigable, when in some seasons we boys had to ride miles to find a hole with water enough to let us swim. Then there were the real farmers, the Hilboldts and Schneiders, one of whom restored to us the beautiful tenor lost in Dittmar, now far away in the forest. From what part of South Germany they came, I do not know; but there was no question of their loyalty to their particular dialect. Having been brought up to speak pure, almost Biblical German, dialect always left me in a bewildered state of mind, although even as a child I enjoyed the peculiar harmony of character and linguistic expression. Of this, Plattdeutsch (Low German) best understood by the North German, was a particular favorite, because mother could read it, so that I understood. To this day Fritz Reuter is a favorite with me. Few people know what they miss by not being able to enjoy his humor. I recall Schneider's appearance only faintly. But as long as memory lasts, I shall hear him sing with the enthusiasm of surrendering devotion those memorable words: "I b-i-i-n ein F-i-i-sch auf tro-o-ocknem S-a-and" (I am a fish on sand so dry); so suggestive of the actual state of some of our disillusioned newcomers, but really calculated to express a much more universal dilemma to which many Americans are now peculiarly sensitive.

To the south of us, just at the point where two branches of the forest reaching out from Mill Creek approach each other, leaving a gap to give us view of the endless prairie, lived Regenbrecht. He had married a Hagemann, and the family was large. He measured somewhere between six and seven feet, inclining to the latter I should say, and weighing not to exceed one hundred and sixty pounds if that much. He was college bred; was in the child's mind credited with rare intellectual powers and devoted his gifts to the not indifferent task of calculating the number of bushels to a small acreage; and whether the supply would last through the winter. Perhaps no one among us was better known for integrity and simplicity of character. He was a welcome visitor everywhere, always sure to brighten spare hours of my hard worked father in days when discussion and conversation were still counted among the social gifts. Less than a mile beyond lived Kluever; small but successful farmer.

All this sounds so simple and gives but a poor picture of the native beauty of the country, dotted with its unpretentious but well kept homes. It was all rather haphazard. The vegetable gardens were of course near the houses, because they had the personal attention if not care of the owners. Beyond that, however, there were pens for the domestic cattle, of which every home had some; and then fields of corn and even cotton, whose growth gave surest indication of the character of varying soils from richest black to poorest sand. But individuality marked location and development. No modern contractor's idea of symmetrical propriety had disturbed our conception of freedom of thought and conduct. This was before the farmer reversed the order of things to turn his place into a business for profit and from that profit to draw enough to feed and clothe his family. The family lived on and upon the farm — the surplus might yield a profit.

Finally, farthest south, on the very verge of the prairie extending far to the Gulf of Mexico as it were, the monarch of all he surveyed, lived Swearengen (Sam, I think). He was little known to us, but in many ways he was our accepted prototype. He stood alone, and I never look upon a picture of Washington now without going back to him — not the picture so much as what he stood for. He was not the only non-German but he was the one to whom we looked as a typical American. Perhaps we were influenced the more by his unwavering position as a Union man, when later on we of German blood were charged with the double complaint of being Union and German — in the parlance of the day, "Dutch" — a term to which we might not have objected, if its true dignity had been understood.

There were a few others of the older settlers not of German blood, but they were poor whites, rather contemptuously called "white trash." How they lived no one knew; they were not within our horizon. They were as clearly beneath our position as we (certainly after the secession issue was raised) were held in a separate caste by the more successful of the older stock. Perhaps one was as undeserved as the other. I do not recall that any of them were ever guilty of misconduct, and I have since then lived to learn that honesty and misfortune need not be strangers. However, Swearengen stood apart. He was a friend of Sam Houston — the idol of Texas youth; had fought with him as rumor went in the struggle for independence, and with him aided to oppose secession. He now lived the life of his conviction, a free American, with his wife, four sons and one daughter, about some of whom there will be more to tell. There were many others, but a youngster's memory is faulty, and some may come to me as I proceed.

Of course, we heard of the nearby towns, and had echoes come to us of the remoter places, with pardonable enthusiasm, called cities. Catspring, a village, aroused no interest in us beyond visions of knives, ropes, fishing tackle — even saddles and bridles and blankets in Soder's store. We may even have wondered whether the cat did really spring at somebody, or whether it merely came to find water. In any event, nothing less than a wild cat could have made so lasting a name. Bellville was the county seat. It held our attention probably because Miller's store was even more alluring than Soder's in Catspring; and because here was a court house in designing which the builder (as rumor had it) had forgotten the stairs for the second story, so that the addition on the outside presented a very prominent feature in the landscape. Also Bellville had a jail, never occupied so far as we knew, until the Civil War; but well calculated to prepare our imagination for an eloquent teacher's account of the horrors of the Bastille. San Felipe was foreign to us, certainly in so far as it concerned pronunciation or spelling. We accordingly took liberties with both, as though we had been brought up in an advanced Americanization school. How much warmer our response for Columbus; not only because of its proximity to Eagle Lake of alligator lore; but because as if by patriotic instinct our hearts went out to the great names of America. I have seen Columbus only twice. Once in our flight to Mexico in 1863, and again in 1909 when I visited the county seat of my native county. How American were the generous and unexpected demonstrations of welcome. I had hoped to slip in and out on the way to my old home, but at the station people were assembled in large numbers, cheering to the tune of a band called "Nagel's Band," composed of young men and old from all parts within a range of ten miles or more. For some occasion not connected with me houses were decorated and a procession was had to exhibit what the immediate county had to show. Of all of this I confess I remember little save fine horses and the skill with which beautiful young women handled them. To keep before me the Columbus of my time, I brought with me a treasured picture of the first Court House of Colorado County, a majestic Spanish oak, with the foliage rich and abundant, adorned with hanging moss, and known to this day as the tree in whose comforting shade the first court trial by American rule was had in Colorado County.

Houston, sixty miles away to the east, then stood for but two ideas, the popular fame of Sam Houston, and the terror of yellow fever. If the fever did not prevail at all times, the danger of an outbreak seemed ever present. It touched us only as travelers passing our way made report, or threatened to carry the scourge. The long lines of covered wagons, as they crossed the plain, and as we see them pictured now, I never saw. But I saw enough to catch their spirit, and memory so gripped me that I was glad later in life to see their reproductions in the movie while the lights were down. For we saw the canvas wagons, usually in pairs, rising over the horizon and winding their weary way towards us along the dusty road, obdurate messengers of good or bad from the great world outside. As they came near us we could hear the rumbling of the wagons, the clanking of chains; could see the long and steady pull of the oxen under the burden of their heavy yokes, head down, long horned and varied in brands as in color; hear finally the strokes of the hoofs on the hard ground; the simple but persuasive "gee" or "haw" from the driver walking beside them, and perhaps the wicked crack of the cowhide whip hanging from the long elastic hickory handle. And then the wagons would stop, for here was the doctor's gate. At times there were only subdued conversations—not for us. At other times the drivers had symptoms that "allowed" examination. Then to our consternation these "suspects" would be taken into our sitting room to be examined, resting on the only lounge we owned. When the verdict was had—good or bad— there being no hospitals, the subject, with such remedies as could be given, went on his way, thinking no doubt that no symptoms was so much to the good, and trusting that bad symptoms did not always prove true; and father, a firm advocate of the theory that yellow fever could not be communicated by contact, would to our renewed terror, continue his much needed rest on the same and only lounge. The canvas wagons moved on, the oxen unmindful of the cause of their respite; and if the driver at last fell victim to the dread disease, perhaps there was no doctor's gate at which to stop, and probably enough in the then state of medical science, it made little difference. Those were the conditions as we saw them; wondering what could induce people to live in the presence of such danger all the time. That was part of the early story of Houston, splendid now in her prosperity, her attractive homes, her academy, her place as a great city of Texas—even of our country.

Galveston, too, could not deny a yellow fever reputation, in spite of her cooling gulf breezes that made our summer nights bearable. But she was far away, too far for easy communication—a seaport unforgettable to father and mother. Although they had made the usual sea voyage of six weeks or more in a common sailing ship from Bremen to New Orleans, they always said that the one dreadful memory of the whole journey was the trip by boat from New Orleans to Galveston. I find this confirmed in letters written by mother and father at the time. One result was that father lost the diary which he had kept of the trip from Germany. It flew out of his pocket, as he jumped for a place of safety, and he never recovered it. A sailor grabbed it, no doubt, taking it for a pocket-book. It may be imagined what the craft was like. No wonder that we caught eagerly at every report and rumor of wrecks and disaster. Among many only one has stayed with me; but through all the later discussions about psychology or kindred subjects, this has persistently held its place. As is always the case, we children listened in on a good many things that were not meant for us; and no doubt some of our most stubborn impressions are gained in just that way. The story was the old one, compelling to young and old alike—told a thousand times, to be accepted, doubted or scouted from different points of view. A woman well known to us and respected by all, knew that her daughter had left Germany to join her. Just when the ship had sailed or when it might arrive she could not even guess in the uncertain state of communications. She had, however, felt no special anxiety until one night she was aroused from her sleep by the appealing call "Mother," and that was all. The call had been so vivid that she could not dismiss it from her mind and so she spoke of it to others. A few days later came the report of the loss of a ship in sight of Galveston, with accounts of the fate of the passengers. Among the lost was this daughter. The account gave harrowing details of how she had clung to a raft in sight of shore, but cruelly tossed by angry waves her strength had finally gone, she had lost her hold, and had gone down with the heart rending cry "Mother." Such details may always and will generally be supplied. But today as then I see the raft, the despairing face of the girl, her failing hands letting go their grasp—all with unerring clearness. If a boy can not picture that, where is his imagination? These are the more essential incidents. The further fact seemed undisputed. At the very time when the daughter was lost the mother was awakened by the call. The older people marveled then, as others, better versed, speculate now; and we children made our wondering contribution. Some years later, about the close of the Civil War, when I was the only one of the children left, and after mother had followed us to St. Louis on the long journey by way of Mexico and New York, she turned to this subject as she often talked with me about questions supposed to be beyond children's ken. Mother was a serious woman; no slave to creed, but religious as I think in the truest sense. She could not accept the story as more than a coincidence of fact and dream, and this was her reason: If such messages were possible she would have heard from Paul. She had not heard, and that was all. It did not seem strange or even impressed me at the time that she named Paul alone, when she had lost two daughters as well. But Paul stood apart in memory as he had in life, strangely gifted with imagination and the suggestion of vision. Probably unconscious of it, but with discernment as true as compass, mother had given the family's unreasoned estimate, and for the rest had left the problem where it was. Such was my picture of Galveston that I never saw until 1909, when the great sea walls afforded attractive walks in sight of the ocean's surf; and protected the now important port from harrowing storms that toss the sea as of old.

Nearer by, and in a sense more closely related, were such towns as Neu Braunfels, Neu Ulm, Schulenburg, etc. But they were out of the beaten track and mostly west, whence travel was uncommon. They were to us only a reminder that there were others of our kind sharing our task and our joy of freedom. Mere rumors that floated to us made up our picture of them.

German immigration was well distributed in Texas, as it had been years before in the eastern part of the United States. It had settled on the Atlantic Coast, advancing in large bodies into Pennsylvania, North Carolina, etc. That story has been told, and is frequently rehearsed by indifferently informed politicians before "German" constituencies. But some German immigrants not often mentioned had gone to Louisiana, as is interestingly told in a pamphlet by J. Hanno Deiler, seldom read. They formed a considerable and an influential part of the early population of that section. Their participation in the development of that country as pioneers and as soldiers would make a fascinating story. Indeed, they should have a far more dignified place than is customarily given them by authors, who unhappily see and read our history through Anglican glasses, or at best are content to restate the story of accepted German achievements in our country. But that is another story. I do not profess to write history; a task for which I am less qualified even than those who have sought to perform it in the past. As a mere background for my story, I am endeavoring to picture a German settlement in Texas, a state that did not engage our country's interest until about the annexation, and containing a population that has had but scant attention from those who have undertaken to champion German influence in our country. Germans had, however, come to settle before Mexico yielded her control of this territory. Some of them fought under Houston against Santa Anna; and at the conclusion of the war were among the pioneers in a country that up to that time had been little more than a happy hunting ground. It is true that the political disturbances of 1848 in Germany were the occasion of a large exodus from that country to this. But it should not be forgotten that long before that revolution large bodies of Germans, impatient of delay, perhaps hopeless of success, in any event moved by a demand for freedom as pure and strong as any that ever animated protest against political rule had found their way to this country and, in part, to Texas. And it should be borne in mind that this difference in time of arrival worked little change in the problems which newcomers had to meet, for, to all intents and purposes, Texas was virgin soil and forest, to be conquered by those who had nerve to come and endurance to survive.

Some of this immigration had been induced as is so often the case by advance agents. With or without previous visits they had published descriptions of this new country. These were often exaggerated, particularly with respect to obstacles to be overcome; as they certainly succeeded to cast into unanticipated moulds many of the lives with which I am now concerned. In some cases this resulted in mild forms of colonization peculiarly doomed to disappointment. Somewhere I have heard or read that for our section one colony was led by a commoner, and another by a nobleman. Some of those who had left the old country in protest of her government, found cause to reflect upon the fact that when it came to the inevitable disillusionment, the former scuttled for home, while the latter stood by his charge, regardless of sacrifice. Right or wrong, I have always associated with these the von Roeders, who were among the earliest comers—fit champions of the cause of that day. They appeared to give little heed to their "von," but I have sometimes wondered whether they and their kind might not have resented Disraeli's scathing rebuke of nobility, that it had preserved its prerogatives, and had forgotten its obligations. In this respect the German "Junker" had something to say for himself.

I can not believe that our settlement was closely associated with colonization schemes. It is true that father and mother, the Dittmars, Litzmanns and the Reichardts came from the same neighborhood abroad. But others came from very different parts of Germany, north and south; some like Amslin had even come from German Switzerland. I have the impression that Charles Sealsfield (author of books about Texas) was a name often mentioned in our home. Still later there came a considerable number of Bohemians. The two elements remained essentially apart, although the newcomers, too, had their castes. For instance, my uncle Litzmann's wife, "Tante Anna," was a Bohemian. Her charm and kindness won all children. My memory of her in later years, with her fair skin, arched brows, auburn hair and strangely gentle expression had me look upon the first canvas by Gabriel Max as an old acquaintance. Generally speaking, however, they provided for those who could afford such luxury, the farm labor and the maids, in which positions they were equally trustworthy and efficient. The German contingent of my memory, on the other hand, represented quite largely the professional class—men and women who had been driven to emigrate from conviction, moved by a demand for greater individual freedom and opportunity. They were not a reckless lot. They had at least attempted to reckon with the chances of their adventure. The impelling force of their hazardous undertaking was the same old dream of liberty which had prompted the earliest immigration to our country; and which we are still struggling to redeem. They were of a high order, moved by the spirit for sacrifice that sustained settlers in the earlier days. These impressions have of course come to me in later years. As a child I took it all for granted, and in any event had neither inducement nor standard for comparison.

But under the pressure of taunt and laughter that met me upon my rather pathetic appearance in the safe haven of the North after our escape from Texas, I began to suspect; and finally concluded that probably I had never been in a community of so high a percentage of college bred men as that from which the Civil War had driven us. My father, for illustration, was a graduate in medicine at Berlin, after having given some time to study for the clergy, including as I have been told even Hebrew. He was certainly at home in the Bible. They had suffered their disappointments; they had been forced to adopt unanticipated pursuits; but they had maintained their self-respect and offered a nucleus for the society of cultivated men and women. In the main a community of small farmers, with here and there as in my father's case a return to the original profession, they had found a happy, peace-loving society in which personal liberty and public order reigned supreme. These were the conditions into which our family had been transplanted (after their brief stay in Saint Bernardo) from old Germany.

There must have been much in the attitude of the older settlers to confirm these conditions. Father's early letters reflect something like admiration for the people he met. In one place he says that he has not seen a fat person in Texas; that the people are thin and fit, and the men, always armed, sit their horses to perfection; also that he has generally been met by courtesy. It is told of one German town in Missouri that it had for years been without policeman or prisoner. Finally, the rumor got out that the old jail had an inmate, and straightway a reporter was sent to verify the strange message. He found the jail empty, but the constable explained that having no deputy he had decided to keep the prisoner in jail during the day and send him home for the night. We must have done better than that, for in the early days I think there was no jail at all; certainly there were no inmates. Nor can I recall personal encounters or litigation, about all of which even children would have heard in a world that had so little of human incident to tell. As I gather from father's letters all his early purchases of land, cattle, horses, material, etc., were carried through without quibble or unfair advantage. It is true that his title for the second home appears to have called for several supplemental payments; but these were probably the first warning of an advancing civilization.

THE OLD HOME IN GERMANY

My parents, Hermann Nagel and Friederika Litzmann, were born in Pritzwalk, Mark Brandenburg, Prussia. Here they were married and continued to live until late in 1846 or early in 1847, when they came to the United States. The two families had lived in Pritzwalk for several generations; but our accounts did not go farther back than the grandparents. Grandfather Nagel had engaged in draining swamp lands (of which there were few in that sandy section), contracted typhoid, and died at the age of thirty-two years, leaving his widow with four boys—father and his three brothers—to bring up. To judge from a portrait he must have been a man of striking appearance—rather of the intellectual, even poetic type—the last man to be engaged in the work in which he lost his life, unless the cause of conservation at that time constituted a peculiar appeal to imagination. Grandmother Nagel was the very personification of North German energy and resolution. She took up her task and met it in spite of every conceivable obstacle. First, she lost title to her little property, owing to frauds committed by some officials, which resulted (so report went) in sending the wrong-doer to the penitentiary, and leaving grandmother without her property; all of which has a modern sound. However, she managed to help three sons to their doctor's degree, leaving the fourth his wish that he might remain free to follow any occupation that would permit him to live with or near any one of his brothers. Perhaps he came nearer to carrying out his treasured plan than the rest, for he certainly was never far removed from his oldest brother; and when I met him years later, his devotion and self-abnegation were pathetically touching. Grandmother lived to be over ninety; long enough to be persuaded at last that going to America did not mean to cut all ties of friendship and affection; indeed, to accept that the dreams of venturesome youth may be more wise than the reason of mature age.

Mother's father, Pastor Litzmann, was the Lutheran clergyman of the town (Evangelical) as his father had been before him. They may have been more than mere clergymen of a particular church; and certainly grandfather's picture would pass for an archbishop anywhere. He also lived to be over ninety, and during the last few years was blind, although he did not on that account leave the pulpit. I gathered that mother was for years his reader; and this may in some measure account for her remarkable acquaintance with books ranging from the Bible to Schleiermacher, the German poets, Reuter, and even translations from English authors. Mother's conception of religion and her attitude to life would make me believe that her father was not a fundamentalist in the modern sense. Of mother's mother I heard little; but since she and my grandfather's first wife had eighteen children between them, her attention to them must have been somewhat divided, and I would not on that account minimize the importance of her position in the family history.

Pritzwalk was then a modest although quite an old place. As I saw it in 1868, on my first visit to Germany, it bore the character of a New England village with its central street, the row of neat white houses of nice design, unspoilt by modern contractors' monstrosities. But in one respect the difference was radical. There were only two church buildings, Protestant and Catholic, I think. As I recall it the steeple of the former was gone, as some one whispered, (probably not true) a reminder of the war of 1813. They even told that grandmother Nagel, then a young, strong woman, had slapped a soldier's face for insulting her father. But there it stood, the church of my fathers, in which two of them had preached, the last one to give my mother a Bible which I now have. Who will say that there is not a deep significance in the preservation of the old House of Worship which one's ancestors have attended, and in which as it were they in spirit join the devotions of succeeding congregations? That at least is what I felt when I came there without a warning thought. Perhaps I had been unconsciously better prepared than I knew. Mother had a way of teaching, without one's suspicion, that the wax was yielding to her pressure. When I caught my first glimpse of Bremen, noticing less the buildings and steeples of the city than the cluster of red roofs set in the green foliage of the country, my first thought was that I had seen it all—that I had been there before. When later in Halberstadt I met my cousins, three boys and two girls (first blood relatives since my brother and sisters had gone) there crept over me a feeling of kinship that more than anything I had known made me feel the aloofness of my life. One of my grandchildren now suggests that kinship with relations abroad. After a brief visit there and a few days in the Harz with all the lore of the Brocken, Hexentanzplatz, Rosstrappe, unprepared as I was for the occasion, I finally came to make my entry into Pritzwalk, which somehow did not work out precisely as was anticipated. Even then I had to leave the railroad to travel some ten or fifteen miles by bus. At that time the prevailing view was upon Brandenburg Sand. When I last visited there, in 1928, the whole area seemed to be covered with forests in the different stages of growth. Indeed my son and I rode from Berlin to Pritzwalk virtually under trees shading the highway. But the first time I suspect the driver knew the importance of his haul, and had plans of his own; one does not bring captive Americans into Pritzwalk every day. We pulled along until it grew to be dusk, and I could see struggling lights in the distance. The town had one main street, but of course also a good many cross streets. It was supposed that the entry of the hero, in Pritzwalk's eye just snatched from the wilds of Texas, would be at the chief cross street where traffic was accustomed to enter. So, as I was told, my Uncle Eickhoff (then the pastor of the old church), was stationed at that point, my aunt at the next street, and my three girl cousins at as many more. To make assurance doubly sure the cook was permitted to patrol the remotest and most improbable point of entry. All was set for a prompt and warm welcome; especially since some part of the town was out, for news travels fast in close communities. The old bus rumbled on, but the driver having in mind the interest of the public and, if you please, its rights, concluded that the longer route would afford the greater opportunity. Perhaps he also felt some interest in the cook. Accordingly, we made our entry at the extreme cross street, and while my uncle, aunt and charming cousins were in due time left to join the curious onlookers, I was with great decision captured by the cook of no small proportions, and was led in triumph as the last word in Wild West exhibit, although in mildest mood, through the dimly lighted main street of the city of my fathers. It was a great moment for the cook; but that ordeal once survived I had the welcome meant for me; had time to wonder which of my cousins I should have preferred as my escort; and in the course of a week's visit had the chance to get my bearings.

How neat and civilized was the clergyman's house; in itself so attractive with white painted rooms and the good old furniture; the little garden with the vines climbing up and the flowers in full bloom. What more could one want

THE OLD HOME IN GERMANY

if one had no call for adventure. In the summer of 1928 my son and I were permitted to visit this old home again. He, a young architect, was charmed and confirmed all my impressions.

We also saw the old church, with a full steeple now—and the cemetery with the tombstones of my ancestors—all so dignified, so simple and so true. In 1868 I visited my Uncle Wilhelm's home—he who would study only what would serve to keep him near his brothers. Now I became the object of his devotion for three brothers. The meals astounded me—all especially ordered, I know—duck and steak and rolls—coming all the way from some central point, no doubt. And then the bed rooms. Royalty in its moments of greatest delusion could not have hoped to sleep nearer the ceiling. I measured six feet three and one half inches but it was still something of an athletic achievement to reach the top of that bed. And then no sooner had sleep claimed me than I was rudely awakened by the nachtwaechter's club on the cobble stones, and the sonorous call to all the world, "Hoert, ihr Herren, und lasst euch sagen, die Klock hat zwoelf geschlagen," (Listen my lords and let it be told, the clock the hour of twelve has tolled) calling down the ages like the command of some ancient Prince.

When during the same visit I went to Spremberg to see my mother's sister, Elise, the wife of a Judge Seemann, my earlier impression was confirmed. It all seemed so sweet and hospitable. My aunt was the oldest, and the beauty of the family. The judge was deformed; but, nevertheless, a man of splendid presence. His parents had died early, and he, as the oldest of a large family of sisters and brothers, had succeeded in seeing them all through school. He had for years been in love with my aunt, but owing to his misfortune never dared to speak until her indifference to other suitors gave him hope. Thus I found two lovers of advanced years, for devotion could never have been more constant than was theirs even then. In the morning when he had been "harnessed" as he called it, we would take a walk and he would talk of literature and pat the trees on the way, with nicknames for many of them. In court he looked every inch a judge, and litigants seemed to share my impression.

A few years after I visited there again. My aunt had died, but he seemed to feel that she was always present. Toward evening he would take me to the cemetery to sit on his bench at the grave and to listen to the beautiful notes of a nightingale. In him I saw first what I have since seen so often. Some persons so afflicted never conquer their grievance, and are often driven to visit their pardonable resentment upon others. But those who do triumph are the most generous, thoughtful and noble among us.

As I look back upon it all I wonder what really did induce father and mother to leave so well ordered a little place, as their old home possessed after all of a charm and comfort just such as we so often in our time strive to find in our new country. But it was not the place; it was the system against which the revolt was aimed; and no doubt father was the moving spirit throughout, although mother's sympathy was not lacking, as her letters disclose. In later years a pronounced law and order man, he was in his youth a consistent protester against the accepted rule of the land. Many are the tales that I have heard to prove the truth of this conclusion. Some only floated down to us as stories will; others were confirmed by father later when it was safe, and were then told with great glee. Still others were first revealed to me when abroad I was mysteriously asked whether I was any relation to the great broad-swordsman Pinne (nickname for Nail or Nagel). As far as I can make out, one of grandmother's chief concerns was to find new boarding schools for father, as he was expelled from old ones. Of course, there are two sides to every question; and while grandmother was wondering how long her purse would hold out, father, a mere boy, was pondering how slavery could be cast off. As the sequel will show, he had some reason on his side, although some of his early remedies were somewhat drastic. It may be all wrong to deny young boys Irish potatoes on the ground that this diet is not conducive to brain development, and in consequence to force them to boil their delectable potatoes in secret in their own room. But it can not be right when such boys are detected in the act, and the ringleader is ordered to carry the steaming pot after the head teacher down a flight of stairs, to have the chosen student suddenly stumble without perceptible obstacle, and deluge the unfortunate teacher while in pursuit of his "duty as he sees it," with the aforesaid composition of Irish potatoes and boiling water. And yet it is told that my father was a participant in such an adventure, and when challenged later on his only answer was, "It was the system."

While I share the common contempt for eavesdroppers, I can not quite believe that the boys had a right to coax their spying teacher as far as possible to the remotest corners of the upper hall, and then and there to the accompaniment of sudden alarm to have their partners in crime nail down the eavesdropper's slippers which had been carefully placed at the head of the stairs for prompt and noiseless exit. The result is inevitable, too precipitate by far — punishment and crime are out of proportion. Again it was "the system."

There were, of course, more innocent frolics, like the cure for snoring boys. This consisted in placing a pulley in the ceiling and running a string fastened to the bed covers of the snoring culprit through it. We thought it the climax of humor that the snoring always stopped when the victim vaguely groped for the cover suspended in midair above him; and we listened sympathetically to the description how the offender settled down for restored peace and renewed effort after the covers were permitted to descend to his welcome embrace. But again the answer was "the system." That a real grievance was at the bottom of all this conduct is made apparent by the final outcome. Grandmother's purse was put to the last strain, and so my father was told that only one more chance could be given; and in order that no hope for success be lost, he might have the choice of the next school. He made his selection, and often have I heard him bless his good fortune, and speak of the head master of that school with profound respect and real affection. As late as 1872, when the teacher was an old man living alone in some remote town or village, my father then attending the University of Berlin the second time, traveled the distance to visit him. There they opened the piano, and the old sage playing the accompaniment, they with a few gathering friends, sang once more the old songs of Germany's tradition and glory, and then said the final goodbye. Quite different were the tales of this school. How the head master would come before the assembled classes on some glorious morning, and after striding up and down in absorbing thought, would suddenly exclaim "Glorious weather"! Receiving no response except in the approving expression of marveling countenances, he would follow up with "Too glorious to be confined in these cramped walls. School is adjourned. Come out to the forest and I will tell you something about its beauty." This was only one of many experiences, any one of which explain the esteem in which the man was held. But the climax was capped by a certain Sunday expedition, such as were common outings in Germany then as they are now. When I participated in the first one, I was struck by the fact that the young people all seemed to look upward, into the trees and the heavens. We had always watched our feet. On the occasion of this outing the entire school was off on a country lark, all on their own. All went well, in perfect accord with the accepted rules, until the return trip. High spirits prevailed; and as the students met parties returning to the country from the city, the usual hilarity was indulged in. Finally, the reckless gaining the upper hand, they unhitched a farmer's horses and proceeded to ride about, adopting the course of a circle, by way of suggesting the circus. Father, mindful of his promise, true to the really admirable record he had made, had in no way participated, although challenges were not wanting. Then came the taunt—worst enemy of youthful resolution —he did not dare, he was afraid, etc. That settled it. He would show them how timid and futile their performances were. Once committed, he was bound to excel. And so he mounted a horse, and after the usual parade straddled him backwards and directing the beast by the tail, proceeded to give his comrades his conception of a modern circus. The climax had been reached; the unsuspecting deriders had been properly rebuked by the sleeping champion. The horses were returned; the students came home as models of probity, and for weeks all seemed well and danger was forgotten. Then one morning the head master, his face like a cloud, opened the session as follows: "I have a communication here from the Police Department at Berlin making complaint of the conduct of my boys on a certain Sunday, six weeks ago. The charges are that their behavior was riotous in the extreme. Particular mention is made of one who rode a horse backwards; and showed especial disregard, etc., etc. Now, first who was the boy here referred to? I ask him to rise." Father felt that he was doomed. He had selected his own school; he had made good; and in one reckless moment he had forfeited all he had won. But there was only one course. He slowly rose and, saying that it was he, stood to receive the final blow. It came in most unexpected form. "Well, I suppose you did, that is a matter for me to deal with. What concern is it of the State police to interfere with the conduct of my school? Indeed, I have had annoyance enough by their interference, and we will consider the matter dismissed." Strangely enough it was, for never another word was heard from any source. What wonder that here was the one authority for which my father had felt respect and affection, and which seemed at least to suggest a wholesome protest against what he detested. And still it remained "the system." It continued so afterwards. In later years he confessed to me that as a young man he had hardly been interested to read a book unless the Government had denounced it. Father attended Halle, Wurzburg and Berlin. Whether the causes for change were the old ones or were made in obedience to custom, following the reputation of professors rather than the fame of particular universities, I do not know. I do know now that there were associations of students. Those student organizations[a] were based in some measure on political affiliation; and the customary duels were fought upon the same ground. In these father was extremely active, fighting many a duel himself, and serving as second in many others. It was not for sport. It was done in deadly earnest, for it still was "the system" that challenged him.

a "Burschenschaften". These student fraternities founded in the 19th century were inspired by liberal and nationalistic ideas and were involved in the March Revolution and the unification of Germany. It was the supression of the revolution of 1848 that led many to emigrate.

That feeling never left him. He was as German a character as I ever knew. He was devoted to his own people, entertained the highest hopes for them; but his very heart protested against the official supervision of personal conduct. So strong was this feeling that while later on he learned to admire Bismarck, I felt at an earlier time that in spite of his strong sense for law, he could hardly suppress a regret that Ferdinand Blind had failed in his attempt at assassination. Again, in the winter of 1872-3, we had been settled in an apartment in the suburbs of Berlin only a day or two when the official inspector was on hand to know whether this was the same Hermann Nagel who about 1842 had occupied a certain room on the corner of such and such street, etc. "That is it" said my father; "he is of course perfectly entitled to know, but I feel as though I wanted to go home." Not very different was his experience when in 1872 he appeared at the University of Berlin to pay his final tuition for the last semester back in the '40s. The payment had been variously delayed by misfortune but in part because he wished to make it in person. The occasion was met in the same old Prussian fashion. The Treasurer hauled out the old ledger, turned to the page, stated the amount and accepted it—and that was all! I sometimes wonder what my father would have felt and said if he had lived with us during the World War from 1914 on. When I think of the humiliation that he would have had to suffer in our country I frankly am glad that he was spared it.

So when I ask what prompted them to emigrate, I must say to myself no doubt father's was the primary influence. Mother was prepared by nature and by training to face and meet her problems as and where they came. But in one of her early letters to father's mother, she expresses her own feeling about the decision. Among other things

Fig. 11: The Nagel House Today

she writes: "You will of course want to know how we like it; but perhaps it will be best to refer you to Hermann's letter. I confidently believe that he finds here what he sought and expected; and more my warmest wishes have not asked. My hopes are in many respects exceeded. Although I believe that we may live satisfied and happy anywhere in the world wherever it may be, I find that here nature comes to our aid, almost guarantees it, provided always we do not seek our happiness in social pleasures and display of our surroundings. The first is partly out of the question; the latter altogether. But to compensate we are surrounded on all sides by forest and flowers—oh Mother! and flowers; even now in March I have seen twenty different kinds of flowers. It is a perfect glory. Even roses bloom here, but that is rare, and I am envied for the rosebushes that I found here." The decision had to come, and if so, then better at once than later. Father could not even wait for the uprising of 1848; probably had despaired of it, and so they struck out for the great adventure of a new world —untried and uncertain—but with the chance and the right to have a hand in the making of it. And thus we finally came to take our place as part of Millheim.

OUR NEW HOME IN MILLHEIM

The new home stood on the top of quite a hill — sandstone and generally poor soil — with its view down upon and into the forest in one direction, and prairie in the other. We were not so close up to wild life as we had been; but the challenge to imagination was greater, as was the chance for real encounter. It lay at the fork of two roads, one the main highway between Houston and Catspring, and farther west with a branch just beyond Constant Creek to Bellville; the other a road to San Felipe. This was a point of real advantage, for we could catch glimpses of the outside world, when modern townspeople can only watch the endless stretch of vehicles or automobiles. Apart from our unfailing interest in canvas covered wagons, there were cattle roaming free. It was for us to spot them and fix their ownership; and to wonder where a neighbor would catch up with a cow that was clearly going in the wrong direction. And then there were riders, some with common outfit bent on ordinary errands; others out for the joy of the ride. For instance, young Hagemann whose father raised the finest stock would pass the house on a spirited horse, with not a trick in saddle or bridle missing, as though his purpose in life was to arouse envy in the heart of an ambitious boy. Life was full of human incident, made richer by the view upon open spaces where eager eyes could often make out groups of deer peacefully grazing in the early morning or at dusk. Our entry into this home must have been very different from father's and mother's at Saint Bernardo. This time the house had been finished before we moved. Not so at the old place. After the terrible voyage from New Orleans to Galveston my parents had come to Houston, again by water through the now well developed bayou. From that point mother travelled by ox team, father having proceeded on horseback; and as though fate would give them no respite from their cruel hardships, they were overtaken by a severe Texas norther. Barring one night when mother and her party were taken in by a Good Samaritan, they were exposed to the cutting winds of the norther, the severity of which no one can know who has not felt it. After a day or two father returned to meet mother and they reached their destination chilled, and drenched from the exposure, with little or no preparation for their reception. Three families had jointly bought a common acreage. The agreement was that the land should be divided into three parts, and that the choice should be made by drawing lots, with the promise that he who drew the one habitable house should give shelter to the others as best he could until they could build their own homes. Reichart drew the home; and while father and mother did thus find protection with him during the day, they were forced to spend the nights in the one log house on their ground. This house had openings in the wall, but no windows; and its roof offered no serious hindrance to a fair view of moon and stars on clear nights, and as little to dew and rain on others. The redeeming feature of their experience was that the home was finally built as other difficulties were overcome; and that it was all done without so much as a rift in the relations between the parties to this quixotic enterprise.

But delighted as we were with our new home in Millheim, it is true that with all the university representation, we had as I recall it no architect. There must have been mechanics, and for the rest we probably relied upon the designs which were carried in memory, or suggested by what we saw before us. Perhaps some good angel had sent crude plans, not unlike the thoughtful Englishman who is said to have provided more or less perfect designs for New England colonies; for the comfort of early settlers and the admiration of intelligent visitors to this day. In no event were we in the competitive list with older settlers like Amslin, whose house had the air of a modern cottage nestling in the shade of protecting trees. But we managed to get our comfort, combined with utility, not unaided by American innovation. Our home was built very much upon the lines of the one at Saint Bernardo, with such additions as growing success would allow. There were the three main rooms, two bed rooms and one sitting room, which also served as dining room when season or inclement weather forbade the use of the porch with its glorious view through blossoming climbing roses, upon open space and the fields of corn and grain. For some time Paul and I slept in the third room, which was also the drug store. Often enough, half in sleep, have I seen mother with the old-fashioned scales in her hand and the trimly cut papers near by, measuring to fill the powders and salves according to father's prescriptions—the very picture of patient duty and loving devotion. Later on the drug store, true to custom, grew in size and variety. It encroached upon our space. Perhaps, too, the strong odors were disturbing. So the east porch was enclosed, and here we had three beds in a row along the blank wall, with quilts for warmth in winter, and with mattresses stuffed with corn shucks for comfort. It was marvelous how yielding the shucks became in a mattress when they had been so stubborn in the field. The size and shape of a boy was as it were faithfully reproduced by the impressions of his body. As time wore on, the undulations assumed shapes more and more fantastic, until a desperate director of a struggling museum might have been tempted to use such a mattress as a reduced model of an imposing mountain range. But at night we lost no sleep over them, and during the day they were discreetly covered with sheets or with cotton quilts — another of mother's many aids to our comfort. These had none of the allurements of crazy quilts. They were two plain sheets with cotton of our own picking, unadulterated by alien hand, between, stitched through to hold the cotton in place. Our house furniture was of the simplest, tables of plain wood, and chairs so straight and hard that later years may class them as rare, for no one would think of reproducing them. In the kitchen tin must have been the chief factor. This was certainly true of our wash bowls. Even so, they were sunk into the wash-stand to protect them from the hazards of awkward boys. We had soap, too, piled up in long pieces like cordwood, and handed out in chunks, cut off as necessity dictated. Soap was a domestic product. As I think of the large kettle with the heated conglomerate of grease and what not, forever seeking consistency under the stirring impetus of a paddle, I come to regard it as the first suggestion for the modern and little less seductive home brew. That soap was as uncompromising and unattractive as fundamentalism. It had no allurements for casual employment. It was meant to take off dirt and say nothing about it. It did both, and was a natural enemy of small boys. In making soap we were sometimes drafted into service. The paddle was entrusted to our hands, with the injunction to give that horrible brew no rest. This no doubt invited some resentment; but it was at all events work — dignified work that men might be asked to do. Very different was it when we were called upon to churn butter. No doubt the advent of woman's suffrage — the one human venture in which superiority persists by the side of equality — has changed all this. But in that age and generation it was the last word of humiliation to have a boy do work that by rights belonged to the feminine domain. To cook in camp was well enough; but to have to work in the kitchen was the limit. There are two things that can not be combined; and these are churning butter and getting lost in dreams. There is time for only one. If I were asked to name a job that would teach a scatterbrained lad the need for concentrated, continued and persistent effort for the accomplishment of a given task, I should say get a churn and put him to it. But we did not know our mercies; did not even know that we were spared the hair brush and to be honest, tooth brush, too. Perhaps that accounts for my full head of hair today, and for the dentist's statement that I have more teeth in my head than any of his patients of my age. But true to mother's rule, I must say "Unberufen" and rap on wood, as I do as I write. There must be some compensation in savage life. I take it ours was the fate of most country boys in the early days. The problem was during the warm season (which happily was long) to keep us out of water, and during the cooler season to get us into water. But that problem was not ours, except in so far as mother's watchful eyes curtailed our freedom of conduct. Perhaps she found some peace in the thought that whatever might be true of this season or that, the general average for the year was fairly good.

The third bed was Hermann Vahl's, an older boy whom father had taken in at the dying request of a stranger to whose aid he had been called at the last moment. It was an altruistic venture which no doubt gave Hermann more than he could have found elsewhere, but which certainly raised problems for our little family that might well have proved serious. Hermann was by nature alien to us; good-looking as only the hero of romance can be; with the clear cut features of extreme southern type; brown eyes and dark hair with a certain wave. He was a born athlete, able to do most things by way of sport, and willing to do only a few by way of work. The very contrast of our common garden variety of cotton-haired boy of Nordic type.

The other bed room was father's and mother's, who had with them Baby Clara. Little Helene had died soon after our coming to Millheim, one Christmas Eve which, in memory of the peaceful little figure lying on our couch, has given Christmas a meaning of its own for me. My recollection of her is very vague, although I think of our playing with her in the open, and feeling a brother's joy in her merry laughter; or perhaps hearing a little cry at some mishap and being touched by her ready response to a brother's concern.

For the rest the house had a few changes from the old one. Above all, the larger fireplace, wide and deep enough for any hickory logs. There was no cellar, happily, for there were dark corners enough for timid boys with home-made candles that always blew out. The one lard lamp was not for us to meddle with. I only remember the scissor-like contraption to trim the wick; and the nut cracker—equal even to a hickory nut—both handmade of course, "made in Germany." The north porch served as our refrigerator. All water was hauled in a barrel laid on a sled, from the cold spring half way down the hill, and was left under the roof, away from the sun. The use of ice was not known to us. A cool spring was, therefore, of first importance, as was the sheltered porch on the north of the house. I remember seeing ice once, just enough to cover a sheet of water so close to the ground that the question of support did not arise. I tried to skate, sliding on the soles of my shoes; but the sliding was not restricted as I had figured and I was deterred from further serious efforts for life. A kitchen was added to the west, made of boards. Here the maid (for this was another new feature) reigned supreme; and here under her kindly care (she was Bohemian) we snatched our hasty breakfasts of cornbread, fresh butter, New Orleans molasses, bacon and milk, before hurrying off for school. It was a great advance — too great to be just taken for granted even by boys given to trust Providence for all good things. But that was not all. We had a smoke house; another wooden addition. Just an enclosure as I see it with a door to enter, and cracks enough for well distributed ventilation. There was always meat enough on the hoof, but there was no Beef Baron to slaughter. To provide fresh beef or bacon was an event in the colony — fit suggestion for intelligent cooperation. Meats were obtained in larger quantity at one time, and were then kept by the several owners in the smoke houses to cure and to preserve. Hams and chunks of beef were hung from rods fastened across the smoke house and near the roof, to keep them within reach of the smoke and out of reach of such intruders as rats and mice. All this sounds very simple, but to cure meats is an art, and like most true arts, calls for care and patience. Anybody can start a fire, but very few know how to keep the hickory sticks alive — not enough to break into a blaze, and just enough to keep up a steady smoke to rise in even column up to the roof, there to envelop the suspended beef and bacon, and then to find its way out by the cracks in walls and roof. All the modem talk of smoke cured hams and nut fed hogs sounds like so much romance to me. It may all be true. But did we not have hogs that scarcely left two fighting boys enough pecans and hickory nuts to supply the family wants for the winter evenings before the blazing fireplace, undisturbed by family conflict as to who should place the log or stir the fire. And as for our smoke, no Cape Cod navigator could keep his pipe at a more steady draw. We have been taught to believe in, almost to worship progress; but there are some things in which wholesale production will never supplant or even touch the individual hand's creation. So at least I like to believe, in memory of the joys of my youth.

Another addition was the barn, surest proof of a farmer's rise to the test of success. When the barn looks smarter than the home, we know the owner's credit is good at the bank, although we may wonder a little about the care of his family, and be not so sure about the feeling of his neighbor. We had no such problems. Ours was just a fair barn built of logs, cracks plastered with mud and straw, enough to keep out most of the rain and draught; stalls enough for horses and mules, of which we had four or five, about which more hereafter. The loft right under the roof had space for corn and fodder, and here it was our joy in winter, when the fresh feed was wanting, to reach down to our pets—every horse and sometimes even a mule becomes a friend —their regular allowance of corn on the cob and dried corn stalk leaves tied in bundles, or hay for greedy meals. When I was there in 1909 that barn still stood, and the manger, out of which our horses were fed, was there intact though gnarled—silent testimony to the fibre of hickory wood. Attached to the barn was the common rail fence enclosure—pen we called it—in which the animals could move about when they were not let out into the larger pasture. Across the road, which passed just in front of the house—a thoroughfare all the way from Houston and then farther west—was another pen, larger, for into it we drove the cows for milking. There was room for many, because the Texas cow of that day was not equal as a milk producer to modern standards.

Just beyond was our garden rich in vegetables, and persuasive proof of the civilized taste and the achievements of foreign cultivation. There we had sweet peas, beans, radishes, turnips, cabbage, cucumbers, beets, sugar corn, Irish and sweet potatoes, onions, parsnips, cauliflower, carrots and squash. We even had asparagus; and well I remember father and mother working with spades to prepare the deep bed with well chosen soil. But asparagus after all remained a delicacy and was reserved for the grown ups, with no pangs to us, for vegetables as such were a disquieting incident in our lives. They seemed to be necessary for some people, and were forced upon us only as a customary urging of older people who professed to know what is good for boys. Somehow color almost as much as taste seems to decide a lad's like or dislike for food. There was—horrible to relate—even spinach standing menace of life, in youth and in old age. Hours of play I lost because I had the option to gaze upon the hated enemy all afternoon, rather than devour him at one desperate gulp. My dislike has never weakened; it was intensified; and to this day one of my nightmares takes shape in the doctor's order that I must at last, after a long battle of resistance come to spinach. So far I am thankful for my mercies. I can not believe that any one honestly likes spinach. When I see people eat it, disguised in milk or vinegar or other substitute, I firmly believe that their smug manner and patronizing look is nothing more or less than the eternal story of the fox's counsel with his tail cut off. For us a meal meant meat, beef or pork in all their forms, venison rarely, veal never, and bread and butter, molasses, brown sugar, with perhaps a potato (particularly a roasted sweet potato) thrown in. What more did man want here below?

Like all youngsters we had a sweet tooth for fruit. I think we had strawberries, but they, too, would go for a delicacy —fit morsel for older people. Our domain was the blackberry patch where sole competitors belonged to the animal world. We put up with wild persimmon ripened in the sun, if we got there before the opossum. Mustang grapes were symbolic rather with their strong vines reaching high up into the oaks, and serving as ornaments to the tree and as swings for adventurous boys. We ate sweet peas in the shell, before they were spoiled by cooking. Sugar corn was a favorite. We would cut the stalk just as the tassel indicated that it was ripening, then strip off the outer rind and chew the rest for the sugar that it contained. The process did not quite lend itself to modern form. But boldfaced chewing was not frowned upon then as it is now, although I am sure we got more out of it than later custom yields. Tobacco chewing was never adopted by the original immigrants. As a native I was made immune by an early and most unhappy experiment — of course under the influence of a dare. And after all, be it tobacco or gum it is chewing still — a habit condemned but not abandoned. We had plums, cherries, I think, and peaches. Children have them in the cities now, picked by other hands, and trusted to ripen in the market. It was our joy to know when they would ripen, and to get them before some one else crossed our purpose. Peaches were the prize fruit, and of these we had great red faced cling stones — Indian peach, we called them. The earliest could be picked from the hanging branches; others by climbing into the tree to reach for those near enough to the trunk or strong branch. But there was only one ideal way; for it marked the boys' advantage. Peaches are still my passion; but I eat them now seeing myself standing in the saddle, my horse under the tree, reaching out for the red cheeked fruit, immune from common touch; to collect them into my hickory shirt, and to enjoy them on my ride. Probably a magnet of every boy's eye was the watermelon. We had very few of the long cucumber shaped melon. Ours belonged to the cannon ball type, of one color, darkest green. We would watch the ripening process with the care of a modern devotee of research—deepening color, state of the vine; until it came to the final test. Some would make it by cutting a small triangular hole into the melon, and drawing out a sample for inspection. But no real worshiper of the melon would use methods so crude, and so sure to injure the fruit if opened too soon, even in so slight a manner. Our method was simple and I think true. Of course, we did as our elders did. We struck the melon with our little knuckles, and looked wise with a far away look as we listened to the sound. But that was not the real test. We touched the vine just where it was attached to the melon. If it snapped the fruit was ripe. If not, the proof was clear—the melon was still drawing sustenance from the vine. But to be sure of the test it was made early in the morning while the dew was still upon the plants; for later in the day under the hot and drying sun even a green vine might snap. We lived by this rule until watermelon later in the season or by the aid of marauders became more scarce. I will not say that under such pressure we did not sometimes welcome the aid of the drying sun, and did not perhaps give the vine a special tug. But even so, true to the methods of modern statesmanship we might neglect the spirit, but we always respected the letter, and we never lost the substance. With that intuition which makes the only true rules of conduct, we aimed to gather our melon in the early morning while the test was sure, and while the fruit itself was cool from the night's exposure. Then it was placed in our cool spring, to be taken out at the proper time. Sometimes we carried melons on our expeditions for several miles, holding them in our hands over the saddle knobs, and cooling them in a stream, for dessert after the swim and camp meal. City people may think they know what watermelon is. They eat them in our clubs as though they did. Often have I tried it in the attempt to fool myself back into the illusions of youth. But too often the melons are spongy, and do not dissolve like sugar on the tongue. He who as a boy has put his knife into the rind of a melon and has seen the running crack in response to the cut; who has had the luscious heart of a melon melt on his palate, will no more be deceived by a battered victim of modern traffic, than will he who has tasted a Rockyford in Colorado or Utah, be intrigued by the cross of melon and squash that is so often served to us. Even today a farmer's life has its advantages, its charm and its pleasures past compare.

HOME LIFE

As I think of our home life, it all seems so simple and so well ordered. The wonder is how it was done. The burden of course fell to mother, with father held for once in Prussian reserve for emergencies. This period covers my life from the age of six to fourteen; brother Paul was two years younger; and sister Clara, only six years old when I saw her last in the year 1863. In the course of these few years our lives, both play and work, underwent what by us were felt to be great changes; but our home's background seemed always the same, under the ever present parental influence. Father's practice had grown fast, and during the last few years of our stay—during the war—covered a circuit of from ten to twenty miles east and west. He had a few books, only a small choice of medicines and instruments; and was therefore quite dependent upon his university training and his own intuition and observation to deal with every phase of medical aid, physics or surgery. But this school is not to be despised. Years after in Berlin, when he was hearing lectures and visiting hospitals, a famous professor suddenly turned to him to make a diagnosis in an obscure case. Father paused and explained that his practice had been limited, so to speak, to the prairies. "For that reason I ask you. Save me from the man who has learned to lean upon others. Give me the man who has won, unaided, in the face of emergency." Father was embarrassed then, but he often recalled the incident.

Dr. Becker, twenty miles west, was the one other physician with whom father consulted from time to time; and for him he felt the deepest personal and professional regard. Father was perhaps an idealist, but he was not given to speculation in the field of occult sciences. He was inclined, however, to believe that Dr. Becker possessed the power to read thought and condition at the bedside. Bits of conversation between mother and father upon such subjects left impressions upon me that were never quite erased, and that without ever doing more may pursue me through life. Later, when mother had joined us and told us of the last illness of Paul and Clara, father found peace and comfort in the thought that everything possible had been done, because Dr. Becker, twenty miles away, had attended them to give the best he had.

As long as we lived in Millheim father made his rounds, riding an abnormally large mule, to the amusement of those who were well, and to the relief of those who were ill. For the mule was as wonderful to behold as he was fast and untiring as a traveler. When I now read of the trips made by camels across the desert, somehow that mule gets into the picture. In truth he looked not unlike a camel, and even his gait seemed patterned after that famous conquerer of distances. But with all his great stride, his fox trot was smooth and easy for the rider. He was the tallest, leanest mule, bar none, I have ever seen, and Missouri affords a chance for contrasts. In appearance he was the least attractive brute of his species and I have seen many. To make his title to this distinction doubly sure, one of his long ears had in his youth been attacked by worms and permanently weakened at the root. These worms were a constant menace to our animals. Every break in the skin was attacked by them. We fought them with calomel but the attack upon the animal's ear was often detected too late. So while his sound ear stood guard to point the danger, the other ear flopped unceasingly to the time of its owner's step. Father had all the presence of a man of military training, which, however, he could not claim. A fractured skull, received in a duel, saved him from ever having to wear the hated steel helmet. His mule was the least military contrivance ever seen on stage or in circus. I can not now wonder at the smiles of good-natured friends and neighbors, for the picture was unique. Astride that grotesque charger sat a figure, athletic in every line, known to be a great swimmer, runner, jumper and ten pin roller, with a name in German universities as a swordsman; with his strong, cleancut features, steady blue eyes, heavy head of hair and long flowing beard, set to meet any storm. If neighbors had not laughed, it would have been a reflection upon their sense of humor. But we, like children, instinctively sensing a friend, knew the virtues of this beast of burden. We judged him not by looks; and we did not laugh. He never threw anybody; he knew no tricks, he stuck to his gait; and he was always glad to be caught in the pasture. We knew a friend when we saw him; and we had reason to esteem him by contrast. As father had lost his grey horse, so had we lost our trusted Sam. Our equestrian exercises were now also restricted to a mule. He no doubt was of the same species, but otherwise he bore no likeness to father's. Where one was tall and lean, the other was small and round as a butter ball. Father's had been raised by us, and needed no brand to identify him. Ours was believed to have been owned by Indians, Mexicans and many white men before he came to us as the untiring tormentor of our youth. His age must have been great, for his body bore brands of letters, crosses and symbols, as countless as they were mysterious. In truth, when later I came to read Blackstone, the phrase "Memory of man runneth not to the contrary" always recalled my early impression of that mule's life. These two most intimate associates had no names, as all respected horses had. One was known as "Der grosse Esel" (large mule); the other "Der kleine Esel" (small mule); and that was all. But the contrast between the two was not left to size and shape alone. It was most pronounced in their characters. Our knowledge about Indians and Mexicans was limited; but as far as tradition and imagination would carry us, our mule was a past master in every trick that any race, in or out of circus, could have taught him. In our long experience with him, we hit upon only one unfailing symptom—docility in him meant trouble for us. I was thrown oftener and in more ways by him, and with less excuse, than by all the horses I ever rode. He had every advantage, endless resource combined with large experience, and a body so round that there were no shoulders to hold saddle or bareback rider. If I rode him down an incline to give him water, he kicked up behind to land me in the stream. If I rode him up the incline on the other side, he reared up in front, to let me slide over his haunches and repeat my bath. If I rode past a bunch of cacti, he shied, to see how near he could come to land me in the thorny nest. A boy's efforts with a lasso he seemed somehow to intercept with his one sound ear; and having fixed the unhappy boy's attention upon the lasso, he became startled by the confusion and deposited the boy on the ground. For, be it remembered, to complete the contrast, that while he, too, had a wobbling ear, the big mule had his on the right side, and the little mule had his on the left. So that when father and I rode out together, each mule with an ear wobbling in time and tune as it were to the click of the hoof of his particular pace, one with an ear erect for signal to his rider; the other with an ear alert to every chance for his rider's discomfiture—no wonder we broke the monotony of our neighbors' lives, and mine as well.

As a rule father was away most of the day. When he came home, any spare time was given to the small cares of the place; and without that he was weary enough to welcome rest and peace. While our bringing up was largely mother's care, she at no time had more than one maid — the Bohemian girl, a fiend for work; always cheerful, as glad of freedom in her sphere as we were in ours. But the kitchen took nearly all her time, because she cooked for the entire household, and for such hands as our little field in some seasons employed. Mother, therefore, had all the burden of the general household, which is now in itself regarded as a cruel task. She also had charge of the drug store, and I do not believe that ever a question arose as to a possible mistake or delay. The vegetable garden was in her charge, with such trifling aid as we children could give. While we were small that came to nothing, and as we grew older we went to school, and when in the garden had half an eye on the watermelon patch. Besides, there was the question of our clothing. Our work day clothes were simple enough — jeans — no doubt a hickory shirt — bought at the store until the war set its bounds. There were probably only a few sizes, and since brother was unusually small and I was uncommonly tall, we had but one choice, and that was the long and the short of it. For shoes, too, we were left no option. This meant the best fit the store afforded, and such quality as its owner approved. Polishing was reserved for state occasions — perhaps when we rode by the side of the lady who broke her brothers' horses. Grease to soften leather and to keep out wet was the thing. Long were the consultations to find ways and means to keep us from breaking our shoes down at the heel. This situation was so grave that even father took part in the conferences. There was but one outcome. Inasmuch as the shoes were not made to stand up of themselves, we had to do it for them; and it was for us to walk so straight that they would not bend out of shape. The instructions were clear, and the penalty in case of failure at least in doubt. No boys ever watched their step better than we did;

and when shoemakers now tell me that the soles of my shoes always wear out in the center, I know how I got the habit. Boots we had rarely; they were reserved for exhibition purposes, with one trouser leg down, the other stuffed into the top of the boot. Spurs, too, were largely ornamental, hung low to strike the ground as often as possible — to make an ominous noise — faint suggestion of the rattling of a scabbard on the sidewalk.

Even so, there was still the problem of holiday clothes, which mother did not leave to choice from a job lot. These she cut and sewed herself. And as the war stringency became more severe, she made all our clothes, finding her only relief from labor in the fact that it was not easy to obtain material to work upon. Even want has its compensations. The matter of hats is most clear in my memory. Store hats were a novelty to us.. Mother made most of ours out of palmetto leaves. These were taken, as I remember it, when young and pliable, were stripped into fairly narrow blades the length of the leaf, and were then platted into long ribbons, which were dexterously turned and sewed into the shape of a hat. We had to submit to frequent fittings, which impressed me as unhappy interruptions. New hats called aloud for hair cuts. This also was mother's task. The operation was simple. Scissors that cut cloth and calico could be trusted to trim hair. There was no fashion to embarrass us. We were as tractable as a modem candidate before a political convention. The aim was to shorten the hair; and one straight cut across would do it. So whether by accident or design we were generally released, presenting a distinct reminiscence of Lutheran custom. As I look back I see only that faithful figure with infinite care patiently striving to have her boys pass muster with the best. This was her work for our care as we saw it every day, and took for granted as children will.

As I see it now, I can not doubt that her chief thought went to our bringing up. Education is a large word, not to be applied to us; certainly not in the sense in which it is now used to describe the storing of facts. But in a more generous sense we must have, between our country school and mother's attention, have had more of it than we could guess. We were certainly helped at home with our lessons, and since books were few, that help must have been of a kind far beyond the ordinary. To remember what had been said at school, to make it our own, and the ability to restate it, was the test. In this we were aided at home by answers and explanations to endless questions. For this mother was well qualified by her very extensive reading, and sustained by her tireless concern for us. Watch was kept even over our handwriting, in the German script, of course. A few of my letters of that time in my possession now are written with the accuracy of lithography. I firmly believe that when later I was irregularly admitted to a high school in the North, it was done largely because I was a refugee asking for a chance, but partly because my writing with chalk showed that I had been under strict and intelligent discipline.

Father was not a great reader then; always rather a man of action. He was in the true sense an educated man; but while his German was otherwise perfect, he retained certain colloquials acquired in Berlin, such as giving "g" the soft sound of the German "j." Mother's reading at that time was necessarily limited by her duties, and by the scarcity of books. One journal came to us before the war — the "Kriminalzeitung," of New York, I think. It must have had much that did not pertain to crime or it would not have been admitted into our home; although I do not remember ever reading it. But there were letters from abroad, correspondence in the old sense, very treasures of information on affairs in Germany, combined of course with the usual family accounts. I remember hearing for instance, that my oldest uncle (after whom I was named) a patriot to the core, had declined an "Orden" saying that his work might rest upon its merits. All of which found a very warm response in our democratic hearts.

Our teacher had a somewhat better collection of general literature, and no doubt mother had free access to this. Our own books, however, were few. Some had probably been lost in the journey from abroad. But these few were fair samples of the ruling taste. Among them I recall Schiller's works, complete in two volumes; Schlegel's translation of Shakespeare (an old edition of which to my deep regret one volume was lost, probably in the course of our travels). Today I regard this translation as a rare reproduction of both text and spirit of the original. Tegner's "Frithjofssage" in the German translation. Gerstaecker's Arkansas hunting stories, also in German. I think "Der Deutsche Michel" although both book and title may be the mere echo of things overheard; and certainly the Lutheran song book with the names of mother's sisters and brothers written upon the fly leaf. I recall no others; but under the suggestive home influence I read in those named to some extent. Gerstaecker's Arkansas stories we devoured. These were actual hunting experiences, telling what we might hope to do any day; serious fights with wildcats, and similar narrow escapes galore. No doubt some of our more or less exciting escapades may be traced to its influence. It is natural that in such an atmosphere "The Robbers" engaged my chief interest among Schiller's plays, with "William Tell" a close second. It is equally natural that this early choice went to a play which I believe Schiller had in the meantime virtually repudiated as crude, if not worse. However, there were heroes in it, as nobody could deny;

and every Texan was at that period in training to be a hero, or at least a hero worshiper. In spirit I am that still; but feel somewhat discouraged for lack of material. In Schiller's Thirty Year War I remember that he regarded teaching history through leaders as the most effective method; which has its merit, and is well enough as long as the supply does not give out. Frithjofssage (at least the first volume) I read from cover to cover, getting out of it, if nothing more, a confirmed love of romance. Today the introductory stanza rests in my memory:

> "Es wuchsen einst in Hildings Gut
> Zwei Pflanzen unter treuer Hut
> Zwei schoenere nie im Nord erschienen; Sie
> wuchsen herrlich auf im Gruenen."

What a setting for the trials and triumphs of romance; certainly for a country lad.

That father still treasured his old student's song book was no secret, but we knew of it only through the singing which we sometimes heard. I had it for years, and have now given it to our only son to have him hold dear the memories of our ancestry. I must admit, however, that my oldest daughter Hildegard[a] is the one who best kept the

a The daughter of Charles and Fanny (Brandeis) Nagel, Hildegard Nagel was born and raised in St. Louis, Missouri. Her early years were marked by the death of her brother Alfred and the suicide of her mother, Franny Brandeis Nagel, the sister of Justice Louis D. Brandeis. Following her graduation from Bennett College in Millbrook, New York, Nagel worked with a psychoanalyst at Johns Hopkins University in Baltimore, where she met her lifelong friend, Ellen Thayer, a magazine editor. A student of Carl Jung and Gerhard Adler, Nagel spent most of her professional life as a psychiatric social worker in New York City. She was a member of the C.G. Jung Foundation for Analytical Psychology and served as president of the Analytical Psychology Club of New York. An edi-

idea alive in the original language. As a mere child she used to recite the story of the Iliad in German, tossing names of heroes to the right and left to revel in the fairy story. We heard father and mother perhaps speak of Schleiermacher, Lessing, Rueckert, Koemer, Arndt, Herder, Klopstock, Kleist, Tieck, Schlegel and other well-known names — no wonder when their section of Germany was really the home of the romantic school. The truth is that not until I had read Willoughby's "The Romantic Period in Germany" did I quite realize the natural and perhaps close association of my parents to the romantic school. Not until then did it come to me that even as father had rebelled against political restraint, so mother had welcomed release from the prescribed form of creed and classic literature. Ornaments and pictures we had none; and that may account for my disposition now to paste my walls with etchings, and to fill mantles and bookshelves with statuettes — making up for lost time. Most of my early reading was had in the belief that a book was not worth while unless it meant work, in marked contrast to the modern movie and kindred thought saving devices. Our home was impressed with the sense of duty — father almost austere, mother devoted to make it sweet and gentle. I like to believe that it is this same spirit that must sustain the German people in their hour of distress. In that spirit I waded through Humboldt's Cosmos before I was nineteen, coming out with no more than awe at the vast-

tor, translator, and writer, Nagel helped to disseminate Jungian ideas in this country, publishing a critique of Jung's essay, "Answer to Job," as well as other papers delivered to the Analytical Psychology Club of New York. Nagel died on February 16, 1985, in Buzzards Bay, Massachusetts. (Hildegard Nagel Papers, 1868-1985; item description, dates. 86-M211, folder #. Schlesinger Library, Radcliffe Institute, Harvard University, Cambridge, Mass - in http://oasis.lib.harvard.edu/oasis/deliver/~sch00754 accessed May 23 2017).

ness of the universe, and admiration for the persistent author. Happily, a kindlier influence led me by degrees to Buckle's "History of Civilization," and Goodrich's "British Eloquence." Then I was persuaded that it would be proper to read Thackeray, Dickens and Bulwer, and, finally, much later, I succumbed even to the detective story. Virtually all of these earlier books are still on my shelves, many of them to read and re-read. Others in sweet memory of what they have given me. Even the best of friends become remote unless they appear to us now and then; and so I get pleasure by the mere presence of titles of books to tell me of what they have given me, and can give again for the asking.

However, the one book which I do not remember ever reading while in Texas, and which nevertheless had lasting influence upon my life, was the Bible, and this again entirely through the influence of mother. I have known a few persons who both ruled and inspired without seeming to do either. She was one of them. Her eyes seemed never to search, but always contemplated, saw and understood. Only in later years do I remember ever hearing her speak about religion; but in some unconscious fashion she seemed in her very life to impress all her surroundings with religious faith. Her belief appeared to be bound nowhere by the letter, and seemed never to miss the mandate of the spirit.

> "Der Glaube ist wie die Liebe
> Er laesst sich nicht erzwingen" (Goethe)

When first as a boy I heard the now half forgotten verse "Twinkle, twinkle, little star, how I wonder what you are," I did not dare to repeat it in my faltering English. The lines were spoken by night under the broad canopy of a Texan sky. With a child's fancy, half sensing the eternal problem, never to be answered, I gazed upon the bright stars far into the very depths of heaven, there to rest. Neither clergyman nor philosopher, nor scoffer can say more than a child could feel. No influence but mother's could have prompted that dream and make it live. To her I owe it that now I can not always reconcile religion and creed.

Years afterwards I was visited by a committee of clergymen who felt called upon to make sure of my religion before giving their support to my candidacy for public office. I did not regard the point as altogether regular, but was glad to waive it. I told them that I had learned my religion at the knees of my mother, a clergyman's daughter. That I could not say how and when I was taught; but that faith had come to me like something given without command or struggle, indeed, consciousness. That I could not recite many parts of the Bible, but felt secure in its spiritual mandates. Finally, I told them that no doubt they could repeat the Ten Commandments, while I had to confess that I could not. But to put our spiritual preparedness to the test, I offered to submit with them to an examination by any competent committee into the conduct of our lives with respect to the Ten Commandments. That ended the interview; and the result of the election seemed to show no evil effects.

When our only son went to boarding school I went with him; the question which one was the greater sufferer left undetermined to the last. He, the prospective victim of homesickness, and I wrestling with that ever recurrent problem, what and how much a father should say to his son. Recalling my own youth, I knew that the one unfailing guide to me had been the thought that come what might, I wanted to be able to meet those large and steady eyes at home. I had tried to cheat them once; but protestations, pleading and, finally, begging, were met by the one unrelenting answer, "Karl, that is not the truth." When at last I broke down and confessed there was neither penalty nor admonition. But there was never another conflict of that kind between mother and me. I made sure ever after to be prepared to meet that look, which followed me through the years of my youth, and stood like a warning between me and many a menace. So I told my son just to think of his own mother, and nothing more. Again years later I had the deep satisfaction of having him tell me what those simple words had meant to him, and to feel how the unspoken counsel from the prairie had stood in the life of our generation.

To say that our family life was serious is perhaps not quite fair so far as it concerns the children. It is true that the North German is apt to take life hard. He is guided by a rigid devotion to principle and duty as he sees them which is not unlike the Puritan as we picture him. Indeed, it may be that the enlightenment of a century or more had made the newcomer more tolerant of the opinions of others, than the historian has us think of the earlier immigrants. However, there was little in conditions to soften the inherited attitude of grown people. Father's profession was no fair weather occupation. Good weather or foul, from early morn until late at night he rode his circuit on the faithful mule. Beating sun, downpour of rain or bitterest norther were faced with no thought of self. I see him now returning from a weary ride, with his long flowing beard tossed and parted, to be swept over his shoulders, but never the turn of a degree of his square, straight features from the unrelenting heat or storm. Perhaps he was even then lost in thought about this or that patient, wondering whether his diagnoses were right, going back to the wise counsel of great teachers in search for the true remedy, and speculating, if all else were correct what prescription his modest assortment would permit him to write. Father had cares enough to confirm the natural sternness of his character, and outside his home he saw little enough to soften it.

Upon mother's share I need not dwell farther, although it would be easy to name the varied cares that are not part of daily routine. The household purchases, the storing of the farm's products for home use, and the preserving of fruit and vegetables, which was done on quite a large scale. For illustration, we used to cut peaches in slices with the skin on, and then put them out on a clean sheet on the roof of the house to dry in the sun. In that task I was always glad to help, because no one cared to keep count of the slices to be dried. I loved them dried almost as well as fresh; and to this day I have to keep my hands in my pocket when I pass a dried peach stand in the market. One day, looking up at our drying peaches, I saw that the roof was on fire, just where it joined the chimney. The alarm paralyzed every one but mother. The Bohemian cook appealed to the Deity, and we boys stood aghast. Mother, however, put a ladder against the edge of the roof, told the cook and me to fill tin pails with water, climbed up the ladder, ordered us to carry the pails up to the roof, which as far as I am concerned was done by some power not my own. She met us at the edge of the roof, carried the pails up the slanting roof to the top, put out the fire, and in the evening upon father's return included it among the happenings of the day.

Finally, in case of illness, mother was the nurse. Who else was there? And whenever I was very hilarious, she would be ready for the next siege with the simple words, "you are too gay; you will have chills and fever tomorrow"; and she would be right.

MAETZE'S SCHOOL

We came to Millheim for several reasons. Father wished to be nearer the more thickly settled community which provided part of his practice and promised a larger one; both parents felt the loneliness of their life, remote from neighbors; and finally, there was the question of a school for growing children. As yet there were very few of school age, because most settlers had come later than father and mother, and as rather young people. But in Millheim there was at least a nucleus, and there, too, was the one man who could fill the place of teacher. So after we had settled there the first steps were taken to enter me. There were a few children and a teacher; but there was no school house; either because it had not yet been built or because it had been destroyed by fire. The answer was simple. Why wait for a school house when the teacher had a sitting room that would hold us, and would save him a walk. Our first "Educational Institution," as we would now call it, was therefore started in Gustav Maetze's sitting room and library in his little frame house, tucked away in a grove of black jack or scrub oak, but not without the welcome of shrubs and flowers. From our home it was not a mile, not far enough at least for any one but a modem automobile slave, to ride. I do not recall all the pupils; but there were the teacher's son and daughter, and no doubt two or three Engelkings—all quite strange to me. I was what we called a regular cottonhead—a full head of hair; blond—almost white—with the blue eyes of the North, and fair skin burnt brown. Free as a lark in the open, I was shy, almost timid with strangers. Even when perched on top of our moving wagon leaving Saint Bernardo, I had been troubled by vague fears of the terrors of which I heard them speak.

Now the hour had come. Father himself took me to the teacher, and I said "Good morning," and gave my hand to this large and serious man. Was he kind, I wondered: I knew he was wise. Only a wise man could look like that. Besides, he was a teacher and must be wise. All I can say now of that first awful day is that we at last reached recess, and that I made an effort to run away. I did this in sheer fright, for that sort of conduct was foreign to us. I hid in the brush, never never to come back; and there the teacher soon found me. Happily for my future state of mind he showed no anger. With simple kindness he sat down by me and talked to me just as he often spoke to all of us—always drawing on his rich store of history, or fairy lore. He told me, too, of games that no boy could play alone, and how recess was meant to give boys a chance to learn and to play new games. He won me, of course, and I today wonder how many teachers in the humdrum life of our crowded schools have the chance or even care to use this "first aid" to teaching. I came with him; and now look back upon those seven or eight years spent under his eye with hardly an echo of trouble in school, and with a vivid memory of stirring sport in games.

But more and more children grew to school age; and even a teacher's library could not make room for them all. While there we became a friendly little group. One for all—all for one. We listened, if we did not always learn together. What was said for or to one missed no one. Every word of praise or censure hit the class. No truer picture of our state have I seen than a well known canvas in which an outraged teacher holds up a page stained with ink blots, scolding the culprit, to the dismay of those comrades who are within the range of the teacher's vision, and to the amusement of those who are not. I could almost name the hour and the offender. All this was now doomed to go.

The demand of expansion was upon us. Not "Light, more light" so much as "Room, more room" was the call. For this is clear; every pupil added must serve to weaken the effect of the teacher's work; however it might widen the circle of our sports.

It was left to Engelking to provide the new or rather the first school-house of which I know, probably because he had three boys to attend—the majority ruling, as we are taught it should. The idea stuck, because he always continued to be a Democrat. He built the school-house at a point to best suit his own boys. He set it down within a stone's throw of his store, right on the edge of his small cornfield and on the border of a deep gulch, which heavy rains tore into forms more and more grotesque. The school-house was painted white, and lives in my memory as a smart little affair not unlike an enlarged modern beach bathing house, and with very much the same general exterior. For furnishings we had several rows of long plank benches with crude little desks in front. To the delight of all, those desks had lids that could be opened, and even had holes for inkstands. The teacher's desk was larger and sat on a little platform. There were a few books for the teacher's use, chief of which was a dictionary; and we had a few primers, still in German. Most of our writing was done on old-fashioned slates; and to their grinding effect on the nervous system, I trace my aversion to discordant noises. Our final proof of penmanship and our tasks in the shape of essays were written with pen and ink. The only other aid to the teacher's equipment was a well polished cane— the size of a small fishing rod. There were a few of us who had reason to regret that it had not been left to serve what was regarded as its natural purpose. The essentials of the study course were the three R's; and in these our showing must have been quite good. Of arithmetic I recall nothing

—a failing that stayed with me through life. Reading aloud to the whole school remains very clearly with me. Our teacher must have thought well of it for I never lost the habit. In writing I clearly excelled—certainly in form. The teacher's method of relating incidents in history; his easy but spirited manner must have been very effective. Some of his descriptions stand out today like paintings on canvas. The difficulties of his task were, however, on the increase. As our numbers grew, the ages of the pupils varied more and more. With one room and only one teacher, there was little chance for classes, although teaching was more and more needed for different grades. I see him now either listening to our recitations or lost in a discussion of some theme or description of some incident, or walking up and down the short aisles inspecting our work, encouraging with approval or admonishing with counsel or warning. He seemed to be a man of strong passion under severe restraint. As a rule we got the benefit of the latter, but on rare occasions the former was given full swing. In such an event, misgivings filled our hearts, for there was no assurance that punishment intended for a particular culprit would be directed with the required precision to hit its special mark. Our teacher had no doubt given more thought to the cultivation of his mind than to athletic training. I will mention no names, but it is true that we had one or two very-nice comrades whose conduct in school engaged our teacher's unceasing attention and provoked his peculiar ire. At one time his impatience must have reached a climax, for we saw hurled through the air a large volume with leaves wildly fluttering— strangely generous spreading of learning, looking as large and ominous to us as a modern dictionary. The dismay on the teacher's face at the rashness of his act was soon relieved, because no one was hit and the book fell to the floor, to be used thereafter with more care and greater wisdom. After all, books were rare, and not to be thrown away on bad boys. Indeed, the teacher did not easily forget himself, and use was not often made of books in that fashion. The cane was the thing. It was cheaper, and also very handy. I would not say that thrashing was a frequent occurrence; but there were some reminders of the ancient custom. The rule was to haul the culprit (in those early days of romance and chivalry, always a boy) into the aisle, and there, holding him at arm's length by the collar, to show the practical use to which a well cured cane could be put for the discipline of a school. Our lack of faith in our teacher's aim was not without reason. There were times when even the cane failed of its mark, and of these I have reason to remember one. My neighbor in school was my age—a dear fellow at play, and the most confirmed shirker of school tasks I ever knew. His chief interest in work took the form of its recommendation to me for my good. Somehow I have been particularly afflicted during my life with thoughtful advice of that sort. People who were wise in making rules for others seemed to feel a peculiar concern for me. Indeed, had I been a better judge of human affairs, I should have sensed the threat of the Eighteenth Amendment many years before I really did; and my measures for its advent would have been far more complete and perhaps provident than they were. But to return to my neighbor on the school bench who caused the whole incident, for the account of which (be it his experience or mine) I must rely in some respects upon hearsay. It is true that I was lost to the world, probably worrying over some problem of addition or division, or worse. My neighbor was recklessly sagging on the bench. The teacher was seen to parade the aisle with measured steps. That the cane was carried at his side was known to only a few. My dear neighbor showed no sign of awakening to either work or danger, and our teacher gave no warning of the ire that was rising in him. He was glad to bide his time. The longer the offender persisted, the more clear the case for punishment. At last the moment had arrived. There was a sudden commotion; the teacher had leaped to a point between the benches, and with one fell swoop the cane came down on my back, not protected by so much as a fair share for my neighbor. The teacher had for some time had his eye on the boy; but he having no eye for books, also kept at least one eye on the movements of the teacher. At the pivotal moment he shoved forward, and left me to take the brunt, without mercy or regret. Well, the cane was not broken; my neighbor had made his escape. The teacher was so flustered that he quite forgot what he had in mind; and I was left to reflect that even great teachers may make mistakes, and, indeed, may have to ask pardon of small boys. Perhaps I even cherished the incident in memory of another act of quick temper at my cost. Only one other time did he strike me, and that, though intended, was done in passion. I was writing in German script and he was watching me. It was in the early days of the school. Still fearing him, my trembling hand gave the proof in black and white, and he struck me on the cheek. To this day I resent it as undeserved and cruel, and I often wonder how many grown people suspect the power for mischief of such an act. It is strange how even the wrong of a speech will linger as when I was timid and awkward about something, our teacher said, "If I were to hand you an inkstand I think you would put your finger in it;" or when my speech in answering him was involved, he said, "Sprich wie Dir der Schnabel gewachsen ist" (Speak as the beak has grown in your face). But these were exceptions that must not be dwelt upon. Quite the contrary, taking the hotchpotch of that school, boys and girls from six to ten, and more, very few books and only one teacher, I marvel at the patience and the tact that kept us in check and held our interest.

Again, the number of pupils outgrew the school house; and this time the new building was erected by concerted effort. It was placed nearer the teacher's home, and to us. It was plain in the extreme, built of rough boards, with the old fashioned shingle roof, one large fireplace, a bare plank floor, all furnished with the old desks and benches added to for the larger attendance. The exterior was almost forbiddingly barren—not even painted. What there was to give went to the interior. The modern conception was still foreign to our people. The merit of a school was not to be judged by the building, and the importance of a discourse did not depend upon the size of the subject. There I received the benefit of a lasting influence. As I look back upon that time, I can not resist the feeling that Gustav Maetze was probably as great a teacher as I ever had.

I need not wonder when I reflect upon the career of this man before he came to this country. Of the details I know little; but he was a graduate of Breslau, and had been deeply interested in the movements which preceded and followed the revolution of 1848. He was not merely a protesting citizen, but he was prominent enough even as a young man to be elected a representative to the Prussian National Assembly. Not many years ago, in reading Bismarck's speeches, I was surprised to find that one of the earliest, in 1849, was made in answer to one Maetze. It turned upon the question of amnesty for political offenses; and I wondered whether my teacher might have remained there so long. I imagine it must have been he, because the movers of the resolution upon which the discussion turned immediately after made their escape to avoid arrest. However that may be, they were both young men then, Bismarck, perhaps, at his most reactionary period, and Maetze no doubt at the other extreme. Thus it happened that when the test came, one remained to reach highest place and to achieve fame in the practical affirmation of his strong convictions, while the other barely got across the border, to make his way to our new country, there to treasure his dreams for himself, and to give to the youth growing up about him the inspiration of his liberal belief. I can now trace many impressions if not convictions to the influence of this man. Of the old country I do not recall more than bare mention. It must in many ways have been a painful subject to him. But with ancient history he was more ready and generous. I have read of the Athenians and Spartans; but their arms I have heard clash only once, and that was when this teacher, all afire with enthusiasm, drew up the opposing lines to engage in conflict; or told how a few men held the pass against an overwhelming mass of troops; or how a messenger, panting from exhaustion, holding his left side with one hand and a wreath of victory aloft in the other, announced the result of the battle of Marathon. Many of us in our little school have since read of heroes in history and in fiction, but nothing can ever efface the dramatic pictures that this teacher then fixed in my mind. Children are prone to take for granted what comes to them, particularly if they like it. I am not sure that I should ever have been awakened to a proper sense of what this man did for us; but for a single circumstance that came to me as late as 1893. During the World's Fair in Chicago, the director of our Art Museum in St. Louis was Director General of the Department of Art. I was a member of his board at home, and he gave me special opportunities to see the art exhibit, perhaps because he and I had a small sum which we were seeking to invest for our Museum. A night or two I slept on a lounge in his office to get a good view of the exhibit in the morning before the doors were opened. At the close of the Fair I think I could have given the position of every painting or piece of sculpture of moment. It was a very feast for one who had once dreamed of being an artist. In my wanderings through these long halls of things beautiful or execrable, I saw objects familiar to greet again or to pass, and things new like revelations. One day I came upon a large bronze statue, "The Messenger of Marathon," by Max Kruse, which is now placed in front of one of the museums in Berlin, where I saw it in September, 1914, on our way home during the World War, and again in 1928. The impression this figure first made upon me was fairly startling. It was not only the intrinsic beauty of conception and the great perfection of execution. It was the manner in which my teacher was suddenly recalled to me. I felt the full truth and force of his vivid descriptions; and quite unconsciously said to myself, "That is the way in which he told it." Never until then had I quite felt this man's influence. Now I look back upon some of his early suggestions as I treasure Goodrich's "British Eloquence," as determining influences in my life.

Probably we were told many things of our own country which I have now forgotten, or which were in time merged in the mass of information from other sources. Perhaps the bitter trials of the Civil War and the tragedy of the Great War in a manner obscured some of them. Whatever the truth may be about that, I recall only one impression of my country—the glory of it. We had it all, we had but to enjoy—a strange attitude for youngsters of our bringing up. We were always right, and we could lick anybody; another conclusion not in entire accord with the outcome of some of our personal encounters. But of this there is no doubt. Imagination about our state and our country was fired to a degree that would make the wordy pictures of a modern Fourth of July orator look pale, faded and shopworn. The very grandeur of the idea made it the more simple. "Sam" stood for Swearengen, for Houston — of Texas, and for the United States. History simplified. What more could a boy ask. Nothing more clear than patriotism. Keep your eye on the goal, and do the rest. Who fixes the goal is another matter; as even we were to know before we were many years older. But even so, the extravagant idealization of Houston was certainly more wholesome than the exaggerated prominence today of baseball and golf heroes.

In a way our teacher of course prompted these rather vague ideas of glory and patriotism. But I bear him no grudge. His impulse carried us away from a world so small that it could be measured by the yard stick. His revolt against too much government may have been too intense; and his enthusiasm may have obscured wretched facts. But there was the all powerful appeal of a man who had us believe that the fight of this life is worth while. No morbid thought was ever permitted to creep in. No cheap slogan was employed as without book or note, with the freedom and earnestness of a true orator, he held us spellbound with his stories of the great, the noble and the true. Perhaps what was said of another great teacher was true of him. Prof Rudolph Eucken, of Jena, Germany, is credited with having had a profound religious influence upon the German people of our time. As is the case of all men and women who have something to give, he had critics, who said that his lectures on religion were all very well; but that he did not reach definite conclusions. Perhaps they expected him to give an account of the beginning and end of the world — it would be such a labor-saving device. I know little of the merits of the controversy, but I read with great satisfaction the comments of an Englishman. He had heard Prof. Eucken lecture. He admitted that Eucken's dealing with things unknowable might be somewhat vague; but he made the simple and to me welcome defense that no student had ever entered Prof. Eucken's lecture room without coming out imbued with a higher and nobler purpose of life. In my own experience the dean of our Law School at one time asked whether I thought I managed to give our students a clear conception of the principles of Constitutional Law. Perhaps I parried somewhat by answering that in view of possible changes by one means or another, definitions too precise might in time prove embarrassing. But I sought to retrieve myself by expressing the hope that no student had ever entered my classroom who had not gone out with greater devotion to our institutions and respect for the Constitution of the United States. This I owe in some fashion to my teacher on the prairie, and I am glad to remember it, although in the meantime my position is in danger of being regarded as quite old-fashioned.

But education does not rest with teachers alone, nor even with parents. The modern playground is more than a breathing place for children that live under cramped conditions. It is a potent influence by the simple method of give and take, to fashion true rules of self-government. Our school was not without its playgrounds. It was not "all work and no play." There was space without limit, and we had but to make it serve our plans, and above all to choose our games. By that time there must have been from thirty to forty pupils, most of them boys. In that first generation boys seemed to predominate, in numbers at least, and, and I recall, they were taller than their parents. We were a mixed, very democratic set of youngsters. Even the children of the educated parents differed greatly in background, tastes and bringing up. This distinction was of course much more marked in the case of children whose parents were real farmers or had more modest occupations; and of these there were many. The school, however, knew no such distinction, as there is no safer leveling process than the playground. I am very conscious of my wish to emulate some of my otherwise less favored playmates. In school I may say that I rather had the advantage of them, but in the open I frankly looked up to them for example.

I had always been a weakling—hardly expected to live, as I have been told. The strength and the endurance of some of the others greatly impressed me, and I soon came to follow where I could and to counter where I might, by bringing into play some of my own unsuspected advantages. In some respects, however, I always remained a gaping onlooker. There was one boy (one of the older ones) rather slow in school, but a wonder on the playgrounds. Among other things, he boasted of his contempt for pain. To prove it he would ask us at the distance of a few paces to throw our rubber ball at him. In those days these balls were solid and hard as wood; so that his claim was not without merit, and the performance was altogether persuasive to us. I have sometimes wondered just how Schopenhauer with his theory that pleasure is the absence of pain would have dealt with this example. Consistently this boy's life should have been one holiday of unbroken pleasure. But it seems to have run very much the common course. Much later, when both he and I were grey, and when I had not seen him for say forty years, I found him sitting in my waiting room. He wore a full beard, and had come North with a shipment of cattle. He stood up, and with a half diffident air said to me, "You will not know me." I asked him to give me a chance, and after a minute said to him, "You and I went to the old school together; you were the boy who let me throw the ball at him. You lived on the way to Catspring on the left where the corner of your fence touched the road. Your name is Hilbodt." All he said was "Well!" and then we fell to reminiscing, even as I am doing now. I knew him by his eyes. There was something challenging in their calm and peace. Similarly some years later, while walking aimlessly in the street of a Mexican village, a stranger suddenly said to me "You are a son of Dr. Nagel. He saw me once when I was supposed to be dying. I shall never forget those eyes."

We were just a lot of boys and girls, with variety enough to provide fun or to put us to the test. In the school room we were one group of pupils. Outside the girls and the boys each followed their own kind of play. Our opportunity was of course limited; the greater the call upon our recourse. We had long distance and high jumping. "Horse shoes" we never played; we had not heard of Chief Justice Marshall, and our horses were not shod in those early days. We did run short distance and even endurance races, and we played ball. It was all very simple, of course, both equipment and performance. We made our own bats; and with that we played the ordinary game of hitting our ball to send it as far as possible, the decision resting with the ability of the field to catch the ball in the air. Very primitive, of course, but destined to develop into our more perfected modern baseball, a game that to me is almost as confusing in the intricacies of the play as it is confounding in the language used to describe it. My favorite game, as I recall it, was "Black Man's Out." The reason for this name I do not know, and can not guess. Black men were almost unknown to us; and the game itself in nowise suggested the state of the black man as we might have heard of him. The boys were divided into two equal parties, which were stationed on opposing bases, one or two hundred yards apart. The point was to have as many as possible of one side reach the opposite base without being tagged by members of the other side. It looks very simple; but it gave chance for a good deal more strategy and skill than appears at first blush. A fast runner and a good dodger had the best if not the only chance. The game was my delight, because I was good at both. I could so to speak outrun anything in the county; and being as light as a deer, soon made dodging a specialty. How I used to rush at once to the very edge of the field, leaving all the slow ones of the opposition, and having only one or two left to contend with, tempt them into a wild dash, only to evade them by a sudden turn behind them, and then unchallenged reach the base. Again and again I would be the only one left on my side to escape.

As I recall it all, it was the first conscious feeling of personal triumph. Here at last was one thing on the playground in which I could excel, a feeling which relieved me in a fashion from earlier humiliations. Like other timid and sensitive boys I had been made the victim of teasing and jesting. It seemed cruel and I suffered from a sense of injustice. At one time older and stronger boys even struck me to see whether I would fight. I was beside myself with indignation and a feeling of helplessness. Getting out my little pocket knife I opened it and rushed at the first comer. Why it ended with that I do not know but it did end then and there. The use of a knife was quite within Texas custom of that time although when knives were used they were larger. But our alien colony had not yet adopted the custom. For a long time I thought with horror of what I might have done; and to this day, I try to judge every act with a thought for its conditions and environments. Nor was leap frog neglected; or wrestling. No boy could go without this friendly test of strength. I did not favor it, because I was not good at it. Of course I took my turn, as all boys did. Agility was my only hope for success or escape. We had not heard of Japanese methods. For that matter we were blissfully ignorant of all rules of the ring. We had one aim, which was to get the other fellow down; or at least not to let him get you down. Putting your foot behind the other fellow and bending his back was the favorite trick. I could not do that often, because I lacked the strength. But my quickness generally saved me from having the opponent do it for me. However, wrestling has no place in my list of triumphs; my length was measured on the ground too often. At marbles I was better — skill not strength was needed. It was surprising at what distance I could hit a marble. I have no bent to speculate about such things, but it is true that in a vague fashion I felt the power of personal will in making the shot. Be that as it may, to this day I love to handle marbles. They remind me of pleasant little triumphs. I must rest content with that memory; for in later years I have never had the suggestion of the power of will over matter confirmed.

Our school was planned only for our own kind. Whatever other differences there might be, we were entirely German. Not even Bohemians attended at that time. But one day our school was thrown into a state of great excitement. There appeared during recess the only daughter of Swearengen, about seven or eight years old, and Angelina by name. How or why she came I can not say. Perhaps she was curious; perhaps lonely, way off at the remotest point of the forest, forever looking out upon the great prairie, and no children to play with. Whatever it was, she came into a strange world. She could not have understood it, and I wonder whether she could have suspected the surprise she brought to us. She never came again, and so neither could tell the other; but I may tell of us as best I can.

We were a crew of sunburnt youngsters. Most of us barefoot, and hats were regarded as a hindrance to freedom. There are differences in sunburn to be sure, and we had among us every grade from cottonhead to jet black. But in contrast to this visitor we were just one lot of the commonest type of brownies. She wore some light fabric, in contrast to the dresses of our girls, probably in color rather than cost. But that visit was all sufficient for the boys. Her hands had not been exposed to the sun, her skin was fair, and her hair hung over her shoulders, blond and wavy. As for the rest, every survivor will indulge his or her own imagination. I swear that as I saw her eyes they were blue, and could not have been anything else. I do not know whether she was handsome or not; but she was beautiful. I had reached the ripe age of say ten years, and I ought to know that she was more of a vision than a person—an impression which was perhaps confirmed by her constrained silence. To this day I treasure the picture; and I have never seen sketch or painting of an artist's conception of an angel without thinking of that girl's appearance among us. Some such feeling was shared by all of us. We were alien as she was. We were not somehow the same kind. Could it be true that we were not quite American, and that to be so we would have to become different? I vaguely felt all this; and, right or wrong, I accept the experience as a most welcome and persuasive process in Americanization, in marked contrast to most of the crude and opinionated proceedings of the present day.

Once more before leaving Texas I had seen that girl. I think a number of boys out on the prairie came in to find shelter from a rough weather surprise. Not acquainted with each other's language, we played tossing pillow cushions. I came away feeling that she stood apart as something different, but that, strangely enough, she liked to play just like common children.

When in 1909 I revisited my old home for the first time, while standing alone thinking of the tragedy of our parting and all that followed, there came up a grey haired rider—of the old cowboy type— and reigned his horse before me. "I came twenty miles to see you, although you do not know me," he said. I answered with the picture of that girl's visit to our school before me, "You are one of the Swearengen boys, which one I do not know now, but you had a sister whom I have remembered. I know that she married a Bohemian, and that they were happy and well to do. Is she living?" Assured that she was, I added "I am old enough to send her a message. Tell her for me that I have never forgotten her, and that she lives in my memory as the artist's ideal of an angel. Please give her my very best wishes for her happiness." "I sure will," he said, "and she will be happy to know it," and with that he galloped away.

At that period the games we played during recess or even after school filled a large part of our lives. Most of our spare time we after all had to ourselves, and in making the most of that time, we built upon the examples and the suggestions of our playmates.

PLAY AND WORK AT HOME

But the change crept upon us; although the beginning and growth of a boy's work on a small farm is quite unnoticed. With a devoted mother, engaged in tasks varied and many, there are a hundred ways in which a youngster can help. I trust I did this, but shall have to leave it with that. My first duties, in addition to bringing in the cows and feeding the horses and mules, were rather restricted to the vegetable garden and the front lawn of our home. Carrying water, and even watering the plants with the old-fashioned sprinkling can (improvised, I think), were among my earliest tasks. We helped gather peas, and even shelling them, with such robbery on the way as hungry boys would be guilty of. We worked with rake and hoe and even with a spade to loosen the earth or destroy the weeds around the plants. We dug out radishes, carrots, and turnips, and even Irish and sweet potatoes, and carried them to the house. When it came to peaches and other fruit, we were not left to operate alone, because fruit must be handled with care, and there must have been a desire to save some of the best for the household. Our lawn was a very modest affair. But we did have the place enclosed by a picket fence. There were the two cedar posts giving support for the entrance gate. Hard as metal they were, as we found one day when father fired a new six shooter at one of them, and to our surprise had the bullet hit and rebound, to fall at our feet on the piazza. Just inside the gate were two gorgeous yuccas reaching high up in the air. I would make myself believe that I saw them in bloom; but perhaps the many others that I saw later on confuse my memory. There were flowers tended by mother, perhaps watered by us, what kind I do not know. The "Kornblume" was mother's favorite, certainly so far as color goes, but I can not say whether we had it. The front of our porch was covered with climbing roses, rich in bloom in spring and summer, and giving protection from the southern sun, so that we took our noon meal out there in comfort. The rest was just grass, left to grow with little restraint, because the sickle meant hard work, and the mowing machine we did not know. So wild was the growth that coming upon a snake was not unusual, although that did not keep us from rolling about upon the grass in play with the dogs or without them.

But the demand upon our work grew with us. Our farm was small, because father depended chiefly upon his practice. We raised what we needed for ourselves, our horses, milk cows, dogs and hogs. Our home stood on the highest hill about, bare as a desert, always dry and only poorly covered by struggling grass. To the west at the foot of the hill was Constant Creek, not to be trusted for water. In the rear was Mill Creek, at that time never quite dry, but varying from a timid stream to sudden rises out of the banks, far into the dense forest. The soil beyond our hill and near these streams, was very rich, black as coal, but soft as though it held oil—perhaps it did. In bad weather our horses were kept in the barn to the east. Just beyond to the pen across the main road the cows were brought to be milked, and here they were sometimes kept over night. Beyond that was the garden, and then came our little field of corn and cotton which with our neighbor's cornfields, was the only break in our view upon the great prairie south. In this field we met our first tasks as farmers in action.

So far our work had been half play, not quite free from a child's curious interest. In fact, I think I owe to that early time my love—perhaps something akin to understanding, for plants. To this day I will fight for the life of a tree, tend it like a living thing, visit it as I would a friend. A tree helped this year is apt to help himself next year. It is not always so with a man. No such sentiment ever took me to the field, although corn at least suggested the gratitude of a beloved animal. Our cotton stretched in regular rows down an incline to the very bottom near the creek. However small our planting, we had every grade of growth from the measliest plant with small bowls and cotton sticking in the cup or mixed with dried leaves, to the richest plant rising high above our heads, with green leaves thick to suffocation, and the bowls evenly opened, holding a wealth of flowing cotton to be easily taken by a deft hand, the smaller the better. But it was labor for old or young. True, the bags were suited to our size, but even so the drag seemed to us a heavy burden. We would start down between two rows with the empty bag slung over the head, but resting on the right shoulder and hanging on the left side. The picking would be done chiefly with the right hand, the left one aiding; and would follow the right row, and one side of that if the plants were too thick for short arms to reach through. The cotton as picked would be shoved into the bag, the first point being to so pack it as to have the bag stand open for easy reach. As the collection grew, the strain of the bag grew with it until finally, between the weight of the bag and the heat of the sun beating down upon us between high plants, we were quite ready to think our lot as hard as Hermann Vahl, with his natural dislike for labor, would have us believe. No doubt most boys have at times thought that some ordered task was unjust. If I have to name the one that stirred me to this feeling, it was this one—always with the aid of this young man whom father had sought to rescue. Only now when I say this does it become clear to me what endless mischief might have been wrought by this alien influence in our home. I could not have been more than twelve then, because upon the declaration of the Civil War Hermann joined the Confederate army, and with the exception of one brief visit after the war, in St. Louis, I never saw him again. After we had gone, and after Paul's death, Hermann visited mother the last time as she says in an affectionate reference to him in one of her letters which reached father long after. I can not well describe my feeling for him. He was grown then, and just the figure to fire a boy's imagination. In many ways his example was good — even inspiring. At the same time I felt even then that his attitude was one of antagonism to our parents, and this, happily for me, I resented. In some ways therefore, the war with all its tragedy for us was a blessing in disguise for me. It set me free once for all from the danger which our parents' charity had planted in our midst. In another way it changed the whole course of my life. But for the war I should no doubt have been sent to school in Germany, partly because our parents knew of no advanced schools in our country; partly because of the respect which they, in spite of grievances felt for German institutions; and chiefly because deep attachment for grandmother prompted the wish that we might see her and live under her influence for a time. Even when we fled it was planned that I might be sent or taken to Germany. I can not but wonder what a German bringing up and the outcome of such an experience might have been. In my heart I congratulate myself upon an escape from conditions the effect of which I should hardly have been able to resist. Where the appeal to imagination is strong, it is not easy to hold admiration in needed restraint or proper relation. With my start in youth, I feel that I can not forget my debt to the influence of American institutions. My education it is true was haphazard at best; but somehow it taught me the most essential point of view—respect for the country of my fathers, with loyalty for my own.

In the cornfield our work was much less tiring. The plough I handled only a few times—making more of an impression upon tender muscles than upon the soil. Here we were at least on higher ground not cut off from the chance of breezes. In kind the work differed. At times we peeled the leaves from the stalk, gathered them in regular lots, and then twisting a few of these long leaves into a binder, made each lot into a bundle for hauling and storage. At other times we gathered the ears of corn by breaking them from the stalk. This called for some art. Perhaps I never got the trick, but I combined a twist and jerk, and usually succeeded. When I did not the mischief was done. It seemed to me that nothing could hang on with more toughness than an ear of corn, and how like a razor the blades of shucks would cut tiny hands. I was young but while an exasperated golf player now has a new language of despair and outrage, our protests missed nothing that we had heard up to that time. After the ear was off, the shucks had to be removed. Here another trial was met because we had once more to break the same bond. When this was done the corn was taken to the barn, and even the shucks were sometimes saved; before they were too dry to be fed to the cattle; at other times, when quite dry to serve as stuffing for our mattresses. In some sense shucks were ever with us, and when I employ the well chosen term now to express disgust, I have rather better reason than is commonly true.

It is not possible for me to say how from season to season the sphere of our labors grew. I left in the fall of 1863, at the age of fourteen, and most of the work of which I speak covered at least a few years. However, the impression that my parents were very exacting, would not be fair. It is true that my father was governed by a stern sense of duty. Mother, though less severe, was just as serious. Both began with themselves in the application of their view of life; and beyond that they sought to bring us up with respect for the rules by which they lived. Among these was, perhaps the chief one, a simple belief that there is no happiness without working for it. To the last day of his life father sought to have me respect personal independence, and to look to self-support for its security. If I did not know, I should gather from their general attitude, that our parents were in part moved by such thought when they had us do the work which we did. But there were other reasons which must often have had them call on us for help. This was the necessity of the case, certainly after the war had begun. A natural scarcity of labor was felt more and more. All young men were gone, either at the front or in hiding. If crops were to be brought in at all, it was for us to help. Father's duties had become even more exacting. To his labors as a physician was added the duty of a friend who was in the confidence of men in sore stress and danger. Mother could not add to what she had done. So we, quite contrary to our supposed position, and no doubt with our parents' regret, were forced as we might to do the tasks of men. Thus during the last few years we had at least a taste of all the labor common on a small farm. We helped milk the cows, the duty being shared by mother and the cook; and here as in hauling the water there was no Sunday holiday. By this time there were three boys, another lad nearly my age had been taken into our family to have him learn German with most unsuspected results, of which more anon. It was easy to divide this labor. Texas cows were more famous for horns than for milk. Each milker could readily take on one cow, perhaps two; and between us we were lucky if we got the needed supply. The real question for me always was which cow would fall to my lot. If I got the brindle (and that was the name we gave her) there was always trouble. Brindle cows were my particular dread. There was something red headed about them. If there was a brindle cow in the herd when I was around, she always broke away and cut for the woods. When I undertook to follow and to head off a cow before she reached the woods and got hooked in the shins, it was of course a brindle that did it. And so when it was for me to milk the brindle, the question was not so much whether I would get milk into the pail, as whether the cow would get her hind leg into it. After the disastrous risks of this conflict became known, safer methods were adopted, and I was spared the ordeal. Black or white or spotted cows were quite gentle with small boys. We milked them in peace and in the absence of a stool to sit on did the best we could. Indeed, we sometimes took advantage of our occupation. We liked fresh milk, the fresher the better. So, horrible to relate, we would at times milk for direct consumption, straight into the mouth. This sounds quite savage, I know; but we liked milk warm and unspoilt. In time we learned to eat clabber; as we put up with cooled milk, but boiled milk was anathema always.

Even the ax was added to our list of tools. I will not go too far. We never really chopped wood, unless it was done in pursuit of our sports, as will appear later. The cut logs were brought to our door, fit for the fireplace in our sitting room. But for the kitchen even the smaller logs had to be split, and this was one of our tasks before school. Most of our work was, of course, done after school, but some jobs were sometimes left for the morning hour. Unless the work had been done in time, as it seldom was, there was no chance to hunt in the woods before school time. This splitting of wood was almost as trying to temper as shucking corn. Hickory is always tough; even oak will do. And so this task was apt to be delayed to the last moment, and was then done under the kindly cook's threat that it was a question of wood or no breakfast. Of course, Anna did not really mean it; and sometimes after watching our hopeless struggle with some knotted chunk of wood, she would come to the rescue, kind and energetic soul that she was. At such times we always discreetly withdrew. We did not care to see her face. The indignation of her back was enough. But our breakfast tasted quite as good; and she served us at the kitchen table with just the same gentle care. The hogs she also fed; unless corn was served them, when it was our privilege to play benefactors. Chickens, fortunately, looked after themselves. Even the bringing in of the eggs mother would not trust to our reckless hands.

Finally, we hauled the water for the day's supply, and this always had to be done in the morning before leaving for school, in order that it might be cool and fresh. The method was simple. We had a large barrel which was laid on and fastened to a heavy wooden sled. It had a square opening at the top to pour the water in, and a faucet at the side to draw it out. Boys, however, preferred to dip in from the top with a tin cup or a hollowed gourd, which would not be considered safe today, particularly on sleeping cars. Our spring was about half way down the hill towards the forest. At first we had only one which supplied cool, hard water, a very relish for a thirsty boy, and giving just the right temperature to a watermelon left in it, after having been plucked in the, morning dew. In the early days this supply was ample, enough even to permit of a little shower in a bathing house. Our contrivance was never patented, although its principles were confirmed by experience. We fastened a large tin bucket to a pulley so that it might be moved up and down. The bottom was punched full of small holes, and these were covered by a false bottom which could be let down or lifted by a pulley. Of course, the workings were not entirely accurate, and it would not do to go near the thing until ready for the bath. Practically, however, it met all the uses of a modern shower, without the option "hot" or "cold." In time we opened another spring on the side of the hill, really to please a desperate neighbor but with the unhappy result that our spring was reduced so as to furnish only the bath, and to leave us dependent for our regular supply upon an indifferent spring of soft water. To this our sled would be drawn by a horse and with the barrel standing slightly elevated some twelve feet away, we would carry the water in buckets until the barrel was filled. It looks like quite a job to me even now, and at the time it seemed hard work before school. Even the horse pulling that loaded sled up hill back to the house seemed to share our feelings, for his task, too, was hard.

As we showed more and more that we could fill our places, we were charged with other work, also necessary but fitting in much better with a boy's notions of farm life. This was riding the prairies, sometimes only to locate our cattle, sometimes to help bring them nearer to our home. Going south meant the use of horses on some quest or message, or merely to roam over the prairie. Going north, on the contrary, meant the company of dogs, and to follow our own sport in the forest. There were it is true ways of riding through the forest by taking clear cut roads. But low branches and thick brush prevented any thought of further venture. Of course, we had heard of Absalom's riding under the tree's branch to be hung by his hair; but that warning we did not heed. Of our horses and dogs, some of the former were in time treated as our own, the latter of the hound type were always at our beck and call, good and true.

The little mule had by this time been given over to brother Paul's care, although in truth the reverse was true. However, Paul got along very well. He not only learned to ride, but by his equable temper and unfailing decision, he seemed to get better control of the trickster than I had had. Certain it is that while he did pay tribute to our little mule's love of frolic, he did improve on my record. But my experience had its value. Having tried every conceivable way of falling off a mule, I had gained some understanding of methods in emergencies. When a real horse was finally given me, I had reason to think myself a fairly safe horseman. Indeed, I do not recall ever having been thrown, unless the horse fell with me, which happened rarely. By that time there were a number of horses on the place. Mother rode very rarely, and used a sorrel named "Lizzie," usually employed about the farm. Father, until the very last few months, stuck to the large mule; but then bought a beautiful bay, which stood out among our stock like a prince among peasants. He had all the gaits known to the south, particularly a wonderful pace, rack and canter. On occasions he was even harnessed in a new buggy — a vision for our eyes — hanging low between the wheels, the picture of ease and comfort without end. We had no German name for it, so "buggy" was good enough for us. It seemed a strange contrivance anyway, with its odd springs and sitting high on the axles. It looked risky to us for travel across creeks and over roads with every kind of ruts. With us the bed of the wagon sat on and was fastened to the axles. There could be no accidents, and if the ride was hard, straw or hay in the bottom of it saved us from jolts. In time our doubts yielded to the joy of a Sunday ride now and then in the buggy when we learned to know that sitting in a buggy properly is just as true a test as sitting a horse correctly.

My fortune I again owed to the leaving of Hermann for the war. He was a good rider, as he was an expert in everything else that he liked to do. His horse was a roan, rather short, of common size. A fast and even walk was his only easy gait, but in that he might have pleased royalty itself. His trot was long and hard; his canter, unless he was in very good humor, equally hard, and his mouth no less so; but with all he was a very answer to a boy's dream. He could outrun anything that was ever put against him. His name was "Barbarossa" which we turned into "Rossa," with quite an Americanized contempt for the possible effect of the change. When I became the happy owner of "Rossa," his name was safe— challenges of his speed were no longer heard of. A year or two back when Hermann was still with us, the last great effort to defeat him had been made, and no pains had been spared. Rumors had been afloat for some time; for even in small settlements the feeling of competition for place is alive and will somehow make itself heard. One day the plan was sprung upon us. Our ambitious neighbor, the storekeeper, had bought a horse for the one purpose to down "Rossa." This was an event for the whole colony. Everybody was on the alert, and as is always true in such cases, people took sides with more or less strong feeling or conviction. In this the horses alone may not have been the sole factor. No doubt the standing of the owners entered into the case. I should say the physician had some slight advantage over the storekeeper, although some sympathy went out to the man who dared issue such a challenge for the entertainment of the settlement. At last the day was fixed, and most persons immediately interested showed signs of nervousness, as has been exhibited on greater occasions of similar character. Hermann's nerve, however, never failed him. He showed all the confidence of the unvanquished hero of a dime novel, and we boys of course lived in the reflected glory of his strength. Race tracks were unknown, as was also, I think, betting on races. We only raced when the spirit moved us or our horses, and the triumph of the run was the height of our reward. In a case of such importance as this one, the track was however selected with some care — we were approaching the ways of civilization. Furthermore, it was important to give chance to the old and young to see the race. So the course was laid along the highway between the homes of the two owners. The start was to be made at the store, and the finish at our gate; which may have given us advantage, for every horse — even the best one — runs better towards home; he knows the limit and likes the place. This course was of a kind to test a good deal more than speed; for although it was little more than a mile long, the track offered every condition from deepest sand to hardest soil. In other ways, it had great variety, in that it was anything but straight, or round for that matter. It started in deep sand, as the boys knew well, from earlier effort to tug their way through. It wound around a sharp and steep gulch, came down a stretch on level ground, past our school house through a grove into a lane between rail fences, and our next neighbor's house and barn, and then under some large trees to the last turn at the corner of a fence, out into the open for the final run to our gate.

I must add that there was no modern race equipment. The ordinary heavy Mexican saddle was used; and in those days the stirrups, covered with long leather wings, weighed as much as a modern race saddle. The bridles, too, were the common hard bit, for snaffle-bits we never used. The storekeeper's horse was ridden by his son, very tall and slight, with legs well adapted to urge his horse in place or in aid of whip. Hermann rode "Rossa;" and by him a whip was scorned. The other horse was a bay about the same size as "Rossa."

The hour had struck, a Saturday afternoon, I think. The course was lined with our neighbors; few grown ups and no youngster missing, I should say. The owners decided to watch the race from the points of their respective homes. Older people do not like to show emotion; but neither father nor mother fooled us. They had a way of moving about with overdone composure. As for us, we were the victims of struggle between hope and fear, for Hermann was at the other end, and we were robbed of his reflected assurance. The awakening came like a shock; there was a shift in the air, as it were, the horizon line moved to and fro, up and down. People were pressing forward, stretching necks to catch an early glimpse of the oncoming riders. We could hear the clatter of hoofs just beyond the neighbor's house, the rhythm of their steady strokes. But who was ahead we had no means of guessing. Then they burst out from under the great trees, the last object between them and us; and it looked like neck and neck. "Rossa" was on the side next to us, but more than that no one could see. On they came, still nose to nose, each at his very best. They reached the last corner. In making it "Rossa" had the sharper and shorter, the other horse the easier and longer wheel. They swung around horse to horse as though they had been trained to run in pairs. Then came the final tug for not more than a few hundred yards, the last test of speed and wind; right down upon us they thundered, a picture of force and dash to make all other races seem like figures on a screen. For this was not a show; this was part of us. But even before much of this last run was covered, the die was cast. Hermann sat "Rossa" calm and firm—neither spur nor whip he used—leaning far over, almost flat on the horse's neck, he might have given points to a jockey. His opponent was freely using a whip; but also legs and arms which flung about like remnants of a broken wind-mill in a gale. All to no avail. "Rossa" shot to the fore, held it, gained and passed the gate an easy winner. Hermann managed to hold him in somewhere half way down the hill, "Rossa" seemingly under the impression that the race had just begun. His opponent stopped readily enough, head hanging as though he felt his defeat and cared for no more. It was all over. "Rossa" had won his last real race—he was never challenged again—and he was our horse.

At the time of which I am writing he was mine, dear "Rossa." No wonder even a boy would put on the blanket and saddle with care to save his pet from the sores that are the horse's torment. To the last with only a trifling exception he remained my only horse. There was a sorrel colt, very promising, which I was finally to have. But he contracted some fistula trouble and, besides, had scarcely grown when I had to leave. However, I rode him a few times, and fortunately for me he was much gentler than his age would suggest. Boy-like, I rode him out upon the prairie. I was alone, armed with nothing but the common lasso. I need not say that my saddle was small, although built upon the usual lines. So also my lasso bore some relation to my size. Here I was out upon the prairie on a new horse all my own. There were cattle roaming about me, taking little or no heed, because this was not the time of year for rounding up, which they probably knew better than I did. But I was out to learn all the tricks of the cowboy, among which the chief ones were to pick up a handkerchief from the ground while the horse is running, and lassoing a steer. I had no handkerchief to tempt me; but there was the lasso to lead a boy astray. The victim for my aim was soon selected. He was young and fat and full of energy. So away I sailed after him on the green nag. Swinging my lasso about my head in approved fashion, with the accustomed luck when no trained eye is watching, I got him by the horns the first dash, wrapped my end of the lasso around the saddle knob as I had seen the cowboys do, turned my horse for the final halt in the steer's mad career; and in a jiffy found myself seated in my saddle still, but flying high up in the air, with my horse peacefully standing by. Needless to say, none of my equipment was made for such maneuvers. The only question was which part would first give way. In this instance it was the girth, which explained my sudden ascent, sitting my saddle still. My position was not without danger. Had the nag run away, my chances for escape were small indeed. For no sooner was I on the ground than the cattle moved to gather about me, with horns lowered and some pawing the ground—all proof of threatening approach upon an unaccustomed figure. Even when cattle from the prairie are penned, a rider may move among them unmolested; but let him go on foot and some moody beast will soon give him a test of speed for the top of the fence. I know because I have tried; and have reason to remember that in my race for liberty I sacrificed only part of my trousers, while my less fortunate comrade was caught under the ribs and spent many weeks in bed. This time I owed everything as is so often the case, to my faithful horse. Though young and hardly broken he never moved, and let me with my saddle (which had been released from the lasso) in one hand take hold of the bridle with the other, and find a place of security standing under his neck. In that position I mended the girth as best I could, re-saddled and rode home, wondering about the stupidity of cattle; how long it would be before some lucky cowboy would salvage that lasso on the young steer, and just what I could have done with my catch if my saddle's girth had not given way.

This was my only experience of the kind. I came near it once more when in a thunder storm, racing for home like a foolish boy, a bolt of lightning struck the ground say a hundred feet in front of me, and I barely kept my saddle, owing to the horse's sudden swerve.

The wonder is that with all my affection for "Rossa," and riding him during those few years when I was old enough to plan for myself, there is scarcely anything particular to tell about him. He carried me where I would go; he beat anybody who invited a run, and he followed cattle in the general round-up or when they were troublesome on their evening return, with the good sense and promptness of a Mexican pony. Only once he and I had a real fall. We had been out for a longer ride, several of us, and we were bringing closer home some of our cattle that were ranging too far away. Our course from the prairie lay between the forks of dense forest in the lowland along the head of the creek and the common black oak on the upper level. As we approached home we came nearer and nearer to the forest, and here we knew cattle would make a break, if at all. People think cattle stupid; but I never knew young or old cow or steer to make for the black oak groves. Always they made the run for the impenetrable forest. And this time not altogether to our surprise, one of the cows, the only brindle in the herd of course, made a bee line for that point. I was the nearest rider and welcomed the chance. Off we were and headed her off; but being a brindle, she turned and struck my shin bone with the point of her horn. A boy must be pretty mad to go on after that. But I was mad and chased her at full gallop back to the herd. Of all things, "Rossa" stepped into a mole hole with his front feet, and turned somersault if ever a horse did. I slid over his neck and went to the ground ahead of him, and he went down, one of his hoofs just grazing me. We were both on our feet in a twinkle; but he had fallen on his back, as my saddle tree was cracked clean through and hung like a shell on him. It was a good price; for we got the brindle, and I got a new saddle. With such exceptions it is all a memory of joy, the freedom of the life on horseback, and the trust in "Rossa," rain or shine, hot blast or bitter norther.

In the meantime we were pupils by imitation of a practical riding school. The original immigrants could by that time ride, of course, but there was little to learn from them. They, it is true, had sat up on a mule or horse; had told us to rely upon the knees without use of stirrups; never at our peril to take hold of the knob of the saddle; and that the true secret of riding is balance, etc., etc. We had heard all that, with the common effect of rules and more rules. Our real tutors were the native born with whom horse and rider were one. The Mexican was the ideal. His pony had endurance without limit, and adroitness unbelievable. His saddle was a marvel of ornament in our eyes, with its low seat, strong shoulders and flat knob, wide as a saucer; the deep wooden stirrups hanging by heavy straps straight down from the seat, encased in leather guards which ended in narrow strips almost grazing the grass; all made useful by a multitude of straps, and decorated every inch by buckles and brass buttons. The bridle was in keeping with its hard bit, and the cruel curb chain to enforce it. The ponies had never known any other or they might have asked the reason for all this extra weight of a saddle and wicked torture of a bit. But to us all this was the goal of our ambition. True, Mexicans did not often come our way, but we had seen a few who brought in herds of goats, in the belief that we ought to like what they did. We loved the kids, and we wondered at the Mexicans. We saw them ride—no rising from the saddle—just one movement of horse and man; no question who was giving and who was taking orders; just the rhythm of unbroken motion. This impression was so strong that I have never become used to the manner of modern riding; perhaps I could not unlearn the old method; but probably because of my feeling for its ease and fitness. There was only one way, figure erect, limbs straight down and feet parallel to the horse. That feeling was confirmed years after when I had a chance to see Indians ride. In camp one morning somewhere between Provo and Fort Duquesne in Utah, I saw a young buck on horseback coming towards us. He had been at a dance, and as he faced the rising sun with all his trappings and regalia he was the very picture of romance and grace. More wonderful still was an Indian boy who stopped his horse before the officers' club house at Fort Duquesne. He gave no sign of recognition or response—true to the tradition of his race—but he sat his pony so that no one line challenged the eye; but all lines were lost in one perfection.

Really we did not need the exhibition of the Mexicans for Hermann was a master himself. He could cut and trim the leather for saddle and bridle; he could cut hides into strips and make out of them the common riding crop, or the long whip which was used in herding cattle. He could sit a horse to arouse the envy of every boy and the admiration of every girl. How easily erect he sat, with his fit legs going straight down like an Indian's, his small feet lost in the heavily guarded stirrup, and his nimble hands coying as it were with the reins. It all looked so easy; but when it came to action, with what precision the lasso went; with what well aimed force the whip was sent to the mark; and how promptly the horse responded to his knees' pressure. There is art in riding the prairie, and call for decision. I have seen Hermann on horseback facing a maddened steer actually keep him at bay by landing the quirt of his long heavy whip stroke after stroke upon the steer's nose. The old trick of lowering from the saddle while at full speed to pick up a handkerchief was in a way new to us, but with the young men it was a regular sport, the trophy always going to Hermann. In the test of placing a coin on the bottom of the stirrup to hold it there with the leg straight, letting the foot no more than reach it, no one was as sure as he to bring in the proof of his skill. Almost a sinister influence in some respects, he was our idol in sports. He did not profess to teach us so much; but watching and admiring what he did, we learned in a fashion to make horse hair rope and cowhide whips. We at least became accustomed to see firearms used and lie around. We too measured the distance between saddle knob and handkerchief on the ground and when a pony was small enough, sometimes got it; and the coin at the foot of the stirrup we brought back often enough, if the distance was not too great. Even so, it was not so much learning to do this or that thing, as it was that we were filled with the spirit of adventure, the wish to do the things which in this new free world appealed to a boy's ambition.

I have spoken like a fair weather horseman. But such were not always the conditions. There were many times when our orders fixed the hour of our going. There were others when going out under a bright sky we were surprised by sudden change. True weather prophets were rare even then. In summer our costume was the same, on foot or horseback—trousers ("Hosen," as we called them) and shirt, generally shoes, and often a hat against the heat. In case of bad weather we took short coats. An overcoat I never had until I was sixteen. The sun we did not mind; nor did the heat oppress us as much as might be thought, because the breezes from the gulf were almost constant during the night and not uncommon during the day. No doubt this early training helped to make me a sun worshipper. Rain we took as it came—part of the game—counting on exercise while it lasted, and on dry clothes when we got home. But for one state of weather we did have holy respect, and that was the Texas Norther. It deserves its name. Perhaps there were wise ones who could scent the coming storm. If so, we were not of them. Father was nearly always away on his rounds ready to meet what came, and like boys we took our chance in the same spirit. As I recall it, a Norther was always preceded by extremely warm if not sultry weather; but one did not always follow the other, and no boy bent on his plans would give them up because the weather might take a bad turn. So out we would ride, miles into the open prairie, without trees to break the horizon line, to offer shade or to obstruct howling weather. There were cattle everywhere (fences for them were unknown) like mere dots in the distance or standing out clearly before us, grouped in that strangely picturesque way as though waiting for the photographer. The vast space was covered with grass or weed, green or brown according to season—rain or drought—and broken only at long distances by streams upon which the cattle depended for water, and to which we sometimes went to camp and fish with the grown people. The condition was familiar to us; there was little to take our eyes away from the cattle, to single out our own—usually by shape and color, or if need be by the cut on the ears and brand on the haunch. For by that time title claim to cattle depended upon the owner's mark and brand. Prairie chicken would fly up with their sudden alarm and mighty whirl of wings, but they were too common to move a boy or scare a horse. A big snake might be killed with our long whips or chased to its lair. Very rarely a wolf might be seen and even chased, just for the lark of it, leaving him wondering what pranks boys will be up to. Or a wild turkey thoughtless of the effect of food in abundance might venture to fly across an angle of the prairie and be forced to alight only to have his speed increased by the hopeless pursuit of foolish boys.

Apart from the sports thrown in to make life worth living, the accepted purpose of these rides was the inspection of cattle — always testing the eye for distant and true vision, or for strength to look straight into the sun. Our attention would be turned to the south — the picture before us. Little did we care what took place behind us; time enough when it came to turn for home. On rare occasions, not more than twice, we might be surprised by a prairie fire advancing upon us from behind; which is not as dangerous as it sounds. Far less dangerous, indeed, than a fire started near our home threatening our houses and fences, when every man, woman and child had to go armed with sticks to beat it down. Out on the prairie the cattle kept the grass fairly low, and the fire itself would not be of serious consequence. The smoke might become so. If driven towards us by a wind, we would be in the midst of it, and while it was annoying, the real discomfort was the biting effect upon the eyes. However, that was all for the moment; and the charge through the smoke and low flame was really an innocent enough adventure.

Not so with a Norther. It came suddenly, with little warning to us. The air would become sultry — there would be an ominous hush — the silence broken perhaps by the chirp of a bird to keep up his courage, or calling for his mate in despair. The first signal of danger was generally given by the cattle, as an animal is always quick to scent danger. We might see an old cow raise her head, sniff the air and turn her gaze to the north. Others followed here and there, far and near. The warning would be confirmed, and the movement was on. Some would go farther south to seek shelter under the lea of the banks of streams. Those nearer home, perhaps accustomed to return there, would turn north to make the forests before the storm reached them. It was a wonderful spectacle—great herds dispersing—moving in the two divisions, first at a walk, with that long and energetic stride of a cow or steer bent upon a settled purpose. They saw as we did the low, very black cloud on the horizon, moving toward us; they heard as we did the dull faint rumbling in the distance; measured as it were the chances of the race and broke into trot or run as the storm came nearer and nearer. That experience was not uncommon and once awake to the danger, with the same instinctive search for safety, our horses were given full rein for home. Complete escape was not possible. It was a question of how much we would get and how long we would have to take it. At first the cloud would lie like a solid black band upon the horizon, and then it would advance upon us with astonishing rapidity. The line between it and the blue sky would be cut as if with a knife. As the cloud came on, the sky upon the horizon might even clear, leaving that solid black body to the mercy of the wind that drove it. Then we would feel the first whiff of chilly breeze, making our little bodies in shirt sleeves shiver with the sudden touch of cold in contrast with the prevailing heat, and having us hold on to our light straw hats as best we might. On would come the storm and on ran our horses, in the race for time and shelter. Faster and harder came the blast, until the cold seemed to cut like knives and make us fairly whimper under its punishment. As the clouds moved above us, the pelting rain would be let loose and would almost blind us and drench us to the skin. With it all we would have to slow up, because even horses grow tired and as we knew it is not well to run them hard into the face of strong wind and rain. As we got nearer home there was before us the picture of just one common movement. Cattle with heads low, long horns touching the grass, trotting or running madly for the forest to be lost in the brush; horses and mules in enclosed pastures, standing under trees or near the fences with their backs to the storm; chickens seeking shelter in any nook or corner; hogs lying close to the trough, with not so much as a grunt of protest; tin pails and buckets clattering over the ground. So we, too, would reach our shelter, unsaddling our horses, putting them into the barn; and finding warmth in dry clothes and before a log fire that mother's care had of course started, and wondering just where father had been caught and how he had made out.

These northers usually came late in the day. The cloud would move over us like a dread messenger, to disappear to the south; and with it the gale would usually subside. The setting sun throwing its rays upon the receding cloud would present spectacles so gorgeous that they might have been fit subjects for a Turner, a Diaz, an Innes or a Bierstadt. One tiny cloud might be left to set off a whole sky of azure blue, even as an artist may save his canvas by one jot of paint for emphasis. Sometimes when the storm came late or had lasted long, the clear Texas stars would peep out from over the cloud as it descended to the southern horizon, and they would stand out against the pure sky like messengers of peace, good will and joy, which they certainly were, to us and all our little world. We may speak of the heavens as we look upon an unclouded sky; but a glimpse of its blue beckoning through a rift in the clouds, or an opening in the foliage of the forest, as a Diaz or a Rousseau would paint it, can set us to dream of Heaven itself. And then we weary and hungry boys would eagerly devour our supper, to enjoy it the more, make a dutiful effort at tomorrow's lessons, fall asleep over the task, and be sent to bed, to dream of hunting and adventure and to awaken in the morning to rejoice in another day.

As I write I wonder at the different kinds of experiences we had. The simple truth is that we were living under strange conditions. Nature was wild, and we were getting out of it all the fun it offered, while our parents were seeking to give us the comforts of civilized custom. All of our comrades did not quite get out of it what we did. They had their own lives. Most of them could do better than I anything that needed strength and endurance, but many of them had less freedom than we, because they were called on for farm work on a larger scale. They were fit for it, and we really were not. Necessity drove us to it, because during the war years there were few young men left, and labor was scarce. So we helped out as we could. As I think back I wonder how many were moved by the appeal of their surroundings as we were. How many felt that the myriad of stars of the Texas heavens had something to say to us; how many would lie out on the grass at night to make sure that the moon had a face, and whether it was kind or harsh; how many traced the shape of animals in the clouds—the bear or the elephant; and how many of them let their dreams wander far into the very mysteries of the heavens.

Our little experiences read almost like fiction, because they are of a past that is gone. They look strange because they are as it were of another world. Children today have a life of their own, quite as alluring—indeed more so. The popular sports of today, even the old ones, were unknown to us, and most of them would have been beyond us had we known of them. For instance, I do not remember seeing a skiff until I crossed the Rio Grande in one late in 1863— and a sorry specimen it was—dug out of a log. Of the ocean we only heard; and to get anywhere in our streams or rivers meant to wade or to swim—sometimes on horseback. Ship or sail I never saw until we reached the mouth of the Rio Grande on the Gulf. The only railroad train I had ever seen, when I got to New York in 1864, ran from Houston, I think, to Allentown, not far from Columbus. It was one of our great surprises before leaving home. Everything about it seemed wonderful but its speed, so we raced our horses against it. It may have stopped at somebody's back door. At all events, we left it behind with a poor opinion of this intruder upon the freedom of our prairie. The rumor was that an irate old lady, who objected to the track so near her home, had taken her revenge, and delayed the train at her door by the reckless use of common soap on the rails. Such reports were hailed by us, and we were ready to believe that she might have been an ally in our race. In any event, the train's speed was never such as to cause the unhappy consequences that were told of the first railroad in a far eastern country. In that case the natives had sold chickens and what not to pay their fare for a ride at the trial trip. At the finish, the owners were faced by an incipient riot, because the passengers contended that the arrival of the train on schedule time had unfairly cut short their full allowance of pleasure.

The sports of this time were as foreign to us as my story will seem novel to young people today. We knew them no more than we knew the English language, and that was as alien to me as a modern newspaper account of a football game. Not that I had missed my chances. Indeed, I made efforts at English during the last two years of my stay, although not even that much was planned. A boy nearly my age whom I have mentioned, had come to our home to learn German, and he from that time on was our companion. The way of true Americanization perhaps never had a smoother course than in this instance. If he ever learnt a German word, I do not recall it; but from that day on I was devoted to the English language "as she is spoke." That I learned his lingo does not surprise me so much, as I wonder now how I ever managed to unlearn it. I suspect that the laughter which greeted me later on upon my arrival in St. Louis may not have been caused solely as I then thought by my clothing of marvelous cut and color; but in part by the lingo which I used. With my parents I spoke German as long as they lived. I therefore regard this new comrade as my sole English tutor in those early days, and I accept the experience as sufficient answer to our alarmists who regard themselves as the peculiar guardians of American patriotism. The stages of my progress I can not recall, but the first attempt at English I shall never forget. Perhaps for that reason I have always read with sympathy Lincoln's account of his own transition from stage to stage in his early life. At that time, among other things, we built the old-fashioned traps set with the usual stick supports with grain strewn about to tempt the birds, generally larks. Having set the trap we of course kept keenest watch. One day while on guard I saw the trap go down, and in my eagerness to give the alarm I essayed upon my first English sentence. Running through the high broom grass, destroying innumerable spider webs glistening in the sun, and soaked to the knees I called out "The fell has fall." Trap is "Falle", and fallen is "gefallen"; and this was my declaration of independence from the language of my fathers. Needless to say I was understood.

I speak of these things to show how limited our field of sport really was; and how this very condition served to have us welcome every new idea, and perhaps in a measure to develop self-reliance and resourcefulness.

I would not, however, have it believed that our parents left us entirely to our own devices, and that many of our little plans were not encouraged and even suggested by them. From mother we knew all about "Struwwelpeter," and heard much of fairy tales. The north German and the Scotch are not unlike in this. She had us ponder over the little problem how we could make four dots (standing for so many horses) and then by two lines have each enclosed in a separate pen and tied to a rope. Under her supervision we wrote letters to a grandmother in Germany, to whom we no doubt gave a clearer impression of ourselves than we were ever able obtain of her. Of all this father did little for obvious reasons. He was engrossed with his duties; and with the exception of great teachers, the masculine mind does not seem to shine in children's sphere. On occasions he did, however, go to great pains to give us treats. When we were still very small the games did not go beyond the old acting of a bear, which we as other children received with a strange mixture of disbelief and dread. Bears were a real thing in our lives, and we readily filled our role of scared children in the play. Father had an oaken desk ("Pult," we called it); the lid opened from the top and rested on arms that were pulled out. It came all the way from Germany, and made the trip to Mexico by sea to New York and to St. Louis, only to be lost there in one of the transfers from one home to another. From behind this desk he would appear, and resting on all fours, moving toward us with his full head of hair and his long beard, the growls of his deep bass voice were hardly needed to set us off in fits of excitement. Even Blind Man's

Buff was played—our furniture was proof against its injury. But there were greater occasions of lasting memory. One day we were told that we were to be taken to a circus. What precise idea we got I can not say, but our minds were certainly set on something beyond the ordinary. I do not recall any of the common circus posters, if there were any, but we were told that there would be a vast tent holding all sorts of strange animals, and that there would be riding of incredible skill. The day was some time ahead, and teacher and parent must have had a period of uncommon trial with us. To attend meant a drive of ten miles—San Felipe was the place. No one but father could take us, and he of course had to complete his rounds before going with us. He rode the trusty large mule as usual, and never did that mule go forth with more fervent prayers for his speed than that morning. The day looked promising. The sky was clear. We believed firmly that when a dog eats grass it means rain that day; but no dog had given warning of danger. School let out early; the demand came alike from old and young; and as the time for our start approached, we three stationed ourselves at points on the three roads that met at our home to give prompt notice if and when father was sighted. My post was on the way to San Felipe, where I could see about a mile to the top of the next hill. Time wore on. Surely there was delay, caused by some mishap. Could it be possible that we would not after all see the circus? And we the only ones at school to miss it? Then I saw a figure rise above the hill. At that distance all men look alike, but this is not true of all mules. A large ear appeared, and that was encouraging. At last appeared the second ear, welcome ear wobbling from side to side, and sending to the winds all doubt and fear. We were saved, and I gave the regular signal—we called it the Indian whoop, in search for some name big enough to fit the noise. We did this by placing our two hands together to make a concave hollow and then blowing into it, which enabled us to produce notes both high or low of great force. The day was ours. Father and mother seemed as happy as we were, and the family party made its way in the common wagon drawn by two horses. I can not give a picture of that circus. I have a vague remembrance of amazing tricks on horseback by men and women in scant attire and of fantastic gymnastic stunts. But in the main it is all one great maze of color and glamor—enough to make me a confirmed devotee of the circus for life. I wonder were there animals, or am I seeing my first circus in the setting of later years? I would almost swear that I saw an elephant there; not because I recall his picture, but because of the effect which the performance of the first elephant I ever saw had upon my earliest information about him. Who my informant was I do not know; but this is what I had firmly fixed in mind. The elephant was a very large and dangerous animal. In his case all ordinary methods of catching wild animals were futile; but the ingenious savages had hit upon a way of bringing him into captivity. It was well known to them that if an elephant fell or lay down on the ground he was lost. The elephant of course knew this as well, and so when taking his rest he took wise precautions. Instead of lying down, he leaned against a tree to get his desired snooze. The natives knew that elephants had regular places for assembly, particularly at night. By finding these places they could easily identify the trees against which elephants were accustomed to lean —the state of the bark would show that. The savages, therefore, used deception; savages always do, as all boys knew. They took their saws—they always had them handy —carried them in their trousers—and sawed these trees half through, with care of course so that the elephants would not notice it. Then at night when all was dark the elephant would come wearily along, half asleep after his day's wanderings, and would lean his tired body against the tree half sawed through. Down would come the tree, and with it the clumsy elephant; and there you are. All the savage had to do would be to take him, as of course he did. The question of how he got his captive away never arose in our minds, or for that matter in the mind of our informant. I am not quite sure at what stage in my young life a real elephant first sprung the surprise upon me to awaken my benighted mind; but somehow this first circus claims the credit for it. This much is true, however. Very early in my life I saw the first elephant go through some of those amazing feats with which we are now familiar. Before my eyes that reckless brute climbed a narrow-stand in imminent danger of falling down and stopping the whole circus. Not content with that he stood on his hind legs, and then on his front legs; and, finally, he lay down, prepared to die as I felt, unmindful of all consequences to us. And then he arose with the air of one who has abused the confidence of his friends. That elephant laughed, if ever an elephant did, and I was sorry that I could not join him. He had not only shattered all my lore of the elephant family, but to him I trace the painful reservation with which I listen to stories of animal life, and with which indeed I read even the history of men.

But whatever may be true of elephants, I know there were clowns. They were without guile, and they will always be the delight of every real boy. I do not recall a face or a trick; I simply laugh as I think of them. The clown is really a natural born actor, and it is one of my dreads that the whole band may find it out and take to the stage, to the irreparable loss of really American audiences. That first impression stayed with me for life. It did not take my children long to sense this weakness for the circus, and especially for the clowns. A circus in town never needed special appeal from young to old. The call was unanimous, and the order never varied after the first visit. We would take a box, and the seating of the family party was so arranged that I could see all the clowns, and all the family could see me—the laughing youngsters agreeing that the clowns might be good, but that my show of enjoyment was better than anything that any clown could do. And so it has gone on until now there are grandchildren, just beginning to catch the note from their parents, and to count upon the combined weakness of an old man for grandchildren and for clowns to take them to the modern circus—popular descendant of the primitive ancestor at San Felipe that left its generous mark upon the life of every pupil of Maetze's school.

Probably we never knew what effort it had cost father to make that circus, and perhaps as thoughtless boys we never suspected how much he and mother enjoyed it with us. But it is true that when it came to things worth while he never failed us. There was one time when father made a great effort to give us pleasure, and as I think to revive memories that had grown doubly dear in the stress of the struggle so void of sentiment. It must have been Christmas time, some years before the Civil War. Little German toys had come from grandmother. I recall only the well known monkey which we could to our delight slide up and down and jump over his pole. Perhaps the Texas store had added a few more toys. At all events, the occasion was an unusual one. There were great preparations; and since it was all novel to us hope was at a high pitch. In story we of course knew about Christmas Eve, but it had never been formally observed. At first we were too young. Then little sister Helene died on Christmas Eve, and in later years the war prevented. This time we had a Christmas tree. It is at least the first and only one I remember in Texas. A few common home-made tallow candles were put upon the tree, and the toys were no doubt placed about its foot, but covered for our surprise at the proper time. So much for the plans at home, which were exciting enough. But the climax was still to come that night—Christmas Eve—which we observed according to the good old German custom. There were whisperings of the appearance of a real sure enough Santa Claus; and we stayed outside and watched for the first sign of his approach. Our imaginations ran wild, for our joy was not unmixed with awe. With Germans great joy is often marked by a certain solemnity, as their art and certainly their music will show. Indeed, I do not know how to express the mood of young and old that evening, without using the simple but very true word "feierlich." Santa Claus might at times come down the chimney, but that he would do later at night when children were asleep, and certainly not when there was a full blaze in the only fireplace in the house. So we watched outside at nearby points, wondering how the surprise would come, when the suspense was broken. Far off, half a mile away in the cornfield we saw a light, just above the little hill. It grew larger and larger as it rose above the horizon; so large that it made the little stars (surprised at this big newcomer) scurry back into the sky. Then we saw the tall figure of Santa Claus, wrapped in a long cloak and hood, and he had a long beard, as Santa Claus must always have. The light was a torch which a tall boy carried to show the way. So they came through the cornfield towards us, and reached the fence between field and pasture. We wondered a little that this strange figure could climb a rail fence; but why shouldn't he if he could go down chimneys in the dark to leave presents for sleeping children? Then they came to the pasture where the milk cows were kept at night, and we saw how the cows looked up and rose to run into the dark, sharing our feeling about this strange appearance. The dogs began to bark. It was time they did we thought. Finally, these two figures climbed the last fence, crossed the road and stood at our front gate. They stopped as though that might be all and they go on their way to the next farm. But no; little lights appeared through the picket fence—there was one explosion like a firecracker—strange contrast to the peace of Christmas Eve; and they entered the gate coming through the front lawn. In our absence mother had lighted the candles and uncovered the presents. And then Santa Claus and his attendant led us into the full glory of the evening, there to open a bag with a lot more of little presents, to the amazement of the youngsters, not the least of which was our recognition of father as Santa Claus and Hermann as his attendant. Father's absence might have been accounted for, but Hermann's we should have guessed. We had had neither mood nor time to suspect or to think. We were lost in wonder at the picture and the riches before us. It was my one child's Christmas Eve. All others have been mere reflections of that strange mixture of pleasure at so many gifts and awe for the holy hour.

Then came the time when father took me along to learn to swim. Constant Creek in one of its rampages during a heavy rain had dug deep holes into the sand, and when the storm had subsided there were left fine swimming pools of clear water. Judged by modern ideas they were poor enough; and we even knew that the banks of these streams were the favorite haunts of the deadly moccasin. But when we did not find snakes, we assumed that they had gone in hiding. Beyond that the water was deep. A bank served the purpose of a spring board, and we trusted to the tradition (perhaps true) that a bite in the water would dissipate a snake's poison before it could make the wound. The claim does not seem so convincing to me now; but counting on it I enjoyed many a bath, and only once did I see a snake near me in the water. Father was a wonderful swimmer. He often swam on his side with an overhand stroke—at least the suggestion of modern methods.

He had told us how he had saved a drowning soldier in a struggle so desperate that he had to strike him on the temple before he could bring him to safety. He had even won in a swimming race abroad. So our eyes were bulging in expectation, with more reason for me than I could guess. There we saw the men take their dives from a great height as it seemed to us, and I saw father make those long powerful strokes that made him look when I saw him swim in later years in larger bodies of water, like a king in his element. Then came my turn, which made my first lesson in swimming as sudden as it was unique. I was simply caught up and dropped from the bank into the pool many feet deep. But such was my confidence in father that I can not recall a feeling of fear. Down I went with the usual snorts and gasps in coming up, only to be caught before I came to the surface, so promptly had father's dive followed me. I had been baptized, so to speak, and was then left to practice dog paddling in a more shallow pool. Once feeling secure in this, the regular stroke was soon tried, and in a jiffy I felt that I had the secret. After that, I was left to do for myself. Swimming became a favorite sport, which I enjoyed all my life without fear or cramp, strength alone setting the limit.

SPORTS ALL OUR OWN

School and the little work we had to do still left a good deal of time for play. But the usual sports were out of question because once out of school we all lived widely apart, to meet only at rare times. We had to rely upon our own devices, and the conditions about us in some respects quite wild, led us to make our own weapons, and finally to hunt and chase. The start was simple enough, but in time we had fights that from a boy's point of view may be called real adventures. Among my early recollections is the Bowie knife, which, however, well known in early Texas, formed no part of our equipment. We had common knives, always the famous IXL. Anybody might have a blade; but only an IXL would invite envy. Even with knives games were played. We practiced throwing them to have the blade stick in the trunk of a tree. But "mumble the peg" (this may be right or wrong) had the call. The knife was thrown by a dozen different ways and the aim was to have the blade stick in the ground. It was thrown from the closed hands, right and left; then by holding the point of the blade between thumb and the several fingers, four times, and having the blade after turning in the air, stick in the ground; finally, by holding it on the head and land the blade in the ground. The real point was this. The winner had the right to whittle a small peg and drive it into the ground with one stroke of the knife handle, and the loser had to get the peg out with his teeth. It sounds like a strange kind of pleasure. But no doubt most of our games were much older than we; and boys will be boys. From the first whittling was our passion. Not the mere lazy cutting of anything that came to our hands, but the attempt to make things of interest. A city child could not guess in how many ways plans came to us. There was of course the fact that if we wanted to fish and hunt we had to find a way to do it. Simple tackle we had, but we had to shape the rod and fix lines and hook. With a gun, even a small one, I was not trusted until the last years in Texas. Again, things that look simple now were quite novel then, and for that reason they caught our eyes and had us imitate them. One day I saw a neighbor's son older than I, who had been to school in Rostock, Germany, drawing pictures. It is true he was only tracing; but I marveled that a mere boy would dare to make pictures, and I took courage to try. In some fashion it was a pastime for many years— the hobby of which we hear; and at last it has become a passion, until I am a very crank about etchings. I may sketch with my pencil at times just for the joy of it but at others to ease the talk of bores, for I do think that the force or turn of a line may say more than speech. It is the suggestion that is the thing, and I owe much to that boy from Rostock. I came to try other things, as, for instance, to make toys. Not copies of our old ones, but new ones that looked like the real life about us. We whittled horses and oxen; wagons with yokes and wheels, simple of course, but all ready to have the outfit move. Neither were the horses always tame. Some of them were in action, with the prancing gait of a horse under a martingale's restraint to our hearts' desire. During the war we did much with our knives, for playthings became as scarce as clothes; at least with us. So our little sister Clara (who then was four or five years old) was surprised on Christmas Eve, and sometimes in between, with presents of our make. After all, mere soap bubbles like others of the species became tiresome. We had only a knife and gimlet—the smaller holes were made with heated wire. But this is certain; we made toys to last, and not to teach waste and not to break, according to modern fashion. We felt respect akin to affection for things. Hand made things are not only the more beautiful. To me they have a human quality, to speak as it were like any other creation. I may cherish a stub of a pencil that has seen me through a hard job; or reading a book wonder at the fun the author had in writing it, or since my children and young friends still welcome me to the court, prefer to play tennis with a Doherty.

By degrees our ambition grew, and we made larger traps and bows and arrows and lances; first for play, then for use. In making and flying kites we became quite expert, and we rejoiced in the grace of the flight, even if the secret of the power was not guessed by us. Our first try at fishing was to catch mice by the use of hook and tackle. A simple string with a bent pin baited with bacon would be let down the mouse's hole in the floor. To our delight we always got a bite, and to our disgust we never caught a mouse. When we pulled in our line we could feel the weight of the mouse and his effort to save himself. Sometimes we got him out of the hole and thought he had wriggled off the hook as a fish would, when the greedy mouse had simply not let go the bacon which he was nibbling and pursuing until he saw us. Those were the first lessons in fishing of which we did more or less when we grew older. Many a nice sunfish, and some larger ones did we get with the old-fashioned long cane, the line fastened at the very point, the simple steel hook baited with an angleworm, and the cork adjusted to the depth of water to show us when the fish made his first attack, and when his stronger pull told us that he was or might be caught. Sometimes we would even get a gar—a kind of shark—or an eel, both an awful bother to get rid of. Worse still were the turtles, for which we had no use, and which when caught meant the loss of the hook; because our tiny fingers could not get it out of the beast's stubborn grip. The small fresh water catfish we thought good enough to eat. When I came north to find catfish not in good repute I charged it to the muddy river water. But even with us the big ones were noticed only for their size. They were no fun; simply so much dead weight to pull up like a cod. More exciting was the sport we had when the water was low and closed pools were formed. Then we would wade in to catch fish with our bare hands, sometimes getting them of very good size. At one time we had a long fight with an alligator about five feet long. We could not hold him; but he was terrified, which confirmed our opinion that the alligator is not to be feared, if boys bathing make noise enough, as they always do.

Somehow we did not do so much fishing on our own, unless it was to catch small fish in the little streams near by. This of course was fun, but it offers nothing to tell about although there was one time when we hiked off without leave and I got one of the few thrashings—not more than two or three —that was ever given me by my father. Mother never struck me, so far as I can remember. Another case of such punishment do I recall. When I was quite small and we were still going to the first school we had to pass the storekeeper's house. On my way home the owner asked me to tell father to call to see one of the children. Half a mile's play and frolic had it slip my memory, and I forgot. When a second and urgent message came my father was very angry; and being a man of quick temper, he punished me and locked me up for the rest of the day. I have never suffered more. Somehow the punishment passed me by. I was so worried by anxiety and remorse. I knew the form of prayer; but this was the first time that I begged in my own way in an appeal to a higher power to save the child and to help me. It was perhaps not a high order of prayer; but even so it might not suffer in comparison as most prayers go. After all, "Prayer is the soul's sincere desire, uttered or unexpressed." For hours I knelt or paced the floor with arms in supplication, saying over and over my simple words of distress, when finally the good news came to my relief. I am glad to think that I knelt and tried in a child's simple manner to send my words of gratitude as I had made my appeal.

But to resume. Real fishing was as a rule a part of longer trips planned by older people. This meant riding horseback or driving in a wagon for some distance; sometimes it even meant camping for a night. On one of these trips we came across an alligator that was to our surprise traveling across country from one stream to another. There was really no reason for stopping at all; but in such primitive times the impulse to kill seems to rule. Just why I do not know, but at first the men tried to lasso him; and I now wonder what they would have done if they had caught him there on a prairie. But they did not succeed, for the alligator with great agility always caught the rope in his jaws. Finally, feeling their defeat, the men just killed him with an axe. Even here he gave proof of the strength of his skull and hide, because it took many blows to finish him. The men went on their way as it seemed, with the feeling that they had done a thing worth while, an instinct which seems to inspire ruthless hunters to this day.

Of camping there is little to tell that is not common knowledge now. There was wood everywhere for the camp fire. But the meals were not up to our date. Canned goods were not known, although we might have a bottle of home preserved fruit, or jelly or pickles. In the main we had fresh beef, pepper and salt, raw potatoes and bread. Sometimes we had only corn meal, and baked our own bread over the fire. It would not pass muster now, but it tasted very good to hungry boys. The potatoes were baked in hot wood ashes, and no home or hotel could do better now. The meat, well spiced with pepper and salt, was toasted on spikes over the flame. He who has tasted such beef and potatoes need not be told that it was good. The quarters for the night were very simple. We trusted the Lord for something. The first tent I ever saw was in the camp of the United States troops at Brownsville, on the Rio Grande, early in 1864. The one time we had material or tarpaulin of which tents might have been made, mother used it in her despair to make trousers for us, to protect and, also, to endure. In our camp we wrapped ourselves in blankets (which made us dream of Indian custom), and lay down on the bare ground, giving what spare time sleepy boys have to watch shooting stars, or to wonder what the little twinklers might want to say to us. It did rain sometimes, and if it did we took refuge under thickly leaved trees that in the season of full foliage were probably as good as most tents, not so stuffy, and very much more interesting. While the pattering rain on the roof has its own charm, even the steady drops on the leaves were soothing so long as they did not come through. Besides, we firmly believed that fish like to search for bait and "bite" in rain; so even rain had its bright side. Fishing proper was mostly left to the older people, because in going out to camp larger streams or bodies of water were chosen. We of course were given safe places on the bank where we might throw in our lines; and we, too, had our catches. Even so, our minds were fixed on the bigger game, which often meant good sized fine fish, but more often the sluggish catfish with its broad head, at times big enough to fill our largest tin pan. On one occasion at least the fishing was done in still another way. Whether or not it was planned I did not know. The method used may even seem cruel now, although I do not believe the fish felt any evil effects, and probably the hunters carried off most of the scars. Some kind of dope covered with bread dough had been put into the water at night, and in the morning a certain kind of fish— Buffalo he was called, I think—seemed to be the victim of the sort of hilarity that is commonly more promptly exhibited by less innocent human beings under like circumstances. With that picture before us, not unlike the sporting antics of salmon in Alaska, the question was who of the men could catch one of these fish with his bare hands. This was no trifling job, for these fish must have weighed from ten to twenty pounds, and their natural aptitude for athletic performances seemed to be in no way impaired. Of course, father was the one we and for that matter all the others looked to. He was our prize swimmer, and to the last he never learnt to disregard a dare. So in he went — we must remember that bathing suits were not then known to us. Such clothes as we had we aimed to keep dry. As I think of it I marvel at the daring of it all. There was a large body of water, such as a river like the Brazos will form. It was not known to us; it was of considerable depth; the banks were covered or fringed with logs, branches and debris from the last rain's torrent; and were no doubt the home of every water enemy known to us, from alligator to moccasin. I see the struggle now. Father with his long stroke towards one of the hilarious victims, actually seizing him in both arms, going down with him and coming up again, without the slippery fish that had of course escaped from his grasp. Again and again we saw the same struggle. No fish was ever landed; but as for the sport itself nothing more exciting had ever come to us, and father, too, seemed to feel that he was more than paid for his effort.

Such were the things to tell about at home, that helped to break the routine of a little farm home. What father did not tell of his exploits mother was soon to learn from less reticent children.

But if some of the waters were not suited to our fishing tackle, there were none near us too large or too deep to swim in. There was one particularly attractive pool formed by Mill Creek, which for several summers meant many a horseback ride, merely for the frolic of a swim, shared by a lot of boisterous boys. Bathing suits were unknown. Neither did we know spy glasses or for that matter people who wanted to look through them. To go there was something of an affair. We would bring things to eat, always watermelon for dessert, after the swim. The pool was large and deep, with very clear, calm water, and nice sandy beach. We used to find or bring stones to see who could make them skip on the surface of the water the greater distance — dancing upon it—touch and go. Conditions were not favorable for snakes, and we gave little thought to them. We might even have dismissed alligators from our minds, but for the fact that at least one made himself known to us. I may seem to return to speak of these brutes too often; but it is natural that they looked very large to a boy, and surely they were large enough as they were. In truth I did not see many of them; since they are not so easily detected by the untrained eye. They have a way of lying very still, with the body below and the nose barely above the water. When very small I was standing with some one older than I on the bank of the Colorado river. A certain object caught my attention and suddenly I said, "That stick just moved." The answer was, "It did move; but that is an alligator's nose." It is no wonder, therefore, that we were on the lookout for moving sticks or stumps, and sometimes in flowing water thought they moved when they really did not. One alligator I did however see to make all others look like dwarfs. One fine day a whole party of boys came to our swimming pool. We were in high glee, all set for a good time, when right there on the very beach from which we were to go in we saw a tremendous alligator. I will not say how long we thought he was, because I do not want to invite a row with the zoo. But he was certainly a whopper, much the largest I ever saw in those days. He seemed to feel his own dignity, too, for he was very slow to give ground. He had been basking in the sun, and as we came on in numbers, shouting and yelling, he very slowly crawled towards the water and slid into it. We now owned the beach, but the question still was who owned the pool. About that we were not so clear, and our shouting was not quite so loud. We held a council of war and, decided that all alligators are cowards, and if they are not they ought to be. To this day I do not know whether an alligator would attack, but rumor had us believe it. No doubt there were doubters in our ranks. With that brute's snout before me I did not feel so sure myself. But as is always the case, doubters are swept along by the firm stand of a leader or two; and this is one instance in my life when I just went along with the crowd. I now know that a good deal of the success of leaders depends upon well timed noise. My experience later in politics has confirmed me in that conviction. So, guided by the best advice we had, we acted upon that rule; and wiser than many victims of political ambition, we trusted our fate to one plank— noise and racket without limit or end. There were no pussyfooters among us; the plan once made was carried out in letter and in spirit. Half a dozen boys or more, without a stitch on them, jumped into the pool at one dash, and yelling, shouting and splashing with the energy of mirth or despair, made racket enough to clear that pool of fish, alligators, or any other living thing for the time. For all intents and purposes that pool was ours. Our way of using it was not questioned; but I am forced to admit that my enjoyment of that swim was disturbed by misgivings as to the precise whereabouts of that alligator. I may as well add that for years the thought of that brute would not let me swim in peace even in salt water on the north shore. True, there could be no alligators there, nor shark for that matter; but that brute's ugly snoot has forever associated the sensation of being gripped by cruel teeth with the act of swimming. So I had my swim that day and, indeed, on many other days; but that alligator had his revenge on me for helping to end his siesta on the sunny beach of our pool. Nevertheless, bread and butter and watermelon tasted good, perhaps the better for the experience; and no doubt the exercise of muscles and lungs sharpened our appetite.

That sort of sport led to others. If we youngsters could scare an alligator, where was the wild animal that we could not fill with fear? Our heads were of course full of stories about painted Indians that we had never seen, and about panthers that we had probably never heard. My particular nightmare was either a fight with Indians when I had no arms, or a panther crawling up on me when I was bound. But that was at night when we were asleep and could not help ourselves. It was different in daylight when we thought of hunting animals that we had seen, although we feared some of them. We all know now that if you play long or often enough with an idea you are almost sure to try it on. If we did not know that rule of life, we at least helped to make or prove it. From very small beginnings we by degrees came to have some fights that were really not meant for children. But one thing led to another. We came to wander in the woods — the haunts of our enemies. As we grew older it gave us no joy to kill innocent animals. We might throw a stone at a moccasin or a stick at a rattler, always at a safe distance, with no chance to hurt them— just the inborn hate of a snake. Or we might follow the trails of the forest, old and dim, made perhaps by Indian or bear, with no trace of either now; or perhaps by deer whose fresh tracks stirred our instinct for the hunt. We might climb into the great Spanish oaks with their hanging moss full of mystery and sometimes the abode of scorpion or other enemy such as poison oak, which never affected me. We might climb into the spreading branches, and from them into the great mustang grape vines, there to sit as in nature's swings to look into the dark forest and to listen to its call. What can a city boy know about the language of the woods, its wooing and its alarm, its cry of triumph or despair. Like music, the language of the forest is for every one—free for all who can hear and understand. The chirp of a bird, the bark of a squirrel, the call of the wild turkey—all have their notes from joy to fear in fullest scale. And when all else is silent, who has not heard and sought to understand the lament of the trees or the warning of the forest? When every whisper in the air, every rustle of a leaf may mean anything from a gentle rising of the breeze to the startled movement of a squirrel or a deer; when every change of light and shadow, every shade of sound is instinctively felt and judged for what it is. These are the things that we learn to feel only when we are young, and which induce city people so often to say how much more quick we are to see every shift of light and to hear every stir of sound in the forest. Nearer and nearer we came to our new challenge, with pity for some, with enmity for others.

Our first efforts in the chase were no doubt suggested and led by our dogs. We had two of the hound type. No dog was ever as near and dear to us as Murf had been; but these were trusty friends who would not molest our cats, but would jump in between us and a rattler at any time.

As I think of them and others I have known since, I feel at times that if most of us had as much good sense as dogs seem often to have, democracy would have a better chance. They were not as free from danger as a common pig, whose thick skin and bristles protect him. But for all that, I have seen a dog tackle a poisonous snake by gripping his body and swinging both ends to and fro with such violence, that the snake never had a chance to bite before his back was broken. Now and then a dog would be bitten and would come home with a swollen jaw; but somehow they would always get well. It was the same with cattle.

But this was not the way we started. Like timid boys we commenced with innocent game that could not harm us. We set traps for birds, for the pleasure of catching them, and to keep them in large cages; only to let them out to enjoy their freedom the more for the restraint they had felt. Our first mark was the lark, of which we caught very many; and how they would soar into the sky when we set them free—away from all human cruelty—back to their world of freedom. With the "Kardinal" (red bird) it was different. He would fight for the king's rights; and when the first one got my finger in his beak and crushed it black and blue, I felt that I had met my first setback in hunting wild things.

In time the dogs led us to follow the chase of rabbits, innocent rabbits, for which I feel sympathy every time I see one. Our dogs were good at finding, but not at catching them. Either the rabbit would get away in the brush, or he would be treed; which meant that he would crawl up the hollow of a tree, too small for a dog to follow. At this point our work came into play, and it was so cruel that I am now ashamed of it, and am glad to admit that our chance was small. One way was to start a smudge under the hollow forcing the rabbit to come down. Another was to use a pointed stick, which was pushed up against the rabbit; by twisting it would become fastened in the skin, and enable us to pull the rabbit down. I hate to think of it, and am glad to say that we did this only once or twice. But one day while we were engaged in such cruel work things took an unlooked for turn and the rabbit got away, leaving us the worse for wear. This is the way it happened. Our dogs had started the rabbit in the open, but had been forced to pursue him into our neighbor's enclosed pasture, where he crawled into a hollow tree. Brother and I had followed and were just getting him down when two sons of our neighbor came to claim the rabbit. I did not then know that this situation raised the old question of law as to who is the rightful owner, he on whose land the game is started, or he upon whose land it is caught. We may at least have sensed the reason of the rule, and felt doubt about it. The uncertainty of it may have had something to do with the indecision of the dispute. The case was aggravated by a grievance of long standing between brother and me and these two boys, Robert and Ulrich. They were just our ages and stronger than we were. But for Paul's indomitable will, Ulrich had no trouble with him, and adroitness alone could save me from the stronger Robert. Our row had several causes. Not long before, Robert, the older, had, while I was at home with chills and fever, whipped brother Paul. This I had resented, and on my return to school had with great success, and not without a sense of self-righteousness evened the score. But of more lasting influence was our complaint about their dogs when we had to pass their house on our way to school. We were afraid of strange dogs, because a very treacherous one had jumped at me and actually run her teeth down my chest and had turned to bite little Paul through the calf of his leg

—a wound that troubled him for more than a year. So violent barking meant danger to us, and no doubt our conduct, by arming ourselves with sticks served to excite the dogs still more. Be that as it may we had several combats every day until finally father in his exasperation shot one of our neighbor's dogs. With the exception of the gate post this was the only hit father had to his credit. But for the time all those conditions helped to create a tense relation.

When we met to settle the right to the rabbit, it was in that spirit the fight commenced. There was nothing said. Each side knew that the fight must be had. No breath was lost in talk; each faced his man, and we went at it. There was only one rule with us, which was to win. We used fists to strike and elbows to guard. We hit under the belt, if we knew where it was; we clinched and rolled on the ground and in the brush; we were up and down, noses bleeding, and strength giving out. I felt that I could not win, but that I must not lose. The same conviction seemed to have crept over Robert, because of a sudden we stood facing each other with hands down. We just looked at each other and knew that we were done. Our brothers followed our lead; and so we turned away for our respective homes, a drawn battle. The rabbit had made this move earlier, as soon as he saw his chance. Somehow I was glad of it; not only that Robert did not get him, but that nobody did. I felt ashamed of our cruelty; never practiced it again; and ever since take pleasure in seeing a rabbit get away, the cute little rascal racing for his cover. Running is his only means of defense, and I wonder why he gives so much prominence to his little white tail. Perhaps he does it to deceive us. They say most animals use tricks to fool their enemies — generally their color is like their surroundings, so that they can not be seen. The rabbit may hope that the hunter will shoot at his tail and not at his head. He could spare one better than the other; one might grow again, the other could not. Why should we say "Scared like a rabbit," when all of us so often are like him; and when the poor fellow has neither means of defense nor moral support? A soldier once told me that there are times when whole troops feel as brave as a lion, and other times when the same troops are as scared as a rabbit. One morning during the Civil War he told me—it was at Stony river, I think—Federal and Confederate troops were drawn up in opposing lines. The morning was frosty, and every man seemed to feel as though his last hour had come. The colonel, erect and stern, rode to the front, and just as he was about to draw his sword a rabbit ran past making a bee line between the two opposing troops. The soldiers silently envied his luck, and the colonel called after him, "Go it, cotton tail, if it were not for a matter of self-respect I would be with you." So there we are. We do what we have to do, and the rabbit does the best he can in his way. My sympathy is with him, and was from that hour; after that I wanted to fight animals whose habit it was to fight and kill others. Other doubts came into my mind. I had licked Robert before; why not this time? Was my case not as clear, and was the sense of right really so much of a factor in the outcome. The truth of that idea I felt then and believe in now. But as we grow older we learn to know that in human affairs right must often lose. Indeed, Providence seems to intend that at times a losing fight for the right shall become a challenge to our moral sense. Even as other experiences may be provided to test our willingness to share with others.

So we entered upon our more adventurous plans. For some time we had made bows and arrows—a natural advance from mere whittling—from simple pleasure we went to more serious business. At first we only shot at targets. We made them by drawing the bull's eye and the circles with our pencils on large sheets. Of course we did poorly, because our little arrows floated helplessly in the air. Experience was our teacher. We loaded the point with wire so as to have it keep its head and hold its course. The next step was to make an arrow that would both strike and stick. So we split the head of the arrow, placed a nail in it, tied it down with twine, and then sharpened it on a grindstone. What more could an Indian do? Our bows became larger and were more carefully made of hickory and sometimes dogwood; and for the bow string fishing tackle was used. It was surprising with what precision we learnt to shoot, and what distance our arrows would carry. With a gun I shot at a target only once, hit the bull's eye and quit; just as in my only game of baseball I made three home runs, and wisely rested with that. When we lost an arrow we had a way of shooting another after it from the same bow in the same state of wind, and often the second would lead us to the first. Having our weapons ready to hand, what would boys do but start to try them out. Our sympathy for innocent life was not yet quite alive, and our first victims were mere birds. To this day I regret that one of my best shots killed a lark; but it was my last crime of the kind. We began to make larger arms for real war upon our natural enemies. We now made lances — long staffs with large sharpened nails for points, similar to the arrows. To this was added a child's axe, which father gave us. Thus equipped, with our dogs to attend us, we set out on our new ventures. My sympathy for Boy Scouts needs no explanation.

It would be tiresome to tell of all the encounters. Strangely enough most of them were attempts to kill snakes. There was game like coons and opossums to attract us, but we had not yet caught the southern taste for either; and, after all, our arrows could never more than wound them. Besides, the opossum's trick to play dead was the source of great hilarity on our part, and it excited no wish to correct his pretense; that is, to wake him up. Snakes were our game. We were moved by the old hatred for them, and they offered a rich field for our hunt. With harmless snakes we did not bother. We would not even kill them with sticks. We used them only to try each other's nerves, by slipping them inside our shirts and letting them crawl around our bodies. I can not claim that I ever became indifferent to this test; but under the customary "dare" I stood it. It was poisonous, dangerous snakes we were after, and I can not now believe that our parents knew in how perilous work we youngsters were engaged. Of course, poisonous snakes were so common that in a manner old and young became used to them. Every one was supposed to know how to protect himself. Besides, we had all kinds of snake lore to warn and to guide us. For instance, there was the black snake that was calmly snoozing under the cover of the man's bed, where he happened to see it first in the dim light of a sputtering candle. Boys might lie down in camp a few feet from a snake's hole, and ask no questions. We did not then know of the Mexican custom to surround the camp with new horsehair ropes, which snakes are said not to cross. But no boy ever got into his bed at home before making sure that he did not have a snake for a bed fellow. This was only rumor, but we knew that Mrs. Hagemann, while reaching under the barn for freshly laid eggs, had been bitten by a big non-poisonous chicken snake, which seemed to share her taste for eggs. We had seen our dogs pick up even poisonous snakes in our own yard and rattle them about their ears until they put them down as dead as a snake could be before sundown. After we got a piano—the wonder of the county—which stood in our common sitting and dining room, and took up as we thought most of the space, we found a copperhead under it. A copperhead is small but very poisonous, and he has his own way of showing fight. He raises his head straight up in the air, say several inches or more, as though he were trying to stand on the end of his tail. This one met all our expectations in this respect, and his small size seemed to fit him for our attention. We gave no alarm to the older people. Neither did we try to charm him with melodious notes from the piano, as we are sometimes told can be done. We took to such sticks as were always handy, and put an end to him.

While picking cotton in the heavy growth of the bottom, just as I was reaching through a heavily leafed plant to get a bowl rich with flowing cotton, I saw a large rattler with his head up as though he were striking for the same bowl. This called for united action and for long distance striking, the aim being to crack the neck just at the head. We got him and left him for dead, or as near dead as according to our tradition a snake could be while the sun was up. All snakes, however injured, lived until sundown, as we believed, and dramatically died as the sun sank beneath the horizon. Armed as we now were with bows and arrows and lances, we no longer waited for the snakes, but we went out in search of them. Perhaps this sounds more serious than it was, but after all we were only little shavers. We did not kill many of our enemies, but we sent fear into their camps. Wherever we came upon one, off went our arrows, often missing but sometimes hitting, for a moving snake is not an easy mark for a boy's arrow. I remember one very large rattler, quite safe on the opposite bank of a stream. He moved along slowly, hardly giving thought to us, when one of our arrows struck him square in the back. Like lightning his head shot back as he coiled for action. We had no arrows to waste, but watched the one that had struck, wobbling to and fro as he writhed and coiled in his wrath. The injury may have been severe — may even have broken his back; but our arrow was not barbed, and the chances are that in time he scraped it off, rubbing against brush and debris. We did, however, finally come up with a real fight, which fills me with dread even now when I think of it. The start was innocent enough. It was a lazy afternoon, the dogs were with us, and like boys we were trying out our little axe. We blazed trees, as though we needed new trails in the forest. Boys and some grown people do not know that every such injury to a tree must be paid for. The tree may be strong and young enough to have the bark grow over the wound, but the chance is that a sore will be left. If the place is not healed over, rot will set in, and in time the tree may become hollow, depending upon the strength of its shell to sustain it in storm, and upon the soundness of its bark to supply the sap. In such cases the only ones benefited are the owls that make their nests in these hollows, or the squirrels that use them for their store houses of nuts which they collect for their winter supply, or sometimes when the opening is low down, for rabbits when they seek quick shelter from hot pursuit. On that day we were following a trail, with nothing further from our minds than the greatest adventure of our lives, when suddenly the cry of the dogs arose, and they were off in wildest scramble. We followed with no idea what had started the dogs, and came up with them at the foot of a fallen giant of the forest. The tree was hollow, which gave the reason for his untimely end. The roots were still intact and rose like great arms in appeal to the sky. Our dogs were near the mouth of the hollow (the bare ground still showing where the roots had been torn up), and were barking like demons. Things looked unusual, but we thought that the dogs had started a rabbit and had been close up with him before he got into the tree, so that their excitement could be accounted for. At all events, we were bound to find out what it was that had gone into that hole. While the opening was very large, Paul was the only one small enough to crawl into it, and this he promptly did. Our suspense was great. The doubt about the inmate of that hollow tree would have been enough; but I think we felt somehow that this time we had something uncanny to deal with. In a few minutes Paul came crawling out backwards, and told us that there was something besides a rabbit in that tree. What it was he could not guess, and it was for us to find out. There was no more thought of crawling into that hole, so we concluded to cut another hole in the trunk of the prostrate tree higher up, and to get a look in that way. That was my job. I was twelve years old, while brother was ten, and the third boy was eleven. I was the senior, and the one to handle the axe; so I got up on that trunk and stood on it like a gnome in a primeval forest. The use of the axe was not novel; we had cut or at least split fire wood. The other two with bow and arrow ready, watched the opening, and I with the axe set to as best I could. The wood was not hard, it gave like rotten wood; the axe made no clean cut. This should have warned me, but my zeal blinded me. I went on when after a few more blows suddenly, suspecting nothing, a large part of the trunk under my feet caved in, and there shot out right along the handle of my falling axe the head of a rattler that will live in my memory as the largest I ever saw. With the instinct that is born of the country, I let go the axe, and falling backward, rolled and rolled until in spite of their alarm, the other boys laughed aloud at me.

So much for that. So far no one had scored, and the question was how the fight was to be made. The snake did not leave us long in doubt. It is said that a rattler will not pursue for attack. I think that an angry one will. This one at least left no doubt that he was ready to try it out with us. He did not stay where he was, or even in the tree; but he came out into the open, and took his place on the bare ground right at the foot of the tree where he could watch us. It was clear that he was mad clean through.

We had never known our dogs to fail, but this time they made no move, and shared our dread of this enemy. I may have seen longer rattlers since, but I can not believe that I ever saw one whose body measured so much around. He coiled for the thrust, and of this we at least had sense enough to take notice. We had not then heard that a rattler can not thrust farther than half his length; but even so he seemed long enough to have us keep at a good distance. The odds began to look in his favor, for with no more than our little weapons we seemed a poor match for that ugly brute. However, we were bound to do what we could. We must at least use our weapons, such as they were. With as much care as excited boys could command, we began to send our arrows at him, and with very good result. Nearly every arrow hit, but they caused no serious injury; and if that were possible, only made the rattler so much madder. The picture was really a great one. The big rattler in endless motion, coiling and recoiling, snapping at the arrows that were wagging to and fro like signals of his pain. I think now that perhaps he was spending all his poison in the many thrusts; but no such idea came to us then. At last our supply of arrows was gone. We had shot the last one, and the rattler showed no sign of giving up. We held a council of war—our one lance was our only chance. I threw it with all the strength that was in me, and hit the heavy coiled body which, indeed, was not easy to miss. But no vital spot was struck, and the pain only added to the fury of the snake. Then in despair, and without giving thought Paul threw the axe at him with the same result, leaving us quite unarmed in the fight. Another council of war was held, and this time we felt that strategy was the thing—of all things a boy's scheme against such a snake. We still had our knives. We cut a long green pole, leaving at its small end the points of two strong twigs, so as to make a short fork. Armed with this, I again climbed upon the trunk of the tree. How we escaped risk after risk is today a marvel to me. Knowing that in these haunts snakes usually live in pairs, that was in itself taking a great chance. But never thinking of that danger, I walked along the trunk of the old tree right up to the great roots, where I could look down upon the snake. The tree was rotten, as we now knew, but it held my small weight without a sign of giving way. The other two stood in front, holding the attention of the rattler. With great care, fully realizing my danger, and how much depended upon the success of my aim, I let the fork end of the pole down between roots, and as luck would have it, caught the powerful brute right over the small of his neck, just behind his flat head, and held him. His struggles to get free are not to be described. Pinned down as he was, he beat the air and hit the pole with all the might of his strong body; but Paul with his daredevil presence of mind rushed in, got hold of the axe, and chopped off the snake's head. With every chance against us, with risks enough on the way to end every one of us, the fight was over, and we had won. As the sequel will show, our venture was not over; but we tied a string around the neck of the snake, and with a feeling of triumph dragged our trophy home. Unhappily for us, father had returned in time to meet us. Both he and mother were thunder struck; but father did not lose his presence of mind and took us in sections for as sound a thrashing as we had ever had. It was my second or third, certainly the last of such depressing experience. However, the glory of such an exploit is not easily dimmed, and in time there were other signs to revive our courage. About the time we were regaining a normal state of mind we saw father dragging that snake and carefully laying it across the road to measure how far it reached beyond the wagon tracks. The result seemed to be a good one, for he brought our trophy back and put it in safety from harm. Coming in he told mother (not to be sure for our ears) that it was the largest rattler he had ever seen; that it had nineteen rattles which, by our method of figuring, meant twenty-two years for the snake; and that he would send the rattles to his mother in Germany to show her what size reptiles we had in this country. No doubt he added in writing later that his boys had killed it; but he did not speak of that at the time, at least not in our hearing.

Soon after but without saying anything about our snake fight, father gave me a gun, and of course bows and arrows from now on seemed rather unfit for the larger field that opened before me. In this I fooled myself, because as proud owner of a gun, I really did not do any more than I had before. We now felt that wild turkeys were best suited to our new weapon; and they were in so far as our sport and their safety went. My gun was a boy's rifle, which, however, I was told never to load with anything more deadly than bird shot, or at the most, buck shot. Our plans were large and nothing was to be left to chance. We had heard that real hunters have a way of luring turkeys by imitating their call, and thus getting near enough to shoot. To do this we were also told they used a particular part of turkey wings' bone. The ordinary whistle, which we made out of willow twigs, was of course useless for such serious business. They seemed to rely not alone upon the imitation of the sound, but also upon some occult influence of the bone, which might have belonged to some close relative of the turkey to be shot. As may be imagined, we did not rest until we had a bone, which our elders told us was just the right one. We practiced the call until we had it down fine, and then went forth to make the woods resound with it. We had the bone. We had a gun, and turkeys there were many, and later all game became bold after more and more young men left for the front. Everything was set for the hunt. Our main trust of course went to the bone. We followed trail upon trail, crossed and recrossed our stream day after day, never failing to call to let the turkeys know where we were. But, the wild turkey is a wary animal; and I now feel that after we had traveled those woods for a week there was not within forty miles of our home one single turkey that was not too lame to limp away. I had just one chance at turkeys while I had that gun, and that was before we had heard about the bone. I really deserved better luck, because I had done a hunter's trick in creeping up on game. Such hunting was done before school. No "daylight saving" law was needed to beckon us, often wading through wet grass up to our waists. I must have been out the first morning with that gun, as the result will show. I saw a young turkey just go into some brush next to a rail fence, not more than a mile from home. I knew every foot of ground there, and also of a rather deep, very narrow gulch which ran along the fence. Making for this and crawling along in the gulch, I got right into the midst of a flock of wild turkeys without being noticed. The thing is almost past belief, unless we recall that game had become so bold that from our front porch we could often of a morning see deer in the small free space that opened out from the woods. So close was I to the turkeys that it seemed to be a question whether I should take one by the leg or shoot at another with the gun. Boy-like I chose the latter; it was so much more like real hunting. Taking careful aim, I pulled the trigger, the cap snapped and the wary turkeys needing no warning, were off. My gun was not loaded—father looking to me and I to him—and I lost my only chance. Not that I never fired the gun at times even at snakes, although such shooting was sure to frighten other game. So snakes escaped, unless they offered peculiar challenge; for even a snake might excite a boy's admiration. Looking across the stream where I took my first bathing lesson, I saw a fine rattler just crawling out of his old skin to make his debut in his new outfit. Barring one other time, I never saw such splendor of color on an animal. The pure gold, in contrast with the deep black, fairly shone in the bright sun, a very glory of raiment, I stood to wonder at it. Years after I read how Baden-Powell had waited for a member of an African tribe at a well known spring. As he lay in the high grass he heard his victim come, and then heard him drink with the deep draught of an animal. When he had enough the savage rose to his feet and raised his lance to greet the sun. As Baden-Powell looked upon his splendid figure, glistening in its splendor under the sun's rays, he put down his gun. He could not kill him, and let him go. I have admired Baden-Powell ever since, and would like to believe that I followed just such feeling when I let that specimen of marvelous beauty go, although it was only a snake.

My only real adventure with that gun I had one morning before school time, when I hoped to meet up with the same flock of turkeys at about the same place. While waiting at a point of the woods, I suddenly saw a bobcat coming leisurely towards me. This was too much. I took aim and fired right at his face. There came the greatest yelp of a cat I ever heard, and he must have gone ten feet in the air, to come down with a thud like a sack of meal. I thought he was dead; but he must have called upon another one of his nine lives, for up he came, scrambled into the brush, and as I could hear, up a nearby tree. I tried to locate him of course, although my one barrel gun was empty, and loading then had to be done from shot pouch and powder horn, the charge rammed down with the rod. I never found him, although I did so reckless a thing as to walk right under the tree, never thinking that an angry wild cat likes nothing better than to pounce upon you out of a tree.

I was ready for another promotion. Father gave me a real gun, double barreled, one side for ball, the other for shot, to use as I chose. With this I had only a few shots while at home. The time was short, and our duties became more and more pressing. But I took it with me on our trip to Mexico later on.

The only wild turkey to my credit I did, however, get with it. Out as usual before school, a whole flock of turkeys ran along a wood road, with that strange movement of alarm and energy. They were getting away from me fast, and taking pot luck I got two with one shot, both hit through the neck. My load of buckshot must have been a liberal one. My luck spoke for itself; for the time I ranked all my school mates.

But again I had the most exciting experience the first time I went out with this gun. It was towards dusk and Paul was with me. We had gone rather deeper into the forest, away from home. The woods were dense in places, leaving open spaces only here and there. The rays of the setting sun streamed through the undergrowth, striking trunks of trees and brush, with the wonderful glamor of evening lights. There was not a sound, not a breath to stir the air, when without warning we were face to face with the most beautiful animal I ever saw outside of a Zoo. He stood very still, not fifty yards away, with his eyes straight upon us. My first thought was that at last I had met a panther; but candor makes me admit that this could not be. His bobbed tail and his alert ears with their tufts of standing hair settled that. Neither was he a wild cat, for he was too large, and his coloring was far too brilliant for a cat. He was no doubt a lynx—no mean enemy in a set-to with a mere boy. However, there he was, and as I was now a bold hunter with a gun that again was not loaded—this time I think father had fooled me—I aimed and snapped the old-fashioned cap. It was of course a lucky day for us. The chance was that any shot from my gun would only have wounded him, and in such an event there is little question what the finish would have been. As it was, I had proof of an animal's contempt, if not magnanimity. He gave us one look and trotted off, snarling a rebuke for stupid boys, the most magnificently graceful thing in the splendor of his colors as they were played upon by the evening sun, that I have ever seen. Zoos are all very fine, but he who has seen a wild animal in his native glory must always feel that the best kept animal, caged, lacks something. Only he who has seen such a play of color can know how true are the lights of a Sorolla or a Zorn.

Once, as I have said, I actually fired with my new gun at a grazing buck; and missed him, as I am now frankly glad to say. At another time I came so close upon a herd of deer at early dawn that I fully meant to fire; but with a boy's eagerness, in raising my gun, I struck the old-fashioned powder horn. In the stillness of the morning the click sounded like a shot, and no more was needed to have the deer scurry away for the safety of the brush. I missed the animals, but not their subtle beauty, as they bounded off with a grace that needs no teacher and a power that knows no restraint.

As fortune would have it, our only fight with a member of the cat family was had under quite different conditions. Hearing our dogs bark in the forest about a mile from the house, brother and I got on our mule to find out the trouble. For once the mule did not cut any capers with us—perhaps he was also curious, as animals sometimes are. We found our dogs at the foot of a rather small tree, in the top of which sat a wild cat—a sure enough wild cat—eying the situation from above. Luckily for us we had not brought our gun. The commotion was so great that very soon dogs joined us from other farms, and we were then followed by other boys, some of them older than we, also without arms. It was decided to chop down the tree and give the dogs a chance at their quarry. This the older and stronger boys undertook to do, unmindful of the danger. How true it is I do not know, but Gerstaecker's Arkansas story (which had thrilled me) said that in hunting wild cat it is very dangerous to get under its tree, because the cat is apt to jump on your shoulder for attack. Whatever may be true, we were no doubt protected by the presence of so many dogs. To most of us chopping down a tree is a tiring and slow task. But in time the trunk was weakened so as to lean to one side for its fall. Here we made our mistake. We should have made a clean cut to bring the tree down suddenly. But we were too eager. So we helped the tree along by pushing, so that it went down of its own weight very slowly. Our surprise was compete. The wild cat seemed not to stir until the tree commenced to descend, when it crawled forward towards the top of the branches; and just before they struck the ground, it leaped with the most graceful and easy movement, first to the ground and then up into another tree. Our dismay was natural, but that of the dogs was tragic. In the belief that they were to grapple with the enemy, they rushed forward, one over the other, through and over the branches of the fallen tree, only to see their prey reach another point of safety. There was no room for tactics. We had merely to repeat what we had done before. But we now had an advantage. The tree had fallen in a direction which did not give the cat much choice. It had to take what it could get, and this was a single tree, standing apart from others. When the second tree came down, more ground had to be covered, and the wiser dogs as if by instinct, gathered at the point of descent. The cat could not repeat its escape, but had to stand its ground, which it did with such courage that it filled me with admiration. How many dogs there were I do not know, probably eight or ten, one more eager than the other. The wild cat in making its lone fight, braced its back against the trunk of a tree and faced its enemies. There was no attempt to run or to attack. It stayed on the defensive. The dogs were wild with excitement, and some of them had to pay the price of first experience. The few that rushed in boldly at first, returned with scratched noses, and sometimes yelped in pain and fury. It looked as though the cat might succeed by striking their faces as they came on one by one. But older dogs used to the hunt, knew how to marshal their forces, how to make common cause. Their attacks were united, and from all sides, making it impossible for the cat to ward them all off at once. In that way one or two dogs got a grip. The others were able to push through, and it was quickly over; the wild cat was beaten by superior numbers. It was our only trophy of the kind, and we took the skin then and there. It was given to us because we had been the first on the ground, and this time we came home in great form, without misgivings as to our reception.

I have related so many of these little incidents, not because any of them are novel or meant particular risk to us; but because for mere kids they were very real adventures, and may for that reason interest other youngsters. If so much is true, there are many similar ones that might do to tell before a blazing fire to willing listeners among children. I have chosen some of the more striking as it seemed to me, because they stand out among the others. They seem innocent enough as I read them now. I can but tell them as they have happened. Perhaps the best that can be said is that we made the most of them. In any event they may give a setting to one side of our life which in most respects was so very sheltered.

THE LIFE OF OLDER PEOPLE

There were many other things to interest us. We had neighborhood meetings. They would probably be called picnics now. Certainly they served the same purpose in providing good things to eat, perhaps even a glass of imported wine; although it must be said that smoking and drinking was done only in moderation. On one of these outings I for the first time tested and felt the effect of wine. There are always persons whose sense of humor calls for victims — the more innocent the better. Father knew nothing of it. He enjoyed wine and cigars but never to excess. Whiskey was not kept in our home; and until I was thirty I had scarcely tasted it. So I must not complain of this early warning which no doubt stood me in good stead. These meetings served more especially to give the women living at distances a chance to renew their friendships. They did not have occasions for meetings like the men. At the store the men had erected bars to let them practice the old gymnastic exercises in remembrance of the life of their youth. Even a ten pin alley they had. We heard it whispered that the game had really called for nine pins; but when the law prohibited this, it had been changed to ten pins to conform to the law's injunction. This may have been idle rumor, but in view of today's legislative futilities I am prepared to credit what we heard with some truth. As we had learned to expect, father excelled in high and distance jumping, in running, and some other sports. But in rolling ten pins (particularly playing in parties) he was good only up to the last ball, when so much depended upon the throw. He was a man of so much strength of purpose, that to this day I can not understand the common remark: "Oh, well, that is his last ball." It must have been a certain nervousness, because of a sense of responsibility to his partners.

Our piano made our home the meeting place for the singing society (composed of eight or ten) of which our teacher was the leader. Once a week they met to sing the old popular or student songs. "Reisst die Kreuze aus der Erden, alle sollen Schwerter werden," or "Steh ich in finstrer Mitternacht So einsam auf der stillen Wacht," or "Morgenrot, Morgenrot, Leuchtest mir zum fruehen Tod," or the inimitable "Ich bin ein Fisch auf trocknem Sand." These and more we heard the men, true pioneers to their adopted country, sing with the spirit which they had brought from their beloved Germany. Years after in St. Louis one Sunday morning father came from his room joining in a hymn that was being sung in a church across the street. The text was decidedly different but the tune he insisted was taken from the student song "Armer Strumpf muss sterben." He was much affected. But in the old Texas home we listened in our corner with a feeling not unlike awe to these songs from the old to the new world, but our little efforts to imitate always faded away when we found that we, too, had listeners. We had no music at school; and until I came to New York I had never heard a woman sing. Somehow "Ein feste Burg ist unser Gott" comes to my mind. But that I must owe to mother. It was within her domain. Perhaps this recollection moved me to recommend to Mr. Busch to give to our Museum a painting by Kuehl which bears this title and which remained on the wall throughout the Great War—inscription and all. On such occasions we learned more of the doings of our elders than on any others. For songs did not occupy all the evenings. What was there told was not quite meant for us, but we were not kept away. So, among other things, we got the story of many of father's pranks, often at the expense of others present, and these were of course of chief interest to us. How we chuckled when we heard that our own father could do such nonsensical things. Not that our mirth ever rose to disrespect—one look out of his eyes would settle that. At the same time, some of my own later pranks may probably be traced to this early revelation, and may in turn have afforded similar motive to my own children, perhaps not to stop with them.

However that may be, our eyes popped out of our heads when we heard them tell, with shouts of laughter, how our serious minded and overworked father had danced like an acrobat through the store, jumping behind the counter, vaulting over it, playing hide-and-seek behind sugar barrels, coils of rope and what not, always pursued by an irate challenger, daring him to come on; father answering that no one could throw him until he had caught him. Our thoughts were not at one until we heard the whole story. A strong man—very much of a braggart—had been boasting of his prowess—how he could throw anybody in the county, etc. No one had doubted him, but still he persisted until everybody's feelings were on edge. It was then that father said, "You can't throw me," and the answer came, "My dear man—ridiculous—I would crush you with one arm—but I would not want to hurt the doctor." One word led to another until father's taunt became as trying as the other's bragging. All was made ready for a trial when father, to the surprise of all said that it would not be necessary to take off his coat for so light a task. To make a long story short, father said that to shoot a bear you must first find him, and that he was not boasting of his strength, but of his agility. After all the language in which challenges can be couched had been exhausted and the wind of the braggadocio had given out in his vain pursuit, the play was called off; and to judge by the telling of the story, the watchers had really enjoyed the discomfiture of the challenger more than father had his success.

They told how father had joined a small party at the store for a game of cards, and, also, to share one rare bottle of wine just received. They were just seated when he was called to the proprietor's house to attend a newly arrived baby. "Penalty of the profession," they called to him, "we will drink the wine in the meantime." They little reckoned who would pay the price of such a jest. In a few minutes a messenger came to fetch the wine at once, because the baby was so weak that it could be saved only by a wine bath. There may have been doubts, but no one dared to say no. The wine was taken; the baby was reported to be hale and hearty, and no one doubted that father got his share of that bottle when it was returned. It was common report how father, calling at a patient's house, had been attacked by a very vicious dog. Indignant he threatened to throw the dog down the chimney. He received a rather exasperating answer, and while his threat was not literally carried out, he did carry that dog up the roof and held his nose over the rising smoke, until there was at least one visitor to that house at whose very sight this dog slunk into a corner. This feat we greatly enjoyed, because we lived in very dread of that dog. One day I had been told to take some medicine to this same house, and I was so scared that I got an older boy to go with me. Passing the store we bought some small nails and wrapped them in packages of brown paper, planning to throw one of them into that dog's mouth if he attacked us. It looked quixotic; but stranger things have happened, and a better shot was never made than my companion delivered that day. Nor have I ever seen a more disturbed expression than I saw on that brute when he fastened his teeth upon those nails.

Fig. 12: Unter den Linden, around 1900

Father's act added very much to the satisfaction of our sense of justice.

But we listened to the exploits of others as well. Kleberg, the justice of the peace or notary, or something associated with writing wills and deeds, was known as the man of great nerve. He was probably not more than five feet and six inches high, his body somewhat deformed, and his head was large and impressive. He always rode a big stallion. When Kleberg was carried down our road by his horse with the powerful rack he looked as though armies must fly before him. It was he whose stoic contempt for pain was known to all of us. Father was really only a physician, but under existing conditions was forced to do the best he could in every emergency, including cases of surgery. One of the most usual complaints was a kind of boil on the finger. It yielded readily enough to lancing, but it was so painful that persons were known to lose a joint of the finger rather than submit to have it lanced. Kleberg presented himself with such a boil on his thumb. Father's method was simple. The patient would place his finger on a table, father would stick the knife into the boil, the patient would jerk his finger away, and the operation was called a success. No exception was proposed in Kleberg's case, and all went by rule and custom until the last act, when the two men stood facing each other in mutual surprise. "Well," said Kleberg, "I thought you were the surgeon," and since he refused to budge with the knife in his thumb, father had for the first time to complete a surgical operation of that kind. It was this man who, riding his proud steed, had been accompanied by father on his horse to Bellville. While there father had been seized with chills and fever, and a great torrent of rain had sent the Mill Creek over its bank. When the rain ceased they started home, but found the creek so swollen that any attempt to cross looked hopeless to father. Not so with Kleberg, who declared that his horse could swim any stream. Father protested but to no purpose. "Wotan" was, I think, the name of Kleberg's horse. So without another word he rode as close to the bank as he could, called out "Wotan" in tone of command, gave his spurs, and horse and rider plunged into the surging mass. Father always said that at one time he lost sight of them altogether, and that he never expected to see the rider again. But up they came, the rider in the saddle, as though all had gone as it should. But the struggle had only begun. The floating wood and debris from the forest got into the way on all sides; and when at last that difficulty was overcome, the question was how to make the other bank, wet and soft and yielding at every effort of the horse to get a foothold. But the stallion met even that obstacle, Kleberg sitting his saddle without sign of agitation. There was one final struggle upwards, a tremendous plunge forward, and they landed on the other side. Father's surprise was great; but it was greater still when Kleberg turned in his saddle with the laconic comment, "Well, why don't you come?" The invitation was not acted upon. Kleberg rode on, the picture of majesty, the monarch of all he surveyed. Father, his teeth still chattering with fever, returned to let the flood subside.

Some of the pranks were rather drastic, but they seemed less so to us who lived in the spirit of the time. In a nearby town there was another store keeper who really was not of the type of men that I have described; and perhaps he was for that reason the more successful in his business. At all events, he was not attractive; his choice of supplies was; and his place was patronized more and more. He was full of guile and pluck, and he had been treated with consideration. He had one peculiarity, which drew common criticism. His statements were rendered in a form which left his customers in a state of hopeless confusion. Modern forms of traders' statements have the same effect upon me now. There had been some remonstrances. One enraged victim had appeared in the store on horseback to present his grievance. But barring a brief abatement, the system continued. Finally, a whole party had come to celebrate in a manner, however keeping careful accounts of their orders. When the statement for the evening was handed them, it confirmed the worst suspicions—an affected state of hilarity on part of the guests had no doubt encouraged the store keeper to go to extremes. This time they picked him up, tied his feet, and putting him in the bed of a wagon, hauled him some distance on their way home and then let him out, with the advice to reflect upon the situation on his way back. This he must have done, for it was said that for simplicity, clarity and accuracy his statements became models ever after; certainly for these particular customers.

Fig. 13: Berlin University in 1850

In this manner we also heard of father's record as a dueling student abroad. We heard the accounts, but not until I spent a year at the University of Berlin in 1872-3 did I really know that in many of them he had been the chief actor; and it was later still before he spoke of them to me. While in Berlin when my relationship was established, the whole truth burst upon me. He had been a well known swordsman in the university days before 1848, when a duel usually meant a class contest of some kind. It was not difficult then to give him his place in some of the old stories. It was he who in one duel had at the very start been cut across the mouth, and had been almost ordered off the field, because of loss of blood; but claiming his right to continue, had finally by blow after blow with the flat blade, brought his opponent to his knees. Certainly he had a cut across his lips, and that was the reason he wore the heavy mustache. It was he who, fighting at Wurzburg with a strange sword, had his skull fractured, and was for weeks despaired of; who half conscious, had heard the surgeon's plan to put a plate in his temple, and had aroused himself only in time to say that he would rather die than have it done. Certainly there was the scar on his temple, which we had scarcely noticed—it seemed so in character with his stern features— like a line added for emphasis, and ironically enough destined to save him from hated military service.

But the duel which was spoken of most freely father only saw. It is the one upon which Winston Churchill based his description in "The Crisis."[a] Many a time have I heard father tell about it, until his small but always sympathetic audience could hear the very swords whistle through the air. It had a peculiar charm for the forty-eighters, for in every phase it pictured the intense political conflict of that day. There was a student at the University of Berlin, tall and strong and handsome as an Apollo. When he and his beautiful sister walked "Unter den Linden" every one stopped to give them one more admiring look. His rank as a duelist was unchallenged, and he was a "Junker,"[b] every inch of him. Contests with him were not sought; but he

---

[a] *The Crisis* is an historical novel published in 1901 by the American **novelist** Winston Churchill. It was the best-selling book in the United States in 1901. The novel is set in the years leading up to the first battles of the U.S. Civil War, mostly in the divided state of Missouri. It follows the fortunes of young Stephen Brice, a man with Union and abolitionist sympathies, and his involvement with a Southern family.

[b] *Junker* is derived from Middle High German *Juncherre*, meaning "young nobleman". The author here seems to be saying that his father was a true "nobleman". In the following text we find him taking on such persons (Ed.). They were an important factor in Prussian and, after 1871, German military, political and diplomatic leadership. The most famous Junker was Chancellor Otto von Bismarck.

was really in search for more triumphs. In father's corps ("Maerker,"[a] I think), there was one of the very opposite type, a serious student, indifferent to dress and form, but well set up and a good swordsman. Fight for fight's sake had no charm for him, and it was known that he had rather overlooked provocations from the Junker. Finally, some insult was so clearly meant that honorable escape was not possible. The challenge went out, and was accepted. On the appointed day the two men met, and there was a great attendance of students. As the two stepped up, the Junker appeared confident of success, while the Maerker, keeping his short pipe between his teeth, looked the picture of indifference. When advised to put his pipe away, he said that it would not be necessary, which his opponent seemed to regard as a further provocation. The first exchanges confirmed the impression that the Maerker was really not interested, and would content himself with a purely defensive fight. But in the second round things took a different turn. By a stroke, masterly in its swiftness and accuracy, the Junker cut the stem of the pipe clean at the very lips of his opponent. The rebuke had been administered, and the change in the picture was instantaneous. It seemed as though the Maerker's most sensitive spot had been struck. His pride was stung into action, and from that moment he took the offensive with

---

a   The Berlin fraternity of *Märker* (lat. *Marchia*) is a merger of the three founding leagues Teutonia, Franconia and Normannia, whose history dates back to 1842. It is the oldest fraternity of Berlin with its own existing house. The name is derived from the Mark Brandenburg, a historical landscape that was considered one of the most important counties of the Holy Roman Empire of the German nation. The student connection life can be experienced at regularly scheduled events such as evening lectures with personalities of current affairs, pubs and common leisure activities. The activities also include fencing, which the Berlin fraternity of Märker has traditionally prescribed. (http://www.berliner-burschenschaft.de/ accessed 24 May 2017. Editor's translation).

so much decision and skill that the Junker seemed soon to see his mistake. The conflict was reversed, and the Junker was never given another chance to more than try to protect himself from the fierce assault. It became and ended a one-sided fight. The Junker parried with great skill, but as the truth dawned upon him he could not conceal his feeling. He grew pale, and retreating more and more before the fast falling blows, was at last forced to retire behind the line, not wounded but a fallen hero. The gusto with which this story was told reflected the strong feeling of a period when social and political lines were sharply drawn, and when even a student's duel was taken as a test of strength between oppressor and oppressed — between right and wrong as they saw it.

Father was often sought as a second. In one case a friend, a dear companion of distinct literary promise, had been challenged, and asked father to be his second. He had never handled a sword, and father advised him that a few days' practice would serve no purpose. He told his principal that his only hope lay with a heedless attack right and left, as soon as the word was given. This was done in full measure. Father with some hesitancy admitted that his principal had been saved from serious disfigurement by timely and perhaps somewhat irregular interposition of his sword at moments of particular peril. Once his principal's glasses had fallen off; another time it was something else. He did not explain just how he justified—probably because the reason of the rule had not yet found full acceptance.

Such stories may have put ideas into our heads. I think we were not really bad boys ever; but we felt the native demand for pranks. While grown people were usually kind, there were exceptions, and sometimes there had been things said or done to which boys are very sensitive. There was one man who became a victim of our particular challenge, and upon him we let loose our first attempt at humor. He slept, as we knew, near an open window on the ground floor. We took some guns, and having sneaked under his window, fired them off at a signal, and made our escape into the dark. We were safe. He came out to his front door, and was greeted by us with mocking shouts. This was to us the very peak of humor; all home made, too. The triumph seemed complete. Our enemy withdrew; and as we started to do the same, we missed one of our number. We had to move with caution, and at last found that the sinking of a well had been started, and our comrade had fallen into it. He was lying low, in the hope that his friends would find him first. We did, and saved him. We were not sure who would be declared winner by a fair judge; but we never doubted the rarity of our humor. Nor did we ever give credit to the native kindness of an injured man who no doubt knew every one of us, and never told.

I wonder at my remembrance of these trifles—things which I saw or heard. But this was our entire world. Rarely did any news or word break in from the outside. Newspapers were of course scarce. Letters from abroad were rare; and apart from the messages of love, spoke of things and persons foreign to us. In view of present day custom, I can not but wonder that none of the accounts of our surroundings that did come to us seemed ever to refer to the women. Somehow they appeared simply to be good —as we expected them to be. Some were nicer than others, certainly to youngsters; but they were all good. As I look back I can not but feel that there must have been a distinct pathos in their lives. The charm of adventure went mostly to the men, while the women had to contend with the unromantic drag of this new life. This would account for the hard lines in the faces of most of them. Not unhappy; uncomplaining, yes; but with little sign of the joy of life. Unquestionably the women bore the brunt in this fight to conquer. The long weary struggle to save for others what they had cheerfully surrendered for themselves, was bound to leave its mark, as it did.

If there was scandal it might not have reached us, but I can not believe that there ever was ground for any. The relation which the men sustained to each other would exclude that. There were likes and dislikes, of course, and some few men were not held in high regard. But I do not recall an act of violence, unless it be an echo from far away — out of another world. Nor do I remember a lawsuit among the people of our settlement. It is true father had to make three payments to get his title straight, but that was the act of a title shark, not a member of our colony. If any occupant of the county jail ever came from our midst; or if any disturbance of the peace among us had ever gotten into a court, we should have heard; and we never did. Our family were Lutherans. I recall the dialects that marked the various sections from which the people came; but I could not with certainty state the religious persuasion of any of them, apart from the common respect for religious teaching which they seemed to feel. Within a radius of say five miles in either direction from us there was no common cemetery, and graves were few. Neither was there a church, although as a community we were impressed with the idea of "Sittlichkeit."[a] As I read father's letters written at a time of profoundest sorrow, I am amazed at his familiarity with the text of the Bible and more still at his broad conception of religious thought. All in all it was a colony

---

a   Sittlichkeit is the concept of "ethical life" or "ethical order" furthered by Georg Wilhelm Friedrich Hegel in the Elements of the Philosophy of Right (PR).

of peace and good will, in which men and women found what they had sought—liberty; and in which they patiently struggled to obtain the comforts of civilized conditions. There was neither self assertion nor apology. Self respect was the key note. No one changed his name to prove his or her Americanization. There was no Rosenfeld to emerge as Rozier. It was quite natural for me to resist the change from Nagel to Nagle so often inflicted upon me in later years.

But the year 1863 was coming upon us, and I was going on fourteen years of age. The consequences of the war were growing more and more ominous. For a time these conditions had contributed to our peculiar sports. We had been made to rely upon ourselves for play and for weapons; and game had become simply reckless because of the absence of hunters. We boys had lived a sheltered life with the lure of the world at our door. Now the change was creeping upon us so that even a child must feel it. The old meetings for songs and exercise and pleasure we missed. The air became tense with apprehension. Even old and close relations in some cases became strained. During the last few years we had been admitted more and more into the life of our elders, particularly our parents, and we could not but feel how by degrees the easy confidence and the sense of freedom were withdrawn. Our own parents spoke guardedly in our presence, and when they were most serious made sure that we were not within hearing. The change did not come like a sudden storm, but like a lowering cloud settling down from all sides to envelop us.

THE SHADOW OF THE WAR

From now on it meant war even for children. Not that we had not known of it, for we had. Upon its declaration most of the young men had volunteered. Father was held in high esteem, and before leaving a body of them called to say good-bye. They knew and respected his position, and he understood and respected theirs. They simply could not deny the call which many a man and woman north and south could not resist; and for which even father inconsistently enough felt a certain sympathy when Texas was finally invaded. In one of his letters he admits that he could not deny a feeling of resentment at the invasion of his State. The young men stood in double line in our room as if they would salute. They told him of their decision, and he said a few words to them. It all seemed very grave and affecting. I remember particularly one bright chap, a little disposed to be jolly; and when we got the report of their first engagement, it said that he had fallen as they thought by the first bullet. We children were shocked; but children forget. Later others returned on furlough— exchanged prisoners, I believe; and still later, just before leaving, I saw Sigismund Engelking, returned from the front in Virginia, hobbling about on crutches, with a shattered leg, from which he happily recovered. After the war he visited us in St. Louis. His grandson is a lawyer in San Antonio now. Of Hermann Vahl only mother heard during that war. From the first the rumor among the children was that the Bohemians were so opposed to war that they would not enlist; that some of them lived in hiding—even underground—and that those who had been forced to join the army would fire too high to hit the enemy. I am the last to lay much stress upon rumor, and a child's mind is easily worked upon; but I fancy there was some element of truth in the report. They were moved by the same loyalty to the Union that prompted my father to take his stand. However that may be, our youth as a whole had answered the call, and for some time we escaped, to all intents and purposes, the eye of suspicion. Texas had been a doubtful state, and but for the position of Arkansas it might have stood by the Union. Idols like Houston were Union men, and whole sections leaned that way. At the same time, our colony was the peculiar object of distrust. Slavery was unknown to us. It has been told that ours was the only section south of Mason and Dixon's line of which that could be said. Besides, we were in the eyes of the older population, still aliens—to be plain—"Dutchmen" with "damned" added, to make it clear. Oddly enough, father, because of his opinions and his long beard, in some quarters earned the unique title of "devil". Altogether our unpopularity was on the increase; and naturally enough the dreaded conscriptors seemed to close in upon us more and more. All this reached the children only by degrees. I got my first distinct impression one day when our teacher with his long student pipe stopped at our fence (such visits were rare now) and had a few earnest words with father. It seemed strange; they were not so friendly. Maetze was a democrat to the core—a state's righter. How he voted on secession, I do not know; but when our state had spoken he accepted the decision and sided with the confederacy. With him went Engelking, the store keeper. From then on it could be no more than the personal respect of political antagonists in war, and that meant a strained relation, which did not escape us. Maetze had come to summon father to see his wife who was ill. She was a favorite with the children, and mother's dearest friend. We greatly enjoyed the story of how she secured a certain cow from Engelking. She had set her heart (so the story went) on owning that cow; and for some reason Engelking had said that he would not sell that cow to her. To make doubly sure, he sold the cow to father, and with the settlement's acclamation father gave the cow to Mrs. Maetze. The great object was secured, all the rules were kept. Mrs. Maetze owned but never bought the cow. We youngsters fairly shook with laughter. Had we been a little older we might have recognized the incident as a pioneer in modern diplomacy. But that was some time ago, and now Mrs. Maetze was very ill. Soon after she died, and for the first time we felt how oppressive can be the silence of a body of friends from far and near at a funeral, and we saw the grief of our parents for the loss of a dear friend. Maetze married again. Our playmates there were stepchildren now. We were welcome as we had always been, but somehow we never again felt quite at home. No doubt Mr. Maetze was a great teacher; but for the home welcome we children had looked to her.

Owing to the need of doctors at the front, father's circuit became larger and larger. He would start early and return late; sometimes in the wee hours of the night. It was whispered that he stayed out at night to attend patients in hiding, particularly the Bohemians, who were determined to escape the draft. There may have been something in that, although he never told me. A few strange missions on which I was sent certainly confirmed my suspicions, and one of these I remember clearly. I could not have been more than thirteen, when one night my father gave me a folded slip of paper and told me to take it to a little hut a mile or two off, on the way to Swearengen's house. It was a lonely place; so far as I knew no one lived there. To reach it I had to ride most of the way in the forest, although the hut was in the open on the other side. I got my horse from the pasture, saddled him, and started on my way, my heart beating with all the dread that a boy's imagination can conjure up. As long as the road led along the old fence which separated our lower field from the forest the ground was not strange and my nerve held out. But turning to the right I had to ride through the forest itself, and that was my dread. The night was pitch dark, and my sole trust was the sense of my horse. This was a part of the forest which we rarely visited and had never gone through—dense as forest primeval. This was the haunt of wild life—wild cat and lynx we knew—perhaps even panther. I made that ride, seeing nothing and hearing only the steady steps of my horse, with the heavy branches of the great trees bending down upon the narrow unused road; and with my heart thumping to the measure of every conceivable terror. "Wer reitet so spaet durch Nacht und Wind" has always seemed very real to me. Then suddenly there came down upon the silence of the night, right over my head as it felt, the weird "Too-hoo-too-hoo-o-o-h" of an owl, its wicked echoes sent back by the great trees. The suddenness and the uncanniness of it all almost undid me. It sounds foolish, of course, but at that age I was as afraid as most boys to go into a dark room; nor was I more immune than they to any sudden scare from behind a door. My horse, however, was owl proof and took me safely to the hut, where I passed the paper to a man I did not know; and returned, still scared stiff riding through that forest, but greatly heartened by the fact that my course was for home.

Father's absences from home were prolonged more and more. One day he was expected early in the afternoon, and long after supper he had not come. Mother was walking up and down the porch, tormented by fear. I mustered my courage, half asserting the rights of an older son, and asked her what made her so uneasy. "I am afraid," she said, and when I answered "Why? Father is not afraid of bears," she said to me with her compelling earnestness, as though to admit me into her confidence, "I am not afraid of bears, Karl, I am afraid of men." That reply marked a turning point in my life. The whole truth was open to me; and from that moment I in a way felt what my parents had to contend with. That night we three got our horses to ride out in different directions in search, and when mother made no objection I knew how great was her anxiety. Each one rode many miles and returned filled with dread and fear, only to find that father had come by an unused route, and was once more with us safe and sound. After that there were not many days without a renewal of that anxious lookout for his return.

The talk of conscriptors became more and more common. Our young minds were filled with visions of riders coming down upon us and taking away whom they could find. There were many tales, no doubt largely made up, of how this or that man had escaped in the forest just in time. But about one of our friends the stories were more direct. He lived at a point south in a little grove looking out upon the prairie. Between him and the main forest there was only a narrow space in which there was one modest farm, over which we looked out upon the prairie from our little hill. It was said that so soon as a strange rider was seen our friend would make his way in great strides from grove to forest. Since he was tall and lean his figure could not be mistaken, and rumor had it that his stalk across that opening was taken as timely warning by all who felt uneasy in their shoes, of whom, however, there were not many left. Be that as it may, there were those who had safety on their minds, and engaged in speculation without end to find ways and means for peace and security. One of them appeared to lay a plan before father, who was of course to be a chief actor in the scheme. In brief the plan was this: He was to be taken ill. Father was to treat him as usual, giving the impression that he had lost his patient, because the first purpose of the plan was to have the friend reported dead. From then on the steps were to be taken according to custom, with this exception that the coffin was to be large enough to allow for the needed breathing space. Father was to attend the funeral, and to make sure that he resurrected the victim in time. The patient's part was risky enough; but father had the double role of announcing his death and keeping him from dying. Thus the story went among the children. Father demurred, but suggested a substitute, which was accepted. The plan was that this man, already a rare combination of great height and lack of weight, should undergo a process of starvation until even the most hardened army doctor would not pass him. The examinations were to be had at the county seat, Bellville; and the starving period was begun. For some reason the date was put off and father was greatly troubled to hold so reduced a body in a proper state. Building up was dangerous to the plan, and further reduction no less so to the man. At last the time was on hand. We children of course only knew of the illness, and that in spite of it all the cruel conscriptors would make the examination. The wagon passed our house, with the patient lying full length on the bottom of the wagon bed. Father deeply concerned, accompanied the wagon on horseback. In later years he told me that when they lifted his friend to carry him up the stairs of the Court House to the second story where the examinations were held, and laid him on the floor, he seemed to be near death from exhaustion. At last he was pronounced unfit for army service, but good enough for herding army cattle. Whether he ever served I do not know, but my recollection is that he was not away for long. Much of this may be extravagance—the saga of a child's world. But in part this story is true, because father often spoke of the alarming appearance of that pathetic figure of his friend. As I reflect upon this account, I can not wonder that much as father was needed as a doctor, there was growing suspicion about his attitude as a public adviser.

Perhaps the strangest feature of it all was that the suspicions directed at us were held almost entirely by civilians. As has been the case in every war of which I know—even in the World War—oppressive measures could rarely be charged to men in uniform. On the contrary, particularly in the Civil War with all the prejudice against us, the soldiers were always our friends, even to giving us protection. "War hath no fury like the non-combatant" was said by Montague, an Englishman of the World War, and it was ever so. Cowards are always intolerant, and like tyrants they abuse their unfair advantage. As I reflect, I can not believe that father ever felt even at the hands of "stay-at-homes" the intolerance which was visited upon some during the World War, for daring to say what many of their former critics now complacently proclaim.

In the early days of the Civil War we enjoyed the account of old Swearengen's answer to the first Confederate soldiers that came our way. It was said that a small troop passed his house, and true to his convictions, he hung out his old Stars and Stripes. "Take it in" was the demand. Back came his answer, "This is my flag. I have four boys in the house—best shots in the county." These were the boys who were tired of shooting deer with rifles, and borrowed father's six shooter for the sport. It reads like an imprudent answer, and would have been for any of us. But it happened early in the war when each side was to win in two months, and could afford to be generous; and besides

Swearengen was a popular figure, well known far and wide.

There was a short conference, and with the final answer "Keep your old flag," the soldiers rode on. Thus went the story, and we were glad to believe it. I am happy to think so to this day; for where could it have happened but in America as I felt then; and what finer tribute could have been paid to a man who had given proof as he had of his

Fig. 14: Robert Gould Shaw Memorial, Boston

love for his country. Even father was treated similarly. Later in the war when feeling had run high, he was called to attend a man who was in jail for some military offense. His right to enter was questioned; but the soldier on duty knew him as one whose hospitality he had enjoyed, and with a cheery "It's all right, Doc," all was settled. As father told us of it, we felt his sense of gratitude in every note of his voice. He was not seeing much of that side of human nature. Perhaps he did not come up with soldiers often enough. His next meeting with one of them promised for a moment to prove more serious. Father had come home for the midday meal, and was stealing a nap, when an officer rode up and gave the customary "Hallo." Father came out drowsy with sleep, worn as he was with work and care. The officer asked where he could get some hay, and father as I thought, in a rather abrupt manner answered that he had none, but that a certain neighbor might have some. Young as I was I trembled for the consequences; but the officer made some remark about men in a bad mood, rode on his way, leaving me wondering. We had, however, seen soldiers from time to time at short range, and need hardly have been surprised at their conduct. Passing through soldiers, perhaps two or three at a time, often stopped with us. There was no room in the house, and they camped outside; but they shared our meals, and after supper would stay to chat with father and mother as soldiers will, and as much as our limited knowledge of the language would permit. How we boys enjoyed these visits, especially in winter when all would sit before a blazing log fire to crack pecans and listen to stories. It is true father and mother's English was very poor, but they managed to make out when the visitors did most of the talking. As for the boys, our German student had by that time taught us enough English of its kind to have us feel quite at home. Of course we listened with open mouths to the story of real war. Sometimes the soldiers would even challenge father laughingly for his well known opinions, and usually the evening wound up with an invitation to have the whole family admire the pictures of sweethearts which, like most good soldiers, they carried with them. Of course, we were greatly charmed with these proofs of confidence and real romance; and I treasure the memory of these men to this day.

Later mother confirmed these impressions. She told us that after we had gone and she was left alone with sister Clara, soldiers would stop for meals, and that in no case had she been shown anything but courtesy and consideration.

Finally, even slavery in its mildest form came to our settlement. We of course knew that black men and women were held as slaves, but it was all too remote to enter our lives. Now and then we saw black men driving teams of oxen that hauled cotton towards Houston or supplies the other way; but they were strangers to our life. As I think of them they always looked serious. Sometimes the lash of their long whips seemed cruel, almost savage. Why was it that they never smiled? Since then I have known many negroes; have met them in most walks of life; have counseled them; conferred with them, and spoken at their meetings. No people can give better proof of pleasure and joy. Years ago, before the influx from the South to the North was so strong, I watched a group of negroes laying a street pavement. They worked in perfect rhythm to the time of one of their popular songs. I never saw a happier group of workmen, and I never knew a street better laid. But see one alone and he will be serious, bearing the mark of the tragedy of his race. It is just this that the Shaw Monument in Boston means to me. The heroic figure is fine. But far greater is the unconscious movement of the black troop. They know not whither; they know not why; but wherever the course it must be for something better than they have.

In or near our settlement I remember only three negroes. They stood for clearly marked phases of slavery of the time. The first was an unusual man. He was the only slave owned by Amslin, father of the girl—heroine of our youth

—who was said to break obstinate horses for her brothers. This man was allowed a part of the week for himself, and, so we were told, was buying his freedom at a fixed price with his earnings. Perhaps his master had bought him with that in mind. He was a fine looking man, dignified and courteous to all, always kind to children. We lived miles away and did not see him often, but we liked him because he would gather us about him and show us how to make things we wanted, chiefly for our saddles and bridles; and how to hang our spurs at a decorative and useless angle. Somehow he appeared to know everything in which we were interested; and certainly he never was too tired to show us how to do for ourselves. It was a beautiful picture as he sat at the foot of a great tree with the youngsters clustered about this calm, kind figure, to listen and to learn.

The other was a cook bought by our store keeper after the war had been on for some years. This was the first and only inroad upon the fixed custom of our settlement. The report went like wild fire among the children. We got it while at school. A black cook had been "bought," and she was in Engelking's kitchen right now. It sounded like a deep mystery to us. No sooner had school let out, when there was a mad scramble to get there first. There we were outside the kitchen, stretching and straining to get a view of this strange thing; and there was a kindly young black woman, with teeth like pearls, good naturedly smiling down at a lot of foolish boys and girls. Of the institution of real slavery that was perhaps the best phase. It stood for all the futile argument that has ever been made to have one man rule another. The black cook probably felt no protest, although she may have dreamed where others have since then been taught to see.

The third negro I knew was a mere boy, poor victim of man's unrestrained power over man. Why it was I do not know, but I was sent many miles on horseback to take some bags of corn to be ground at a mill. I had been there because I remembered the calm mill pond in which some of us had had a swim, and I had swallowed an unbelievable quantity of water when a boy pushed me over the safety line. This time I came alone, and as I watched the clear water turn the wings of the wheel to the rhythm of its flow, there came this black boy about my age on the same mission. While the mill owner was busy inside, I had cut some sugar cane and was eating it as we boys always felt free to do. Seeing me with my piece, the black boy followed my example. As we were both waiting enjoying our feast, the owner came out and saw us. He did not say a word to either of us, nor did he seem to resent what I had done. He went back to his mill and came back with a rope and long whip — the kind with which you can bring blood from an animal. There was no word said, but the boy seemed to know what was in store for him. He was taken by the arm, led to a post, stood against it and lashed to it. The boy kept his sugar cane in his hand and seemed to take it all as an act of daily routine. Then the man stood off and struck the poor boy with that whip, lash after lash. I was so horrified that I see little but the one general picture now. But this I remember; whenever the whip came down, the boy would draw up his bare legs to save his poorly clad body, and with every blow his yells would ring out to the forest. Finally, the agony was over, the boy was let go, and walking away with the air of a stoic, he finished what was left of his sugar cane. Soon after we both left, he perhaps to feel that if he had not been cowhided at the mill it might have been done at home, and I boiling with a sense of injury that would have made an abolitionist of me if I had never heard an argument.

Closer and closer came the pressure of the war. Our heads were filled with rumors of the doings of conscriptors, although we saw few if any and there was little material left beyond the old and the lame and the halt. But the young boys were coming along, and the question was at what age they would be taken. It was more and more clear that as a colony we stood apart, and that the rules made for others might not apply to us. I was aware that young and by no means strong, as I was, some concern was felt for me. Indeed I have reason now to think that father left largely if not chiefly to save me from being drafted although his own precarious position must have entered into the decision. Even if not taken at once, no one could guess how long the war would last; and here we were shut up in a vise. There came the word that the army needed beef, and we were to furnish part of it. That meant that our steers would have to be collected in the prairies and brought in droves to certain points. A number of the men left in different parts formed a party to carry out the plan, and to my delight I was permitted to go. Most of these men were really strange; there was at least no one to put himself out for me. I was to do a man's part, herding by day and camping by night.

Camping was of course had according to well known and simple rules. A boy's good appetite was taken for granted, but he might also help and bring in wood, perhaps lay it, or even light it. To this day I cherish the belief that I can lay and start a fire. Our family is not small, and I am sure of its affection. But in spite of every care, there is not one member who would agree with me on that point. My answer is that they all hold the same opinion of each other; and I believe that upon this subject turns one of the accepted conflicts in all well regulated families. In fact, it has been said that a census would name this as the most universally recognized cause for amiable but persistent rivalry.

Our equipment was the usual one on like trips. Such provisions as we took were carried by others. I had my horse "Rossa," my tiny saddle, bridle and spurs, a large blanket for camping, rolled and strapped on the saddle, just behind the seat. A smaller blanket—my raincoat as it were—rolled and strapped just inside the saddle knob, and adding to the snugness and firmness of the seat. No lasso, only the usual long whip with a short handle, and a rope with a stake to put my horse out for the night. As we rode through the prairies we would pick out the steers of our brands, collect them and go forward, driving them in herds. In the beginning this was rather simple, but as we moved on we added to our herd as we found more steers. The animals became restless, and again and again some of the more troublesome ones would try to break away. This meant a chase by the nearest rider, and often it meant a fast run to head off, to turn back and, by constant pursuit from side to side, to return him to the herd. Most of this work was done by the horses. They were so trained that without as much as a touch of the reins, guided perhaps by slight pressure of the knee, they would turn and dodge, leaving the steer no choice of his course. The only help the rider had to give was a liberal use of his long whip when the chance offered. The first day was perfect; the weather was fine and all went well. The second also, as I remember. How the herds were kept together at night I do not remember. Probably the only boy was left to sleep, while some men were always up to watch the herds that under normal conditions were ready enough to graze or to lie down. Our first destination was San Felipe, where we would find pens to hold our steers that were growing more and more restless. This we hoped to make on the third day. It turned out to be terrible weather. All day it poured rain, with no end of thunder and lightning. The water stood inches deep on the flat prairie. Every one did what he could to protect himself. My little blanket was a wonder. It was of Mexican make, very light, with all the colors of the rainbow, and under ordinary conditions, water proof. It had a hole in the center, and by slipping my head through, I would be kept dry to the knees. But not in such weather, for in a few hours every one was drenched to the skin. The steers became more and more nervous, driven away from their grazing grounds, amid the thunder and lightning, and wading in water they grew desperate. It was a day of plunging of steers here and there, and chasing after them as best we could. At last we arrived near San Felipe and got our herd safely into the enclosure of the usual rail fence pen. We were still a short distance from the town proper; but there was a new home in sight, and all seemed well. I did as all the others, unsaddled my horse and took him off to stake him out. I had taken with me a stick and with that drove the iron stake into the soft ground, and left "Rossa" to do the best he could. The next step was to get dry and warm, and so we went to the one house in sight. We seemed to be welcome. There was a blazing fire in a large stove, and we thought our problem was solved. But we had no change of clothes, and some of the party, not content to dry their clothes while they had them on, tried to hasten the process by taking some of them oif. They went too far, and we lost our welcome. The owner objected, and we were all, right or wrong, simply turned out. No one questioned the right of the owner; and off we went to get our horses, re-saddle and start off for better luck. The rain had stopped and the sun was just going down upon the horizon, amid clouds that seemed to be scattering and scuttling away as though they had done all the mischief they could, and were ashamed of being caught in the act. Just then we were met by something of a stampede of the herd of steers. It was the only one I ever saw, and while we managed to keep control, they did break down part of the fence, and at one time it looked like a getaway for the night. It was a very startling sight; and no one who has not seen and heard the movement round and round, of such a herd, with the long Texas horns clattering against each other, can have any idea of the din and of the real menace of the scene. But we held control, and then I was sent on to San Felipe for the night. I landed at a store and was taken in with open arms by one of father's patients. He started a fire in his stove, put some blankets on the counter, put me to bed there, got me some warm supper, promised to take care of my horse, and left me for as dreamless a sleep as ever a boy enjoyed. In the morning my clothes, all dry, were on hand, and after getting a great breakfast of eggs, bacon and cornbread, I rode off with many messages for father, to join my party. After all, a boy seemed to have some advantages over the men.

When I came up all was ready for another day. It had been decided to drive our herd to Bellville, ten miles away. So far as the herd was concerned, the day was uneventful. After the excitement of the night, the steers seemed to be weary and moved along quietly enough. But for another reason we were greatly disturbed. There was a report that the conscriptors were at home waiting for us. I believed it, and was tormented all day with the thought that on reaching home it meant goodbye and off for the army. I shall not dwell upon it, for I recall only the dull feeling of doom upon me. We crossed a stream, the water dirty and muddy from the fording of the cattle. We drove on and on, straining our eyes for strange riders, but reached Bellville without seeing a sign of conscriptors. Near the Mill Creek bottom we rode through grass so high as to half hide horse and rider, and cattle. Our heavy stirrups fairly obstructed our progress. Only a Cazin could give the effect of the waving grass played upon by the warm sunlight. There I had my one trial at riding a steer bareback. It was of course a dare, and simple enough. If the men of the party had been father's friends it would not have been done. But they were strangers, bent to try me out. I was timid, perhaps too timid to refuse a dare. So I was put on a young steer, with only one possible result. I survived the first bolt; but the second landed me on a heap of hay, from which I climbed to safety on the fence, with my reputation saved. We got home at last, only to be told that conscriptors had been there but had left the day before. Thus ended my only regular herding and camping trip; and it was to be the last before our flight.

Not long after I was sent with another message to a Mr. Meissner[a]. He lived some fifteen miles or more away, and father told me to go one day and return the next. The way turned to the right from the main road after crossing Constant Creek, passed near the swimming pool where the alligator had left the beach to us, and then continued through woods of black jack and similar timber. The road was not often used, and I remember no farm house on the way; mere squatters we did not count. At all events, I had no trouble in finding the place, and reached it by night. It

---

a Meissner, Maximillian Alexander (1837–1905). Maximilian "Max" Alexander Meissner, attorney and state representative, was born in Brandenburg, Prussia, on January 3, 1837. Meissner immigrated to Texas in 1854, settling in the vicinity of Bellville, Austin County. (Handbook of Texas Online, Aragorn Storm Miller, "Meissner, Maximilian Alexander," accessed May 24, 2017, http://www.t-shaonline.org/handbook/online/articles/fmelb. Uploaded on June 15, 2010. Modified on April 27, 2016. Published by the Texas State Historical Association. Accessed 24 May 2017.)

seemed a nice, orderly little home, way off there in that hidden section. Mr. Meissner met me with a kind greeting, and impressed me at once, as I learned to know him as a man of character. I was made welcome, had a good supper and, because of the cramped quarters, was given a blanket to make myself comfortable for the night in the hay loft of the barn. I was very sensitive, if not imaginative. Even today everything I recall presents itself in pictures, perhaps good enough with a better pencil than mine. Our home was never demonstrative, and I remember breaking into tears merely because a dignified stranger put his hand on my head and said a few words of kindly approval. We were never able to speak of our lost ones, although later I found that here mother had only deferred to father's feelings. I went to the strange barn with some misgiving. Of course it was very much like other barns. There were the cows lazily resting on the ground chewing their cuds. I could hear the horses stamp their hoofs inside. The moon was doing her best to make amends for the absence of the sun; the stars almost laughed to keep me in good cheer. But it was all so strange; the unrest at home pursued me — another message this, and I alone off there in the dark barn. Like other children I had heard ghost stories and half believed them, and no doubt that night added a few of my own. I could hear the mice in the grain; they seemed to be holding a meeting, perhaps making ready for an assault upon the store of ham and bacon in the house. It was all uncanny and leery, when, Great Scott! another one of those owls made night hideous with its weird Too-hoo-too-hoo echoing through the woods. Of course, it came to nothing beyond playing havoc with a nervous boy's fancies. Sleep, best solace for troubled boys or men either, finally claimed me, until I awoke to hear the cocks crow their insolent notes of superiority, and saw the sun's first streaks at break of day. After breakfast, with many messages, I returned by the same road. There was joy in that ride once more. "Rossa" was at his best. I can now feel under me that long, strong stride of an eager horse on the homeward stretch, with grasshoppers and lizards scurrying right and left on the parched ground to escape the dangers of this ruthless and unbidden visitor. I loved him and little dreamed that this was to be my last ride on my Rossa.

WE LEAVE HOME

That the trip to Meissner had some serious meaning I could not doubt, but all I felt was a vague dread of what might come next. In a sense we children shared a common fear. We were a part of a distressing situation not suspecting how important our part was in the minds of our parents. All the people were different, everything was strange, and anything might happen. Like children we thought less of the fate of the men who had gone than we did of the chance that we might be sent on the same way. Our thoughts were bound up in the one word "conscription," and our one answer was the hope of escape, which meant not to be caught at home. More than fifteen miles we had never been away; that was our horizon, and beyond that neither fear nor hope ever had us go.

As I write this account of our situation at that time, I can not but feel how entirely inadequate it is. The bare facts carried in a boy's memory can hardly provide more than a background; and the atmosphere which really gave character to that period can not have been more than remotely sensed by him. As I reflect upon it all, I recall clearly enough the feeling of suspense, particularly after the war was on; but even so I conclude that we must have been the victims of well founded apprehension rather than actual wrongs. Perhaps the true realization came to me in later years, just as I learn to understand my father's attitude to the old country more clearly after my own observation had me appreciate that his conception of a "system" was by no means an abstraction or prejudice. He might indeed have continued to live in his old home without being molested; but he could never be sure if and how long he might exercise the privileges of freedom as he understood and claimed them. He might have avoided restraint; but its constant threat was to him like a state of slavery, humiliating and intolerable.

So it was with us in an ever growing sense from 1861 to the end. As I have said, barring the conscription terror we were really not molested. Indeed, in many ways, the treatment shown us was very considerate. But this very statement shows clearly that we at all times felt at the mercy of others. If we fared fairly well, we owed it to considerations that were welcome enough while they lasted; but that always held within them the possibilities of change for the worse without fault of ours. No doubt there were causes and influences that would not occur to a boy, that perhaps were not fully appreciated by older people, but that nevertheless must have been potent in our behalf. In a remote sense, the position of the German section of our people during the great war was not unlike that in which we found ourselves in Texas during the confederacy. But the parallel holds only in appearance. With a few exceptions in the early stages, there were no such cases of violence and persecutions in Texas as took place in the United States generally during the great war. The explanation for this may be found in the fact that in reality the conditions were entirely different. After all Texas was a new state — a vast territory, very sparsely settled. With a few exceptions, such as San Antonio, Houston and Galveston, the only centers of population were mere towns in scattered locations, and giving little occasion for easy communication, or, for that matter, for concerted action. The feeling for the Union was profoundly impressed upon the people in Texas, and was warmly championed by the accepted popular idol, Sam Houston. He was Governor when secession was voted, and while he had been deposed because of his persistent official and private protest, he still enjoyed very considerable following. Opinion was so sharply divided upon the subject of secession, that probably the isolated position of the State had more to do with the final decision than arguments upon the merits of the problem.

It must be remembered that the population was at that early time predominantly what we designate as American. There were other elements—French and Spanish, or rather Mexican—but if they were not disturbed this was because of the common acceptance of American rule. The Texas star was the symbol of our patriotism. This was the environment into which the German immigration found its way—mostly between the years 1840 and 1850. Their arrival could not have been altogether a surprise. As has been true in other newly opened territory, newcomers were invited and welcome in Texas, where as has also been true in other places more importance was attached to the size than the character of the population. But for the arrival of the Germans particular preparation had been made. Lovers of adventure or impatient champions of personal liberty had come to Texas at an earlier stage, and had been active participants in the struggle for independence. These pioneers from Germany had made a good impression, as indeed they might, because in every phase of life they were of the spirit of that day. For the influence which induced the larger immigration we must however look farther. This was exercised by comparatively few men who had come to Texas—not so much in pursuit of adventure, as in search of the truth about immediate conditions and ultimate promise in this new territory. Among these Sealfield's[a] publications were perhaps the more significant,

a Refers to Charles Sealsfield who was the pseudonym of Austrian-American journalist Carl (or Karl) Anton Postl (3 March 1793 – 26 May 1864), an advocate for a German democracy. He lived in the

both in point of literary merit and immediate influence upon the minds of prospective German immigrants.

Fig. 15: Charles Sealsfield 1864

His description and appeal were meant for thoughtful readers. Whatever the explanation may be, there is no question that the immigration which now came to Texas was marked by a definite purpose and plan. These people did not come to seek adventure, although they were prepared to challenge it whenever and wherever it stood in the way of their chosen pursuit. Indeed, in many respects

> United States from 1822 to 1826, and then again in 1828/1829. During a final stay from 1853 to 1858 he became a US citizen. Sealsfield is best known for his German-language Romantic novels with American backgrounds, and also wrote travelogues. He returned to Europe about 1829, living in Paris and London before settling in Switzerland in 1832, where he resided for most of the rest of his life.

these men and women left their old homes in search for the chance to found new ones, in very much the same spirit, and often under similar conditions of hardships that had prompted and had been overcome by the earliest migration to our Continent.

Again, I can give only the vaguest impression of the character of these people; and even so am restricted to a locality which did not go far beyond our immediate settlements. We knew of course that beyond us, particularly to the west, there were towns like Neu Ulm, Neu Braunfels, LaGrange, Bastrop, etc. Most of these and similar towns were composed largely of German population. Some of them were as German as our settlements; but in addition to these homes of the German element there was a considerable sprinkling of German settlers in other towns, and even more upon the farms that dotted the land between them. Upon the whole it seems safe, therefore, to form an estimate of this new population by judging them as akin, if not a part of our own immediate community. After all, distance was not always a barrier; now and then a visitor would turn up and give welcome report of the doings at other points, to listeners, always interested in the fate of their own kind, and ever hungry to hear from the outside world. What did not come in this direct fashion came by way of rumor—grapevine messages they were called during the Civil War —and perhaps they were as reliable, if not as comprehensive a guide as the accounts that come to us today by the modern method. At all events, we knew that the aims, methods and fate of all these colonists were cast virtually in one mold. They as we had their schools, their singing societies, and their gymnastic paraphernalia—some better or more pretentious than others, but that was all. They kept up the German language; in fact lived the life of Germans in this new setting; gradually and unconsciously yielding as we all did to the Americanization process by adopting and seizing as their own what this new America offered on every side.

All in all our position was unique in its advantages, so far as it concerned our relation to the outside world. These colonists came as peaceful bands of men and women. They settled at points where no encroachment upon their interests was possible. The aim was freedom and happiness rather than profit; so that they restricted themselves to the thorough cultivation of small tracts, and even cattle raising was limited to the needs of all farms. While protest against the dictatorial regulation of life was a large factor in their decision to leave the old country, they were very guardians of law and order in the new. Controversies to engage the attention of law courts were virtually unknown; and less important differences must have been of a trifling character. While, therefore, some if not most of them may not have found everything that glowing accounts had promised, they were at least free and unhindered to enjoy all that this virgin land had to offer.

We lived under conditions that were peculiarly our own. We stood apart; and were regarded as aliens in the adopted country. Father was perhaps more in touch with the outside world than any one else; but even his practice, while covering a fairly large territory, was limited to the German element. His very indifferent acquaintance with English would determine that even where other influences might not be felt. We children vaguely sensed this situation, and perhaps our feeling is best expressed as one of a half conscious desire to be American. It had never seemed to me that this feeling had a note that was in any sense unworthy. There was no suggestion of apology; but there was a very positive desire to be an accepted part of the new association.

At a later period, after I was a member of our Bar, a colleague said to me in a casual way that he would never have thought of me as German, because my attitude seemed to him to be so entirely American. The statement gave me a distinct satisfaction. "American" seemed to stand for a new people, never to be monopolized by one race at the expense of others.

No doubt our parents appreciated the problems more clearly, and knew that in time the question would have to be met, where to yield and how to persevere in the great process of amalgamation. They could not have realized that race feeling could ever have been carried to as high a pitch in our country as has since proven to be the case. But even so, some toll was bound to be exacted in the process of adjustment; and that toll must necessarily be highest for the newcomers. Minorities must preserve rights; but in the last analysis wisdom is their best protection. We were such a minority, representing one very distinct phase of the problem. Our Bohemian element, that settled largely in our localities, no doubt faced the problem in more acute form than we did—they seemed even more alien But, on the other hand, we were less amenable than the settlers of Spanish or French descent, whom earlier association with Americans had rendered more or less pliable.

During the early period—covering the fifties— we were greatly favored by circumstances. There were few causes and certainly no occasion for friction. There was room enough for all; and little or no inducement to prescribe rules of conduct by any one to any one. Means of communication were indifferent. As tax payers we were reliable;

the prompt application for naturalization was proof of the proper patriotic spirit; and the manner of our cultivation of the soil and treatment of stock made it clear that ours was not an invasion by competitors. We were not primarily in search of profit; but our mission was to find security and comfort and freedom. Even the attitude of the German immigrants to the institution of slavery was not given any particular attention then. No immediate effect was felt; no political issue was imminent, and we were good naturedly tolerated. In a way it was all expressed in the rather deprecatory term "Dutchman and even that may have been little more than a clumsy rendering or translation of "Deutschmann." In a word, doubt and danger belonged to a remote future; and for the present the sense of freedom found expression in the right to sing songs that had been suppressed, and to rejoice in the response of their very echoes. All would probably have gone well, as indeed it did, but for the controversy about slavery and union, which became more and more keen, and at last penetrated even our remote haven of peace. Sentiment and opinion were well divided; and until the issue pressed for decision, the German element, although it could not escape attention and criticism, found satisfaction and protection in the fact that its sentiments had powerful and aggressive champions in some of the popular leaders of Texas. But after the decision was made, that picture was changed. Competent champions were silenced; and those who had sought and found protection with them, were now left to fend for themselves. On both great issues the German element was completely committed to the unpopular side. The dream of union, and the failure to achieve it in the old country had induced them to come; and the opposition to slavery was traditional with the German people. So long as the Civil War lasted, they were therefore in a precarious position. But even so they were largely saved by the fact that the call for troops was answered by the very generous response of our young men. In some parts of the State, as, for instance, in San Antonio, some of the men refusing to fight against their State, sought to escape to neutral territory. But in our section fealty to the State determined the course of the young men of German ancestry. For a considerable period the situation was relieved. The eye of authority was upon us; but for the time we had done everything that was required. We could not, however, expect to be trusted. We did our duty; but we did it regretfully. Our heart was on the other side. It was known that in the North the German element was overwhelmingly for the Union; and that a very large percentage of the Union army was made up of that element. Conscription was tightened throughout the South. Not only could we not hope to escape rules that were made for the entire confederacy; but we had every reason to apprehend that exceptions, if made at all, would be made against us. Every unknown rider was assumed to be an enemy; and if he wore no uniform, the dread of the non-combatant was that much greater. I marvel at how little really happened to us; but a moment's reflection presents our situation as a truly pathetic one. We suffered all the privations of the Southern people, and these were grave enough; but in addition we were the victims of uncertainty and doubt. Communication with the outside world was cut off; there was no word to or from our relatives abroad. At home we were not trusted, and we did not trust persons or report. We were in a vise, prepared for any sacrifice from danger to father, to conscription for me. At last father and mother must have been worn by the unbroken and ever growing anxiety. This no doubt was the subject of the long and serious talks when we were not within hearing distance; and this finally brought them to the desperate decision to have father and me attempt the escape even at the risk of leaving mother and brother and sister to await the end of the war, with no one to look to but mother's courage and our faith in the South's traditional protection for a woman.

To me the awakening came without warning. The visit to Meissner had been a summons to join a party of men, who hoped to make their escape to Mexico. How long the plan had been under way I could not know. When I did hear of it from mother it came as a great shock for she had to tell me that I was to be one of the party. One day after my return from school she called me to her. I could not but know that I would be asked to meet more than had so far been my part. She was sitting in one of our stiff backed chairs, and had me kneel before her with my arms resting upon her knees, our eyes searching, trusting, unafraid of whatever fate might have to say. Holding my face between her hands—no longer as soft as they had been—with gravity and affection struggling for mastery, she told me that father would have to leave for his safety. For so much I was in a way prepared. But then she added that since I was so tall and might be drafted at any time, I must go with him. That was all. It was said in a very few words and was so final, for no woman was ever more brave than she. Only her "unberufen" while knocking on wood was an echo of old time superstition. There was no question and there were no tears, and no better proof of family discipline in a time of stress and fear could either of us have given. Some question by look, caught as though it had been spoken, made mother add that she would be more safe along than with us at home. To the credit of the South, be it said that this was true then as it has perhaps not been more true in any other part of the world; and of this her lonely life during our long separation gave ample proof.

Mother had warned me not to speak of what she had told

me to any one—not even to brother Paul. I was to go to school next day as usual, to be ready to start in the afternoon. When mother had told me some time before while we were anxiously waiting for father's belated return, that she did not fear bears but men, I felt vaguely that she had taken me into her counsel. Now I felt charged with a secret full of ominous foreboding. It was for me to take my place and I must have kept faith, for not even brother Paul suspected when on that afternoon of November 3, 1863, we met for the parting.

Our family affection was I think very profound. It is true we were not given to demonstration; but that may be an acceptance of the poverty of words—indeed almost proof of the depth of feeling. While we children went by our real names, and mother always called father Hermann, her name with him to the last was "Rieckchen," an endearing abbreviation of Friedericka, in every note a symbol of protecting affection. The buggy was waiting at the gate and we were all on the front porch. From it we had so often looked out upon our little world that had seemed so large, filled as it was with our joys and our sorrows. Now with one cruel wrench it was all to go—go forever without mercy or hope. Father and mother had made their fight and had themselves well under control. My feeling must have been dead for the time, so stunned was I by it all. Some new relentless power was at play. This was fate and we were its victims to be tossed about like so many dice. But Paul and Clara had no warning; and their distress was heartbreaking. A child's instinct seemed to tell them more than we could know, and made it for them a last goodbye, as time at last proved it to be. For years and years it remained a dream—never quite real. I did not shed a tear, until during our flight I would wake from sleep in camp, crying bitterly. Many years afterwards—in 1909—when for the first time I came back to the old home, and the school children passed by me all in line, the picture of Paul and Clara came to me so clearly that I broke down like a child, and had my first unashamed tears for that parting. When at last I was left alone, I went to the graves upon the side of the hill looking down into the forest—scene of our boyhood sports. How protected they seemed under the great tree and the warning yuccas. As I came up, a rabbit bounded out, final proof of the peace that dwelt in that one spot, the only ground to which mother had retained title when, nearly two years after our separation, she left to follow us.

Some of the party had started a day before. Father and I were to follow; as was true of Kluever, who had a covered wagon. We left our home November 3, 1863, in the little buggy drawn by the saddle horse. I had no look of farewell for Rossa or dogs, or any other animal or thing dear to me. Life had been sweet there. Really no one had been cruel to us, but now mother and sister and brother were to be left alone. We went by an unusual road leaving our pasture garden and field on one side and the forest on the other, past Swearengen and say ten miles farther, to spend the night at Reichardt's farm house within a mile from the place where I was born. These were old friends who knew what our dilemma was. Little or nothing was said. They and my parents had come from the same section in Germany. However different in association there, they had been brought together as immigrants, by a common bond. No doubt thoughts traveled back to the time of their coming, to the dreams that prompted them, and ended with the sense of despair that no one could conceal. Our plan was of course known to them and indeed can hardly have been a secret to any one. We heard of no purpose to hinder us. Even those who had become estranged were no doubt glad enough to keep their counsel.

The following day near Columbus we joined the party which was composed of Meissner, Langhammer and Soder, Kluever joining us later. His delay caused a great uneasiness. It was felt that he might have been stopped by authority. But the cause was nothing more serious than a broken wheel; and this was mended in time to have him join us. Of our party two may have been within draft age, and a third had, I think, been in the army, and was certainly young enough. The fourth was the deformed storekeeper, who was of course unfit, and no doubt went to make purchases in Mexico. My memory is not so clear as to details. We had one canvas covered wagon drawn by a horse and the large mule, the latter was with us I know. There was our horse and buggy and there may have been still another smaller wagon. It was a unique outfit, poorly adapted for such a trip; and the party itself was certainly a strange combination. By way of clothing we had only the most meager supply. Besides my ordinary suit I had an extra pair of summer trousers, and to keep out wind and weather, I had a blue Spanish cloak or mantle that might have excited the envy of a foreign dandy. Provisions we had in plenty; and we relied upon our camp fire to prepare them. Thus equipped we made our way westward. The road was well known. The shippers of cotton to Mexico and of supplies from Mexico had attended to that. We followed the beaten track. The first part of the trip was really not eventful. Our buggy followed lazily along, I picking nuts on the way when I could. In fact, much of the time we walked, so slow was our progress. We had the common mishaps to our wagon but managed to repair them although we afterwards learnt that we were reported as having decided to return in despair. What addition to our supplies we needed we were able to get from farmers on the way. At night we staked out the animals or hobbled them, and slept under the sky with our feet to the fire. It was just the routine from day to day and night to night, with scarcely an incident to disturb us; nothing to hold our thoughts but care about those at home and the chances of our venture.

One night, however, we were surprised by a norther. As usual the animals had been staked out on long ropes, to give them every chance to graze. We had made our camp near the highway, indeed I slept on the highway. The night was very beautiful.

I remember as I lay wrapped in my blanket, how clearly the stars stood out in the heavens. But a tired boy does not dwell long with such pictures, and I soon went to sleep. The others had probably done as well, for when the storm broke upon us, all seemed to be unprepared. The cold blast was so sudden and so fierce that the embers of our fire were sent into the air. Everything that was not fastened down was torn away; and worst of all, the frightened animals tried to break their stake lines. Hobbles which were well known to us we had not used that night. It was pitch dark, but every one was out to make the animals secure. Horses may be nervous, but there is nothing like a mule's snort of alarm. No one took time to put on shoes. Indeed, it would have been difficult to lay hands on them. In bare feet we ran out to find to our surprise that in places there were thorns—Texas stars we called them because they had five points, every one effective. There was no excuse to stop; the animals were very panicky, but had not gotten off. After calming them down, they were taken to the camp and tied to the wheel so as to give them the protection of the wagon against the blast. We made out as best we could inside. I spent the night, asleep of course, lying across the wagon bed, with nothing but one blanket between me and some heavy chains. In the morning I just rolled out, too stiff to climb; and never did blazing fire feel more comforting, or warm breakfast so restore my spirits. Northers are mostly short-lived, and soon we were off on our monotonous way.

At another time we came upon a swollen river, which one I do not know. To try to cross it seemed dangerous; but after much doubt it was decided to try. Whether a smaller rig went first, I can not recall; but the canvas wagon started in, and father and I in the buggy followed. In a moment the water rushed over the bottom of the buggy and carried away father's saddle bags in which he kept what he most cared for. We were really in a serious position, for once in that water no swimming would avail. Even in that emergency our attention was diverted by the antics of the little man Soder. He had wisely reasoned that the large mule rose highest above the waters, and so had decided in this instance to ride this huge animal. A more ludicrous sight than this little deformed man perched upon that monumental mule was never seen outside of a circus. Once started he was eager to get across. He was at the head of the procession. The waters became more and more turbulent, the mule made a misstep, and came within an ace of losing his grotesque rider. It was then we were startled by his desperate cry, "An diesem Tage bin ich zum Unglueck geboren" (on this day I was born to disaster), repeating it over and over again. Amid all the threat of danger, the men could not control their laughter. It seemed to cheer them to new effort. We finally made the other bank, and with a sense of relief for ourselves and abundant ridicule for Soder, we took up our journey as before.

I can not say how far the party had gone when we heard rumors that our route had been cut off by the retreating Confederate army under General Bee. About that time Federal troops had landed at the mouth of the Rio Grande River and had moved up to Brownsville. The Confederate troops, not strong enough to resist, were therefore coming our way into the interior. The question was what to do, for our dilemma seemed very serious. Upon reflection now I really do not see that a retreating army was more of an obstruction to us than the same army stationed at Brownsville. However, we decided to stay where we were for a time and to wait for developments, keeping in hiding as best we could in the meantime. Our camp was made in a grove away from the road, and none of the men showed themselves outside. I will not be positive that we saw soldiers. I should say, however, that we did see some men pass at a distance. If we did not, it may have been because no stragglers of the army happened to come our way. We felt sure that they were in the vicinity. I was permitted to go out with my gun, perhaps because I was a mere lad, and probably also with the faint hope that I might be able to get some game; which second reason I was lucky enough to confirm. The first afternoon I saw four wild ducks on a small body of running water. I fired and got two. As I went to take them, a fair sized alligator plainly moved in the water towards the same point. As the second barrel of my gun was loaded with ball, I aimed at his head, and there was no mistake about my hitting him. To kill an alligator with a shot is not likely, and I have no reason to think that I finished him. But that fellow rose high out of the water, showing the white under him, and his contortions generally left no question that his feelings were too much hurt to give any further mind to the ducks. So, I hauled them out, and was warmly welcomed in camp, although two ducks for six persons were not much more than enough to give flavor to our supply of food. My luck stayed with me the next day. I was alone, wandering about without real aim, when I saw a wild goose flying pretty high but towards me. This I believe is a rather difficult shot; certainly only accident had me bring her down at my feet. This time my reception in camp was very warm because six persons can get some satisfaction out of a whole goose unlike the German peasant who said it was such a pity about geese—one was not quite enough, and two were too much. However, the unrest of the men grew day by day. The situation looked more and more grave to them. All their time went into conferences with no result. After a few days we started once more, but did not go far before another stop was made for a final decision. The men met, a dejected lot, still speaking only German as they had throughout, and finally the conclusion was reached. We started east on our return trip, for the venture was given up as lost. We could not hope to pass the retreating army. Our way to Brownsville was cut off. I sat next to father in his buggy, and he looked like a broken man. After about half an hour's drive he suddenly turned to me, "I can not do it"; and with that he hurried forward and told the others that he would not return; that if he did he would have to live in hiding, and that he would rather take his chances where he was. His change of mind created some surprise, perhaps doubt, but no more. Each one had thought it out, and after a very brief final exchange we said goodbye and parted, going in opposite directions. The four men who had at least some experience in practical affairs, lost heart and returned, taking with them the wagon, and even our mule. Father, who had little experience outside his profession, with a fourteen year old boy on his hands, and nothing but a buggy and a horse to carry both, persisted, perhaps because he knew little of the actual risks. I never saw any of those men again, and what

I heard later may have been largely fiction. I was told that two of the men were tried, for what offense I do not know. Apparently Meissner's case took the more serious turn, for he was said to have been sentenced to death. It was told that on the morning set for his execution he had to be roused from his sleep to learn that he had been pardoned. Also that he was so beloved of his neighbors that to set the petition for pardon in motion many people had taken gold out of their hiding places. In relating this I feel sure of only one thing, and that is the esteem in which Meissner was held by all the people who knew him.

I can say very little of our wanderings after father and I were alone, beyond the fact that our course was entirely aimless. We drove through roads of heavy sand, which made our progress slow and tiring. At one time we went to a point on the Gulf of Mexico, Indianola, I believe, and there I saw the ocean for the first time. Father's despair must have been great, for he went there in the vain hope of seeing some sail that might take us off. We saw nothing but the vast expanse of the Gulf, neither boat nor sail; luckily for us, I imagine, for heaven knows what hands we might have fallen into. So we turned back in a northwesterly direction. I have no way of telling how many days we spent in this aimless search; how we managed at night, and where we got our food. It is all one blur of the feeling of wretched doom. At last father decided to give up; there was no other way. But instead of following the others home, he took the way west to San Antonio, there to submit to whatever might be in store for him. We must have been quite near, because we did not travel long before one afternoon we reached San Antonio, little dreaming what strange fate fortune had prepared for us. We looked for the worst, the sole question being what form our penalty would take, when we literally walked into the arms of an old friend — Urban. This was the man who had worked on the little farm at St. Bernardo, sometimes taking care of me as a baby, and who twelve years before had left the place on foot with all his fortune wrapped in a red bandanna handkerchief tied to a stick and slung over his shoulder. This meeting meant a great change for us. Urban was then a rich and respected man in his section. Some said that he was in good standing with the authorities. However that may be, he had influence enough for us, as the sequel will show. We were at once taken to his home, which in point of comfort was beyond anything I had ever heard described. Mrs. Urban was not German, but she and her children took us in like long lost friends. Country boy that I was, I even thought that the little daughter liked me. The kitchen was in charge of a black mammy, who treated us like starved refugees to be fed up. She was not far wrong. I at least felt like a stray kitten rescued from the street, lapping up milk before an open fireplace.

San Antonio was then a modest place but it looked very big to me. A modern skyscraper would meet my estimate of some of the houses. There were regular streets running through the city, the better ones lined with homes and stores, and a large school house; the others further back with adobe homes of Mexicans. However modest San Antonio even then had her East Side and West End, and what not; for class feeling is quick to draw the line. The city was also the headquarters of a Confederate colonel, who was attended by at least some soldiers. But we were not troubled in any manner; and for more than a week we lived the life of shelter and plenty. We of course knew that mother must feel great concern about us, and from San Antonio we sent our first letters. I wrote to Paul. I have the letter among the papers mother saved and brought with her. Perhaps he received it; probably not. We did not know until much later that he had died within a few weeks of our leaving. It was always a comfort to father that his friend, Dr. Becker, had come the distance of twenty miles to attend Paul, although he had been unable to diagnose the ailment. Mother firmly believed that Paul's illness was caused by homesickness for us, which he had never been able to overcome. The sadness of the whole situation I can picture but not describe. Until I took courage many, many years after to read the correspondence, I could not fully understand my parents' anxiety and sorrow although I was an immediate party to it all. For at least six months mother wrote not knowing whether any of her letters had reached us, and whether we knew of Paul's death. Half dreading, half hoping that we must know she writes again and again to tell the state of her agony as best she might. During all that time she knew nothing of our whereabouts. When we separated from the rest of the party father had no plans, and mother was left torn with doubt as to whether we had reached Mexico, perhaps gone to Germany, where she preferred to have us, or whether we had been entirely lost. Father's position too was desperate enough; for although he had abiding faith that mother and the children would be safe, he had no letters to confirm his confidence. Much of this would pass a boy of fourteen by, but our family attachment was very close and I was old enough to share the anxiety; and if more were needed father's gravity and care-worn look were bound to be reflected in me. I can remember only on rare occasions to have heard him laugh or seen him smile during the entire trip. At that time he still wore a long beard and as I think of him, he was a picture of sadness and severity in one.

No doubt owing to Urban's influence we felt perfectly free in San Antonio. Father met some of the more prominent men, among them Baer, the head teacher of the school, who had stayed although some of his friends had made their way to Mexico. For the time father's horse was mine, and I was free to ride him out on the roads at will. Soon after we left he died, as a result of too severe a ride and neglect. Strangely enough, Rossa had died about the same time at home as mother's letters received much later told us. Coming back from such rides my horse would wade the San Antonio River, whose waters seemed as clear and blue as the sky. I think I saw (perhaps too vivid an account is playing with my imagination) how that river comes gushing out of the ground as a great spring, the water so clear that one could see a coin at the bottom.

One of the most interesting men we met was Degener. He had been in prison for a time on the charge that he had aided a number of young men in their effort to get to Mexico soon after the Civil War began. One evening father took me with him to visit the home. He was a distinguished looking man, who received us warmly. The two men evidently knew of each other. In those days report and rumor traveled fast. Some of the memoirs of soldiers speak of the "grapevine" method, by which secret information was carried long distances with great rapidity. Under our conditions such a system was of course well developed; and what engaged these two men was no doubt more detail than general fact. There was one son about my age, and he told me how the boys played war in the open streets. San Antonio must have been fairly divided in opinion for a long period just as the State of Texas was. While we were chatting and the two men were lost in conversation, I saw in the next room the mother in black, lying on a bed, utterly crushed by the tragedy of which my father was no doubt then hearing the details. It is a long story which I now have in pamphlet form, written by John W. Swanson, one of the survivors. I will not repeat it literally but will try to give the account substantially as he states it and as it came to us at the time.

At the beginning of the war and for some time after there were many young men who wrestled with the problem which way duty lay. They were Union men. They could not support the Confederacy, and they would not fight the citizens of their own state. They felt no doubt like the Bohemians in our section; and unable to accept Lee's decision they tried to meet the situation by going to Mexico. Some sixty men, the large majority of German blood, formed a party to carry out this plan, among them two of Degener's boys. It was, I believe, for aiding and counseling this expedition that the father had been imprisoned. They went on horseback and were armed. Their purpose was to go peaceably to Mexico. They were followed by a body of Texas soldiers or volunteers, and were early one morning surprised in camp. Without warning one of them, while on his way to fetch water from a stream, was shot down. A demand to surrender was refused by the men in camp upon the ground that their purpose was a peaceful one; and with that the fight opened. They were surrounded, and were really in a helpless position. Most of them fought to the last and were killed in camp, among them Degener's two sons. No quarter was shown, and rumor said that the wounded refused to accept so much as a cup of water from their assailants. But this agony could not have lasted long, for all of them died in camp, with the exception of a small number who made their escape. Some of these were captured within a few days, were lined up and shot on the spot. Still others were overtaken and shot while crossing the river into Mexico. Among the few who survived was Swanson who had been of the party and wrote the account. It was of this the two men were speaking, and it was no doubt the risk of similar experience that had moved father to leave.

Soon after the war Mr. Degener came to visit us in St. Louis. He had been elected to Congress and was on his way to Washington, where he made an honorable record. I heard it said that he declined a second term because he believed the election to have been irregular. If so his judgment had not been clouded by the injustice he had suffered. Very few others visited us in St. Louis, but among those was Mr. Maetze who, true to his old principles, came as a Cleveland delegate to the St. Louis convention: and so at last he and father voted the same ticket once more.

But our rest and security had to come to an end. One day father and I were sent to appear before the Colonel at headquarters. No doubt Urban had paved the way, for father seemed to feel no anxiety, and I had a boy's faith in good luck. The colonel was in the second story, and while father went up I chatted with the soldier on guard. Soldiers had always been kind to me. My innocent effort was brought to a sudden halt. The gun caught my eye and I put my hand on it, only to be scared stiff when the soldier drew back, raised his gun and very properly and sternly told me that that sort of thing was forbidden. Soon after I was sent for to join father. The scene there was in no sense disturbing. The colonel, a fine looking man, was quite at his ease and was putting father through a line of questions. I recall only one, but that with its answer made even a country boy look out of the window to hide his surprise. Why did father want to go to Mexico? The answer was that he was out of quinine. The officer seemed to be much impressed by this doctor's wish to keep in stock this medicine so greatly needed in Texas; and we were dismissed as quickly as we had come. Soon after Urban told us that the old plan must be abandoned, but that we could reach Mexico by taking a more northerly route to a point which I think was Piedras Negras[a], now opposite Eagle Pass[b]. I can only guess what had been done. Father did not know or did not want to tell. To say the least, the plans in all respects suggested that Mr. Urban had, as usual, done what a desperate situation called for. One fine morning he and his family bade us goodbye. At the door stood what was called an ambulance, a conveyance upon springs with four seats beside the driver's, capable of being closed, and drawn by four mules that would attract attention at a Fair. To make our safety doubly sure, we were presented to an officer in uniform who we were told would go with us, as he did. In other respects our outfit was the same, but we were now assured of safe conduct to the border, and of food supplies in abundance. We were now leaving the last point at which there was so much as a chance to hear from mother, and from which we could hope to have our letters reach her. I now know that after learning of our start from San Antonio, she did not hear again for perhaps a year. We, barring one note written the day after our leaving home and received on the following day, never heard from mother until long after our reaching Saint Louis when we had the first word of Paul's death.

a   On June 15, 1850, a group of 34 men (commanded by Andrés Zapata, Gaspar Salazar and Antonio Ramírez) met with Colonel Juan Manuel Maldonado to give the news that they had created a pass point at Piedras Negras, to the right of the Rio Grande, south of Fort Duncan.
b   Eagle Pass was the first American settlement on the Rio Grande. Originally known as Camp Eagle Pass, it served as a temporary outpost for the Texas militia, which had been ordered to stop illegal trade with Mexico during the Mexican-American War. Eagle pass is so named because the contour of the hills through which the Rio Grande flows bore a fancied resemblance to the outstretched wings of an eagle.

This trip was too well planned to present any points of interest to be held in a boy's memory. The fact is that it was part of a system that had been in force for some time, and that may have involved more or less doubtful operations with Mexico. Of this I at least knew nothing, and suspected only after we came to learn with how much care our further tour into Mexico had been arranged. It must have taken a week or more to reach the Rio Grande. The weather was fine always. The day's run was timed by former trips; our camps were made at selected places; and but for the ever present care, it might have been an expedition of pleasure. The driver was a negro, an old hand at managing mules and at cooking meals in camp. The officer was always courteous, and he and father got on very well. My seat I need not say was with the driver. The scenery was of course very different from that to which we were used. At home vegetation was rather rich. Here drought appeared to be the natural state. The water supply for us and the mules seemed in large part to decide the length of the run. Cactus and other desert plants made up the greater part of the growth. Years before I had seen the first jack rabbit, advance agent to tell of a great drought in western Texas, only to be followed by herds of cattle in search of water and food. Here too there was less and less of animal life, until we saw no sign of it at all. Even a lad would feel the bleakness of the scenes. How could he help it if he were young enough to remember how he had tried to put salt on the tail of birds with the promise of his elders that if he did it he would get the bird; or how even in winter time myriads of blackbirds would in large flocks move here and there like driven clouds or would suddenly rise and turn and swoop down like twisters in a storm. Of course it all seemed bleak to him. One day we did, however, come upon a wolf—so at least he was called—and he gave a chance for my last shot with my Texas gun. At sight of him the driver stopped, the officer took down his gun—for we were of course armed—fired and missed. As the mules were starting, father told me to have a try. I did and shooting right over the mules got the wolf, much to my delight. There were a few words of praise, but to tell the truth I did not need them.

Traveling in such unaccustomed comfort, we finally approached the Rio Grande River, at Piedras Negras it must have been. It was early and the day was forbidding, rather dull and cold. We could see everything on the other shore—an old ramshackle house and near it two men. One of them father at once took to be Dr. Herz, a man rather prominent in our eyes because he had sought safety in Mexico. The other a handsome figure, but a stranger to us. Father no doubt knew something of the future plans, but I knew nothing. The officer told us we would be rowed across, and with that we parted, never to meet him again. It was said afterwards that minus his military buttons he had joined the Mexican colony; but in those days careless talk was as common as it is now. In a miserable skiff (in truth a dugout) father and I were rowed across the Rio Grande one crisp forenoon, out of Texas and its danger, into Mexico with the hope for safety; but still left to wonder what fate might have in store for us. Urban's hand had not been withdrawn. We were met by a well set up German, clearly a man of some position, who told us that we (he being of the party) could start that day for Monterey, in the interior of Mexico. Again there was an ambulance drawn by four fine mules, with a negro driver. But this time the arrangements were much more complete. We had four armed Mexican guards on horseback. They were the delight of my eyes. How they sat their ponies, and how they seemed to enjoy the prospect. It turned out that this German was a trusted agent, who delivered goods and carried money from point to point. No doubt he had carried gold on this trip, in one of the boxes in the wagon. Before starting father had talked with the stranger whom we first saw. He had been in the Confederate army, was in Mexico in poor health—with no more than ten cents; and with him was a friend in the same dilemma. During the landing of Federal troops and the inevitable disturbances many men had escaped capture by crossing to Mexico. Father I need not say did not have much cash; but he offered to pay their way, so the passenger list was made to five. Father had of course thought of taking the short route down the Rio Grande to Matamoras, but he was told that such a trip would be very dangerous, because of marauding bands of Indians or Mexicans. Besides, it would have been difficult to find means of transportation. The conveyance offered was of the best, and how eventually to get from Monterey to Matamoras father was glad enough to leave to chance. And so we started on the third round of our journey.

The fact is that by one means or another we always escaped, although we did have some very anxious moments; and perhaps I should not go into so many details. But the truth is that even this trip was no expedition of pleasure. We were well equipped in one sense, but the season was going into the latter part of December, and even Texas and Mexico call for protection from weather then. Besides, Mexico was torn by Civil War, and every road was reported to be infested by marauding bands.

As I think of it, I can not quite account for father's failure when there seemed to be a chance, to provide us with more and better clothing. However, he was very reserved about such matters, and having accepted so much he would never have asked anything more of his benefactor.

Indeed, I have no idea whether the means by which we made our trip meant simply the right to go at a given rate, or free passage. However that may be, we still had our original outfits which mother had made for us. Even father's overcoat was her work, built upon the lines of an ordinary quilt, and generous enough to cover a giant. My Spanish mantle alone did not come from her hands, as its crying contrast to the rest of my clothes loudly proclaimed. In other respects, things were greatly improved, and we had no real fear on the score of weather. But that was not the only or the most serious condition to keep in mind. We were told, as we had a right to know, that this route, too, was not free from marauding bands. Nor could it be doubted that the nature of our host's trips was known, and of course offered great temptations. In other words, our mounted guardsmen were not there to please a rich man's fancy, as I should have been glad to believe. They were there to protect the party; and any doubt that any of us might have felt was soon removed by what we saw. It was the custom then, perhaps still is, in Mexico, when a traveler is slain to put up a cross at the point where he is found; as a rule it is fastened to a tree. The number of crosses upon which we came, and the cluster of them at certain places, left no question of the truth of the warning that had been given us. Neither could we believe that these crosses recorded past history, in the face of the new appearance of some of them. The character of the scenery had changed greatly. Much of the time we traveled through forests of yucca, plants which rose to great height, and for that matter offered good protection to an enemy who wished to shoot a member of the party. Our safety lay in the fact that we were so large a party, larger than a band of marauders is apt to be in winter. This assurance we were at least given, and the result seemed to bear it out. At the same time these were only promises, and we therefore moved along from day to day knowing that we might be attacked at any time. Fully aware of this danger the driver, guardsmen and all of us watched with anxious care every cluster of growth or grouping of yucca that might furnish a point for an ambush. Our suspense was therefore constant and intense, as we were all subject to the influence of conditions about us. There was scarcely any animal life; no birds, not a sign of a walking or crawling thing for a day at a time. Water was so scarce that at one time we had a run of some sixty miles from one supply to the next, and had to carry as much water as we could even for the mules. Nor was there any question about the caution of the guardsmen. Any idea to make light of the situation or to wander away from camp was at once vetoed by them. We acted as though we might at any time be attacked. That this caution was not without reason, was soon made clear to us. As we came upon a small cluster of shacks, we found that a lone traveler had just been killed—he could have been ahead of us only a few miles. At last one night we had proof that could not be doubted. I think it was at the end of the sixty mile run which we had made without water on the way. Here there was quite a large stream; and on our side of it was a small village, larger than we had seen so far on this trip and in appearance more habitable. Of all this we had been told by the German agent, who was of course familiar with the route and had seen the place only a short time ago on his way out. We soon saw that there was something out of the way. The driver and the guards made that plain enough by their exchange of looks, even the mules seemed to scent trouble; and nothing is quicker to signal the presence of an Indian than a mule. So at least they told us. As we came nearer we saw or heard nothing to show the presence of human life. All was as silent as death, and then our suspicions were confirmed. The village had been sacked. There was not a person left to tell what their fate had been. The first feeling of horror soon made place to thought for our own safety. The drive had been very long, animals and men were weary, and night had come on. There had been no anxiety about the river, because of course the plan was to camp on the village side. This idea was scrapped at once. We dared not remain there; the river must be crossed at any risk, because it alone gave hope of protection against a night attack. The attempt to cross the river in the dark, however, had its dangers, and no one knew that better than the driver and the guards. It had a passage of shallow water running over a rock bed just about wide enough to support the wheels of a wagon. On the right side looking up the river the water became deep, and on the left side the descent was abrupt as they said twenty feet down, and without indication on the surface. One of the guards rode ahead to give the driver his course, and slowly our ambulance with all the passengers in it, followed. I sat in front to the left of the driver, with the strange feeling that it must all come out right. We had gone about half way over when one of the leaders became unruly or lost his direction in the running water. At all events, he moved to the left, and disturbing the other mules, they carried the ambulance far enough to one side to send the left front wheel partly over the rim of the ledge. Thus we hung in suspense, and I was right over the wheel that was down. There was nothing that we could do but to sit tight, which we did. There was, however, real excitement. The driver did what he could to pull the mules to the right, so as to hold the ambulance where it was. And then with great splashing of horses moving in the water, and Mexican denunciations happily unknown to us—one of the guards actually passed to the right on that narrow ledge, got the off leader by the bridle, and between his pulling and the driver's whip and his American exclamations—more familiar to us—they succeeded in getting the wheel back on the ledge, and in a very few minutes we were out on dry land, ready for camp. So much was done, but there was real concern for the night. As was often done, because there seemed to be danger, we made no fire for the night. For supper we did the best we could. The mules were tied out very near the camp, and our blankets were placed for the night without special order, but not far apart. Every man knew that we might have trouble, and

Fig. 16: Cerro de la Silla (Saddle Mountain) near Monterey today

father told me that since I could use a gun, he wanted me to stand to my post. How well the others slept I do not know. I was too tired after that long ride to do anything else; and was off very soon. The first thing I remember next was a great racket in camp. Those mules and ponies, credited with being the truest warners of the presence of Indians, were snorting and stamping like mad; and the Mexican guards were whistling and calling to them; but as soon as they had called, they would jump away from the spot where they had been. The excitement lasted for some time. But of myself I only remember that I held my gun in place, and wondered what in thunder would happen next.

Fear it seems is always greatest in anticipation. Finally, the mules and ponies calmed down, the guards became reassured, and we settled down as best we could for the rest of the night, several of the guards keeping watch. We had no more trouble. In the morning we found that we were in an open space near the bank of the river. There was no objec-

Fig. 17: Emperor Maximiliano around 1864

tion to a fire now; so we had it and enjoyed our breakfast the more for our experience.

After that we traveled much more in the open. We were getting into the country of plateaus. In fact, the scenery was very wonderful. These plateaus were at times quite high, but the surface always seemed to form a straight line against the sky as though some power had cut it off with a knife when the earth was still soft. One was pointed out to us as the property of a governor. They said the plateau had only one narrow entrance easy to defend. That it had abundant water and grazing, and that the governor kept his herds of cattle up there. In every way nature became much more attractive; and our sense of safety was restored because we found many more little houses, and even villages along the road.

About the time we left the river one of the guards was taken ill, so he was taken into the ambulance (which at last deserved its name) and placed in father's care; and I (Oh! joy) was made a substitute for him as a guard. True, I had never used a six shooter, but I carried one now; and what more would a boy of fourteen want out there in that strange land, where there might be Indians any time. I kept this place for most of the rest of the trip. The guard was quite ill, but as luck would have it, father was able to help him. Never shall I forget the gratitude of those Mexicans. They showed it even to me; but father they treated with attention that bordered on worship. I had never thought or heard of such thoughtful care of one man by another. Poor father was quite embarrassed, for they would not let him get out of the wagon alone; they half lifted him down. Nor would they let him sit on the simple blanket at the camp fire; they fixed blankets for a cushion. In every manner they did for him, until the many ways in which a man can be waited on must have been a revelation even to a doctor. But the motive was so genuine that it was not possible to object. Besides, the patient got well, and I was a sure enough guardsman, fully armed on horseback, in the wilds of Old Mexico.

By this time we entered another change. The Christmas

season was on, and a new world was opened to me—a real challenge to my imagination for which I was in no sense prepared and had not so much as dreamed of. The first surprise came to me before we reached Monterey, and it still lives in my memory. One evening we made camp near a little village. After supper I went there with nothing in

Fig. 18: Zachary Taylor

mind, and was just in time to see my first religious procession. There were torch bearers to light the way as the forms moved in regular order through the street, with their emblems held aloft, so solemn and, as I felt, so holy. I looked with wonder upon the many and varied colors of their garbs, their bright badges and brilliant regalia, all lighted by torches reaching up, only to be lost in the heavens. Unused as I was to anything but the most plain and severe, the silent pomp of that procession filled me with a sense of awe. I feel now that he should think himself blest to whom it has been granted to see the good and the beauty of things about him; and this with all our limitations mother and father had done for us. The memory of that evening has furnished setting for many a discourse to which I have listened, and color for many a canvas that I have seen, giving light to one and warmth to the other. No doubt some of it was crude and perhaps it was not all good, but coming to me as and when it did, it was like a revelation to guide and to strengthen in the struggle between right and wrong.

As if to confirm me in this feeling, I had another experience soon after, most unexpected and very simple, but for all that more unforgettable. It was just before we reached Monterey, and near Christmas day when we camped, with only a modest shack in sight. The sky looked threatening, and father had told me to make myself as comfortable as I could in the ambulance. The weather took a bad turn, and nothing gives less protection against cold than the bottom of a conveyance such as ours. Father was concerned, and rousing me took me to the shack to ask that I might lie in a corner of the one room. How he made himself understood, I do not know. Probably my appearance was argument enough. At all events, I was admitted, and, wrapped in my blanket found a corner for warmth and peace. Although the soundest of sleepers, I was suddenly wide awake some time in the night, to look upon a scene more like a vision than real. A young woman holding a baby in her arms was kneeling in prayer before a crucifix, lighted by two candles. That was all. There were no doubt many like prayers offered at that very moment, but was there an impressionable boy lucky enough to see it all, and to carry away to guide and to guard him, the simple vision of something beyond? I have seen many a painting of sacred subjects, and have looked upon them with sympathetic eye. I have been at many a service, both modest and splendid, and have come away strengthened in purpose; but no influence can ever do what that unconscious woman's silent devotion did for me. What was but an impression then has in time become conviction, for tolerant suggestion is always so much stronger than self-righteous argument.

MONTEREY

The next morning I was back at the side of the driver, for we were not far from Monterey, and he and our host could tell us things in language that we could understand. More and more the plateaus yielded to irregular formation, the larger range of mountains lay before us; until at last we were in view of Saddle Mountain[a], against which Monterey is nestled in the valley. It is true the highest peak looked like the seat of a saddle, and this of course had its own charm for me, aside from the fact that I now, for the first time, saw real mountains; and heard them talk of Zachary Taylor[b]'s battle. The mere thought of the American success warmed a boy's heart. It was a wonderful sight on that clear, fair day; so much so that with my eyes riveted on the scene above, I have no recollection of how we got into the city. I have only a vague picture of peopled streets, although I saw at once that here Mexicans did not live on side streets in adobe huts. Here they were the masters. It all seemed so colorful and so warm—so different from our life, alien but attractive, enough to save me from a sense of racial feeling; or worse still complacent intolerance. We were taken to a hotel. Of this I will make my account discreetly brief. Apart from its very primitive character, I have to admit that here we first met new ene-

a   The Cerro de la Silla is a mountain and natural monument located within the metropolitan area of the city of Monterrey, Nuevo León, in northeastern Mexico. Named for its distinctive saddle-shaped profile when viewed from the west, it is a well-known symbol of the city of Monterrey, despite being located in the adjacent municipality of Guadalupe.
b   Zachary Taylor (November 24, 1784 – July 9, 1850) was the 12th President of the United States, serving from March 1849 until his death in July 1850.

mies of the animal species, in which the place abounded. The table did not offer much choice; and what food we had was spoilt for me by the liberal use of red pepper and spices, which to say the least plagued a boy who had hardly known the use of any pepper outside of camp. To give raw meat a good taste in camp was one thing, but to disguise all sorts of strange mixtures in a hotel, was quite another. From this ordeal there was no escape for many weeks. We had at times felt the want of food, but from now on we were to suffer from its makeup—the more things entered into it, the worse it seemed to taste. As usual there were compensations; perhaps Emerson heard about them. In the court of the hotel there was an orange tree. Whether it bore fruit I can not now say, but in any event we were offered oranges, only to be taken. We had always had fruit in plenty, but oranges and apples were a luxury simply because they were rare. Something less than a week we spent there, in the height of the Christmas season, with the chance to see and hear strange and startling things from morning to night. Nowhere had we seen anything of the Mexican revolt against Emperor Maximilian[a] which was then under way; we had really gone from one rebellion into another. I did not even know in which jurisdiction we were. There were the stores with new and fascinating things, jolly toys and blankets of many hues and saddles of marvelous make, bedecked with ornaments. But most interesting of all were the throngs of people with their colorful clothes, their light-hearted spirit as though life was good; or solitary figures with their blankets easily thrown about them; so different from what I had known. This at least was what we saw in the main streets. The

---

a   Maximilian (Spanish: Maximiliano; born Ferdinand Maximilian Joseph; 6 July 1832 – 19 June 1867) was the only monarch of the Second Mexican Empire. He was a younger brother of the Austrian emperor Francis Joseph I.

churches seemed like appeals to heaven when the bells, summoning great throngs of people, mostly women and children attending in meek response, sent their compelling peals over the housetops to the hills, those silent sentinels forever on guard to give back the echoes for peace and good will. It is so long ago that I sometimes wonder whether I heard the bells; or, indeed, whether there were any. We sometimes see more in a canvas than the artist puts there. But it is all so vivid, that it must be true.

How much is left to time and chance. I had never heard chimes from a church tower. Had I heard them from babyhood they might have become a part of custom's monotony. Had I heard them later in life they might not have broken the crust of fixed commonplace. As it was, they helped to build the very fibre of my being. Years after they gave charm and meaning to the chimes of the Halberstadt Dom that greeted me on my return at sundown from the foothills of the Harz. It is the memory of them that makes me pause now to listen to the chimes of Christ Church in my own city. Be they Catholic or Lutheran or Episcopal or any other denomination, for me they spell religious feeling always, with not a note of discord.

Going in sudden change as these Southern people will, from sombre mood to gay, the same throngs would the next moment as it seemed crowd the streets to applaud a passing circus. Here I could be counted on, for a circus was not so novel—not even the scantily dressed performers on horseback, nodding their acknowledgments for the greetings of the populace. But all this was as nothing to the scenes at night in the crowded plaza. Probably the lights were dim enough although they seemed very brilliant to me, surely bright enough not to let me miss anything that was to be taken in. The street sides of the floor rooms around the plaza were generally open. Some were shops of some kind, but many were gambling places. Around crude tables (right in the open) men sat lost in the games, with the proof of gain piled up in silver coins as neatly as a modern bank cashier would ask. We heard of quarrels of course, and although I never saw a fight, some of the faces certainly suggested them. Passion, in triumph and in defeat was marked on many of them. It was all so strange; in such contrast to what I had ever seen or heard, that these groups of men, particularly one table, were impressed upon my memory. I at least had heard enough of frontier life to wonder why, if there was any fight in them they did not start it then. But I never saw one. The picture that really held me I can hardly describe, because it was just one general view of the people there moving about in endless change. I remember the ease and the grace of it all. Our young people were wholesome looking, with clear skins, bright eyes, rich hair, strong and capable. What a contrast to what I saw here. These young women moved about like fairies, floating over the surface from place to place, charm and courtesy everywhere. To me it was but a scene, to give me what I would make of it; and I was happy enough to take with me the memory of rare grace and beauty.

Something of the other side we saw at a bull fight—my only chance to attend one. The place was in the suburbs, and as we got there—part of the general crowd, we were greeted by the lamentations of many beggars. In general, the spirit was one of hilarity; but the note of supplication was never drowned. At the entrance beggars, mostly old men, were kneeling to the right and left of the coming crowd, and with hands upraised they filled the air with the singsong of their pitiable appeals. What success they had I do not know, but the sight was miserably abject. At home we had no beggars; even white trash, whatever else might be thought of them, never begged. If they ever took anything it was probably a pig, and then a razorback owned by no one. Of the spectacle I was being taken to see I had only a dim notion, but about one thing I was clear. I wanted the bull to win—the fight was not fair; about that there could be no doubt. The horses were protected and the bull was not. The arena, of course, looked large to me —a kind of an oblong circle, with a sort of small structure in the center. The enclosure was made of heavy fence rails, quite high, the rails leaving spaces of say two feet. Behind these rails the crowd was seated. Those who were high up could look over the fence. Those below, as we were, peeped through between the rails. Everybody, old and young, rich and poor, seemed in high spirits; and the better dressed ones had tiny charcoal ovens which they kept between their feet. The weather was crisp, and I thought they were sensible people. The entrance for the bull was way at the other end, of which we, however, had a good view. The first act that excited me more than all else that took place that day, was not on the program. We were about three tiers up, and I saw a small child (perhaps three or four) leave its place, crawl between the rails into the arena, and start to make its way across, no doubt to join some other children there. For a moment it was not noticed; its mother may have been busy fixing her charcoal oven. But just then the first bull came in, and in a moment pandemonium broke loose. There were shouts of cheer or despair, or both, to stop the child or to urge it on, I do not know which. Whatever it was, the noise I have no doubt saved the child. It toddled along with no thought but one, making a bee line for the playmates that had lured it to the venture. The bull had stood to sniff the air, and the uproar had startled him. With his head up, he gazed at the mass of shouting people; never a look to the ground, never a suspicion of the presence of an easy victim. And thus the suspense was broken. The child finished his run, crawled out through the fence as he had crawled in, and was hailed by the plaudits of the people, without knowing any more than the bull what it was all about. Everybody settled down; the first round like many triumphs of chance had gone to the people's liking; they were now ready for the next. The charcoal stoves were given a final shake, and the toreadors entered, one on horseback and one on foot. My sympathy for the bull was confirmed; there could be no question about it. This was not to be a fair fight. True, the man on foot relied only upon his fleetness of foot; but there were two, and the horseman had a large stiff rawhide hanging from the saddles, which gave protection from attack. Compared to other bull fights about which I have read, this must have been rather a tame affair. Perhaps the Christmas spirit softened some of the savagery. Several bulls were let in. One would not fight at all, he seemed to regard it as a put up job. None fought as well as the first one, who was really a fine specimen, and acted as though this was his first entry. He rammed the dry rawhide, and made the decrepit pony behind it wince. He chased the man on foot, and forced him to climb the fence. He charged about, and made his enemies dodge right and left. But impetuous as he was he was struck by some darts to madden him and to drive him into more reckless action. I imagine the show had all the setting of a bull fight, with few of its terrors, and must have left a hardened habitue feeling very much as an old timer feels at a legalized prize fight. However, I had all and more than I could ask; to feel that I had seen any bull fight was really the chief point. Then there had been fighting, and the tricks of the toreador on foot had been wonderful; and, finally, the bull had not been killed, which was after all the chief satisfaction. The show was over, the chatter of many voices again filled the air, the charcoal stoves and babies were taken up and carried with tender care; the crowd pushed and pressed for the exit, and we made our way out, to the accompaniment of the doleful lamentations of the horde of wretched beggars.

In the meantime arrangements had been made for our next trip. We had been there probably less than a week, but had seen something of the bright side of a lighthearted sunny people in a holiday season; and we had at least some acquaintance with the kind of fare that was to keep body and soul together for the immediate future. Even father had some relief from his constant anxiety. The impressions of the city and the presence of our new companions could be trusted for so much. Very different reasons had brought us to Mexico, and our feeling about the war at home was in direct conflict. But father's very indifferent knowledge of English rather hindered discussion of controversial topics; and besides a common lot such as ours was makes for good will and an eye for the common cause. We had of course had no word from home and under such conditions no news is not always good news. We assumed that mother knew from Urban of our start for Mexico, and we hoped that when we reached Matamoras we might find some one who had made his way through the lines of the army and who could give us some report. This was all the consolation we could muster and take with us as we made ready for the next and last journey on land. Our conveyance was the usual one; not so good, but of the same kind. Urban's hand may still have been in this arrangement; but the German agent was no longer with us, and local conditions had to be reckoned with. Perhaps the revolutionary war had better use for superior ambulances. We were four in our party, and to this was added one stranger, no doubt a Spaniard, and a man of some culture;

master of several languages; possessor of a good tenor voice; always courteous; ever ready to help kill the long hours by song or conversation, and as we afterwards heard, no doubt spy for one side or the other in the war which was then on in Mexico.

We were now on our fourth round of the trip bound for Matamoras, on anything but a holiday trip. The men may have had some inkling of the true conditions farther south; but I doubt whether they were prepared for the whole truth. Our experiences were many, and though varied, all of them were part of the general effort to make our way through a sparsely settled territory, occupied by people whose allegiance was no doubt as uncertain as it was unknown to us. Our conveyance was in poor repair. But for the lack of rain we should have had a mean time. Even for cold weather we were poorly prepared. That food would not be to our taste we knew; and almost our whole provision against that condition consisted of oranges, with which we had filled the better part of the bottom of our ambulance. Whoever wanted one took it. They were very much to my liking — an acquired taste which I may trace to that trip. Even our fine looking Spanish companion had no other supplies. For meals we had to stop at wretched looking shacks, and every stop meant at least two conflicts. The first was to eat enough of the food to keep alive; and the second was to settle with the owner about the amount to be paid. As to the latter, the Spaniard was our good angel, for when the overcharge was too clear, he would object in language that proved as convincing to the owner as it sounded forceful to us. On one occasion he came to father's rescue just in time. Our meals had been of so dubious a character that father was ready to go any length to get something better, when behold there came a Mexican who said that he had been lucky enough to shoot a turkey. The thing looked plausible enough; more so because the head and feathers had been removed. Negotiations were opened in the sign language, the bargain was about to be struck at a very high figure, and all tongues were out for the luscious morsel, when the Spaniard stepped in and proved to all concerned that father was in the act of buying a crane for our promised feast. He saved the money but we had no turkey; and we were again left to our daily diet, some of us I suspect feeling that even a crane would have been a relief.

There were other problems, however, in which even the Spaniard was helpless. He who has not seen it can never know what it means to sit by and watch an old Mexican hag prepare tortejas for your next meal. The basic substance, I think, was corn. Having been soaked, it was ground between two stones, one in each hand. When reduced to the consistency of mush, this was lovingly patted between two hands that to all appearance were strangers to water, and surely would have gone up in protest at the suggestion of soap. This process was broken only by the sudden release of one hand or the other in search of threatening symptoms in the hair of the head. When the concoction had finally been baked in some fashion over a flame, or on a hot stone, all was ready for such meal as we could make of it.

We did not always fare as badly as that; but this is a fair picture of the general conditions under which we traveled. In the meantime the weather was growing worse; and after we had gone about half our way, we were visited by another norther. This time there was no means of shelter for all of us, even by using the ambulance as a refuge. The only shack in sight was hopeless. It had little room, and was no doubt kept in a manner that would make our choice between it and bad weather an easy one. Father was taken with a chill, and we were in bad straits. Finally we found two rawhides, and leaving the others to make out as best they could in the ambulance, we found shelter between these hides. Placing one on the ground, covered with a blanket, and putting on what clothes we had, we drew the other hide over us, and let the cold wind play as it would. It worked to a charm for the night, because the hides became stiff from the cold, and the wind driving the sand upon us, we were as snug as could be in our den. But the morning was bitter. Going over to the shack I felt the wind cut as I never have since. We were given some concoction for coffee, which for once I took because it was warm. The meal was the usual corn composite. Father felt so wretched that he paid one dollar for an egg, which proved to be too far gone to eat. That day was really cruel; but we had to go on, traveling was no colder than lying around; and we had no time to lose.

From that time on our trip took a new turn. We at last got into the region of real war in Mexico, with no chance of knowing with which faction we were in touch from time to time. We could not but see that our charming passenger was growing uneasy. The songs with which he had cheered us earlier ceased altogether, and even his conversation became more and more spasmodic. Then a messenger on horseback met us, handed him some papers, and was off. These messages became more and more frequent, until the riders came in such haste that their horses would be fairly covered with sweat even in that season. The effect was very clear. Our companion was in a complete funk. He said nothing but when we at last reached our goal—Matamoras—he shoved a paper into father's hands, asked him to keep it until he could call for it, got out and was gone. The rest of us never saw him again; but father told me that a few days later, while he was in a barber shop the man suddenly entered, asked for and got the paper, and was off again. I have often thought of this incident as one of father's many providential escapes from dangerous situations to which he was an innocent party.

Matamoras[a]

When we reached the border of the city we found that we could not enter in our ambulance. The streets were barricaded with cotton bales, the property as we were told of Americans. So taking on our shoulders what few possessions we had (father one small bag or trunk and I my gun), we walked, climbed over the barricades and made our way to a place called a hotel. Here we spent a few days, amid turmoil as chaotic and terrifying as only a revolution in full blast can produce. We soon learned that the situation was this. In some sections there were two governors who fought for control in behalf of one or the other of the two armies then at war. This may have been the situation in Matamoras. However, both had been kept or driven out by one of Mexico's greatest bandit leaders, Cortinas[b], who if not in control was at least in Matamoras when we got there. Needless to say pandemonium reigned. Everybody seemed to be at the mercy of any member of this band. Two of our friends who had started before us and had reached Matamoras by the old route, had been killed on the street, one was found with fourteen bullets in him; the other stabbed to death. My Uncle Litzmann who had come

a Matamoros is a city and seat of the Matamoros Municipality located in the southwestern part of the state of Coahuila in Mexico.
b This seems to refer to: Juan Nepomuceno Cortina Goseacochea (May 16, 1824 – October 30, 1894), also known by his nicknames Cheno Cortina, the Red Robber of the Rio Grande and the Rio Grande Robin Hood, was a Mexican rancher, politician, military leader, outlaw and folk hero.

earlier had been robbed of everything but a summer suit, including our small mule loaned him by father, and now returned (as tricky as ever I trust) to one of his earlier environments. We never found uncle Litzmann nor did we meet anyone from our section in Texas. The last hope to hear from home was therefore gone, and the next time we now knew, we would have to leave without even a chance of hearing for a long period of time. This was our introduction to the new situation. Only once did I see these bandits move through the streets in a body. They looked almost black; their clothes were ragged, their horses in wretched condition; but what they did not carry by way of sabres, guns and pistols was never shown in a museum. What a picture Dore might have made of them! Not in oil; but in black and white, drawing the lines of the hard faces with the same contrasts of light and shade that would give emphasis to the protruding bones of ill-treated horses. A desperate crew they were, without hope of mercy for him who fell into their hands. Generally they went in pairs or even singly, pretended to ask for small coins, and often shot or stabbed. A man who later joined us, a Jew and a consumptive, was in a position to describe the method in all its details. True, he had not been shot, but his loss in coin had been rather generous. He used to tell it to amuse us; for when he was well out of it, he was glad to have us laugh with him. I saw only a few cases of real violence, but they were quite drastic enough to satisfy me. While we were still in the hotel I was in the office room on the ground floor one day when men rode up and fired off their guns outside. They may have had no special object in mind, but when I saw one of them making for the door on horseback I did not wait to find out. At another time I saw one of these bandits ride into a great crowd of people, which literally filled the plaza, seize a man, throw him across his saddle, and gallop off with him. It may for aught I know have been a rescue, but that was not the impression he made. One day I was leaning against a cotton bale lying on the ground with others near the river, lost to the world, watching United States cavalry troops drilling on the Texas side of the Rio Grande. They were the first Boys in Blue I had ever seen; and perhaps the natural feeling of a boy for real soldiers on his side was somewhat worked upon by our troubles. When up rode one of those brigands and asked me for a coin. Well, coin was not my strong point, but running was; so I took to my heels, and without aim or intention, was lost in a flock of geese that cackled like mad, flapped their wings, and scattered in all directions. If our teacher had not told us how geese saved Rome, I should be tempted to record my gratitude to those geese for saving me.

However, we were no more alarmed than every one else seemed to be. The whole population was in a high state of excitement. With us the question was how and when to get out, and how to secure our safety in the meantime. It was felt that the hotel was no place for us, surely not at night. So we still went there for our meals; but at night we met in a vacant house, away from the center of the city. There we slept on some straw, with such clothes as we still had. The few nights there were hideous. We could not tell when we might be detected; and the very fact that we were in these quarters was ground enough for any act of violence. But nothing happened to us, although sound sleeper that I was I would be roused by mad riders tearing through the street firing their pistols or guns and shouting "Vive la Mexico."

Before leaving, I made one expedition of my own that father would have vetoed if he had known of it. I had seen the men, horses and tents, the army on the other side of the river; and without more, I found a way to get across to see them. This sounds more difficult than it was; for the river is low at that season. How I did it I do not now recall, but in any event it was a rash act. I found more than I looked for. Having watched some troops drill, I sauntered along until I came to the biggest tent that I could see, and going up to it was met by an officer. He looked impressive, and he was very courteous. "My boy, you look hungry," he said. I said I was, and had been for some time. "Well, we can fix you up right here," he answered, and asking me into his tent he ordered a meal for me. Here was another colored cook to come to my rescue. He shared my dislike for things disguised—the whole hash family. There was not a thing on the plate that a country boy could not greet as food, and call by an honest name. I have forgotten what was served at many a great dinner that I have attended, but I shall never forget that day's meal. Ham and eggs, and biscuit and butter enough to build up a boy for a week. But not too much; for my weakness for this menu is still the same. The officer hoped I liked it, asked me to join the army, and sent me off with a few kind words. I started on my way back, but soon after was told that I had been the guest of the commanding officer of the army at Brownsville, General Davis[a]. Many years afterwards, at the Republican Convention[b] of 1880 in Chicago, this general again showed me a great courtesy. I had not

a Edmund Jackson Davis (October 2, 1827 – February 24, 1883) was an American lawyer, soldier, and politician. He was a Southern Unionist and a general in the Union Army in the American Civil War. He also served for one term from 1870 to 1874 as the 14th Governor of Texas.

b The 1880 Republican National Convention convened from June 2 to June 8, 1880, at the Interstate Exposition Building in Chicago, Illinois, United States, and nominated Representative James A. Garfield of Ohio and Chester A. Arthur of New York as the official candidates of the Republican Party for President and Vice President, respectively, in the 1880 presidential election.

forgotten him and had, indeed, in the meantime been at a meeting to hear him speak. In Chicago I was in a dilemma. Grant was a candidate, and for a young man I had been rather active in opposing a third term. As every one knows feeling ran high. The delegates from my state (Missouri) were all for Grant[a]. I would not ask a ticket of the chair-

Fig. 19: Edmund J. Davis (1827-1883)

man, and would not have been given one if I had asked. I was wandering through the corridor of the Convention Hall when of all men I ran into General Davis. I spoke to him to remind him of his kindness to me in Brownsville; and to thank him once more. His answer was "You know,

a Ulysses S. Grant (born Hiram Ulysses Grant; April 27, 1822 – July 23, 1885) was the 18th President of the United States (1869–77).

I remember that, and what can I do for you now?" Nothing could have surprised me more; but I replied that I could not accept anything because I knew he was a candidate for vice-president on the Grant ticket, and I was opposed to a third term. Quick as a shot he came back, "What difference does that make? I will fix you up right now"; and with that he gave me a reserved seat for the

Fig. 20: Ulysses S. Grant

week in the third row from the front of the speakers' platform — Senator Hoar[a] presiding. I was able to hear every word spoken in that Convention, which probably presented as stirring a picture of a political conflict as was ever seen in this country. I never saw General Davis again; but for many years I could recall the chief incidents of the Convention, and could repeat with fair accuracy the more

---

a George Frisbie Hoar (August 29, 1826 – September 30, 1904) was a prominent American politician and United States Senator from Massachusetts. Hoar was born in Concord, Massachusetts. He was a member of an extended family that was politically prominent in 18th and 19th century New England.

important parts of speeches made by Conkling[a], Garfield[b], Logan[c], and by others less known but perhaps as effective in shaping the decisions of the delegates. When a youngster I had read about the uprising of the German peasantry, armed with pitch forks and inspired by romantic purpose. Father had put a cruel damper upon my enthusiasm, which at heart he shared, but the manifestations of which even his brief experience had taught him to regard as so much grist upon the dictator's mill. During this one week I had a chance to observe the violent shifts of public sentiment. The outcome was entirely to my liking. But it could hardly be traced to the ripe deliberation of the multitude; if judged by the demonstrations of that great assembly of people swung in a few days from craziest adulation for Conkling to wildest acclamation for Blaine, and finally settling down to the sobered approval of Garfield. Even so, there was one note which finally won and which is democracy's chief hope. In the face of all the froth and delirium, by degrees popular admiration was withdrawn from the masters of political horseplay, and support went more and more to men who from the start

a   James Cook Conkling (October 13, 1816 – March 1, 1899) was an American politician and attorney from New York City.
b   James Abram Garfield (November 19, 1831 – September 19, 1881) was the 20th President of the United States, serving from March 4, 1881, until his assassination later that year. Garfield had served nine terms in the House of Representatives, and had been elected to the Senate before his candidacy for the White House, though he declined the Senate seat once he was elected President. He was the only sitting House member to be elected president.
c   John Alexander Logan (February 9, 1826 – December 26, 1886) was an American soldier and political leader. He served in the Mexican-American War and was a general in the Union Army in the American Civil War. He served the state of Illinois as a State Senator, a Congressman, and a U.S. Senator and was an unsuccessful candidate for Vice President of the United States with James G. Blaine in the election of 1884.

had counseled restraint and reason. But that also is another story.

All was again ready for our next and fifth round of the trip, which was to be short; only to the mouth of the Rio Grande. We were now five. The Jew had joined us, and we liked him. We got away in a small conveyance, so we had to leave some things behind; among them my gun and powder horn, which so far I had managed to keep with me. It had to be left behind because it would have been risky to be caught with firearms. We went at night, and there was a good deal of anxiety lest we be challenged. But we got through, and arrived some time late in the night at one of those little towns of wooden shanties that spring up like mushrooms when there is a sudden chance for trade. We may marvel at the erection of these temporary shacks; even at the collection of ill-suited boards and planks and posts which go to make them up. But the real wonder is from where the human beings which constitute their owners may have sprung. With the certainty and promptness which marks the buzzard's search for a carcass these representatives of all races and conditions are assembled. They come as if guided by instinct to feed upon the weakness of men starved by seclusion's denial, and hungry for adventure, however cheap. The arrival of the Union Army was the occasion here.

We had gone just in time, for that night there was, as we were told, a pitched battle in Matamoras for possession. It was said that Union troops came over to protect U.S. citizens and property. About that I do not know. We did not even learn which faction won out.

As I look back upon the last week or two, I can not but feel that I have said little or nothing about the character of the country through which we came. The reason is simple. My interest in the scenery was not awake at the time so as to have my memory retain impressions. As far as Monterey, we of course knew that we were never out of danger; but from Monterey on we felt that we were always in danger. Without tent or camp fire we made out as best we could. Add to that the hardships of weather, the lack of proper food, and everything else took second place. A boy's mind is apt to be taken up by one thing at a time. To that fact I owe my ability to record as much as I have. He may take notice of this or that other thing, but only the chief objects imprint themselves upon his memory. After Monterey there may have been mountains. If there were, no doubt I saw them; but they gave me no joy. They were no part of the great game at which we were then playing. I should say that most of our way we traveled on rather level ground and through barren territory. But the weather forced us to have the curtains down, and we were bent on getting through as soon as possible—even the Spaniard while his good spirits held was little more than a welcome diversion. Father's state of mind no doubt had its effect upon me. I wonder now where he got the courage to go through with it. Probably because he had it to do. We were going farther and farther away from home; means of communication were virtually cut off; plans for the future were very indefinite in purpose and in hope of fulfillment. We were out of Texas. In Mexico there was no place for father. Where to turn and how was the question.

Of Matamoras I really remember only the human struggle. Vaguely I see a church tower looking down upon the scene of a lone rider pressing through the crowd to take his victim off hanging over his saddle; but I heard no chimes, and the church did not seem to mean anything. My memory of the character of the country at the mouth of the Rio Grande is just as dim, probably for the same reason, that there were so many other things to think about. I see an old shack or two, perhaps more, but the broad picture hardly includes them. That shows the new shacks, hammered together of rough and new boards, untrimmed and unmeasured; any old way to keep out most of the rain and wind. There was an emergency to be met. The Federal troops had landed on the other side; here was a chance for a new station for supplies. Apart from all the rest there were Texans enough, who felt the twofold desire to keep their person out of reach of these troops, and to have their wares within hailing distance of them. The spot had necessarily become something of a trading center. There were Mexicans, of course. I should have said, judging by the bills of fare that the cooks were all Mexicans. But the trading was no doubt done chiefly by other people, the usual mixture of haphazard and selfish adventurers. Our meals we took in one of these shacks. I stuck pretty close to grain products, whatever their name. Vegetables I do not recall; but they had never made a good impression upon me. Meats became more and more suspicious; I was sure that whatever the appearance or dressing, it was all young goat meat. That was too much for a boy who had kids as pets, given to him as present by Mexicans who had come into Texas with their herds of goats, and who wanted to show a kindness to the doctor's son. That sentiment for a young animal is a very real thing. No man would kill a fawn. We had never even killed a calf. They, too, had become pets in a way, although we had seen them cruelly branded and marked. When later I saw butchers drive calves to the market, I would stand on the sidewalk with pity for the animal and curse for the man. After all, what could one expect of people who tortured horses by cutting off their beautiful tails. This is all without reason of course; but what has reason to do with a boy's impulse, molded and shaped in the young years of his life. To this day, when venison is served, I see the trusting, appealing eye of the animal — always the question, "Why did you have to do it?" I could not eat kid meat; and when pressed too hard, it was the spice and pepper that gave the excuse, and they were perhaps excuse enough.

In the matter of sleeping quarters, we may have felt secure against further surprises, but we were mistaken. Even our two companions who had seen service in the army admitted that. We lived in a grain warehouse; no doubt by leave of the owner's kindness. I recall only two features of this hospitality. We slept on top of piles of filled grain sacks, putting our blankets to the best use we could. Our presence was very much resented by the original inhabitants, chief among which were hordes of rats. Early in the evening we could hear them gnawing at the grain and scrapping among themselves. As night advanced they seemed to have "satisfied the inner man" and, according to custom, became frolicsome. As far as we could make out, they played at races or "Bad Man's Out." Be that as it may they apparently had laid their course across the sleeping intruders. If there was any language of peculiar American emphasis known or unknown to me, I certainly heard it on the first night when one of our friends made attempt to give full expression to his sentiments. But all to no purpose. The rats played at their games, and we had to sleep — a contest in which a tired and drowsy boy no doubt had the advantage. There was of course no way to supply heat in a warehouse. Our sitting room was a bare space near the entrance which had no door, with the ground for a floor, and soap boxes for chairs. In this we built a fire place. It was made of a soap box filled with earth; and upon this hearth we burned broken cigar boxes, and warmed our cracked hands over the modest flame. I rather think that one of the results of this demand for firewood was to create an abnormal taste for cigars in our party. There was of course nothing to interest old or young in such a place. The one joyful moment I remember there was when by some favor I got an apple to eat. It must have been lost and strayed my way.

We were again waiting to start on our next trip, this time by water. So much I knew; but of details I knew nothing, and I doubt that father knew much. How we came to be taken off remained a mystery to me. Somehow I associate with the plans the name of Schmidt. Its owner was one of the smoothest Germans I ever saw. He visited us in the old home, and was said to be a trader in cotton on a large scale. He was small and alert, with a winning manner. He had a wife who was large and jolly, not German, perhaps English or Irish; who rode about the country at our Texas home on a fine grey racking horse. We were much impressed by both of them. I do not recall seeing him at Matamoras; we saw so many things. But I can not get it out of my head that he must have had us taken on board the ship. This is the way I reason. When we were taken to the ship, there came with us a nice looking hunting dog, setter, I should say. He did not go on with us, and I always associate him with Schmidt, who loved these dogs. Hence my conclusion that Schmidt was not far away. In other respects, he cut a large figure in our affairs. I am sure he had helped make the plans for our direct trip to Matamoras, and probably beyond, even to the present time. Unhappily, he did not stop there. When mother, a year and a half after we had left, decided to follow us alone, she sold all of the property which represented father's savings up to that time under a power of attorney he had left with her. She was advised by Schmidt that it would not be wise for her to carry the money with her. She acted upon the advice of this friend (so experienced in large business) and left the money with him for safe keeping. We never saw Schmidt again, nor do I remember hearing of the money.

However, we were told that some day soon the ship would come in and take us off. So we made our daily walk to a point as near the open sea as possible, there to watch for its coming. The prospect was not reassuring. Far out the water was deep and no doubt calm enough; but the approach was over breakers—ceaseless and treacherous for small schooners under sail. It was said that when the Federal troops landed there had been many accidents. A great number of animals had been lost, and sharks had assembled in large numbers. I never saw one there, but in my mind's eye they looked awfully big, and I did see enough to have my fancy played upon. The entrance to the river gave sufficient proof of the losses that had been suffered. When I asked why so many poles were sticking out of the water, I was told that these were masts of schooners that had gone down; and this was the kind of schooner in which we were to cross those breakers. Of course, the account was made vivid for my benefit by the further statement that in case a boat capsized there was no hope for passengers; that the sharks were always on hand, and because of the scarcity of food since the finish of the troops landing, they had become aggressive and ravenous. This was not all fiction, of which a tragedy that I witnessed gave proof. Father and I were on the lookout as usual, when a larger ship came in sight and anchored. They said it was an English frigate. This may not have been correct, but I did not know one ship from another. We saw them lower a row boat, manned as I should say by a crew of six or eight. It started for our shore and soon struck the breakers, apparently without thought of defeat. The boat took the breakers head on, and seemed for a time to make good progress. Suddenly we saw it rise so high that it fairly stood on end, the oars all in regular formation, but mostly out of water. There was no sign of faltering and the boat came down so straight that it entered the water in perfect balance. But there came another shock. Again the boat rose as before; but this time a second wave struck its side and sent it down, throwing out the crew and capsizing it. We saw men struggling in the water, some climbed onto the boat, which was rolling bottom up; but they, too, soon lost their hold and as far as we could tell, every man was lost. We were told that the captain himself was in the boat, and that his wife was on deck of the ship watching the tragedy. I had no further doubt about the meaning of those poles sticking out of the water, and looked forward to our first sail with nothing more than the faith of a boy, who trusts that his luck will hold out; not unlike soldiers who feel that danger is for the other fellow. We did not have to wait much longer.

WE GO TO SEA

Soon after another ship came and went to anchor, and this was to be ours. Goodbye to kid stewed in red pepper; goodbye to the home of the rats and the soap box hearth. It took a day or two to unload or reload or both, and all was ready. We made up a unique passenger list. Father still had the small trunk or bag which in an emergency he could carry as he did. We made our exit; father with his huge grey overcoat. I had my aristocratic Spanish mantle flung over my shoulders to conceal a hickory shirt and to offset striped blue pants; the two ex-confederate soldiers were penniless, and clothed accordingly. Our Jewish friend probably well off was in the last stages of consumption, going to the North by a rough sea voyage of many weeks. And, finally, a widow in deep mourning and her young child. Thus we set out. Schmidt may have gone with us to the ship. That the dog did I can not forget. Near the mouth of the river we boarded what they called a schooner—a one master, painted yellow, whatever else it may have been. Room on the deck was contracted, so the dog and I were sent to a little cabin below, "downstairs," as I called it. This was another first experience. All went well as long as we were in the river, but when we struck the breakers, the response was prompt. I could see that dog turn pale, and felt myself doing the same. We were of one mind—to struggle against a condition like that was wasting energy. With one accord, dog and I, paid tribute of which no fair-minded Neptune could complain. It is said that victims of seasickness have a desire to die or drown or for anything that will put an end to their misery. That was not true of me. I wanted to be saved, and was filled with a sense of danger. I had no confidence in that outfit. Only one fact gave me assurance. While the sail was shaking and flapping without reason, I could feel the body of the boat scraping the bottom most of the time. I was sure that as long as we were near to the ground the danger could not be great. They told me later that the keel had done it; so that what trust I have placed in keels since then rests upon somewhat modified reasons. However, we got across the breakers, reached the ship and were made fast. Going on deck meant to climb a rope ladder that had been let down to us. Years afterwards I saw a play by Field and Weber[a]. They were making a balloon ascension and got stuck midair. A rope ladder hung out from their basket part way down, and Field thought Weber, being the smaller man, ought to make the climb to hasten the descent of their balloon. Weber's face was a study. When looking over the edge of the basket he protested as I recall it: "That air looks awful deep to me." My sympathy was with him. That is the way it looked to me, only the air looked "awful high" to me. But they went, the three well men, one carrying the child, the consumptive and the widow; I just did crawl up and once on deck, lay down completely done. There was some delay, and by the time we started, the world put on a more kindly face. We were on a two mast sailing ship, commanded by a captain and aided by a mate and, I think, a crew of six. The little cabin below served as sitting and dining room, the captain presided at our table, and the mate came to second table. The bunks opened into the cabin, and were of course not built for passengers. The sailors must have doubled up in some of them. The fare was very simple, but it was at least American—its character was not obscured by foreign

---

a   Joe Weber (11 August 1867 – 10 May 1942), born Joseph Morris Weber, was a vaudevillian who, along with Lew Fields, formed the comedy team of Weber and Fields. The young men had a "Dutch act" in which both portrayed German immigrants.

tricks—and I made up for lost time. The early part of the voyage was rather calm, which was lucky for most of us. After the first sudden distress, we got used to the motion and did pretty well, even when very severe weather tossed the ship about later on. But it was an altogether new world; only the sun and the stars and the sky belonged to the world that I had known.

When things look darkest, the mood of a company may be saved by the most trifling thing. One passenger—the one whom we had first seen upon crossing into Mexico although not then in good health, was really a fine looking man. His figure was strong and erect and his features were regular; but a quite strong nose was rather radiant, a symptom which we were assured was not to be traced to the suspected cause. He was young and wanted to know whether something could not be done. Father was not busy, and thought it might. So he painted that nose with iodine. Everybody on board knew, and awaited the result in suspense. The effect was equally pronounced with doctor and patient. Like a beacon light it shone in the sun; and I wonder whether anything short of a real pirate would have dared to board our craft. What the immediate consequences were I do not know; but the diagnosis must have been right, for the remedy worked better than we thought. I saw our friend often in later years, and there were no signs of the old symptoms.

We had our first surprise while we were still in the Gulf of Mexico. We came on deck one morning to find that we were becalmed. The ship did not move an inch, there was not a flap of a sail, and this lasted for about two days. The weather was so warm that we moved about in shirt sleeves, and watched the sailors scraping the boom and cleaning up generally. It was the one perfect view I have ever had of the depths of the ocean. We sank open bottles, and they went down as straight as a leaded line. We could watch them in the clear calm water until they were lost to sight as little dots going down into the depths. Most fascinating to me were the different varieties of fish, swimming about as unconcerned as though our craft was an accepted part of the exhibition. But one day there was an interruption in the performance. At the very side of the ship there rose high above the water's surface, two huge fish, (one a sword fish[a]) in fierce conflict. They went at each other like two bulls engaged in combat, but came down as far as we could see unhurt; and as though startled by the apparition of the ship, disappeared. This calm, of course, meant rough weather; so after the breeze came up again and we had sailed along for some time, a strong wing arose and soon lashed the sea into a very fury. The waves were so high that one moment we would seem to see all the world, and the next the horizon would sink out of view. In the midst of this storm we saw another ship very near by, and I could not account for the commotion on our deck at sight of it. I never knew under what flag we sailed. We may have had several to meet war emergencies as they arose; and we must have had one regular one because we did enter New York Harbor. There was a great deal of rushing to and fro on deck, and many questions and answers through speaking trumpets. But there was no result that I could see, unless it was our captain's gratitude that the state of the waves made it impossible for the other ship to come closer than it did.

We were now nearing the western coast of Florida. The weather was still unsettled, and I was below, when we

a   Swordfish (Xiphias gladius), also known as broadbills in some countries, are large, highly migratory, predatory fish characterized by a long, flat bill.

were startled by a tremendous commotion on deck. All rushed up, to find that a sailor had caught a beautiful and as they said a rare fish—Kingfish[a]—they called it. They were in high glee, because they told us that this kind of fish meant good luck. The coloring of this fish just out of water was certainly very wonderful; and as for the good luck I accepted the superstition gladly. The next commotion was perhaps not greater but much more serious. The mate was alone at table, and I had tarried with him. Like a bolt out of a clear sky came the command "All hands on deck!" The mate put one foot on the bench on which he was sitting, the other on the table, jumped across it, and was up the stairs like a shot. I followed and saw the ship just coming about under shifted sails, and to the left we saw the reefs barely covered by lapping waves. The lookout had seen them only in time to have the ship's course changed; and as we moved away the waves seemed to be beckoning us to a danger so narrowly escaped. For the most, during this part of the journey, we had the monotony of such a trip, as regular as all ship life is.

As we rounded the southern arm of Florida real winter weather set in, which lasted for the rest of the voyage. It was about the middle of January—of the hard winter of 1863-64. Bitter winds blew from the north, and from that time on we tacked to and fro, day and night. One day we saw the open ocean or perhaps Cuba, and the next the coast of the United States. We heard the sailors talk of Cape Hatteras and no wonder, for they knew what to expect. The ship looked like a chunk of ice, and when the sailors went into the rigging, I wondered why the frozen

[a] Menticirrhus americanus, the southern kingfish, southern kingcroaker, the king whiting, the Carolina whiting, or the sea mullet, is a species of marine fish in the family Sciaenidae. It lives in shallow coastal waters on the western fringes of the Atlantic Ocean.

Fig. 21: The Blücher Memorial in Berlin, Unter den Linden

sails did not crack. It all looked very dangerous to me, for I had hardly ever seen ice. To the end it was the same steady fight against that wind, always tacking to keep the sails full, with perhaps some misgiving among the older people as to the safety of the ship. At last one brilliant morning we were in sight of New York harbor. The air was clear and crisp, as it will be after the violence of a storm has ceased. The weather had quieted just in time; as though it would make amends and give our hearts full swing at the finish of this long and arduous voyage. Three weeks we had been out when we landed. What became of the passengers (all but one) I do not know. The widow and the child were met by friends. Father looked up our Jewish friend once more, and found him in good hands. Our two companions from Mexico had to be treated with more discretion. As ex-confederate soldiers they could not go home, but found shelter with some loyal relatives or friends who protected them until the end of the war. Father, himself a fugitive from the Confederate South, had brought them safely through with no thought of what the consequences to himself might be.

In the meantime he had been persuaded by our Confederate friends that St. Louis was the only place to go; and with no other plans to act upon, that was the decision. The boarding house in which we stopped seemed like a haven of rest. Perhaps it was a general shelter for immigrants. If so, it was better than many others that I have seen since; and in one sense we belonged properly enough to its regular patronage. It seemed very clean — my standards had suffered, and no doubt stood in need of mother's admonition. The food was very much to my taste — lots of meat and bread and butter; and if there were vegetables, there was no one to point them out to me. Everybody was kind and thoughtful. Father became a center of interest. Men came to see him; and I would watch them sit apart, conversing over a glass of wine. Even I was sometimes honored with a look to indicate notice; to which I was not indifferent although I had not learnt to be sorry for myself. We were even taken to the opera, my third great experience in the rise from circus to bull fight, and now to the stage. Tickets were scarce or expensive, and we took our entertainment standing. The scenery amazed me. Once I thought that the stage forest looked like real woods. There must have been solo singers. There always are, for the supply never gives out. I can neither see nor hear them now, be it lack of appreciation or good judgment. But the chorus is unforgettable. I had never heard more than eight voices sing the old student songs at home. Neither had I ever

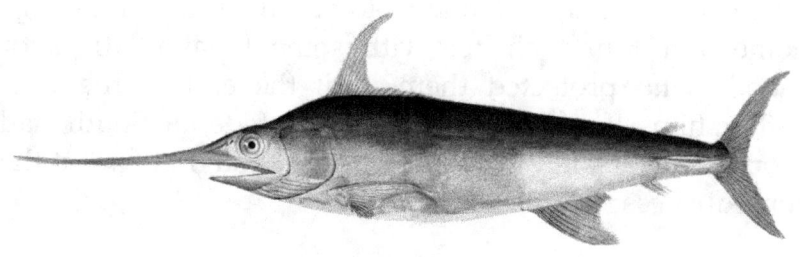

Fig. 22: Swordfish (Xiphias gladius)

heard a woman sing; which until then had not seemed strange. Here there appeared to be hundreds of voices, male and female, just crowding upon the stage; and how they did sing at us and at each other. I could not make out whether they were glad or mad, but there was something wrong. Then there came a royal figure. I thought it a woman, but it may have been a man, because to my rural eyes all ancient cloaks and robes looked alike. Nor did the attitude of command or the picture of strength tell me more. The royal figure approached a great tree in the midst of a forest, on whose trunk a big gong was hung. As summons or warning of some kind, he or she struck that gong several times, the echoes ringing all over the place.

Fig. 23: Menticirrhus americanus (Kingfish)

This seemed to excite the chorus still more; and they went at it hammer and tongs, sparing neither the audience nor themselves; reckless of all consequences. But like all storms, this one gradually let up and receded. Now and then there would come a spasmodic shout of revolt or exultation—I never could make out. A drum would rumble way down in the depths; a fife would send out a high note, almost like a shriek; others would remonstrate or rejoice; and by degrees they would all unite, voices and instruments, in a gentle accord and subside and leave the stage. I never knew what opera it was, but I did not wonder that it took so many people and so many different kinds of instruments to make so much noise. Some years after in Berlin modern music was quite the vogue. Even as late as 1872-73 students would engage in heated discussions whether Wagner was a false prophet or the father of "Zukunftsmusik." At the time a statue of Bluecher[a] stood as it still stands near the Opera House. One morning,

---

a Gebhard Leberecht von Blücher, Fürst von Wahlstatt; 16 December 1742 – 12 September 1819), Graf (count), later elevated to Fürst (sovereign prince) von Wahlstatt, was a Prussian Generalfeldmarschall (field marshal). He earned his greatest recognition after leading his army against Napoleon I at the Battle of the Nations at Leipzig in 1813 and the Battle of Waterloo in 1815.

while at the University, the story went that a placard had been found, fastened about Bluecher's neck with the following inscription: "I am accustomed to the furor of battle, and can bear what is necessary. But if this useless and senseless disturbance in the Opera House is to be persisted in, I ask to be transferred to another place." So perhaps my early difficulties were not without sympathizers.

Fig. 24: A statue of Gambrinus with a goat at the Falstaff brewery in New Orleans

Of the wonders of the city—and New York must have had

wonders even in 1864—I saw nothing at all. I was taken to "Brooks" once, and here father bought for me cloth trousers, a very jewel of an outfit, wide enough at the hip to encompass a devotee of Gambrinus[a], and narrow enough at the foot to satisfy a southern dandy. It was said to be the fashion then, and here was my first bow to that common enemy of society. I had those trousers for some years—a sort of dernier resort, but I scarcely ever dared wear them. They did not seem to go with my Texas outfit —first symptom of that awful test, which provides so much discomfort in life. Besides, they were stylist and I was afraid to appear in them, another unhappy sign of social awakening. However, we had come to the end of our stay in New York; indeed the very appearance of father's purse was warning enough. We had to move on. So one night we started on our sixth round in a day coach for St. Louis by way of Cincinnati, which reads like the Baltimore & Ohio. We were not more than half an hour out, as I sat given up to my first sensations in a railroad train, when we ran into another train that was crossing at a right angle. The collision was not serious, although everybody was up with the exception of one private soldier right across the aisle from me, who kept his seat as though he was used to just such accidents, and had been rather looking for this one.

The trip to Cincinnati is a blank to me; changing of trains, I imagine, and getting out for meals at more regular hours than had been the custom, and nodding in sleep to the discomfort of whatever neighbor there happened to be. Arriving at Cincinnati we found that we had lost our only

---

a Gambrinus, is a legendary European culture hero celebrated as an icon of beer, brewing, joviality, and joie de vivre. Traditional songs, poems, and stories describe him as a king, duke, or count of Flanders and Brabant.

trunk. Somebody had come through the train and asked for trunk checks; and father, trusting man that he was, gave up his check, and got nothing in return. We spent two days there in a search, and at last in despair we landed at what was said to be the president's office. The common idea is that all railroad presidents are hard-hearted. Perhaps so, but there are pictures that even they can not resist. This rather impressive looking man took one look at father's overcoat and my mantle, and in a twinkle was changed into a Good Samaritan. Orders were given, and at the time named for our return the trunk had been found. I have been told that burglars have returned fake jewels. Perhaps a disgusted holder of this trunk check had made the search easy for the officials. At any event, we were now ready for the final run to the only city in the United States to which we ought to go, as our friend had told us. Our start was so arranged as to have us arrive in the morning. Early on February 4, 1864, we reached the east side of the Mississippi opposite St. Louis. We changed to bus, and were off once more. The ground was frozen, and going down an incline the bus, with brakes all set and horses sliding, by chance or design landed on the deck of a ferry boat. The boat in turn made its way through the icy waters, and landing at last, the bus moved up the wharf over cobblestone and other like obstructions. I can now hear the wheels rumble and rattle. Our destination was a hotel, the Green Tree Hotel[a], on Second near Walnut Street, owing its name, I suspect, to a brewery miles away, of the same name. It was really not a hotel at all; but it was a decent boarding house, well kept and providing wholesome food generously. I was so encouraged that I ventured to wear my distinguished "Brooks" trousers; but one glance from the girl who brought the meals in from the kitchen broke my confidence in them forever. I never wore

a See note below.

them again. That girl's look might have wrecked a whole tailor shop. Everybody was again very good to us. The German element had not yet lost its prestige of 1861, and father's story was of course listened to with sympathetic ears. Strangely enough, he came upon a Mr. Koenig, a house painter, whose brother father had known at the University of Berlin. He lived with his sister, a spinster; many a good Sunday dinner did I have at that home, over a grocery store on Franklin Avenue. In that home I became a devotee of soup, bouillon in particular. The real influence for the time in my life, however, was the proprietor of a saloon, no doubt a "Green Tree"[a] customer. By his advice father rented an office in a frame house on Sixth Street between Franklin and Wash Street. It was on the ground floor and had a little nook for a desk under a staircase that led through the room to a photographer's shop upstairs. After we could afford it we had our pictures taken there. The office proper had space for a small table and several chairs, and adjoining was a room large enough to hold a bed and wash stand. I had in the meantime, in obedience to the same saloon keeper's advice, been left at a boarding school in the southern part of the city, several miles away, on Jackson and Barton Streets. It was Glaeser's School, which had a large number of pupils, girls and boys of all ages. With me there were four or five boarders. We had one room, the loft in the third story. The roof came down to the floor on two sides, there was one window in the gable side, and one door opposite leading to the hall and the stairs. We slept two to a bed; and for warmth we relied upon a cannon stove—either stone cold or red hot. So we were settled at last. Father had just fourteen dollars left of

a Green Tree is a borough in Allegheny County, Pennsylvania, United States, and a suburb of Pittsburgh. Settled in 1793, the area stayed rural until the late 1800s, with paintings of the time showing farmland and a vineyard. The community took its name from the local Green Tree Hotel

all his hard earned savings, and he was now to start life over again. From home we had never heard a word, and while in one sense we were at peace, we were in another sense now much more the prey to anxiety. The constant unrest on our trips, the risks and the doubt at every point had in a manner been a protection to us. This was at least true of me, because my attention was naturally riveted upon the changing and novel experiences until now when I had time to stand at the sole window of our room, to wonder how they were at home, how long the war would last, and whether the Confederates under Sterling Price now as far north as the foothills of the Ozarks, would take St. Louis and us after all.

In the meantime we had not forgotten our chief mission to St. Louis, which was to tell the family of our Confederate friend what we knew of him. We had the address of a foundry on Second Street, and to it we found our way. We were of course still clothed as we had left Texas; and as we entered the little office on the ground floor, the owners seemed to succumb very much as the railroad president in Cincinnati had. There were three; the father of our friend, his brother-in-law, and a brother. Only the first made a distinct impression on me. A heavy head of dark hair, clean shaven, and clear cut strong features, altogether a figure of true dignity. Perhaps with no reason at all, this man and Swearengen always come to my mind when I see a picture of Washington, they seemed so typically American. Father managed to explain to him that he must see him alone; and this done, told him in a very few words that the son was safe in New York. There was no sign of emotion; he felt most grateful, and father was quite embarrassed in having to decline all offers of help. To my surprise I was sent out to the home to break the news there. The old gentleman may have meant to pave the way for a family that was more given to demonstration than he was; or he may have planned wisely enough to give them a first taste of what he thought was in store for them. To a gentleman of the old school, with a keen sense of obligation, the situation must have presented some problems. I went. The home was on Olive Street about Fifteenth. In those days most homes were built upon the same pattern; stone steps leading up to the vestibule, protected by storm doors. The inside doors opened into the hall which ran to the rear of the house. Stairs (mahogany banisters) leading straight to second story. Double "parlors" to one side; a dining-room behind them; and then the kitchen, pantry, etc. The second and third stories, as I afterwards saw, were arranged upon the same general lines, excepting that the front rooms took in the hall space; and the rooms over the kitchen belonged to the servants. The plan was mathematically correct; and, indeed, was convenient enough. Knobs were always on the same side of the door, and were so accurately placed that light or dark, the halls and rooms could be navigated with equal safety. The monotony of the design sometimes had me wonder whether it was intended to serve the convenience of unwelcome intruders, or the safety of belated members of the family. The plan of this home was of that kind. I was received by one of the daughters, Ella, a young lady who was out of school, and who at once gained my confidence by telling me that she was fond of horses. Broken as my English was, I had less difficulty in relating my story than she had in suppressing merriment at my appearance. However, all went comparatively well but for my inexperience in the art of saying goodbye. There was a piano in the "front parlor," and somehow I got glued to the piano stool and could not disentangle myself. I managed to whirl around at odd moments, but could not sever connections. It was all a question of getting started, and that is where I lacked the required resolution. I did finally get away, or would not be here to tell the tale. But as I now think of the young lady, I am more sorry for her than I was for myself then. I carried with me many good wishes, which were made good a hundredfold as time went on.

At school my first appearance in a class room broke up the meeting. The girls were the worst; they were merciless, seated as they were on one side of the room facing the door. They were of all sizes and ages, it seemed to me. There was one very cute brunette who simply giggled; and one very handsome blonde who only smiled. I could have forgiven them. But there was one who seemed to grow fat on laughter, without having any suspicion of her ailment. She got completely out of balance, a helpless victim to the effects of hilarity. Soon after her father was triumphantly elected as Justice of the Peace. His opponent was an Irishman, who had a better explanation than most defeated candidates. He said that no one could beat a man like that. He was Michelle to the French, and Michel to the Germans, and Michael to the Irish. And so he was, and to judge from his decisions, continued to be. I really did not blame them so much even then, for I had seen enough of "the world" by that time to know that I was out of tune. Any lingering doubt upon that subject was soon removed by the more drastic methods of the boys. But I found my place; and the school being German, it did not take the teachers long to give me my rank, and to give my critics all the chance they wanted to challenge it. The fact is that before leaving this school I took my place in the front rank, and for the first time had an inkling of the excellence of my teacher in Texas. My attendance at school was very soon interrupted. Measles broke out and I fell an easy victim. They did not take the normal course with me, and within ten days after being there, I was taken down with pneumonia in our garret room—no doubt with the exasperated blessings of the head of the school. Of the illness I do not remember much, and it would not be worth telling. I think of poor father, several miles away in his little office, waiting for patients in his new start in life, and practically without means to come and go. Here was I with the fever rising in hot competition with the cannon stove when it was going, right next to my bed. Of course, all the boarders remained in the same room; one of them for a good part of the time shared my bed, and being a husky fellow got most of the bed cover. I do remember father coming once or twice every day (there were no nurses then for such a case) until finally he brought a consultant with him. They stood there exchanging views—I can see them now as they decided that the fever must be checked. That seemed perfectly sensible to me. So I was wrapped in cold cloths and put back under the covers. As I gathered, if you react you are all right, and if you do not you are not all right. Well, I did. How the perspiration did break out, and how relieved I felt, everything seemed clear and in its proper place again. From then on it was the old story, care and patience. My risk was not the usual one. There was no danger of my eating more than was necessary to keep alive. In spite of the experience of our trip, I was still sensitive about food, perhaps as much to appearances as to taste; and when I could take the grease off the soup in layers with the spoon, I somehow lost my taste for things. Then one day I had visitors. Phil, brother of our Confederate friend, called, bringing his cousin David. The one tall and strong and good natured, the other handsome, with a baritone voice, as I afterwards learned, a combination which at last made a music teacher of him. They seemed impressed with my surroundings; but they brought a bottle of preserved peaches (home product) which gave us something to talk about, and which accounts for my fondness for preserved peaches to this day. They say gratitude is one of the highest virtues; and I have no difficulty in living up to this one. They came several times, always bringing delicious fruit; and the last time Phil told me that when vacation commenced he was coming to take me to the country for the whole summer. Father had refused to accept anything, and had even declined to be their family physician. But when it came to me he could not resist; and the gentleman of the American type was getting in his work. For a few months more I dragged along—a little school work here and there—out in the open as much as possible. On Saturdays I generally visited father—a walk of four or five miles there and back. Sometimes this would be repeated on Sunday with a prospect of a dinner at the Koenigs. One day father was not in his office and I saw an open letter on his desk. Not for a moment could I doubt that it was from mother—the first word, some five or six months after we had left home. There it lay before me—a very symbol of despair, somehow telling me the worst as though I had read it. When father came back his look was enough to tell me what I had felt, that Paul had died. Since then I have read that letter, as I have read some others which I now have. It is a long letter written in sorrow and suspense. The first page tells it all in these words:

"Millheim, December 27, 1863

"My dear Hermann:

Fourteen days ago I sent my last letter to you to St. Antonio. I hope that you have received it with all its sad message. I say I hope, because some day you must learn it all, would to God I had your answer to that letter. As all the people stood about me, and felt sorry that this blow had struck, alone as I am, I could again and again think only of you two, and of the time when you would learn it. Might I only have been with you. I always think it would have been better for you. I am much more calm than you may believe. Elly's death tore me out of carefree peace. I had never given it a thought that this child, won with so many sacrifices, could be taken from me. It is different with Paul. I have always known, although never clearly expressed, that I would not see him as a man. From the first day he was not like other children—. And then to see a child calmly and softly, without thought of its death, slumber into the beyond is not so hard, when one has seen it once as we have. The happiest time, and this is childhood, Paul has lived. And above all I feel 'das Leben ist der Güter hoechstes nicht.' At least not for ourselves. Do for Carl what you can as I shall do for Clara what I can to preserve her happy and cheerful. The oldest daughter of Litzmann's will probably be here for fourteen days. If Carl A. does not return then, because he may have to take care of the farm, I shall try in some other way to have a child in the house. Clara shall not be alone, that would be too dreary for her.

"The Christmas tree Clara did not ask for, but I had to promise to light all the candles, and to give the dolls new dresses. All this I did and found some other trifles that would give her pleasure." These few words tell it all. No word of mine could add to the picture, even if I had the heart to write it.

Many months later, probably in July, Phil came for me with a barouche drawn by two horses. I was ready; no longer dependent upon my Texas clothes. I had added to my outfit in a manner to make a pessimist turn handsprings. Knowing that my next meeting with strangers would have something of a social coloring, I had asked father for enough money to buy a coat, and he had given

me what I wanted. How the sum was fixed I do not know
—perhaps I had felt my way. At all events, I remember
what I got. I hit upon a brown cloth cutaway (I was still
fourteen, and of a figure that would make a saint laugh).
The man said it was a "fine fit," and he would let me have
it for three dollars because it was "a little" moth eaten.
That man was a salesman, and my thoughts go out to him
whenever I pass the old shop which still stands. Well, it
was moth eaten, but I did not know what that meant. The
bargain seemed a good one because it left me a balance for
rounding out my outfit. I got a pair of shoes—also a "fine
fit"; so fine that ever since I have had no comfort without
shoes made to order. To make sure I got a black felt hat for
fifty cents, and a thin black tie to set off my blue hickory
shirt. All seemed well at last—father had given me full liberty; and if he had not, the outcome might have been no
better. So on that day I struck my highest note. Trousers
made, as I now think, of tarpaulin material, a heavy blue
stripe and a light one, alternately, up and down, about
four or five in the round of the leg. I was as thin as a rail;
and even so was barely able to get into them. The shirt was
the well known hickory type, and with these went a black
tie, a brown cloth moth eaten cutaway; shoes too short,
and a black felt hat. The outfit would have consigned Don
Quixote to second place. Nobody laughed. Phil was a gentleman, although at that stage his anxiety must have been
more grave than mine. We drove about seven to ten miles,
talking easily about the war and when and how it would
end, and landed at the gate of a country place. The house
was far back near some trees, and was covered with vines
and clinging roses. In front were a number of very large
trees, the rest was lawn. So much was all very well; but on
that lawn several games of croquet were under way. There
were young ladies, some from Philadelphia and Baltimore,
Phil told me, and young men; and younger girls and boys,

all having a good time; and all dressed for summer outing. I got a panic, and was for one dash back to the school. But Phil drove in, solemnly past all these, with friendly greetings for them and had me get out at the house. By that time I was helpless. I found a last corner of a bench on the piazza, and waited like a trapped animal. No one paid attention to me until the old gentleman came out, sat down beside me and took me by the hand. "Charles," said he, "your room is upstairs, I will show it to you." "I can't go into the house" was my answer. And then came his reply, so kindly and so final. "Charles, you are my guest, and until my guest comes into my house I can not go in." That was all, and I knew what I had to face come what may. Then he took me to the great barn and showed me the horses. "That horse is Charlie; he belongs to Ella (the one I had first met); she loves to ride; none of the rest care about it; so if you like she will be glad to have you ride with her. And that horse is Jule. She belongs to my son. No one has ever used her since he left for the war; she is yours now for your vacation." And so the ice was broken. I went to my room; and met a party of family and friends at dinner, with never a look or a smile from any one to do aught but to cheer me on at a meal such as I had never tasted in my life. I was there all summer — guests came and went — but my welcome and my feeling of perfect ease was never broken. I did give them one more shock, for I had an extra pair of trousers in reserve for special days. To them mother in her despair had devoted one or two tablecloths (no doubt brought from Germany). They were white with the usual dots and figures woven into them. Table cloths must have been more abundant than tarpaulin; or, perhaps, one was not enough, and two too many. At all events, this outfit was as wide as the blue one was scant. But the chief trouble was this: The laundress, knowing the character of the material, treated it as though its purpose had not been changed. She starched those trousers to make the legs stand up like two balloons. When I disturbed the peace of a lovely Sunday morning by my sudden appearance upon the lawn in full view of the assembled family and guests, encased in this Siamese twin outfit, I confess some evidence of suppressed amusement could not escape me. But I saw it through that day. So did the rest of them. Nothing was ever said by them or by me; but I had enough. Those trousers, too, were discarded. They went the way of the "Brooks" pair, and no doubt served a better purpose. The laundress was colored, and it is my guess that those Sunday trousers reverted to their original use, and in due time adorned a table on special occasions, for the delight of invited guests, and to the comfort of a proud hostess. After that I relied upon the clothes in which I had arrived; in part at least of my own choice — first venture in a long and checkered career of selections past understanding.

From that time on I was treated like a member of the family. That is not quite true, because I was really treated better than that. The old gentleman could never do enough for me; and at times created painful moments by his approval of me at the expense of Philip, who was about my age. It is true that Philip was not consumed with a desire for school work; but it was generous of him to save my feelings by never so much as resenting his father's comparisons. My life at this old-fashioned country place was like a dream. I was free to do as I pleased, and to build up my health; and there is little doubt that but for this life in the open at that time, my chance for real health would have been small. Some time later father said as much to me, and added that there was now no reason why I should not become well and strong, if I would observe three rules: Walk straight, sleep full time, and never take medicine unless it was necessary. I think I may say that I followed his counsel.

This life in the country, however, was not without times of real excitement. For instance, Phil and I were sent on horseback for days at a time to collect bills for mowing machines sold to farmers. This was very simple, especially as we did not bring in much cash—we were rather easily gotten rid of by farmers who have an instinctive estimate of human nature. But at that time the roads were reported to be frequented by highwaymen, and no doubt there was some truth in this rumor. What was lacking in truth our imagination supplied, particularly when night approached and we were riding in sparsely settled parts of the country. Many were our encounters in the mind's eye; and one stream—now in the midst of attractive homes—I never pass without recalling the feeling with which we approached it one dark night. Perhaps bandits knew more of the state of our purse than we suspected. We were never molested; and generally brought home at least enough to cover the feed of our horses. The old gentleman must have seen some advantage in keeping two boys out of mischief. On those rides much of our time was given to comparing the merits of Grant and Lee. Our sympathies were keenly divided; so we compromised by agreeing that Grant was more of a soldier, and Lee was the greater scholar. The war being still on, I added as many flourishes to the picture of a scholar as I could muster up, and felt that the soldier would probably save my cause.

At another time we had a competition of mowing machines. The foundry company was the Missouri agent of one of the competitors, the "Buckeye." One of the others had the advantage in name, the "Champion." The day was perfect. Our machine was placed on a common farm wagon drawn by two fine horses, driven by a negro factotum (Carter) a giant of a man with a real sense of humor. Phil and a cousin from Ohio (true to his native soil) and I, all on horseback, made up the guard of honor. The trial was had on a wheat field about seven miles away. For us it had all the interest of a horse race or a modern baseball game. The umpires looked very solemn, and, judging by the result, must have been just as impartial. The "Buckeye" won hands down; the award was unanimous; we were given the blue ribbon, and our enthusiasm knew no bounds. This of course resulted in more or less reckless horsemanship. Each one of us boasted of the faster horse, and short dashes were made to try conclusions. I rode "Jule"—of the pony type—round as a butter ball, of endless endurance, and with a mouth that was proof against any curb bit. Phil knew all this; and bent on mischief, he would start race after race to see "Jule" get away from me. He succeeded beyond expectations. During one of these spurts we were passing under a railroad bridge while a train was just coming along. The locomotive gave one wild whistle, and that was the end of the race, so far as naming the winner was concerned. "Jule" gave a snort, took the bit in her teeth, and was off on a dead run for home. She seemed as crazy as a horse in a fire, going helter-skelter, without aim or sense, regardless of obstruction or guide. Just then I saw a herd of cows ahead of us crossing the road, with that indolent and superior air of cows well fed, lost to all the world, with the one thought that they are about to be milked. I had some doubt as to what Jule would do; but she had none. Hers was also a single track mind with only one idea, which was to tear for home. There was no escape from the conflict. One or two cows made a last minute rush; but there was one whose serenity was not to be disturbed. She sauntered across the road with the air of sole proprietorship, with no thought for impending challenge. The impact was terrific. Jule struck that cow a broadside, knocking her down, going over her, and charging on in her wild career, to the chagrin of her helpless rider. I lost both stirrups, setting them free to bang right and left, driving Jule into further madness, and leaving me to the inglorious fate of holding on to her mane. Owing to her rotund body there was nothing to retard the forward movement of the saddle. As I sat, feeling it gradually slip upon her neck, vainly tugging at a useless bit, with my long legs extending to the point of her nose, my thoughts were carried back to the little mule (Kleiner Esel) menace of my younger days. How familiar it all seemed; how he would have enjoyed it; and how sure I felt that my being thrown was only a question of time and place; when all of a sudden Jule's energy gave out. Slower and slower became her pace, until she stopped before a shady tree, letting me get off to lie flat on the ground holding her by the reins, as glad to rest as I was. Phil and his cousin explained their delay in coming up by saying that they, too, had been forced to lie down on the ground farther back, convulsed with laughter at the amazing exhibition of Texas horsemanship. However, they had to admit that I had not fallen off. We still had the blue ribbon tied to the machine on the wagon, driven by the inimitable Carter, who as he came up made no effort to hide his white teeth, because for aught I could say he might still be enjoying the triumph of our machine. The expedition ended with a run around the circle in front of the home, to the cheers of the assembled members of the family, maids and farm hands.

The general prospect for pleasure riding was more than fulfilled. It was true that Miss Ella was fond of it, and that she had the horse to have her enjoy it. I did not have to be drafted. So we had many a ride through the country, she having her fine saddler set the pace, and I keeping up as best I could on a nag whose gait was as individual as her temper was unique. But all went well for me, as it would for a boy who felt flattered at the very thought of being taken along on these rides by a young lady. My powers of conversation were not severely tested, because Jule's gaits usually had me too far ahead or behind to keep me within hailing distance. We may even have admired a sunset together, or perhaps other scenery; but to me it was the joy of freedom in the open, as I had not known it for so long. One evening, coming back, not more than two miles from home, Miss Ella looked back at me and said, "Charlie, you can't catch me," and with that she dashed off. A boy did not have to come from Texas to accept that challenge, and so off was Jule after her. We were then at the top of a hill which sloped down to a narrow wooden bridge. Suddenly I saw that Miss Ella had lost control of her horse; her hat had come down, and she was pulling hard at the reins.

I urged my horse to the utmost, but she looked back and called out not to pursue because she would not then be able to stop her horse. I thought of the narrow bridge; and right or wrong I felt that I must go on, as I did. After all, Jule had endurance in a hard run. By degrees we crept up and got abreast of the other horse. The curb had broken, and Charlie was pulling on what was no more than a snaffle bit. I got hold of the rein, and by pulling my way and speaking to the horse, gradually helped to settle him down to a canter, in which we crossed the bridge. The up grade on the other side did the rest; the horses were both glad enough to come to reason. We got home without special notice, and nothing was said; but I did not see Miss Ella at a meal for three days.

In other respects the life was a little of everything on a

farm. One day I would shoot at a hawk, if judged by results to determine how many feathers could be shot loose without hurting the chickens' enemy. At another time I would find my old enemy, the rattler, under a sheaf of hay. I would be sent to the city, and sometimes ride back on a big roan—the greatest racker I have ever been on—one who made you feel that owning the county was a mere beginning to the conquest. But much of time was spent in the field, sometimes running the mowing machine, usually gathering the hay in small stacks, or pitching it to the wagon for stacking. I was not compelled to do anything, and felt free to do everything—such a time of rest and revival.

When alone I always felt serious. The separation was ever present, and with it came doubt and fear. I knew that Paul had died within a few weeks after we left and the long silence since then was a natural cause for apprehension of further sorrow. At such times I first began consciously to wrestle with the question of religion. I would not dwell upon this phase because religious conviction and belief is made of sterner stuff. It is true, however, that riding the roads alone, I thought of the meaning of Christ, as most children have, and why it was thought so difficult to live in his spirit. Much that I had heard from mother in her way of teaching; many things that I had seen, among them the impressions of Mexico, had left a very definite influence which as I think back may have gone deeper than I could then know.

My stay on this farm covered more than one year's vacation; I was there several years, among others in the cholera year, of 1866. Mother had at last been able to join us, in 1865, having made the trip by way of Mexico and New York, but by a shorter route. She had however come alone, with sorrow and grief as her sole companions. Clara had died about a year after Paul and of this we had heard only shortly before Mother reached St. Louis. I remember coming to the office and seeing another open letter that told father of her death. The first we knew of mother's coming was a short letter from her written in New York. The day of her arrival was fixed but not the train hour. I was on a nearby street and without warning saw her in a bus. Fortunately she did not see me. Although I was then going on sixteen I could not have met her alone. Her face seemed to tell it all in so sad and tragic a way that I had not the courage. After a few minutes I returned to the office where she had found father. There they were like lost souls holding hands and looking into each others eyes searching for an answer. Not a word did I hear beyond Rieckchen and Hermann. When I was there they would not give way; they always sought to save me. I never heard father speak of their sorrow; and mother never did when father was about. In later years she gave me her confidence and let me share her feeling. She seemed to gather comfort in speaking of our lost ones calmly and in affectionate memory. After mother's coming we had taken a small house on the same street, and there we lived in the center of what became perhaps the worst cholera district. Father again insisted that cholera was not contagious and struggled from morning until night gaining the confidence and sometimes the affection of bewildered people; and at last laying the foundation of a larger practice. In 1866, the cholera year, father and mother got me out of the city, and so I was again in the country, to give them the sense of security and, boy-like, to live blind enough to the very real dangers at home.

One of the features at the farm was the negro servants—rather a new experience to me, in spite of my coming from the south. The farm hands during the harvest were white; but the domestic servants, and the coachman, were black. There was little Charlie, who polished the shoes; and there was his older sister, who helped out generally. Everybody was kind to them, and they were always cheerful. Some years after the girl died, and Phil and I, taking flowers, went to the funeral. They were no longer slaves; but they were colored still; and the relation between them and their former masters was less and more than a white servant could ever accept. The old black cook has become a mere memory of the past—a dear memory to me because I cannot believe that any such steaks, biscuits, butter and cakes as we had daily on that farm were ever served to others. Finally, there was Carter, a character all his own. Never forgetting his place, he was wise to all things. It did not take him long to find out why I had come North; and so he was not afraid to speak to me about things that for him were counted as forbidden. Naturally, he would never speak other than with respect, even with affection, of his old master. Indeed, his fate had been most happy and he knew it well. But one day he gave me what he knew of Camp Jackson. He had really not seen anything; but all other accounts have seemed tame to me by the side of this one. I can not do him justice; but his picture of it has stayed with me. He was a real artist. There was not a suggestion of malice or even amusement, and no suspicion of the impression his vivid account was making on me. This is the way he told it. "Camp Jackson! Don't know much about it, but can't forget that day. I was in the stable washing the carriage, as was my place to do. Mars George, he don't come there very often; knows pretty well that this nigger can be trusted to do what he ought to do. But that day comes Mars George with trouble in his face. He looks at me kinder sarching like. I knowed full well that I hadn't done nothing, so I kinder looks at him, wondering what was the trouble. Well, Mars George, he steps out and walks up alongside the house to the very front. There he looks up and down the street as though he was expecting something. Then he turns back, and just walks up and down in the yard with his hands folded on his back and his head bowed down. He sure was mighty oneasy about something. That was not like Mars George—never saw him just like that before, and so I kept my eyes on him. All of a sudden he moves clean out on the pavement, and stands there looking west up the street. His hands wasn't resting on his back no more. He looked mighty concerned about something. So I went up kinder slow to find out what it was. Mars George had no eyes for me, and I got out where he was. Didn't see nothing, but suddenly I heard 'Tap, rap a tap tap—Tap, rap a tap tap!' That sounded mighty like trouble to me. I didn't know nothing about Camp Jackson. Nobody ever told me nothing; but there was something in the air dat a nigger can feel. I was looking where Mars George was—right up the street, top of the hill, when I saw some bright spots just on the skyline. They kinder blinked at us. Tap, rap a tap, they said to us, as though I could understand them, which I didn't. Then the spots got longer, and rose higher. Lord a mercy! them was bayonets. That meant soldiers; and soldiers meant war. Nobody never told me nothing, but I had heard mighty loud whisperings; and was that what they said. Up and up rose the bayonets, and then I saw the guns and the heads of men. They bobbed up and down—kinder wobbly as though they wasn't used to it yet. On they came at last—four abreast, over the top of the hill, looking mighty serious like, as though they was going to fight. I had seen parades; but nothing like that. Down they came on us; and Mars George he never moved a step. Then I saw that some had guns and others did not. Two in the center was without guns; and those on the outside had guns, and wore something like uniform. That was it, was it? Prisoners! Lord, that war must be on right now, and where did this nigger come in? On they came, and then come the surprise. Right there in the front among the prisoners was Mars LeRoy, Mars George's brother. Sure enough that was he—our side had lost. Tap, rap a tap—they moved mighty steady and solemn-like seemed to me; and just as they came up to where we were, Mars LeRoy he sorter moved to our side, as though he wanted to say a word to his brother. 'Git into line thar,' says a rough voice to him. That sure was a Dutchman. I don't know any of them; but I heard of them in these whisperings going round. Well, Mars LeRoy, he lose no time stepping back; that procession goes right on down the street. Tap, rap a tap, goes right on, sounding more and more far away, as the long column swings after them. When the last man had passed, the sun was just sinking over the western line —seemed that it was all over. Things felt mighty solemn, as though the universe might bust anywhere. Mars George, he looks white as a sheet; sure something awful had happened. Guess it did. I don't know nothing about Camp Jackson or war; but something in my bones says to me that Mars George had lost, and that I had won. I never can forget Camp Jackson."

THE FINISH

To get back to my boarding school after my first vacation in the country. I must not give the idea that any one was unkind to me. That would not be true. I got as good as there was; and the head of the school and his family helped me where they could. But the contrast in fare was marked—to a hungry boy almost cruel. The garret room was very different from the cheerful room in the country, although better than camp in Mexico. The pool of water below our one window was just as dirty as I had left it; and to judge by the conduct of the mosquitoes, they had made the best of their time. Besides, they could always draw reinforcements from the many pools and lagoons between us and the river only a few squares away. After my return from the country the weather would still be hot, and since bed clothes seemed to be about the same, winter and summer, the boys sometimes sought refuge at night in the open space below, where we had swings and bars and like contrivances. The instruction must have been fairly good. My chief teacher was a young man—young enough to cherish some of the ideals that prompted him to choose his profession. He lived in the school house and befriended me outside of the class room, in a way most helpful to me. Among other things, he had me use my pencil copying famous pictures, from which I have derived great pleasure since then, for myself rather than for others. But one problem in my relation to the other boys had still to be settled. I was an alien; and in one way or another, I had to give an account of myself and claim my place. That is the herd instinct. I had not long to wait. My ridiculous outfit had of course caused many a jeer. I took that with disarming meekness. After all, it was not of my making. Disappointed in this, the boys came to taunts more personal. They called me a barbarian from the wilds of Texas. That was too much. So I up and told them that my old home was the most civilized place I had ever been in, and that it had a higher percentage of educated persons than the people among whom I now lived. The issue was drawn, and the only question was when I would get my first licking. Again I did not have to wait long. Of course, I was a lonely boy. Father I saw about once a week, and real companions I had none at school. So I would wander off in the evenings, particularly to Union Park where people were merry; and where I could be cheered or depressed as a looker-on. While there one evening, looking at the moon far away in my dreams, as though I saw her in the skies of Texas, I was struck by a boy who had come up behind me. They told me that he had used iron knuckles slipped on his hands; and when people speak of "making the sparks fly," I always know what they mean. I bled freely, of course; but my feelings were hurt even more. It was not only unjust—it was mean. I nursed my grievance for some time, and somehow have never been able to feel that there is not some virtue in revenge. Certainly at that time the idea of holding the other cheek did not appeal to me. I was out for satisfaction, and by degrees the other boys in the school came to feel that I meant business. I was such a tall, thin object that they had never credited me with such a purpose. So they asked me to a council and told me that if I wanted to fight they would tell me who the boy was and how I could come up with him. This was nuts for me, and so I was posted. The boy had to come every other day in the afternoon to the bakery across the street. I chose my post and kept watch with the regularity of a light-house keeper. My conduct won friends, and before long the offender was pointed out to me. Do not tell me that there is nothing in being right. At first sight of me that boy took to his heels—guilty conscience, of course! He had never seen me run or he would have met the case where he stood. It serves no purpose to give the details of a boy's fight. Not content with the cuffs to which he offered little resistance, he made the mistake of following me back to the school house. This cost him a few whacks with a well saturated scrub broom, which an otherwise thrifty "hausfrau" had left on the sidewalk. The incident was important to me because it was the occasion of my first applause in Missouri, to which I have never yet become indifferent. I was admitted as a full fledged comrade, and never again had to fight at that school. Even the girls did not giggle at me any more; and they are the cause of the worst humiliations and fights and sometimes triumphs.

But there were moments of sweeter triumph. During the war St. Louis had the great Mississippi Valley Sanitary Fair. Mr. Yeatman was, I think, the prime mover in this charitable undertaking. Certain days were set apart for particular schools, and our day had come. All of us, big and little, had formed in regular line to march several miles. We had a band. Heavens and earth! how those brass horns could make the air shiver; and glory to me, I was to carry the United States flag. Perhaps that is the first time I heard "John Brown's Body." We know not the reason why; but way down deep a boy feels for the cause for which his parents have made the great sacrifice. Perhaps it was not fair, for my bed fellow was the only child of a widowed father who served as a private in the Union army, and who afterwards fell in a last skirmish fought after Grant and Lee had agreed upon terms of surrender. No, it was not fair; but an eager boy asks no such questions. Probably I did not think of them then. Weak as I was, I would have died rather than not carry that flag. What was the Fair to me, when I was guarding the Stars and Stripes? I remember the march through the streets there and back, the tooting of the brass band; my only care was to hold the banner aloft and to make sure that it was kept floating in the breeze. Of the Fair I have only a vague picture of hundreds of marvelous things—with the old woman in the shoe, as big as a house—ruling supreme over the whole show. I was now quite at home with teachers and pupils, getting as good as there was of comradeship and lessons and fare. But in another way my position had been greatly improved from the earlier experience before vacation. Every Friday evening I was expected at my friend's city home on Olive Street to remain until Sunday evening. I do not think I ever missed a day. Six meals there were, a good preparation for the following week, and the family's kindness was after all very different from what I could find at boarding school. Beyond that, I saw something of city life as it was then known. I went to church "religiously" for three years—my first experience. The church was Presbyterian, and the clergyman was well known for his learning and his literal belief in hell and all its accompaniments. The plunge was altogether too sudden for one who had known only mother's teachings. I attended, of course, largely out of respect for my friends. The sermons were so extreme, however, that I was in no danger of being convinced. Nevertheless, the constant threat of fire and brimstone was not without effect and added to my otherwise rather elaborate list of nightmares. I attended as long as decent consideration required even after I did not go to the home so regularly; but then followed the usual experience with such extreme doctrine, and for years I did not go to any church at all. Since then the way of persuasion has been somewhat devious. The first barriers were removed by the Unitarian Church. A natural impulse was encouraged by the Ethical movement; and now feels at home in the Episcopal Church. The fact is that my earliest church experience was so repugnant to my feeling, that I now fail to see why one can not worship wherever his brother worships. I can hear today a marvelous voice in the synagogue in Prag, holy it seemed to me. Some years ago I thought a service in Westminster Abbey beautiful beyond words. I could not forget the mere sight of Cardinal Gibbons[a] in the Washington Cathedral, nor his finished speech on meeting him. Phillips Brooks' sermon on the meaning of Christ will leave its impress as long as memory lasts. Eucken I never met; but I have read some things which he wrote. Some Englishman has said, "What is your religion?" "The religion of all simple men." "And what is that?" "Sensible men never say!" It is not necessary to accept this literally to believe that a little more tolerance and flexibility would help many churches of today.

But my new outlook was not confined to the religious field. Phil had his associates, and it is not necessary to say more than that some of them were rather colorful. Somehow I was accepted as his loyal companion—seeing a good many escapades, and participating in none. Pool was a favorite game even among such youngsters. I saw them play often, and sometimes saw them imbibe; but by common acceptance I was counted out in both. Perhaps admitted lack of money was excuse enough. Besides, there was some wisdom in always having at least one reliable friend to lean on, a protection which was not necessarily monopolized by my host. I mean this literally, in remembrance of one evening's effort to steer one of these companions home. I had not noticed that he had gone too far. When we came out, however, the weather had turned cold, and the pavement was as slick as a skating rink, although not quite

---

a   James Gibbons (July 23, 1834 – March 24, 1921) was an American Cardinal of the Roman Catholic Church.

so smooth. I was promptly disabused of any doubt about my charge's state of mind. He took just one sniff of the frosty air, and let out a war whoop that would have brought an Indian camp to its feet. Fortunately, police were even more scarce than they are now, and we were able to pursue our exercises without hindrance. My charge told me that he was a first rate skater; in fact could skate anything on land or sea. Unhappily, he was not a mere boaster, for he at once proceeded to give proof of his accomplishments. He would not have hurt my feelings for the world, but he never knew to what trials he put me; and I never suspected how much he weighed until I had for the fifth or sixth time brought him to his feet. Our progress was slow and laborious, although I succeeded in keeping the general trend in the right direction. Between desperate objection to walking when skating was so easy, more war whoops to summon the dispersed clans of the pool room, gentle remonstrances on my part, followed by pledges of eternal devotion to me, we finally reached a city market house. This offered good shelter, and so we met up with a policeman. My charge was arrested. What better means of reaching a station with a warm stove. I did not then suspect that I was marked for the law—perhaps I was not—but I never made a better plea for the right of self-determination in my life. The officer admitted that I was sober; that my companion was safe in my hands, and that home was the best place for him, and would be for some time. So we were sent on our way, under promise that war whoops were to be cut out. That is the only promise he kept that night, until we were out of ear shot. We still had three squares to go, which we covered skating on one foot, and stumbling on the other. By the time we reached his home the ground was covered with snow. He sat down on the stone steps and told me that when he was "not feeling well" he always took off his boots outside; perhaps out of regard for his family's susceptibility to foreign noises. Argument was wasted. Off came the boots, with the request that I carry them while he navigated the dangerous territory. We were about to start on our venture, when in a startled voice he told me that he had nearly forgotten a most important thing. It was this. When he was "not feeling well" he always wound his watch before going into the house. I never argued—the point was to get done what had to be done as soon as possible. There may have been stem-winders in those days, but not to my knowledge. He fumbled in his vest pocket and found the key. My offer to assist in handling this minute treasure was rejected as a reflection upon his mental status; and after one or two struggles to adjust the key to the watch, it fell into the snow on the steps. He said that this was too bad, because he really would like to go to bed, but could not enter the house before the watch was wound. I found that key— necessity knows no law— and the watch was wound. The latch key was not regarded as sacred, and I was permitted to handle it. With a pair of boots in my left hand, and giving what strength I had in my right to aid him in his ambitious efforts to skate up the staircase, we landed in his room at last. There were no more war whoops, the silence was ominous, the submission absolute. My task was done, I retired, and I never afterwards heard a reference to the episode from any source. Now this was really not as bad as it may sound. It served, however, to show how foreign my new environment was to my old one; for many things came within the range of my vision. If I ask myself what guarded me, I can only say that it was not fear of father, but rather, as I have said, mother's influence; and perhaps, to be frank, the often hopelessly crude conception of pleasure.

But my experiences had a wide range, and in some

respects they were quite irreconcilable. During the first Christmas week in 1864 I sold toys on a sidewalk on South Broadway. I think if mother had been there I might have been prevented. But father was so glad to extend a helping hand to a friendly merchant who was pushed for help that he asked me to do it. It was cold and I can not think that my aid came to much. But our will was good; and the South Broadway merchant must have felt this, for soon thereafter he absconded without taking along any of father's new savings, which he might just as well have done.

My time with my great friends was coming to an end. This was true at least of the very absorbing part which they had in those few years of my life. Some time in 1865, after mother had come, my position was entirely changed, and in the meantime there was not much to tell beyond the routine of a protected life which a boy enjoys under such conditions. I do recall the day Lincoln was assassinated, when I happened to be at the home of my friends. It was again Carter who told me, and his look and voice made me feel that lucky was the man who had a flag to hang out. It was no day for trifling or for jest. Out went the Stars and Stripes from the second story window of the home, and although my old friend had no doubt been a Southern sympathizer, his looks and words left no question about his regret for reasons of both sympathy and wisdom. That day Phil and I went down town as boys would, and I saw for the first time an American crowd in all its power and self-restraint. Up and down the streets the people moved in dense masses—just one steady stream always at the same measure—not a loud word and nowhere a light note —sorrow and decision strangely mingled. This, I think, is characteristic of our people still. Some years ago, early in the Great War, a much traveled foreigner coming with me out of a circus, remarked that he was always impressed by the well ordered and even good-natured conduct of an American crowd. This time there was just one rude interruption. At Fourth and Morgan Streets a powerful man came down the stairs, and on his gray felt hat was a "C.S.A." metal star[a]. He did not more than reach the pavement when he was so to speak "devoured" by the mass of people. What became of him I never knew. He was simply gone — perhaps to be rushed away to save him from his foolhardy act. That would have been in keeping with the sober mood of that crowd. With that exception I saw no sign of violence — men, women and children just moved as though they were in line to join the great National funeral of their beloved leader.

When the war was over, I remember the return of our friend from Mexico to his old home. Smart and upstanding without suggestion of the past. I had been repaid — many times — for father's aid to him. About that time father, true to the feeling that had always been his, took me aside and gave me advice by which I have tried to live my life. "My son," he said, "the war is over. We have suffered, but you must remember that the Southern people thought they were right; that they fought a brave fight and were defeated. I ask you never to let hate enter your heart. If there must be hatred, there will be plenty of people to supply it." Never in his life did he say anything that had a more profound influence on me. How seriously he meant it he proved by joining the Liberal Republicans in Missouri to restore the suffrage to disfranchised Southerners, and by voting for both Tilden and Cleveland for president. The impression upon me is shown by the fact that I, too, joined the Liberal Republican movement, and through many years of campaigning never would discuss the war issue;

---

a Confederate badge

but insisted that no descendant of an ex-Confederate would be moved to become a Republican by criticism or abuse of his ancestor.

From then on I was to see less and less of these good friends. My last visit to the country home was made years later, after I had graduated at Law School. The old gentleman was ill, and I called to inquire. They said he was sinking and I must remain. His family was called in for a final blessing, and then he missed me. True to his custom he treated me as one of his; and put his final seal upon the many evidences of his kindness. The very last day I was called in to prepare his will, which I did, writing at his bedside, formulating as best I could his wishes. I had many misgivings, particularly about the form of unessential things. But the regular adviser was sent for, and much to my relief, approved of what had been done. He died the next day, and as he was carried out there was one mourner who had reason to remember what this man had been to him.

To return to the early days of 1865. The old boarding school life went on with little change. By degrees I came into my own. The teachers were thoughtful and helpful; and to the pupils my appearance offered less provocation for merriment. Besides, there had been a time of great anxiety, which seemed to unite us all in common concern.

General Price[a] was moving up from the south and the question was whether St. Louis was to be snatched from

a   Sterling Price (September 14, 1809 – September 29, 1867) was a soldier, lawyer, planter, and politician from the U.S. state of Missouri, who served as the 11th Governor of the state from 1853 to 1857. He also served as a United States Army brigadier general during the Mexican-American War, and a Confederate Army major general in the American Civil War.

the Union. From the day of our start from home, luck had attended our movements, and although I listened to the accounts of his progress, and in a way shared the fears, the feeling of fatalistic confidence never left me. In the evening I would go to the Soulard Market[a] to watch the "Home Guards"[b] drill, my father among them. They were all very serious, but neither then nor since then have I associated "Home Guard" with much danger to a regular enemy. Happily the danger passed. Price was turned back before he had to meet the "Home Guards," and we settled back into the old routine.

I have had some good friends dear enough to become part of my very life. There was never one more warmhearted in his friendship than Phil. He might have resented my frequent appearance in response to his father's invitation, but, on the contrary, he welcomed it, always to make me feel easy in his company. With some satisfaction I look back upon the time when in the same trusting way he appealed to me in the hour of his need, and I was in a position to meet his wishes. So fate would have it that his advice marked in a fashion a turning point in my boyhood life. We were walking down the street one Sunday after-

a The Soulard Farmer's Market still exists today and is the oldest west of the Missouri. The Soulard district of St. Louis is named after Antoine Soulard, who first began to develop the land. Soulard was a surveyor for the Spanish government and a refugee from the French Revolution in the 1790s. Ed.

b In the American Civil War the Home Guard or Home Guards were local militia raised from Union loyalists. In Missouri after the start of the Civil War there were several competing organizations attempting to either take the state out of the Union or keep the state within it. Home Guard companies and regiments were raised by Union supporters, particularly German-Americans to oppose the secessionist paramilitary Minutemen, secessionist elements in the official Missouri Volunteer Militia and eventually the secessionist Missouri State Guard.

noon with no object in mind, so far as I could see when he stopped before the old Central High School, on Olive and Fifteenth Streets, and without more said "That is where you ought to go. I go there. I hate it, but you would like it." I was willing to admit Phil's dislike for any school—he was a born machinist; to him the ordinary school was a hindrance, it gave him nothing but boredom. His enthusiasm for me, however, surprised me and I have sometimes wondered how much of it was suggested. The real interest of his people in me could not be doubted. His conservative father would be reluctant to suggest; but his mother, and also his married sister, would not stop at such barriers of mere convention. They were very religious, and to them that "Dutch" school of mine must have seemed like a besetting menace for helpless youth. However that may be, Phil's advice was very persuasive—his teachers he said were fine, and the boys and girls were great. That was enough for me. I lost no time. That evening I went to see father and laid the case before him. He was easily convinced—had never heard of so fine a school, which both of us took on the say-so of Phil, who frankly hated it.

It was on a Monday morning early in 1865 before mother had arrived, indeed before we knew of her coming, that father and I presented ourselves at this school. It was cold, and in all essentials we still appeared in our pioneer attire —that sort of clothes wore well. It is true father was getting along, but it was slow work. He had rent and school to pay, and he was saving as best he could, and had in mind better quarters in the hope that mother would soon be able to join us. On the first floor of the High School we met a young girl, no doubt a pupil. She must have been a lady, for she almost suppressed a smile, and in the nicest way directed us to the room of the principal on the next floor. We went up not without misgivings, approaching awe. The principal's desk was in the room of the senior girls. Their desks faced the entrance; and as we came in the customary response was instantaneous. I shall not attempt to repeat a scene to which I at least was not new. They were nice girls—some of them I met often in later years, when we were all graduates of the High School. But nice as they were, all human nature is akin, and the effect of our unheralded apparition was not unlike the first stampede in the boarding school. With the principal it was different. He was tall and slight—wearing a black cutaway, I think, which helped me to feel at home. I had one, too; mine was brown. His hair and beard were dark and wavy, setting off features as regular as a Greek's. A kindly smile played about his lips as he took my hand. The mission was soon told in father's broken English. There was ground for hesitancy. We applied in the middle of the year, which was against the rules; besides admission was conditioned upon regular examination. I could not meet a single one of the rules. But we were in America, and we were fortunate enough to strike a respecter of the reason of the rule. He gave me a piece of chalk and sent me to the blackboard. Father's condition in his quilt overcoat must have been akin to the effects of a Turkish bath. But I had no thought of him. I was on trial to get into the school Phil had told me about. The principal asked questions, and to the tune of unmistakable suppressed laughter, I gave undeniable evidence on that blackboard of my unpreparedness. But the principal was a man of resource. He saw one cause of my trouble, and turned to German. That was my salvation. I could write German to have me bless my stars that no lithographer ever captured me as an apprentice with the prospect of designing visiting cards for life. "Well," said he, "about some things you know nothing; about others you know more than half the junior class, and since you are a refugee, I will give you a chance." In that fashion I was admitted. As we left he said to me that I must come to his house in the evening, so that he might show me how to catch up and use my books. How "American" it all seemed to me; and how "American" it was judged by the modern rule ridden methods. I did go to his house quite often, only to be taken aside for a moment's questioning, and to be sent in to his family to join in their games — kind and gentle way to overcome my shyness. In that fashion he kept his eye on me to the end. Now and then he would appear unannounced before the lower classes to try them out. One day he asked a question of our class, which was met with common silence. With that well known twinkle of his eyes looking at me he said "I know one boy who can answer my question"; I did — and I never knew whether I was more grateful for his generous help or for the rare luck that carried me through. But the luck of a refugee did not stop there. At the end of the school year we had the usual examinations. I made them all but one. Grammar was and is a mystery to me. I never knew why natural speech should be complicated by so many conflicting rules; to me they always seem like obstacles to free expression of thoughts. I read the paper of questions; and certain that I must fail, I took it to the teacher's desk and said that I could not answer a single question. "I know you can not," he said, "and we will not say anything about it." He never did, and I did not for fifty years; but at the time I thought how wonderfully "American" it all was. Since then I have hesitated to mention this experience. Graf Luckner[a] at one time told me that he had lost popularity

a I imagine that the reference here is to Felix Graf von Luckner (9 June 1881–13 April 1966), sometimes called in English Count Luckner, was a German nobleman, naval officer, author, and sailor who earned the epithet *Der Seeteufel* (the Sea-Devil), and his crew that of *Die Piraten des Kaisers* (the Emperor's Pirates), for his exploits in command of the sailing commerce raider SMS Seeadler (Sea Eagle) between 1916 and 1917. It was Luckner's habit of successfully wag-

with German mothers who insisted that their boys relied upon him as proof that to achieve success it is not necessary to attend school. Upon this subject I have no illusions. Whatever might have been true of particular things taught I would not have missed the general influence of that school—the association with members of my class, and with the faculty who counted among them not only the principal, Mr. Childs, but his assistant, Horace H. Morgan; Davidson, a Greek scholar known in this country and abroad; Miss Schaefer, afterwards principal of Wellesley College; Denton J. Snider, etc.

I was admitted to the second class, and showing some signs of progress, I was urged by my classmates to try for first place. This was done less because of interest in me than a desire to defeat an unpopular member. I made the attempt. Three times I paired him in the examinations; and then I went down with typhoid fever. I had just finished a dime novel—all about a "white lady," and knowing her safe in the care of her hero somewhere in Mexico, I turned in and spent a good many weeks rescuing her over and over again from Indians and bandits and what not—everything that my imagination had ever conjured up by way of trial and peril. Two of us had contracted the fever and the principal came to see us. My classmate died, and the principal contracted the disease. He came back to school too soon. The last time I saw him was one bitter morning when the school building was on fire. There he stood, without an overcoat, fighting the flames with the water turning to ice on his clothes. He won that fight, but had a relapse, and we never saw him again.

ing war without casualties which made him a hero and a legend on both sides. Ed.

I was walking out of my boyhood days. I was at the High School about two and one half years. During the last two I laid the foundation for my independence by collecting father's bills on a commission. His highest charges were one dollar and a half for visits and one dollar for an office consultation. But father graded his charges according to conditions always insisting that some charge, however small, helped to preserve the self-respect of most people, so that items and sometimes bills for fifty cents and even twenty-five cents were not unusual. My commission was ten per cent. To prove that father's practice was large I need only add that from that time on (barring board at home) I paid my way, including law school and later six months at the University of Berlin. Father's district was bounded by the river on the east, say Twentieth Street on the west, Morgan Street on the south and Mullanphy Street on the north, and was inhabited by people who were either poor or of small means. I felt that I knew many of the people and most of the dogs, and having the Germanic trend to philosophize I concluded that they represented about the same diversity of character. Dogs were good or bad just as they had been in Texas although here some were smaller and others larger. Some of the people were also mean enough to waste much of my time. One of them kept me at bay for a long time by pretending that they had a case of small pox in the house, and it never occurred to me that even small pox must end one way or the other. But most of them were kind and self-respecting. I remember the cleanly scrubbed floors, and father speaking of the endless kindness and help shown by different families to each other. To that time I owe my first sympathy and understanding for people who have to struggle for existence. But I must bring my story to an end, although the temptation to record the continued kindness of others is not easily resisted. Again I was asked to carry the flag. Our school gave a play to raise a fund to lay the foundation for a Public Library. The play turned upon the Civil War. I felt sorry for the girls who took the parts of the Southern states — the prescribed declarations did not seem to come natural to them. I adored the girl who represented the Union—the very one that had almost fallen off the front seat when father and I first invaded the senior room. How the spokesman of war did make the windows rattle; and how gentle and quiet he really was. How the company could drill and march under the severe discipline of a classmate who had always made a joke of everything serious. But however interesting it all was, it seemed as nothing compared to the fact that I was again bearing the Stars and Stripes every night for a whole week in a large hall packed to the guards. I was not even dismissed when the first night, marching across the stage, I hooked the gas chandelier, all ablaze, with my flagstaff, and came near precipitating the stampede of an admiring audience. The refugee boy had his day—errors were overlooked, credits were marked large. The rest of these school days belong to another period. "That is another story." Our class was a chivalrous one—natural champions of the girls. I had my one big fight to resent a careless remark about a girl classmate, and to take my place in the esteem of my class. I wrestled with the studies—wondering now what trigonometry and calculus could possibly have meant.

We had German, a little Latin and French. Two of us (the other, Fischel, who afterwards became a distinguished physician, and my dearest friend for life) even sent a whole school into hysterics by our performance—in French—of the duel scene in Moliere's "Tartuffe."[a] My

a Tartuffe, or The Impostor, or The Hypocrite French: Tartuffe, ou l'Imposteur, first performed in 1664, is one of the most famous

Fig. 25: Tartuffe

friend never commented on my French, but in dueling he thought me rather realistic. Declaiming was at its height then. We still took patriotic speeches very seriously. I had some advantage in that I could saw the air more promiscuously with my long arms than my less favored classmates. Willis' "Prometheus" was my specialty; and after I had for the first time gone through the suffering tortures of that recitation, my classmates held out great hopes for my

> theatrical comedies by Molière. The characters of Tartuffe, Elmire, and Orgon are considered among the greatest classical theatre roles.

future. I have since then been at great pains in public speaking to keep my arms and hands from interfering with what I am trying to say. Salvini in Othello's address to the Senate confirmed my growing convictions upon that subject. Otherwise, all moved along in a beaten track of common harmony. I made many friends, chiefly in my class, and have much to remember in gratitude. How much they gave me in just accepting me as one of them! I was made quite unconscious of my German ancestry. "Dutch" had been eliminated from my life. Not even the Great War revived it. When and how I came to substitute "Charles" for "Karl" I can not now say. Certainly the motive was not to become Americanized in the modern fashion, for I have stood at all times for the integrity of my family name—in both spelling and pronunciation. I learnt to regard with equal contempt, submission to criticism of German ancestry and any effort to capitalize it for any advantages, and this had continued to be my rule of conduct. My escape from grammar was rewarded by my selection as valedictorian by my classmates. My subject was "True Manhood." I held forth to an audience that was not entirely new to the ordeal. Teachers were as relieved as I was at having me recite my piece without a breakdown. In that audience sat father and mother—united once more— grief not forgotten, but happiness undenied; and with that the Texas refugee boy walked off the stage.

APPENDIX

1935

I.

With this the excuse for writing about myself seemed exhausted. But the few persons who have read the story are not content to let it rest there. The account of a mere boy does not seem to justify itself. In a practical age like ours the real question is what became of him. Was all the care and indulgence shown him wasted after all; and, if not, how did he meet problems when they were left to his own decision. Accepting this challenge as further excuse, I shall try in brief outline to give my approach to the challenge of early manhood.

I was nearly nineteen years of age—perhaps the oldest member of the graduating class. A zigzag course consumes time. Although old enough to be drafted for the army, I had not given a thought to a decision for the future. The commissions earned by the collection of father's bills met incidental expenses, and would probably continue to do so. The protection of the home was accepted as a matter of course. After all, to graduate from the High School seemed achievement enough for the moment; and having done this, fate might be trusted to make fitting disposition. It never came to me until later that I may have suspected myself of having an education; and not then until I had a chance to observe the attitude of graduates of more advanced institutions.

However, I was saved from an all too sudden disillusion.

It was decided to send me abroad for a brief visit—first proof of fate's kindly intervention. The original plan to have me attend German schools had been wrecked by the Civil War. Grandmother, whom it had been Father's hope to have me see, had died in the meantime. But the old sentiment persisted; and while savings were still very modest, there was a certain fund of six hundred dollars which father and mother decided to devote to so dear a purpose. In the early days Father had sent his mother that amount to dispel her fears of the hopeless fate of her dear ones in Texas. She had fallen a willing victim to proof so overwhelmingly convincing. When she died her meagre estate was given to Uncle Wilhelm to insure his comfort, with one reservation. The principal of the historic fund was returned to Father. It proved to be a rare exception to his other early investments, and was now used to carry out a long treasured plan, perhaps not without the hope that some youthful misconceptions about education and general preparation for life might suffer some modification.

The plan was to have me make the trip alone; but once more chance came to the rescue. At school I had found a friend—Washington E. Fischel[a]—who became the most constant friend of my life. We had been in different divisions, he taking Latin and I German—to me the easier course. Our friendship had started during the last year or two. But as soon as he heard of my plan, he not only approved, but at once enlarged upon it. Enthusiasm for a just cause was the key to his life; and what cause could have more human appeal than to have him go with me and then remain to begin the study of medicine. I was a lit-

---

[a] Washington Emil Fischel 1850-1914. Cf. "In memory of Dr. Washington E. Fischel" by Shapleigh, John Blasdel, 1857-;Washington University (Saint Louis, Mo.). School of Medicine.

tle taken aback, because his earliest ambition had been to be a drummer in the Federal army; and when the end of the war closed that door, he had shown some disposition to become a butcher. It seemed to me that he should at least show a preference for surgery. But in the course of a few days he decided for medicine, and that Germany was the one place to prepare for his career. So everything was set, with the exception that my friend had no money. There was no doubt the memory of a grandmother, but there was no fund associated with it. His family lived in very moderate circumstances, and could not help him. But he had two married sisters temporarily abroad, whose response was prompt. He now had three times as much money as I had; his whole scheme was underwritten, and we were off.

An old lady from the East had visited some of his friends — remote relatives, and she was entrusted to our care. Chivalry was our specialty; and she was to be protected. We had not read Don Quixote; but we were no strangers to the impulse. The lady had a berth as far as Indianapolis, and we were charged with securing her accommodation beyond that point. Knowing that competition would be strong we essayed forth — two crusaders for one berth. The excitement was great; an auction for old furniture could not be worse. We won; we got the berth; but I never recovered the watch which Father had given me ten days before, and of which I had been relieved in the melee. The educational process was under way. My friend was highly indignant. Injustice was like a red rag to him; even passengers and attendants on the train were not above suspicion — particularly the porter. However, we arrived in Brooklyn without further mishap, and were received as guests in a hospitable home. We had some difficulty in persuading our hostess that she did not owe me a watch; but to us the excellence of the meals and general kindness provided ample compensation.

When finally my friend emptied the best part of the contents of an inkstand on a highly decorative bed spread, all parties felt that the scores were settled, and we departed to board a North German Lloyd steamer of small proportions for Bremen. The trip was uneventful—fourteen days of sea

Fig. 26: Unfinished cathedral, 1856 with 15th-century crane on south tower.

so smooth that not even the memory of my first voyage could work up real distress. If others suffered discomfort they must have been on the upper deck, from which we as second, if not third cabin passengers, were excluded.

Fig. 27: Bayard Taylor

In Bremen we parted — my friend to join his sisters at Dresden, and I to visit my uncle in Halberstadt. Of my first impression at the sight of Bremen I have spoken earlier. Also of my Uncle Carl's home, and of the walks with Aunt Marie in the Harz. All the folklore and the myths seemed so real, and yet to belong to a world of imagination that had managed to survive in our home. When I read of the Romantic Period of Germany now I do not wonder that so many of the leaders of that school came from a section that offered scenery and story to inspire Goethe and Heine, and our own Bayard Taylor[a].

But we did not come to bask in the sunshine of family kindness, so we arranged for our first tour. Fischel had agreed to take his nephew William, and our start was to be made from Dresden. So far as I was concerned, I got the

a Bayard Taylor (January 11, 1825 – December 19, 1878) was an American poet, literary critic, translator, travel author, and diplomat.

greatest pleasure of the trip before starting. We heard an opera—Huguenots, I think. We saw a play—Ein Glas Wasser[a] charmingly given. We were to learn soon that as a result of the division of Germany into many principalities, most cities, big or small, have concerts, theaters, even opera and museums. Dresden was a relatively large city, essentially residential, with a section known as the English quarter. The museum was and no doubt still is outstanding. To me, untrained and unprepared as I was, it was a revelation. My brief visits there not only aroused my interest, but gave direction to such appreciation of art as I have since then had opportunity to show and to enjoy. The key to the collection seemed to be the more beautiful examples of great artists, such as Raphael, Titian, Correggio, Holbein, etc. I was a convert from that day. It was the most distinct impression that I brought home with me. Before returning, I had collected photographs of every favorite painting and piece of sculpture that I had seen, and many more that I had not seen. They filled two large albums that William T. Harris[b], the Superintendent of our Public Schools and afterwards U.S. Commissioner of Education,

---

a By Eugène Scribe, set in England during the reign of Queen Anne.

b William Torrey Harris (September 10, 1835 – November 5, 1909) was an American educator, philosopher, and lexicographer. He completed two years at Yale, then moved west and taught school in St. Louis, Missouri, from 1857 to 1880, where he was superintendent of schools from 1868 to 1880, and established, with Susan E. Blow, America's first permanent public kindergarten in 1873. As Commissioner of Education, Harris wrote the introduction to then Commissioner of Indian Affairs, Thomas Jefferson Morgan's, Bureau of Education Bulletin (No. 1, 1889) on Indian Education. Harris called for the forced and mandatory education of American Indians through a partnership with Christianity in order to promote industry. It was Harris who called for the removal of Native children from their families for up to 10 years of training for the "lower form of civilization" as opposed to the United States government's policy of exterminating them.

to my delight declared to be the best collection he had seen.

The only time I ever saw that museum again was in 1928, when I visited it with my son and rejoiced to find that my first impression stood unshaken by the growing influence of modernistic art.

From that time on our tour offered little more than the customary sightseeing and tramps, although these were no doubt more novel then than they have since become. The visit in Muenchen was hasty, and I have only a blurred memory of walls of Rubens, with the one exception of Piloty's painting of Seni before Wallenstein. In Nuernberg, a visit to the home of Duerer and the tiny shop of Hans Sachs[a] struck a more intimate note. Even untutored youth might catch inspiration from the story of such men as Duerer, Sachs and Fischer; each great in his particular field, and equally great as leader in the cause of the Reformation. We were of course not spared the "Folterkammer" (the Chamber of Horrors), but perhaps it took the brutalities of later periods to have me believe that such cruelties could have been practiced.

At last we reached the real object of our trip—Switzerland. Here was the time for wonder, for health and for joy. We climbed the Rigi as others did, saw a marvelous sunrise, and marched down again in a drenching rain. We saw Thorwaldsen's famous lion in Lucerne; not without a boastful confidence in American liberty. We rode to Geneva, and by a guide were taken over some glacier, stared at the great Matterhorn; enjoyed the beauty of Interlaken and the view upon the Jungfrau, and in all things

---

a Hans Sachs (5 November 1494–19 January 1576) was a German Meistersinger ("master singer"), poet, playwright, and shoemaker.

did as best we could and as long as our purse held out, what throngs of tourists have done ever since. Youth might catch the spirit and exult; but if more is asked it

Fig. 28: Photograph of Johann Strauss II by Fritz Luckhardt

takes a poet to describe it. The one clear conviction we took with us from Switzerland was that one might meet an Englishman half a dozen times in as many days without the remotest sign of mutual recognition from him. And this in the face of the fact that we, to make an impression, had registered with some remote justification as coming from Missouri, California and Texas.

Whether the Rhine is more beautiful than the Harz may be

doubted; but that it is more symbolic of Germany is certain. To come home without having seen it would have been almost sacrilegious. So we made for the first point where we could take a steamer and, stirred by the eloquence of a "Kellner" at opportune moments, contributed our share of enthusiastic admiration for what was pointed out to us. No doubt the natural scenery was the more significant; but as true sons of a new freedom, our eyes were riveted upon the impressive examples of man's creation — silent evidence of a past, both glorious and ignored. There was the diminutive Maeusethurm suggesting an invasion by a horde of mice; and Ehrenbreitstein with its note of military tradition. The Koelner Dom[a] was still unfinished, and of course we had to climb up to see the men who were engaged in building one of the spires. One of them was glad at last to meet real Americans; he had a brother over there, and he asked us to deliver a letter to him — somewhere in South America.

Our party broke up at Bonn. We had our first impression of disfigured student faces — enough to disperse any party of "Innocents Abroad." Having found our way to one of those delightful inns so common in Germany, my friend and his nephew insisted that their spirits could be revived by nothing less than beefsteak. As treasurer, I reminded them of the low state of our exchequer. My pangs were at least suggestive of the feelings of a staunch defender of constitutional government at the sight of a modern federal budget. But they were obdurate; and I yielded upon condition that we dispel our doubts about the meal with a bottle of superior wine and that they give me a hearing upon the state of our finances in the morning. That agony over, we

a   Cologne Catherdral construction commenced in 1248 and was halted in 1473, leaving it unfinished. Work restarted in the 19th century and was completed, to the original plan, in 1880.

celebrated in the best dinner of our trip, and awaited the revelations of another day. The result was the usual one.

Fig. 29: Thousands of gravestones are crammed into the Old Jewish Cemetery in Prague.

Something had to be done—the sooner the better. With more of an eye to actual conditions than is customary with modern commissions and committees—international or domestic—we reached a prompt decision, both drastic and effective. We bought a ticket to Dresden, and giving the nephew small change for at least one meal on the way, put him on the train. When we last saw him he was waving a fond farewell to us; his gesture was unduly emphasized

Fig. 30: The Old New Synagogue in Prague

by a sudden gust of wind that sent his hat sailing into the air as a last proof of undying enthusiasm.

However, my friend and I had cares of our own. We got as far as Hanover, from which point we could make Halberstadt in one night. Here we bought our third class tickets first, spent most of the balance on one meal between us, visited the then famous Tivoli Garden in the evening, and boarded the train for one of the most uncomfortable nights of my experience. The Leipziger Messe was on; and the mixture of travelers in that direction was equalled only by the variety of tobaccos they smoked. We reached our destination about five o'clock the next morning, recuperated as best we could by sleeping on chairs until seven; and then, having not a penny left, walked a mile or two to my uncle's home. My Aunt Marie was a sympathetic soul; very religious and highly musical. We must have been a forlorn looking pair. There was none of the glow of mountain air. Our straggling hair, the unrestrained growth of which we had regarded as a fitting imitation of student custom, was no doubt accepted by my dear aunt as final proof of the deprivations we had suffered. During our walks in the Harz many weeks back, she had tried to persuade me that the ministry was my call. After seeing me that morning she never referred to the subject again. My appearance must have been more persuasive than my arguments. Her sympathy was the greater. We were treated like princes who had found unexpected shelter. After a few days my friend returned to Dresden, and I remained as a member of my uncle's family. Uncle Carl's conversation was a happy mixture of philosophy and humor. He never preached. He talked like an unconscious teacher—tolerant always, and never flippant. He was over ninety years of age when he died. Feeling unwell after a bicycle ride, he called his two doctor sons and asked for a report on pulse and respiration. Having heard it, he simply said "that pace is too fast for me," and passed into a sleep from which he never woke. Some days when he was free the whole family would walk out to the Dünen— foothills of the Harz mountains. There we had a bite of something, with coffee or perhaps even beer. It was all very informal; not even music to disturb us. The modern resort to thought-saving devices, was unknown then. As sunset approached we would start on the return walk, watching the coloring of the sky and listening to the chimes of the bells in the Halberstadt Dom. To me it was all like an advanced course of training, not to say education. But one excursion uncle did not permit me to escape. Somewhere in Prussia there is a salt mine. Uncle felt that it would hardly do to let me return without seeing this mine. Upon our arrival we were promptly clad in miner's garb and each was given a miner's oil lamp. The descent was taken by way of a miner's ladder. We were told how simple it was. Two ladders, with rungs twelve feet apart paralleling each other moved in opposite direction, up and down, so many feet each time. All the visitor had to do was to step from one to the other as they stopped for the transfer. I felt in my outfit like a hobbled animal, but managed to make the first few transfers. About the fifth my

Fig. 31: Gardekürassier about 1830

lamp gave a violent gasp (sympathetically I suspect) and went out completely. Awkward enough and now in the dark I hesitated until the ladders moved, leaving me with one foot on each. If there was room enough between the two I was in for a descent of seven hundred feet, as they told me. But I managed to avoid that test by clutching some bar in the dark and letting myself down to the next rung, where I stood until rescued. I got some consolation out of a miner's comment: "If that fellow had not been an American he would be dead"; got a fresh lamp, went down, looked at the work below with pretended interest, and breathed a sigh of relief when I got out again.

That is the only time Uncle Carl turned to anything so drastic for my entertainment; and, indeed, my visit was rapidly coming to an end. Fischel was now in Wien preparing for his start in the study of medicine. He wished me to join him, and I went. We had a delightful week together. The hospitality of his friends seemed to be only a part of the common scheme. One day we went out to the Prader, and there was the great Johann Strauss[a] conducting a concert of his own music. He played his violin as he danced about, apparently unable to resist the rhythm of his own melodies, directing his orchestra with his feet as it were, and making us feel as though not only his great audience in the garden, but all Wien[b] was dancing with him. To watch the inspiration and sympathetic response of an audience one simply had to be in Wien in those days of her glory. I saw it again one night in a theater. The play was a comedy, called, I think "Number 26." The star was evidently sure of her audience which had succumbed long ago in obedience to the general verdict of Wien. They laughed or sighed or sobbed at her every whim. There was one scene of peculiar suspense. The actress was to try on a new shoe, upon the result of which the theme of the play seemed to turn. She treated the moment with the required importance— curiosity, doubt and hesitation were patent. The audience shared the anxiety; but it seemed to me that

---

a Johann Strauss II (October 25, 1825 – June 3, 1899). He composed over 500 waltzes, polkas, quadrilles, and other types of dance music, as well as several operettas and a ballet. In his lifetime, he was known as "The Waltz King", and was largely then responsible for the popularity of the waltz in Vienna during the 19th century.

b Vienna.

Fig. 32: Polish uhlans from the Army of the Duchy of Warsaw 1807–1815 January Suchodolski painting

the craning of necks indicated an interest in something more than a mere settling of an abstract question. Having worked her audience to the very height of expectation, she replaced her chair, turned her back to us, and after a tantalizing struggle, laughingly told us that the shoe was a perfect fit. The response was so prompt and sympathetic that it sounded almost grateful in its appreciation.

But our time was up. Leaving our hotel we were much impressed by the separate charge for candles, and wondered how we could have managed to use so many, for we had certainly not been given to burning candles at both ends. But reflections upon the reputation of Wien were not to be tolerated; certainly not in matters so trifling. Probably we had seen what we wanted to see. If truths that were apparent to others had escaped us we felt no regret. There are times when the microscope does not contribute to happiness, and even helps to give distorted pictures.

Fischel was going to Prag[a] to hear his first lecture in medicine, and I went with him—final proof of youthful comradeship. We visited the old Jewish cemetery[b], where we found the tombstones over the graves of some of his ancestors—some of them distinguished Rabbis, I believe, buried as I recall centuries ago. He was no longer of their religious persuasion; but I never knew a more loyal man. He was frankly proud of his ancestry—and I was deeply impressed with the unmistakable proof of his emotions. As we reached the street he was made to feel the cruelty of time's contrasts by a Jewish gamin[c], who begged of us

a Prague.
b Old Jewish Cemetery is the largest Jewish cemetery in Europe and one of the most important Jewish historical monuments in Prague. It served its purpose from the first half of 15th century till 1786. Renowned personalities of the local Jewish community were buried here; among them rabbi Jehuda Liva ben Becalel - Maharal (ca. 1526–1609), businessman Mordecai Maisel (1528–1601), historian David Gans (ca. 1541–1613) and rabbi David Oppenheim (1664–1736).
c Street urchin.

with all the servility of a cowed being. The next day we went to the synagogue[a] and heard a voice so rare in its power and beauty that it came to us like a message from another world.

He took me with him to hear his first lecture in an amphitheater. I understood nothing; thought of little but my friend, who was entering upon a profession of which he became a distinguished member, and to whom I looked in after years in times of joy and care as friend and as physician. We parted at the door, and in another day I was back in Halberstadt, to look once more upon the sky by night through the spires of the Dom[b], to be taken into the Dom by my aunt's brother Paul Krueger, to hear him play great church music on the organ, and to enjoy his fine baritone in accompaniment. He was a follower of Schopenhauer, which seemed to be reflected more in his general unhappiness than in his lack of appreciation of a good table and wine. I also visited him in Braunschweig, and one Sunday he drove me out to a "Gut" (an estate) which was owned by a noted disciple of the same school of philosophy and said to be Schopenhauer's dear friend. It was a special occasion, the philosopher's birthday, I think. There were some thirty guests, among them I the only black sheep. My observation, that what is commonly regarded as pessimism, presents no obstacle to the enjoyment of good food and fine wines, was fully confirmed. The courses were elaborate and excellent, quite beyond

a The Old New Synagogue or Altneuschul (Czech: Staronová synagoga; German: Altneu-Synagoge) situated in Josefov, Prague, is Europe's oldest active synagogue. It is also the oldest surviving medieval synagogue of twin-nave design. Completed in 1270 in gothic style, it was one of Prague's first gothic buildings. A still older Prague synagogue, known as the Old Synagogue, was demolished in 1867 and replaced by the Spanish Synagogue.
b Cathedral.

anything I had seen or tasted. The wines were superb, and the cheerful animation of the guests left nothing to be desired. Finally the host brought out a "pokal[a]," which he had once presented to the philosopher and which had been returned to the giver, I was told, as the only fit recipient of so cherished an object. I gathered that the founder of the school had not been indifferent to the good things of this world. The "pokal" was filled with the contents of several bottles especially reserved for the occasion. It was passed down the line of guests as they were seated at the table; each to take a sip or draft as taste might incline. For the first time I knew what aroma meant, for taste was hardly needed to confirm the quality of the wine. As a result I at least read some of Schopenhauer's works, generally preferring his shorter productions, and always admiring in these his wonderfully clear and beautiful style.

I returned to Halberstadt only to say goodbye. Of course I had visited Pritzwalk — the old family home, but of that I have spoken earlier. Perhaps I may add now that during that visit I had followed a sham battle on a large scale from early morn till late at night. Prince Friedrich Carl[b] commanded the losing side. There I saw a charge by a Kürassier regiment[c] coming out of a wooded hill and

a   Cup such as given as a prize..
b   Prince Friedrich Carl Nicolaus of Prussia (20 March 1828 – 15 June 1885) was the son of Prince Charles of Prussia (1801–1883) and his wife, Princess Marie of Saxe-Weimar-Eisenach (1808–1877). Prince Frederick Charles was a grandson of King Frederick William III of Prussia and a nephew of Frederick William IV and William I. He was born at Schloss Klein in Berlin.
c   The Guards Cuirassiers German: Garde-Kürassier-Regiment) were a heavy cavalry regiment of the Royal Prussian Army. Formed in 1815 as a Uhlans regiment, it was reorganized as a cuirassiers unit in 1821. The regiment was part of the Guards Cavalry Division and fought in the Second Schleswig War, the Austro-Prussian War, the Franco-Prussian War and World War I. The regiment was dis-

pouring down upon retreating infantry with the rising sun upon their metal armor that made me think of powers of another world. The feigned attacks of the hussars, the steady stand of the Dragoners[a] and the easy strength of the Uhlans[b] was all very absorbing—so much so that once I discovered a haystack just in time to escape the consequence of an unexpected right wheel of charging cavalry.

Our parting was had at a family dinner. Even my aunt's parents were there. I had visited them, and recall their home with its old furniture and well selected engravings as the most carefully kept house I had ever seen. There was also my aunt's sister—widow of an English clergyman, and her very attractive daughter Martha, whom I had heard sing the Lorelei in the Harz mountains. Perhaps it was this influence that made it possible for my aunt, way off there in a comparatively small place to assemble enough young people to take the parts of one of Shakespeare's plays, and to have it read aloud in the original. Wine was rarely served in my uncle's home, but this time the tradition was observed. My uncle raised his glass, and all standing they drank a fond farewell and Godspeed to their first relative visitor from America.

The next morning I was on the train for Bremen, absorbed less this time by the landscape with its villages, farms and

banded in September 1919.
a The word dragoon originally meant mounted infantry, who were trained in horse riding as well as infantry fighting skills. However, usage altered over time and during the 18th century, dragoons evolved into conventional cavalry units. In most armies, "dragoons" came to signify ordinary medium cavalry.
b Uhlans (in Polish: "Ułan"; in Russian: Уланы; "Ulan" in German) were Polish light cavalry armed with lances, sabres and pistols. The title was later used by lancer regiments in the Russian, Prussian, and Austrian armies.

church steeples than by the reflections upon the experiences of the last few months. These meditations were broken in upon by the appearance of a young man—a very picture of gravity and contentment. He was a Russian, who spoke English or German, probably both, as so many Russians do. In any event, I could talk with him, and soon found that he was going to America on the same ship with me. Another sea trip, and that in the stormy month of November suggested the question whether he feared seasickness. With a smile of superior confidence he assured me that he felt perfectly safe, and that such conditions were governed entirely by the exercise of will power. In view of my experiences I felt the rebuke, but also gathered hope that after all something might be done, and decided to seek advice. To consult a doctor seemed humiliating. Perhaps the steward might prescribe a diet. Waiters are known to have an uncanny intuition for knowing the real needs of their victims. The result was that the head steward told me he knew of only one sure cure, and that was to restrict myself to herring for the first two days of the voyage. He admitted that the cure would be hard. I figured that two days of discomfort for twelve days of relief was a good bargain; particularly since the first days in the North Sea were as good as lost for me anyway. The treatment was put into effect at once, attended with as much confidence as ever inspired a hopeful patient. By the time we reached Southampton my condition was such that the distracted steward summoned the ship's doctor, and he in turn seemed to have more difficulty in dispelling the apprehension of the steward than mine. He told me that what I really needed was a little common sense in the selection of food, and proceeded to supply what I obviously lacked. I can not say that I enjoyed the sea voyage—that triumph came later in my life—but felt comfortable enough to read several books. When upon our arrival in

New York we were assembled on deck to leave the ship I of course knew no one. A passenger who had been virtually confined to his cabin and that in the cheapest class, was still a stranger. But at the last moment I detected a familiar figure. It was my Russian traveling companion. He was slowly coming up the stairway, pausing now and then with his hand resting on the railing. He was as woebegone a spectacle of shattered confidence as I ever saw. There was no sign of mutual recognition. But when later in life I tried to read philosophic dissertations, the inevitable observations on the power and part of human will never quite escaped the interpretation of this picture of my Russian companion.

In New York I found a letter directing me to go to the home of Urban in Brooklyn. He was the same man who had taken Father and me into his home in San Antonio when we had given up all hope to reach Mexico. Once more I was one of a wholesome family circle. But the truth is that I remember little more than the good meals. Nearly two weeks of enforced moderation must be my excuse. Seasickness may suspend appetite only to create hunger — at least in youth. It is said that Dickens alone could lend dignity, and even give a touch of poetry to a meal. So I shall let it rest there, with the feeling that some descriptions can not exceed the truth.

The next morning I was on a day train for St. Louis, with only a seat, for the cash balance was low. I have the one recollection that again and again I would wake up with a start, to find other passengers enjoying my vain efforts to sleep sitting up straight in the chair. I could not resent it then but have been amused by similar exhibitions by many other helpless victims. At home I could only tell in more detail what I had tried to write. My parents were interested, not only in accounts of their son; but mine was perhaps the first report from any one who had actually seen members of their family since they had left Germany over twenty years before.

It may be said that I did not keep in mind the purpose of these added pages. In a sense that is true. But if I am to tell how I came to choose the course I did, this is a necessary introduction. Those few months did much by elimination and by emphasis to give direction. To that time I trace all the joy I have had in encouraging art, and in having in my possession modest examples within my means. Always the beautiful had appealed to me — in nature and in man's creations. Ugly facts had to be faced, but their reproduction could hardly deserve supreme effort. Above all, the belief in human purpose and the desire to have a part in its achievement was definitely impressed upon me. Whatever future's task might prove to be, it was sure to seem worth while.

II

The truth is that the real job had not appealed to me. I was looking for something that would provide interest as well as support a living. Early dreams about becoming an actor or an artist were dismissed long ago. True artists had destroyed that illusion. But there remained an abhorrence of anything like mere drudgery; I felt a desire for something that would set the imagination free at times. Our confederate friend of Mexico, no doubt at considerable trouble, found a place for me in a foundry office, which I declined with such promptness that there was a coolness for a long time. I think I may say that not even then was I moved by extravagant notions—certainly not by ambition. During a long life I have held a good many positions; some political, others in the field of education, etc. Such enjoyment as they offered me was never marred by the knowledge that I had sought them. I regarded them only as a chance to serve something in which I believed; and today I know that this instinctive feeling saved me many a heartache. No doubt it also stood in the way of many an opportunity. I did care for approval, because that alone made the burden of office tolerable. Deeply interested as I am in politics, my unfitness for sustained service, particularly in its immediate development, is quite pathetic. My aunt's desire to have me become a preacher has come true. What I regard as fundamental is now received as mere abstraction. The position of a representative of public opinion and interest was never free from questions of conscience; but to be a confessed delegate whose conduct is determined by its effect upon the next election, was and is to my mind self-imposed humiliation. Lincoln seems to me to have been right when he said that public opinion must center upon some ideal; and our abandonment of that principle lies at the root of our present political confusion. Of course I did not reason it out; but that feeling was

Fig. 33: Isaac I. Hayes portrait by Mathew B. Brady, circa 1860-1875

vaguely at the bottom of my indecision.

We had moved into a better home, still on Sixth Street just north of Franklin Avenue—a section long ago deserted by every one who made any pretense to social standing. Small retail stores encroached more and more, and gave some evidence of prosperity. Only one old church challenged modem encroachment.

Father's practice had been greatly increased as a result of the cholera in 1866, but was still practically confined to this district, and commissions on the collection of his bills continued to provide my general expense. For a year I had very few associates. My classmates were scattered, and there was little chance for new friendships. My friend Fischel did not return until about 1870 to enter one of our medical schools. He had really returned to see his family once more, the highest medical authority having told him that the condition of his heart was such that he had only a few months to live. This opinion was confirmed by doctors at home. We accepted the decision as final, until at my suggestion he consulted my father, who admitted that he had heart trouble but pronounced it to be a case of "circus" heart, which need not interfere with a long life. This advice was more readily accepted by us and my friend entered the medical school here, and lived to become a noted member of his profession.

But all doors were not closed to me. I became a member of a rowing club with headquarters at the other end of the city. The current of the river was stronger than we thought. At one time we were carried into the wheel of a large steamer, and by extricating ourselves before the wheel started we saved among others, the life of a very popular librarian of our Public Library. Again four of us undertook to row an eight oar boat up stream for about five miles at night. We did it. I got home about three o'clock in the morning, found my parents in heart-breaking anxiety, and quit. A Washington University team had me play as substitute in one game of baseball. Modern baseball is a mystery to me. At that time hitting a ball and running like a deer was probably of relatively greater importance. I could do both, made three home runs, and retired on my laurels. Among other things, a member of an older class at school and I did a good deal of fencing with rapiers, without injury. We had no instructor to urge us into rashness. On occasions I would help a policeman take an obstreperous prisoner to the station. Our neighborhood abounded in opportunities. During a course of lectures for the Public Library I acted as ticket taker, and heard the lectures free. Among them was an explorer, Hays[a], who impressed me by his observation that he ascribed his full head of hair to the fact that he always raised his hat when greeting people. I might now say as much; and I might add that my home training to take off my hat on entering a room, often won cordial greeting from otherwise austere lawyers. The historian Freeman[b] dwelt upon the growth of language and customs. He gave examples of the similarity of words in maritime life, and added that the sailors of Hamburg and Liverpool had no difficulty in understanding each other, while engaged in their work. I wondered then why landlubbers could not profit by the example, and believe now that this points the way to international peace. Another told us that the

a It seems that the author here is referring to Isaac Israel Hayes (March 5, 1832 – December 17, 1881) who was an Arctic explorer, physician and politician.
b This seems to refer to Edward Augustus Freeman (2 August 1823 – 16 March 1892) who was an English historian, architectural artist, and Liberal politician during the late-19th-century heyday of William Gladstone, as well as a one-time candidate for Parliament. The reader may find his essay on race and language of interest.

proper way to pronounce Himalaya was to put the accent on the second syllable. I have often tried it, but not always without challenge — not an uncommon experience.

In the main I was left to my own resources. Like most young men sentimentally inclined, I tried to write poetry, with the usual result. The one real satisfaction I got out of making pencil copies of photographs of favorite paintings. My instruction in drawing had been most simple, but here I found absorbing work. By degrees I tried to make cartoons on passing events. The habit to draw character sketches of faces never left me, and has helped me to survive the tortures of many a bore. My interest went entirely to representations of human life. Appreciation of landscape was left for a later period. A few years later, while a member of our Legislature, I drew a cartoon of a member who as we felt was too generous with his advice. Carelessly I let it travel down the aisle, and was saved from a personal encounter only by timely intervention of other members.

Finally I stumbled upon something real — books. That which was handiest came to me last. I can not explain why this was so. Our teacher, Denton Snider, whose hobby was Shakespeare, had certainly not let us escape his dissertations. Mr. Martin, our teacher in rhetoric, had us recite orations old and new. Thomas Davidson[a], a noted Greek

---

a   Thomas Davidson (25 October 1840, Old Deer – 14 September 1900, Montreal) was a Scottish-American philosopher and lecturer. After graduating from Aberdeen University (1860) as first graduate and Greek prizeman, he held the position of rector of the grammar school of Old Aberdeen (1860–1863). From 1863 until 1866, he was master in several English schools, spending his vacations on the continent. In 1866 he moved to Canada, to occupy a place in the London Collegiate Institute. In the following year, he came to the United States, and, after spending some months in Boston,

scholar, whose classroom I never entered, often in his home and on walks stirred me with his accounts of ancient glory. Our principal, Mr. Morgan, had even given me editions of Hazlitt's British Eloquence and Heine's works. I listened and admired, but somehow was afraid to cross the threshold—that world was not for me. One day a former classmate told me that novels might be perfectly good literature, and could be read with both advantage and enjoyment. She was the daughter of a very exacting churchman; told me that she spoke from experience, and recommended Thackeray. The combination of learning and pleasure appealed to me. Vanity Fair broke the ice. Pendennis, The Newcomes, etc., were inevitable successors. Then followed Dickens, with the Pickwick Papers, to make me a willing convert to this form of intelligent employment. In my then state of mind, Micawber's optimism seemed to me to have more to say for itself than the author indicated. The rest was easy. Hawthorne and Trollope, etc., followed. My eyes once opened I never stopped. From novels I went to poetry, and soon I had cheap editions of Scott, Pope, Dryden, Burns, Dante and, above all, an old edition of Shakespeare in two volumes, with hundreds of sketchy illustrations. The rest need not be told. With the ardor of a convert, I loved books for their own sake; and bought them second hand whenever my purse permitted.

In the meantime Fischel had returned and we started a reading club. The instigator had been a member of our class, and resigned to help support his family. Perhaps in consequence he had become wise to the value of books

> moved to St. Louis, where, in addition to work on the New York Round Table and the Western Educational Monthly, he was classical master in the St. Louis high school, and subsequently principal of one of the branch high schools.

sooner than we had. At all events, it was he who recommended Buckle's History of Civilization. This was at least a reminder of my earlier conception of the object of reading. But it was a decided impetus for more of the kind — Emerson, Macaulay, etc.; and even Hegel's Philosophy of History.

But I appeared to be no nearer to a decision about my own fate; and this was finally made by an accident. To browse around in second hand book stores had become a habit, which grew upon me until it was sheer joy in later years to go into the old book store, corner School and Washington Streets in Boston, and into Little-Brown across the street. There I asked year after year for a copy of Alexander Hamilton's works, for which, however, I had to wait for many years. No one ever asked you to buy or offered to show you. You were just a welcome visitor, and as a rule bought because no one had asked you. There was a second hand book store, of all places on Franklin Avenue, in St. Louis, owned by a German hunchback. Here I was always welcome. One day I came upon a volume in a condition to suggest cheapness and with an impressive title, "Goodrich's British Eloquence." I bought it for sixty cents and retired to my room, which in better days had no doubt been the quarters of a trusted Negro slave. Here they were in all their glory — Pitt, Burke, Fox, Brougham, Macaulay, Grattan, Curran and others. A few days' reading settled it all. Many of the same speeches were contained in my volumes of Hazlitt's British Eloquence, but they had seemed forbidden ground. This time I had dared to enter, and felt as though I had been admitted into the inner circle. This volume, the Federalist, and Lincoln's speeches have come to be my political Bible. But I must not forget Burke, whose Bristol speech was one of the early examples of political wisdom and courage confirmed so often on other pages of his works.

For two years after leaving High School I had vainly groped for light, and here at one stroke all doubt was gone. The law was my choice. By it I might live, and at the same time find some opportunity for public service. Without saying a word at home I went straight to Nathaniel Myers, who was a Jew, and would have been called homely but for a marvelous forehead, brow and eyes. He had been two years ahead of me in school, and I had heard him declaim in the best style of the day. I can hear him now, with his long arms swinging in the air, as we were taught "What's Hecuba to him or he to Hecuba, that he should weep for her." There could be no doubt about his genius, and he was now a lawyer about whose success vague rumors got abroad. I stated my case, and long before he spoke those large eyes indicated his sympathetic, even sorrowful answer: "Charlie, you must not try the law; you are a confirmed dreamer, and you would never make your salt." I tried to tell him how deeply I was impressed, but he countered by telling me that the profession was a hard one, for which in his opinion I was not made. I asked him what I could do when this was the only pursuit that had ever filled me with enthusiastic hope; and he finally agreed that perhaps I had better try it. At the fall term 1870 I entered the St. Louis Law School, and equipped with a copy of Blackstone, inkstand and pen and a highly colored paper weight, secured as was customary desk room in one of the well known law offices. Fortunately, Nathaniel Myers kept his eye on me. After three months he came in to tell me that a desk had been vacated in the office of Glover & Shepley, with whom he was associated. Gathering together my possessions I was rushed over to these new quarters. There I entered upon a relation with men and affairs that in more ways than one had a lasting influence upon me, one evidence of which is the fact that the youngest daughter of John R. Shepley[a], one of the two partners of the firm, is now my wife.

When I went to say goodbye to the old firm I met unexpected kindness. The junior congratulated me and added that they were rather crowded and he had hoped for a better place for me. The firm of Glover & Shepley was easily in ability and character one of the first in the State; Mr. Glover, a Union Democrat, and Mr. Shepley a Republican. In those days to be in an office was to be of it. There were two large rooms and a small one (once a passage way between them). Mr. Glover had the large one at the rear, Mr. Shepley the small one, and Mr. Myers with two or three students, the last one, which was also the reception room. Confidence was hardly avoidable, and good will was the order of the day. We students studied when we could; we learnt by contact, and made friends for life among the best known citizens of our city. We acted as messengers, and copied documents. The latter often meant real work. Typewriters and stenographers were unknown, the latter being introduced by degrees in the court rooms. I remember writing for three days at one bill for a foreclosure—a separate paragraph for every promissory note sued upon. As a rule longhand writing invited brevity, but not in so formal a document. Nevertheless, I think it a true observation that dictation has encouraged verbosity and sometimes confusing repetition. We were even invited to the homes of the members of the firm, which occasions, at first however gratifying, had a note of embarrassment for

a   John R. Shepley is recorded as taking the oath of allegiance of the United States on the September 6 1865 in the County of St. Louis. http://cdm.sos.mo.gov/cdm/ref/collection/CivilWar/id/46976, accessed May 29 2017.

me. New Year's day was then celebrated in the old fashion. From morning until night visitors thronged homes to extend their New Year greetings, and to partake of the good things offered. Eggnog was almost mandatory. On such a day I made my first venture. Mrs. Shepley was a very impressive presence. She came to the office rarely, but by common consent of the students was called the "Queen." The prospect of meeting her in her own home was enough to have spent a more or less sleepless night in anticipation. As the event proved, I had not exaggerated. Her gracious reception was simply demolishing. And then there appeared an unlooked-for daughter— smart as a whip, and obviously unable or even unwilling to conceal the humor of the situation. Even a glass of eggnog could not restore me; and I had my second experience of getting attached to a piano stool from which I could not find ways and means to sever connections. I got away, and looked upon the visit as a forerunner of many more or less calamitous experiences. The members of the firm were less awe inspiring. They entered in the morning with a preoccupied greeting, called on us for help as occasion offered— always informal and considerate, and commanded the respect and admiration of the young men about them. As much was true of many of the clients, who treated us with that ease of manner that contributes so largely to a young man's comfort. I remember meeting General Hancock away from home, and his friendly greeting upon the strength of having seen me in the office. General Grant (then President) called one day when I was alone. He was a man of few words, but very courteous, and my impression then was confirmed by what I read later. So it was with most of the well known callers. Democracy may have introduced a more familiar manner, but in those days real gentlemen were true democrats.

Our office was not without its humorous phases. Individuality is apt to produce idiosyncrasies. This was particularly true of Mr. Glover. He was rather sensitive about his handwriting, which to us was nothing less than mysterious. The word "notwithstanding" would be spread over a line and a half or more; and when we in the hopeless effort to decipher such rather expansive words went to him for help, he would explain with an air of indulgent amazement at our lack of ingenuity. He always used purple ink; and in his absent-minded and energetic movements to and from the inkstand, much of it went to decorate his immediate surroundings. In this process his countenance did not always escape, and his hands never. There were times when his unannounced appearance might have had us believe that Indian warriors had not been exterminated in our part of the country. He was a frequent sufferer from erysipelas[a], for which a generous application of iodine seemed to be the accepted remedy. I was sometimes entrusted with messages to him at his home. Once or twice I struck him when he had been freshly and ruthlessly decorated. As a doctor's son I had heard of contagious disease; but this was nothing compared to the sight of a colorful display of iodine, hair standing on end, and a tortured man's impatience at the breaking point.

The equipment of the office was in keeping with the period. For the protection of documents we had a safe and a wardrobe. But inasmuch as the safe could be opened with any nail, valuable papers were, so far as I could make out, entrusted to the wardrobe; probably upon the theory that thieves were not as wise as we were. Sometimes

---

a Erysipelas "red skin"; also known as "ignis sacer", "holy fire", and "St. Anthony's fire" in some countries) is an acute infection typically with a skin rash, usually on any of the legs and toes, face, arms, and fingers.

papers did not enjoy even that much security, but were stuffed away in a coat pocket. Of this we had a signal illustration. One morning Mr. Glover stormed into the office, the market basket which he habitually brought to be replenished on his way home swinging with ominous energy on his arm. We knew that he was engaged in a trial, but this appearance was distinctly beyond the ordi-

Fig. 34: *Euphrosyne Parepa-Rosa*

nary. He stalked past Mr. Shepley's desk into his own sanctum, from which we heard protesting mutterings, which although not unusual seemed to have a touch of peculiar emphasis. Directly he reappeared at Mr. Shepley's desk and demanded a certain document. When Mr. Shepley, also preoccupied, pleaded entire ignorance of it, he answered that this document was the first exhibit he had to introduce that morning and he must have it at once. Demand and denial became more and more pronounced until Mr. Glover, despairing of any hope of assistance in his dilemma, returned to his room to institute a search of

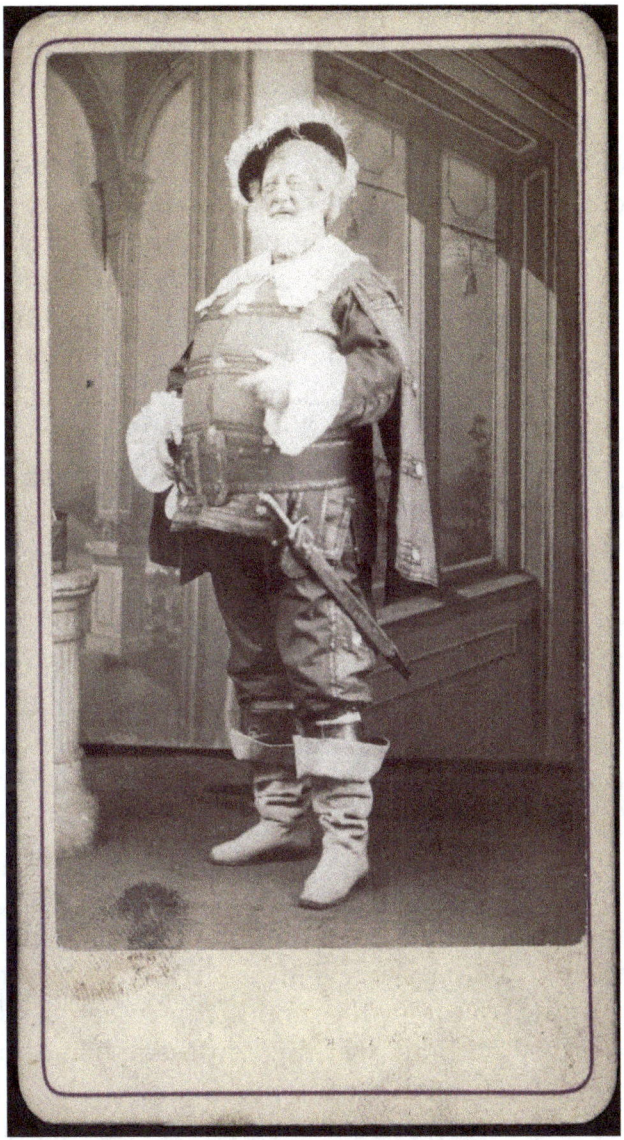

Fig. 35: Ben DeBar as Falstaff

his own. He had a swayback desk which was yielding to the weight of its overloaded pigeon holes. To make sure that he overlooked nothing, he started with the first one — of the vintage of about 1860 — and brought the unoffending papers down with a crash. The cloud of dust that greeted him and indeed the whole office, left no doubt of their antiquity. Mr. Shepley had said that he was busy and continued to write; but Myers concluded that the time for intervention had arrived. He actually persuaded Mr. Glover that the paper in question could not be found in those pigeon holes. Having agreed upon that point, the attack upon Mr. Shepley was renewed. Then I witnessed a piece of real diplomacy, worthy of Machiavelli himself. Myers told Mr. Glover that he thought he could find the paper if he were given a free hand. "But, Mr. Glover, you must promise not to be angry with me." "Now, how could I be angry with you?" So after several more protestations of mutual confidence, Myers reached into Mr. Glover's inside coat pocket, took out the paper and handed it to Mr. Glover, whose expression was one of mixed disgust and relief. We retired to our desks, Mr. Glover to his room from which he immediately emerged, the storm in no sense abated, disappearing through the door with the final declaration, "Shepley is the darndest man I ever knew." No one could have been less concerned than Mr. Shepley, for they were the warmest of friends. But these were mere explosions of intense and perhaps overtasked men. The same man might break the silence of the Law Library by suddenly reading aloud in exultation or derision of some court decision. Or passengers in a street car might turn with appealing eyes to the conductor when a distinguished lawyer without warning proceeded in subdued indignation to rehearse a contemplated speech or argument. But there was never a sign of preoccupation or absentmindedness during the real presentation of a case before court or jury. Those were men of unyielding conviction and just indignation, as their attitude during the Civil War had shown; and of infinite kindness, as every one of us could testify. Mr. Glover took me into the first case that gave me a chance to appear in the Supreme Court. When in great distress I asked Mr. Shepley how I might tell a U.S. judge of my inability to furnish bond in a receivership, he impatiently asked for the bond and signed it. The only other comment I ever heard from him was that the court had not allowed me enough of a fee.

In the meantime we were supposed to be studying law, in my case with such side issues as engaged my attention. I was still earning my commissions on Father's bills, and so meeting my general expenses. This expense account was by degrees indicating a larger sphere of interests. Best of all I was seeing more and more of young people. Fischel had returned and was attending a medical school. He had large connections, among them very interesting persons — men and women. I was accepted into the circle with great cordiality, and look back upon that time as one of the many causes for gratitude to my friend. Life was offering more and more. No great performer came whom I did not hear. Ristori, Booth in Hamlet and Richelieu; I think Seebach in Gretchen about that time, etc. The singers, Parepa and Parepa Rose[a]; Janauschek in Deborah, came later. In those days what we now call the parquet was the pit, reserved for the cheaper tickets. How they used to cheer old Ben DeBar[b] in the role of Grave Digger. And well they

a   Euphrosyne Parepa-Rosa (7 May 1836 – 21 January 1874) was a British operatic soprano who established the Carl Rosa Opera Company together with second husband Carl Rosa. Her achievements were recognised by the Philharmonic Society of London (now the Royal Philharmonic Society) with the rare award of their Gold Medal in 1872.
b   Benedict ("Ben") DeBar (1812–1877) was a prominent American actor-manager. He is associated with operating a major theater in St. Louis, and for portraying the role of Falstaff. He was also connected by marriage with the Booth family of actors. She married violinist Carl Rosa in New York City in 1867. Together they quickly established the Parepa-Rosa English Opera Company

might for he was fine, even though as proprietor of the theater he was only a local genius. Hazlitt says somewhere that one can not be angry with a face in the pit. That part of an audience is amazingly quick and responsive.

To cap the climax I was a member of a singing society "Arion des Westens." This was a tribute to Father on part of both the conductor Froelich and myself. Father loved music, and had insisted upon my taking instruction in both singing and piano. To this day I could not carry a tune if my life depended upon it. My teacher of course turned out to be a rogue and absconded, happily for me, before irreparable damage was done. But in that brief time my efforts had been sufficiently energetic to crack my voice so badly that it took several years to recover. To please Father I was nevertheless admitted to the society, and for lack of a better place I was assigned to the second and probably least risky base section. As a matter of precaution the conductor enjoined me never to start singing before the chorus, and always to stop before it did. By way of recompense I was elected to carry the flag in processions, and while my weakened voice was harmless enough I suspect that these were the only occasions when the conductor enjoyed perfect peace of mind with respect to me. No doubt my present support of our Symphony Orchestra if not more effective is at least less disturbing.

Beyond that, politics began to interest me. My start had been a poor one. During the campaign for Lincoln's second nomination the German element turned rather strongly to Fremont; and influenced by the Principal of the German school which I attended in 1864, I marched in one of the processions. I was then fifteen years old, and per-

> there, which became popular, and which introduced opera to places in America that had never staged it before.

Fig. 36: Henry Hitchcock

haps need not take my remorse too seriously. In any event, I was shown at an early stage how. much importance should be attached to such demonstrations. The movement for Johnson's impeachment[a] quite carried me off my feet when I was really old enough to know better, particularly since our family had never felt any animosity for the South. Fortunately, wiser counsel set me right in time, just for my peace of mind. But in 1870 I came of age, and felt a sense of duty, such as might serve a good purpose at present. I lived in a city ward which I think was known as the "Bloody Ninth." Perhaps I am wrong, but can not believe that any other ward had better claim to the title. A Republican meeting was called, for in those days the direct primary had not yet prevented us from assembling in a room or hall and saying what we thought of questions, or for that matter, of each other. I went, if not full of expectation, at least of purpose. There were others who had their eyes on that meeting, because the best known reporter of the Republican newspaper was there; also a notorious

---

a The Impeachment of Andrew Johnson occurred in 1868, when the United States House of Representatives resolved to impeach President Andrew Johnson, adopting eleven articles of impeachment detailing his "high crimes and misdemeanors". The impeachment trial was in fact unsuccessful and did not lead to a conviction. This was the first impeachment of an incumbent President since creation of the office in 1789. The culmination of a lengthy political battle between Johnson and the Republican majority in Congress over how best to deal with the defeated Southern states following the conclusion of the American Civil War, the impeachment and the subsequent trial were among the most dramatic events in the political life of the nation during the Reconstruction Era. Together, they have gained a historical reputation as an act of political expedience, rather than necessity, based on Johnson's defiance of an unconstitutional piece of legislation, and with little regard for the will of a general public which, despite the unpopularity of Johnson, opposed the impeachment. There would not be another serious attempt to impeach a President for 106 years when, during the Watergate scandal, Richard Nixon resigned from office, rather than face impeachment and trial. The only other impeachment trial of a President would occur 131 years later with the impeachment of Bill Clinton.

party manipulator. All seemed as peaceful as a May morning, when without warning as far as I could see, we were

Fig. 37: Thomas McIntyre Cooley

in the presence of a heated wrangle. The transition was so sudden that I was dumbfounded. The last thing that caught my eye was the glitter of the barrel of a revolver; and the lights went out. I saw a window in the rear of the room, jumped through it into an alley, and went home to reflect whether I would abandon my political career or persist in it. In a mild way I did the latter, although even so it was not the last political disturbance which I saw or took part in.

In contrast to our Law School work these mere incidents may be given undue prominence. But they were very real to me, and had their very decided influence. Besides, well ordered school work does not provide much material for special mention. Our Law School was only a few years old. The faculty was made up of volunteers, although the following year the dean received compensation. Among them were as prominent men as the bar had. Still others served as trustees. Henry Hitchcock[a], a nationally known lawyer, organized the school, and was the first dean. For years Mrs. Hitchcock paid the deficits. The method of teaching was simple; very little lecturing; chiefly searching inquiry into the care and understanding with which assignments had been read. This method was peculiarly effective because our class, drawn from many States, did not exceed fifteen; and every man might expect to be called upon during each session. In addition we had the advantage of a personal relation with every professor—a privilege of which we did not always avail ourselves. For illustration, one professor, whose appointment must be traced to conventional recognition, surprised us at the first session with the statement that "pleadings are the legal reins by which the other legal horses are held in check." Our class was composed of a rare conglomerate of ambitious youths, and to be fair they were all in earnest. We had one member who was an Irishman, Henry I. D'Arcy a graduate of a foreign university, and a man of culture; and there were several other college graduates. The Irishman told me that such a statement might pass me who with my German ancestry must be accustomed to mixed metaphor, but he could not stand for it. I was greatly impressed. So about six of us held a protest meeting, and in obedience to solemn resolutions, notified the dean that we would not

a   Henry Hitchcock (3 July 1829 – 18 March 1902) was a lawyer from St. Louis, Missouri. An early president of the Bar Association of Metropolitan St. Louis, Hitchcock was a co-founder of the American Bar Association

attend those lectures. We were told that we might not get our degrees, answered that we would take the chance, and never heard of the incident again. Our course was only two years. As the examinations approached I felt the usual dread, and was glad to be one of the three who laboriously went over every subject by way of preparation. For my thesis I took the first subject suggested to me, and got second place. The examinations I passed without difficulty, and at the commencement we were addressed by Thomas M. Cooley[a], Professor of Law in the University of Michigan, then the most noted authority on Constitutional Law, and thus I was supposed to be prepared for the practice of the law.

---

a Thomas McIntyre Cooley, LL.D., (January 6, 1824 – September 12, 1898) was the 25th Justice and a Chief Justice of the Michigan Supreme Court, between 1864 and 1885. Born in Attica, New York, he was father to Charles Cooley, a distinguished American sociologist. He was a charter member and first chairman of the Interstate Commerce Commission (1887). Cooley was appointed Dean of the University of Michigan Law School, a position he held until 1884.

III.

Once more I was saved from an immediate test of preparedness. Father had been successful enough to carry out his plan to revisit Germany once more. The inducement was the greater because as a result of the war of 1870 there was real hope for a united German people. To Bismarck whom he had once hated, he became quite reconciled. I was made one of the party, and some time in July 1872 father, mother and I sailed from Baltimore for Bremen on the North German Lloyd steamer "Ohio"[a] (called O-hee-o by the sailors). I had spent the night before in complete collapse from sunstroke—the second attack that summer, and as usual saw little or nothing of the passengers. After our arrival the first few months were naturally given to relatives. Father met old university friends, some of whom were in the public service, and mother met some of her friends. To me it was a repetition of my visit a few years ago. It was all very enjoyable; but a sense of real responsibility had sent me into a more and more serious mood. I was by that time engaged to be married, and the prospect for our union was very remote. I suffered from a throat trouble, which had harassed me ever since the singing lesson. Protracted and severe treatment by a surgeon had not helped me—had perhaps aggravated it. My friend Fischel was now a doctor of medicine. He joined us in the fall, and instead of treating me himself, advised me to consult a

---

a The Ohio was built in 1869 and sold to shipbuilder in part exchange for new ships, resold to Italy and renamed Amazzone. Norddeutscher Lloyd (NDL) (North German Lloyd) was a German shipping company. It was founded by Hermann Henrich Meier and Eduard Crüsemann in Bremen on 20 February 1857. It developed into one of the most important German shipping companies of the late 19th and early 20th centuries, and was instrumental in the economic development of Bremen and Bremerhaven.

young physician in Berlin. I saw him only once. He assured me that I was essentially sound, that the muscles of my throat had been seriously weakened, and would have to be trained back. The method was reading aloud, beginning with ten minutes and increasing to several hours. He gave me two or three years as the probable period for recovery. I lost no time; my gain was obvious. I read aloud many of the best known novels, and finally found friends who regarded it as a privilege to listen. In the course of a few years; that is, while a member of the bar, I regained my voice sufficiently for my unimportant court business; and finally spoke before quite large audiences. I never had a setback, and now the loud speaker has made it of little importance whether I have or not. Nevertheless, I avoid it when I can. It affects me like a bar between the audience and me.

We rented a floor in a new apartment on the outskirts of Berlin. It was all comfortable enough, although Fischel and I, in our desire to have ends meet, rather forced the issue. The house had not been occupied. Everything was spick and span. For all but breakfast we went out for our meals. So we occupied the kitchen as sleeping quarters. A second hand iron bedstead met the case, and we were housed as two prospective students. Our noonday meals we took at a restaurant, made attractive by its low rates. It was largely attended, and we discovered only a few months before leaving that the popular steaks were really horse meat— probably from animals that had survived the 1870 war. A statue of Hegel in the immediate vicinity was hardly enough to restore our equanimity. One day a week I lunched with Father and Mother in the "Rothe Schloss," where English fare prevailed.

Within two days after we were settled the gendarme

Fig. 38: Rudolf Virchow

appeared to verify that Father was the same man who as a student in 1845 had lived in a room at such and such a street. That was the first time I heard Father impatiently refer to "the system," from which he had at one time fled. Some time later we attended at three duels fought officially by officers of several corps who had never met before. Once more Father referred to "the system," and added, "I want to go home."

Early in the fall three of us registered at the university— Father and Fischel in medicine, and I for a mixed course, selected with the assistance of Bleecker Miller[a], who afterwards as a lawyer worked under James Carter[b] in opposition to the then proposed codification of the laws of New York.

Father heard a few particularly selected professors, and with one very distinguished one visited the hospitals as a member of the class.

Of Fischel I only remember that he heard the great Virchow[c], whose first lecture was given as I recall at eight a.m., and that in time he established very close and highly advantageous relations with him. I heard four professors regularly. Mommsen[d] I really did not hear; but what is more to the point I saw him lecture; and a copy of

a Rutger Bleecker Miller (July 28, 1805–November 12, 1877) was a United States Representative from New York. His father was Morris Smith Miller, also a U.S. Representative from New York.
b James Coolidge Carter (1827-1905) was an American lawyer, a partner in the firm that eventually became Carter Ledyard & Milburn (CL&M), which he helped found in 1854. He helped create the The Association of the Bar of the City of New York.
c Rudolf Ludwig Carl Virchow (13 October 1821 – 5 September 1902) was a German physician, anthropologist, pathologist, prehistorian, biologist, writer, editor, and politician, known for his advancement of public health. He is known as "the father of modern pathology" because his work helped to discredit humourism, bringing more science to medicine. He is also known as the founder of social medicine and veterinary pathology, and to his colleagues, the "Pope of medicine".
d Christian Matthias Theodor Mommsen (30 November 1817–1 November 1903) was a German classical scholar, historian, jurist, journalist, politician, archaeologist and writer generally regarded as one of the greatest classicists of the 19th century. He was also a prominent German politician, as a member of the Prussian and German parliaments. His works on Roman law and on the law of obligations had a significant impact on the German civil code (BGB).

APPENDIX

Fig. 39: Franz von Lenbach Self-portrait (1903)

Lenbach's[a] portrait of him hangs in my room today. At the

a Franz Seraph Lenbach, after 1882, Ritter von Lenbach (13 December 1836, Schrobenhausen – 6 May 1904, Munich) was a German painter; known primary for his portraits of prominent personalities from the nobility, the arts, and industry. Because of his standing in society, he was often referred to as the "Malerfürst" (Prince of Painters).

risk of exaggeration born of youthful enthusiasm, I thought his presence a very inspiration. Prof. Wagner[a], the economist and the rage of the day, I never heard. I got as far as the door, but sudden and explosive popularity always brings my reserve to the fore. Instead I heard Dühring[b]. He was blind, and had to be led to and from the lecture room by his wife, unlike another perhaps more typical professor who required like guidance without

Fig. 40: Adolph Wagner

a Adolph Wagner (25 March 1835–8 November 1917) was a German economist and politician, a leading Kathedersozialist (academic socialist) and public finance scholar and advocate of agrarianism. Wagner's law of increasing state activity is named after him.

b Eugen Karl Dühring (12 January 1833, Berlin–21 September 1921, Nowawes in modern-day Potsdam-Babelsberg) was a German positivist philosopher and economist, a socialist who was a strong critic of Marxism. Dühring was born in Berlin, Prussia. After a legal education he practised at Berlin as a lawyer until 1859. A weakness of the eyes, ending in total blindness, occasioned his taking up the studies with which his name is now connected. In 1864 he became docent of the University of Berlin, but, in consequence of a quarrel with the professoriate, was deprived of his licence to teach in 1874.

being blind. Dühring was a socialist of the continental school. His countenance was as clean cut as a chiseled statue. His style was incisive and clear; sometimes satirical, bordering on the bitter. Years afterwards in conversa-

Fig. 41: James Coolidge Carter

tion with Dr. Felix Adler[a] I learnt that he and I had heard

a   Felix Adler (August 13, 1851–April 24, 1933) was a German American professor of political and social ethics, rationalist, influential lecturer on euthanasia, religious leader and social reformer who

these lectures together, although we never met until later. As much was true of Dr. John William Burgess[a] who attended the university then, but whom I did not get to know until later, and whose books I read with great admiration without suspecting the incident.

In Medical Jurisprudence we had a young professor who afterwards gained a great reputation in the treatment of mental disturbance.

In Roman Law I heard the noted Karl Georg Bruns[b]. He was strictly a lecturer; I still have my note books and doubt whether I could understand them if I tried to read them now. Which need not prove that I failed to carry something away with me.

The professor who gave me most was Rudolph Gneist[c], Dean of the Law Department, and then perhaps the greatest authority on the English system of law. I am told that

    founded the Ethical Culture movement. Felix Adler was born in Alzey, Rhenish Hesse, Grand Duchy of Hesse, Germany, the son of a rabbi, Samuel Adler, a leading figure in European Reform Judaism. The family immigrated to the United States from Germany when Felix was six years old so that his father could accept the appointment as head rabbi at Temple Emanu-El in New York.

a John William Burgess (August 26, 1844–January 13, 1931) was a pioneering American political scientist. He spent most of his career at Columbia University and is regarded as having been "the most influential political scientist of the period.

b Karl (Eduard) Georg Bruns, also: Georg Bruns (24. February 1816 in Helmstedt-10. December 1880 in Berlin) was a German lawyer and professor of law. (Translation by editor from Wikipedia.de).

c Heinrich Rudolf Hermann Friedrich von Gneist (13 August 1816–22 July 1895), German jurist and politician, was born at Berlin, the son of a judge attached to the Kammergericht (court of appeal) in that city. Gneist made significant influence on his student Max Weber and also contributed to Japan's first constitution through his communication with Ito Hirobumi.

he had a very decided influence upon the later development of the German code. He spoke without notes to a very large body of students; and his address had much more the character of personal communication. Some of his books upon English subjects have received high praise in England, and a few of them I have passed to the library of our Law School. Professor Gneist took particular interest in students from the United States, and laughingly told us that we were either the best or the worst. He would invite us ever so often to his home, have a cold meal served, and would then hold us spellbound with his informal discussions. They covered a wide field. He spoke English readily and indeed visited England frequently, and at least once the United States. He was also a member of Parliament. Extending to us a surprising confidence, he would not only treat of immediate political conditions, but would give his unreserved estimate of noted persons ranging all the way from George Eliot to Prince Bismarck. No doubt these visits gave me more than all the lectures. Finally, I took some lessons in drawing, and if I ask myself what I learnt in the whole process I should say in the school sense, little enough. The foundation was lacking. In another sense I gathered what for me was of incalculable value, in point of view, general attitude, perhaps inspiration. Above all, a perfect realization of how little I knew.

In saying this I must add that many advantages came to me besides those offered by the university. Into those eight months were crammed more suggestions for interest and impulses for action than ever came to me in years at any other time. Nothing matured. Upon not one of them could I have passed a prescribed examination, any more than in grammar. But somehow at some time all of them helped to make my decisions. The Parliament of the new German Empire was only a few years old. It was the first legislative body I ever saw, and I was in the gallery quite often. The proceedings when I saw them were orderly and dignified. Some of the brief speeches by leaders of the center (Catholic) party were marked by great power, and some of the socialists were no mean antagonists. I missed many opportunities but always hoped to hear Bismarck—the great figure of that day. It is said that he was never an attractive speaker. His voice was disappointing; and in the early days his style must have been involved. His published speeches show a marked change. As parliamentary action developed he, as it seems to me, yielded more and more to the English method. His sentences were shorter and his expression more terse. He was always a hard hitter, not only in action, but also in driving home his point. When as I recall it the United States Congress adopted resolutions in criticism of Germany's conduct with respect to Lasker, a German member who died during a visit in our country, he declined to deliver them to his king. On the occasion of a ceremony in memory of their distinguished member, socialists had attacked him for this conduct, particularly in case of a friendly power. He answered that, as was well known, his feeling for the United States had always been particularly warm, but that he could not be asked to deliver to his king a communication that was nothing short of an insult; and whatever else might be true he at least had never been guilty of playing politics at the grave of a dead friend. On another occasion during a warm debate, a noted socialist protesting his patriotism, declared that in the hour of need his support would be as loyal as that of any man. Replying Bismarck expressed his great satisfaction at this assurance, but added that whenever men of the speaker's convictions drew the cloak of patriotism about their shoulders, they seemed somehow always to disclose the red lining. But I never saw him in Parliament or heard him speak, although I have the printed edition of his speeches, and have read many of them. I saw him once. The king's palace was just across Unter den Linden from the university. From Professor Bruns' lecture hall I could, by looking under the horse's head of Rauch[a]'s statue of Frederick the Great, see the king at his desk. His absences during the morning hours were rare, and here he had many of his conferences. One day I saw Bismarck with the king. This was signal enough for me. I waited near the main entrance until he appeared, and have been glad that I did not miss my chance. As he stood there in military uniform, he was as imposing a figure as I ever saw—a personification of power — physical and intellectual.

Of other prominent public men I saw only a few. Among them Professor Virchow, an unassuming presence as he walked down an aisle during a session of Parliament. He was then regarded as one of the most eminent scientists in the world, a pronounced liberal in politics; and as a member of the City Council of Berlin, the father of its revolutionized sanitary system. General Moltke[b] was there on one occasion—why I do not know. He stood in distinct contrast to most of his surroundings—slight, very erect and, as I thought, notably aristocratic. It was no surprise to read years afterwards that the letters which he wrote as a

a   Christian Daniel Rauch (2 January 1777 – 3 December 1857) was a German sculptor. He founded the Berlin school of sculpture, and was the foremost German sculptor of the 19th century.
b   Helmuth Karl Bernhard Graf von Moltke (26 October 1800, Parchim, Mecklenburg-Schwerin – 24 April 1891, Berlin) was a German Field Marshal. The chief of staff of the Prussian Army for thirty years, he is regarded as the creator of a new, more modern method of directing armies in the field. He is often referred to as Moltke the Elder to distinguish him from his nephew Helmuth Johann Ludwig von Moltke, who commanded the German Army at the outbreak of World War I.

young attache to the German Legation at Constantinople, were distinguished for their clarity and purity in style.

I heard only one set speech in that Parliament, and this was made by a comparatively young member, Lasker. He would have been regarded as a very effective speaker in our country, and was no doubt a forerunner of that type of eloquence in Germany, where so far little occasion had been offered for its development. He died some years later while visiting the United States. It was the resolution adopted by Congress on the occasion of his death that gave rise to Bismarck's set-to with the socialists. He had made a bold and most disturbing attack upon the Minister of the Treasury. Public response was unprecedented. He had demanded the appointment of an impartial committee to investigate the situation, and to this the government had promptly acceded. Within two days Lasker followed with another broadside, and this is the speech I heard. It was powerful, but could not escape the impression that the speaker was capitalizing his distinction. This was made clear at once upon his close. War Minister Roon responded. He was no speaker, but demonstrated how restraint and dignity may triumph. He spoke very briefly. In the simplest possible manner he said that Lasker's demand had been granted, that a committee satisfactory to all parties had been named and was now prepared to act; that in all fairness the result of that inquiry should be awaited; that a second attack under these circumstances was unjust, because Mr. Lasker must be aware of the power of his eloquence, and to employ it as he did now was equivalent to asking a conviction without a hearing. Not another word was said, tranquility seemed to be restored, and the regular order of business was taken up.

During that period the report was current that the Crown

APPENDIX

Fig. 42: Frederick III, German Emperor

Prince Frederick William[a] had been poisoned at a banquet. Probably this was the first intimation of his final illness. After protracted uneasiness he and the Crown Princess Victoria[b] and some of their children were scheduled to

a Frederick III (German: Friedrich III., Deutscher Kaiser und König von Preußen; 18 October 1831 – 15 June 1888) was German Emperor and King of Prussia for ninety-nine days in 1888, the Year of the Three Emperors. Friedrich Wilhelm Nikolaus Karl, known informally as "Fritz", was the only son of Emperor Wilhelm I and was raised in his family's tradition of military service. Although celebrated as a young man for his leadership and successes during the Second Schleswig, Austro-Prussian and Franco-Prussian wars, he nevertheless professed a hatred of warfare and was praised by friends and enemies alike for his humane conduct.

b Victoria, Princess Royal (Victoria Adelaide Mary Louisa; 21 November 1840 – 5 August 1901) was a German Empress and Queen

Fig. 43: The Marriage of Victoria, Princess Royal and Prince Frederick William of Prussia, 25 January 1858, by John Phillip.

return to Berlin. The streets from the station to the Schloss were simply packed. The popularity of Prince and Princess seemed to be very great. Suddenly the royal party appeared. They had avoided all reception committees, and were as it seemed to me making their way through the throng of people, in ordinary coaches. The scene had a distinctly democratic air and the popular acclamation was as great as I have ever seen. That evening the students of the university had a torch-light procession in their full regalia and stopped in front of the Crown Prince's Palace to sing patriotic songs. The ovation which greeted the Prince upon his appearance on the balcony beggars description. It is necessary to witness such a scene to understand the German's love of such demonstration, and also to appreciate his ability for effective arrangement. It may and no doubt does at times deteriorate into the trivial and absurd; but in

of Prussia by marriage to German Emperor Frederick III. She was the eldest child of Queen Victoria of Great Britain and Ireland and Prince Albert, and was created Princess Royal in 1841. She was the mother of Wilhelm II, German Emperor.

its more wholesome manifestation it is an undeniable national asset.

During that winter offering of the stage was particularly rich. I heard once more Seebach in "Gretchen"; this time not without an ample supply of handkerchiefs. I may have suspected even then that Goethe's Faust was essentially a philosophic drama, but Gretchen's fate I felt to be unbearably tragic. Today it seems to me that Shakespeare selected situations to present persons, while Goethe used persons to picture conditions. But take Gretchen as a person or symbol, the effect was equally appealing. I revolted against the social injustice just as I now do before Sorolla's great painting of "Another Marguerite." Of other plays I remember particularly Goethe's "Egmont"; and this because the shortest part was taken by their best actor. In a few words, most effectively spoken, he seemed to give the key to the whole tragedy. But I remember the occasion especially because I saw how very punctilious Germans were about attending performances. It was announced that the program would be preceded by Beethoven's Symphony to Egmont—a double treat. I was the guest of an aunt's stepson. She was the aunt who gave me a gold watch on my first visit abroad to compensate for the silver watch which I had chivalrously sacrificed at Indianapolis. He was as charming as he was interesting; an only child happily married to a beautiful young woman, and independently rich. I saw her again fifty-six years afterwards in Berlin. After the great war she had lost everything; and smilingly told me that she now lived on the difference between the small rent which she paid for five rooms, and the higher rent which she received for three of those rooms. They had two lovely children, and he had for several years promised to present his thesis for a doctor's degree. He loved good things. Not that he forgot himself in their indulgence; but perhaps he was forgetting other things on their account. That night for some reason we were late for dinner, which was unceremoniously abandoned before its completion, in order that we might be in our seats before the first note was heard. No attendance at church could have been more religiously correct.

Another attraction was music. The charming concert on Christmas Eve I heard only once, but the military band at the Guard House between the university and the Museum I heard almost every day. The opera was at its height, Wagner was coming into his own; but there was still strong opposition to him, and its manifestations were sometimes drastic, as is apt to be the case in Berlin. I had occasion to witness such a conflict of judgment and emotion. A concert of Wagner music was announced, with the added attraction that Wagner himself would be the conductor. Here was a call for battle. The house was packed. Students were proverbially impecunious, and in that respect at least I could qualify. We occupied the loftiest gallery— perhaps the third, which was not as bad as it was in the Opera House, where the highest tier, called Himmelsleiter (Heaven's ladder) gave us as good a view of the stage machinery as it did of the performers. The first long intermission was the signal for battle. "Zukunftsmusik" was tossed about with ardent praise and derisive laughter. But for the resumption of the performance, beer mugs might have been turned into weapons of battle. As one of those persons who enjoys music and indeed may be swayed by it, without a suspicion of understanding so far as the conventional interpretations go, I rather leaned to Wagner. At all events, I was deeply impressed. I have read that he was not a great conductor. As I think of him he seemed restrained but intent; and I can recall no distinguished person who looked more unmistakably like his

APPENDIX 399

Fig. 44: Albert Niemann

published portrait. Perhaps the situation was made the more persuasive to me because in the audience was seated near the front the great Franz Liszt in the customary setting of a circle of adoring ladies.

But the opera was the high mark of enjoyment. Niemann[a] was probably as great a Wagner tenor as ever lived, and

a Albert Wilhelm Karl Niemann (15 January 1831 – 13 January 1917) was a leading German tenor opera singer especially associated with the operas of Richard Wagner. He gave important premieres in France, Germany, England and the United States, and played Siegmund in the first complete production of Der Ring des Nibelungen (Bayreuth Festspielhaus 1876).

he was permanently engaged in Berlin. He had a magnificent tenor voice that could stand the strain of the severest role. He was a man of splendid presence, and withal he was a good actor. For a Wagner hero I never expect to see such a performer again. Lucca[a], the great soprano, was in America that season, and substitutes are not expected to quite fill the bill; but every part in the cast, including the ballet, was creditably presented. The houses were crowded. I missed no important evening. As far as great music could help me, I got my share; and as far as one more enthusiast could help Wagner, I did my part.

Finally, I had a chance to pursue my interest in art. The "Neue Museum" as it was then called was near the university, as was a small one, the "Bijou Museum." The interior of the latter showed beautiful design. It had some fine exhibits, among them a very remarkable mask of Frederick the Great. I did not go there often; took it in as I would Schlueter's statue of "Der Grosse Kurfuerst," his warriors marks in the Zeughaus, Rauch's Frederick the Great, and other examples in Sans Souci, and Kinkel's Amazon at the entrance to the Museum, which after all was a chief point of interest. This museum I visited several days every week, and when I left Berlin I could have given the position of every painting and piece of sculpture that I regarded as of any importance. A replica of the "Betende Knabe" (Adorante) which Frederick the Great purchased, I took particular pride many years after to give to our museum. I was no longer buying photographs to any extent. Both need and taste went more to books, and of these I made a small collection to take home with me. April of 1873 was approaching, and this was the time set for my return.

a   Pauline Lucca (April 25, 1841 – February 28, 1908) was a prominent operatic soprano, born in the Austrian capital of Vienna.

Before starting I had a great surprise. Nathaniel Myers, who had so thoughtfully warned against the law, wrote that if I would come to his office (he was now on his own) he would give me fifty dollars a month. I could hardly credit it. All cares were lifted; my start in life was guaranteed. After saying my farewells (including my parents who were remaining) I started once more from Berlin. This time there was no Russian passenger to embarrass me and, indeed, the sea was less cruel to me. I was at least able to read, giving most of my time to Kugler's History of Art, and to some volume by Grimm. Michael Angelo sticks in my memory; perhaps I read it then. How he gained a commission from the Pope by drawing a perfect circle with a painter's brush. If I am mistaken about the particular artist, the statues of David and Moses and the paintings in the chapel were enough to make a hero of him for me. And particularly did I enjoy reading how Michael Angelo, to avenge himself upon an unfair critic, a Cardinal, I believe, had pictured him as Satan in his painting of The Deluge.

Again with my exchequer very low I landed in my home city, to stand the practical test of a member of a profession. But again that is another story.

IV.

From now on my experience was of course largely that of other beginners, with this exception that I had no associations to which I might look for employment of any consequence. With me Mr. Myers had in his employ Fred Wislizenus, a classmate at the Law School, who had also been in the office of Glover & Shepley. He had been away in Rome with his uncle, the U.S. Minister there. He was a university graduate, a well read man, and a most sympathetic companion. We worked under immediate direction of our chief, although when he was away on summer vacations we received the needed communications, and in consequence had some anxious moments. Mr. Myers had an active practice, largely in bankruptcy matters, and prompt action was one of the requirements. I lived in a small hall room in South St. Louis, walked to and from the office, several miles each way, and soon learnt that fifty dollars a month might be a restraint upon extravagance. Our position was as good as could be asked in the capacity which we occupied. But after a year or two Wislizenus and I decided to start on our own as partners. We rented a small room and bought a large desk. We hung out the customary "shingle" — a rather large tin sign — and for some time the creaking of that sign on the breeze was perhaps the most marked proof of our existence. It has been said that Mr. Lowell gave up the law because he concluded that his was a profession but not a business. Our provocation was the same, but we did not have a literary career to turn to. About the time we were established, so far as location was concerned, the Southern Hotel just across the street was destroyed by fire. That meant a change, and still having an eye to low rents, we selected a third story room, which no prospective client without a combination of sagacity and indomitable will could have found. We contemplated each other, discussed such abstractions as suggested themselves, and concluded that we were not a promising combination. My partner was more independently situated than I was, and started alone. What little experience I had was at times encouraging, and again discouraging. A kindly real estate agent gave me a case for President Grant. The thrill was great, as the fee was small. No doubt I owed the distinction to the fact that the amount involved was trifling, and the issue beyond dispute. The same agent employed me to represent, as I recall it, a Princess Cavaletti (Italian) against one Montague (Irish). Ignorance of Romeo and Juliet alone saved me from a double thrill, although one was enough. The Princess' property in St. Louis was then devoted to what was perhaps the worst drinking brothel in our city. Having been taught to be polite, I made personal demand for the rent, and was glad to get away without threatened assistance. When told that Montague had a police record, although so far he had been known to murder only one person, I brought suit before a Justice of the Peace, and bought a pistol. Montague appeared at my office to offer an amount that I could not accept. I can not say that I felt like a true Texan during that interview; but I kept my hand on my pistol, and finally tried the case similarly equipped. I have heard it said that justices of the peace have a peculiar humanitarian instinct, but it is hard to guess what shoot it will take. My relief was great when this time I happened to be its object. I won; collected the money; remitted it, and had reason to believe that my princess client's mind was never again disturbed by this tenant.

At last there came a client on his own so to speak — drawn perhaps by some incautious word said about me. He spoke only German; had a vegetable stand in an open market, and was sued before a justice of the peace by the owner of the adjoining stand—a woman; which was ominous. We tried the case and lost it, he cheerfully paid the fine and a fee of five dollars, and all seemed well. A few weeks afterwards the client appeared to tell me that he had been sued again by the same woman, before the same justice. She seemed to enjoy it, and as far as I could gather, he did. We went through the same process, with precisely the same result in every detail. In another few weeks I was again asked to represent him in exactly the same circumstances. I protested that he must get some one else; that certainly he could not fare worse. He seemed to be disconsolate, saying over and over again: "Ohne Sie gehts nicht" (without you it can not be done). I feared that he might be right, but finally yielded. The humanitarian instinct of this justice was obviously against me. The result was the same in all respects, with one exception. The client did not pay me five dollars, and the next time I met him on the street he made a face at me. It was all very disillusioning, and the remembrance of the impressive counsel Nat Myers had give me before I decided for the law, was distinctly disturbing. Funds ran very low. Often enough I went without lunch; and at other times the price of a nickel would get me a glass of beer and a fine slice of roast beef.

It was then that I again met Henry I. D'Arcy, the Irish classmate who had at Law School led the protest against Teutonic mixed metaphors. We formed a partnership, and moved into a small room nearer to the area of possible clients. Again I was happy in my association. Mr. D'Arcy was a highly educated man of ready wit, and a most engaging talker and speaker. He almost demolished an author whom I knew by the simple comment that he judged the importance of his dissertations by the size of his subject. We can not be said to have been much of a success, but for me the experience was of great value. In this instance as in many others, it was my good fortune to be in daily contact with men whose training was much better than mine; for there was no field in which I could ever feel a sense of security. But for him I should never have had the courage to prepare the first paper that I was asked to read. Perhaps I owe as much to a Unitarian clergyman (Mr. Learned) who after hearing me came to our home to offer congratulations and encouragement. After the ice was once broken, I readily committed myself to many another such heartache. D'Arcy's English was perfect, whether he discussed Aristotle or Gladstone, or his friends Parnell and Dillon, or our own affairs; and as usual I gathered wherever the chance offered. That much I had learnt.

We made a bare living but no more. After a few years Mr. D'Arcy was offered a rather large case on a contingent fee, which would call for most of his time. This meant our separation. He assured me that it was best for me, and in this he was right.

The weakness of my voice had at first kept me out of court whenever possible, and naturally his admitted ability threw most court work into his hands. In addition, I felt a hesitancy about appearing in court which I have never quite overcome, although in the course of time I have made hundreds of political speeches and addresses upon other subjects. The ease and self-reliance with which great lawyers like Joseph Choate and John G. Johnson and Henry Hitchcock presented their arguments always had a particular charm for me. Perhaps they made the unattainable too obvious.

No sooner was I thrown upon my own responsibility than

conditions seemed to improve. Here and there a client came who was a man of affairs, and who might mean more than an isolated case. The first important employment was given me by a widow who turned a considerable estate over to me, as I believe because she liked my mother. As luck would have it, the estate about doubled in my hands while she remained abroad with her family.

Next came one of our best commission houses, that remained with me for many years; in fact, until they retired. Then came a large mining concern that has been in our office for more than fifty years. Finally and some years later came Mr. Busch, who in effect underwrote my professional existence. I met him by chance. After a meeting of stockholders, in which I represented a mere trifle, he invited all those present to join him at a well known restaurant. The weather was oppressive, and he ordered a very attractive but insidious drink. I had never before met him, or the drink, but he turned to me from time to time and spoke first in German and then in English.

Like a bolt out of a clear sky he suddenly said: "They have been telling me that you are one of those stay-at-homes; but I think you can drink with any man I ever met." We soon parted, and I had no thought of meeting him again. Two days later he sent his first case. I tried and lost it, and then settled it for a trifle. He said it could not have been won, and six months later he employed me as his regular counsel. That is about fifty years ago. Since then I have been counsel for his son; and today our firm represents his grandsons in the same business. He made me brilliant offers — employment for life, sick or well, for half my time, at handsome compensation. When I declined upon the ground that he could not afford to have doctor or lawyer who might be afraid to say no, he called me crazy, but

Fig. 45: Oscar Wilde - Photograph taken in 1882 by Napoleon Sarony

upon reflection said I was right. That interview really became the bond of our mutual confidence. But in most respects after my real start, professional employment increased with me as it did in the case of others. After leaving Mr. D'Arcy I remained alone for some years, having no one but Kirby, a graduate of our Law School, in my

Fig. 46: Self portrait by Keppler

office. Some time in the nineties I formed a partnership with him. He is in effect senior partner now, while I am still called "Chief." For a good many years I was quite active in helping to nominate judges; in fact, I managed judicial campaigns in several instances. That alone of course eliminated me from the list of possible appointments to receiverships and gave me a status which remained unaffected by changed conditions.

Fig. 47: Carl Schurz is Don Quixote in this cartoon by Thomas Nast from Harper's Weekly of April 6, 1872

But as my education, such as it was, consisted chiefly of trespassing into many fields without ever gaining ownership of any, so throughout my life the role of dilettante in pursuit of the most varied interests was never thrown off. Wherever the water seemed fine I ventured a dip, waving to others to share the sport if they would. It is said that law is a jealous mistress. Even that saying dare not be taken literally. Distinction in any sphere is rare without broad interests and a fair degree of general knowledge. This, however, was not my case. Nor was it mere search for digression. It was more like indulgence of diverse tastes which went to form the basis of personal happiness.

In the early days soon after the Civil War we had a club, the "Germania." The best representatives of the German element were members, and they gave balls and performances to which invitations were gladly accepted outside of the membership. To use a broker's term, I was still long on time, and for some years was chairman of the Entertainment Committee. We frequently gave plays of the lighter type, in German. Our more pretentious performances were tableaux. Romeo and Juliet was a favorite, and was repeated several times. We had Don Carlos, Wallenstein and, finally, the first part of Faust. To fill the roles we were not restricted to membership, and no draft was needed to gain the participation of outsiders. No distinction, no profession or business offered immunity; and for the roles of Juliet and Gretchen the choice involved no less than a beauty contest. For Juliet we had Emma Kohn, my friend Fishel's niece, and she was certainly made for the part. As Gretchen in Faust we had Miss Morrison, a recognized beauty and a ready wit—not a member. Joseph Pulitzer, the founder of the New York World, took the part of Mephistopheles, with enthusiastic approval. The success was so great that a second performance of Faust for a

Fig. 48: Rutherford B. Hayes

charity was demanded. Unhappily for me, Mr. Pulitzer could not serve, and as the responsible chairman I had to substitute, and did as I am glad to add, with generous efforts to disguise my identity. The deception must have been indifferent, because one rather discerning young lady was heard to say that if it did not look any worse than that below, she was not afraid to go.

In our masquerade balls we were less fortunate. The disposition to assume a part got out of bounds. There was some reason in having persons pretend to be what they would be least suspected of being; but after all there must be some aptitude for the counterfeit part. One year we had an overproduction of Hamlet; and when we became aware of the scarcity of butchers, we wondered whether there might be some relation between the conditions. There is no

Fig. 49: Columbia wearing a warship bearing the words "World Power" as her "Easter bonnet", cover of Puck (April 6, 1901)

telling what people may do to get away from themselves. There was an attractive young woman — a visitor — who destroyed the equanimity of the whole assembly by her impersonation of "Topsy." She afterwards married a clergyman. I can get a laugh at any time from my family at my expense, by reminding them that I was once awarded the first prize for my representation of Oscar Wilde[a]. This was at the peak of his reputation. We decided to restrict ourselves to masquerade processions, for which every one to avoid duplication had to be designated for his part. Keppler[b], who afterwards became the very successful publisher of "Puck"[c] in New York, arranged the processions, assisted by Mr. Kummer, a painter. Keppler's office I sometimes visited to watch him draw cartoons while Puck was still published in St. Louis. He selected me for "Don Quixote" — evidently Myers' original estimate of me still lingered. There was of course a Sancho, who was as broad as I was thin. As a target he was irresistible, and after I had speared him several times he remonstrated that I was unreasonably realistic. I have known men in public life who were idealistically inclined, and whose desire to be practical fell below the required standard. I told Sancho that obviously he had not read the book — neither had I at that time; but he became reconciled to his fate.

We also had a group of alumni of German universities.

a   Oscar Fingal O'Flahertie Wills Wilde (16 October 1854 – 30 November 1900) was an Irish playwright, novelist, essayist, and poet. After writing in different forms throughout the 1880s, he became one of London's most popular playwrights in the early 1890s. He is remembered for his epigrams, his novel The Picture of Dorian Gray, his plays, as well as the circumstances of his imprisonment and early death.
b   Joseph Ferdinand Keppler (1 February 1838 Vienna – 19 February 1894 New York City) was an Austrian-born American cartoonist and caricaturist who greatly influenced the growth of satirical cartooning in the United States.
c   Puck was the first successful humor magazine in the United States of colorful cartoons, caricatures and political satire of the issues of the day. It was published from 1871 until 1918. A collection of Puck cartoons dating from 1879 to 1903 is maintained by the Special Collections Research Center of The George Washington University.

Graduates were scarce, so we admitted any one who had registered. This included me. We met and, armed with sabres and beer mugs, and decorated with cap and ribbons which I for one had never worn, sang the old songs ever new to me.

However, we had had a Civil War, and prosperity was on the way to justify its sacrifices. Old and elaborate homes were deserted, warehouses succeeded, and railroad yards with clang of bells and volumes of smoke encroached upon the once sedate neighborhood. The Germania Club could not even be converted to modern use. The building was leveled, and the spirit that had once reigned there is of the past.

New fields of employment, if not entertainment, had to be found, and what reservoir is more rich in the variety of its offerings than politics? I always resent that the term politics has been permitted to sink to so low a state that its true meaning is almost lost. My approach was very tentative. I was on the point of being nominated for the school board once when an imported band took possession and named someone else. In spite of this and similar disillusioning experiences, politics stood in my mind for something like a sacred cause.

Missouri was a border state. Few states were so evenly divided upon the issue of the Civil War; perhaps none furnished proportionately more men for both armies. The successful struggle to hold her in the Union had been fierce, and it would have seemed natural to have the political alignment drawn upon those lines after the war. The contrary was true. The organization of the liberal Republicans in our state was based upon the idea that the war was over, and that the franchise should be enjoyed by all citizens. In this fight Carl Schurz[a] was no doubt a leader, and as had been true before the war, he inspired the German population for his cause. My father was an outspoken supporter. To me it was little more than a sentiment. I was barely of age. I heard Schurz make one of his impressive speeches in the rotunda of the old Court House, pleading for personal liberty as the foundation stone of all self-government. There was tremendous enthusiasm. As I came out the night was clear and I saw standing half way up the steps Joseph Pulitzer[b], then a reporter on a Republican German paper. He seemed to me an impressive figure, tall and slight, the very symbol of a challenge.

The crucial fight was won by the Liberals, and Carl Schurz became a Republican senator from Missouri. At the next election the Democrats took control, and as a result the old guard Republicans came back to power, to retain it for many years. I had started on the victorious side, but for a long time paid the penalty of my alignment. In the Senate Schurz made his attacks upon President Grant in his sec-

a   Carl Christian Schurz (March 2, 1829–May 14, 1906) was a German revolutionary, American statesman and reformer, U.S. Minister to Spain, Union Army General in the American Civil War, U.S. Senator, and Secretary of the Interior. He was also an accomplished journalist, newspaper editor and orator, who in 1869 became the first German-born American elected to the United States Senate.
b   Joseph Pulitzer (April 10, 1847–October 29, 1911) was a Hungarian-American newspaper publisher of the St. Louis Post Dispatch and the New York World. Pulitzer introduced the techniques of yellow journalism to the newspapers he acquired in the 1880s. He became a leading national figure in the Democratic Party and was elected congressman from New York. He crusaded against big business and corruption, and helped keep the Statue of Liberty in New York.
Today, he is best known for the Pulitzer Prizes, which were established in 1917 by money he bequeathed to Columbia University to recognize artistic and journalistic achievements in the United States.

ond term. The Whiskey Ring and other cases were tried in St. Louis. I sat through them and gloried in the righteous indignation of the District Attorney. We were not yet prepared for such disclosures, but we were in the process of being broken in. The verdicts were only a partial triumph for the Government. The next presidential nomination was had in 1872. Secretary Brewster was the hope of the Liberals, and upon his defeat we were treated to the conglomerate losing ticket of Greeley and Brown. We read that Schurz had sought consolation by playing the piano, and no doubt many of us regretted that we had no instrument to play upon. Things were not going well for a budding politician. He might be tolerated in a local convention here or there, but there was little or nothing for a dreamer to fasten upon. Grant's second term came to its end, and in 1876 a concerted effort was made to name Senator Edmunds as the Republican candidate. Again the selection of Hayes was a mere compromise, and the great Hayes-Tilden contest[a] barely bridged the chasm, and left the American people wondering for what they might have to be prepared.

a   The United States presidential election of 1876 was the 23rd quadrennial presidential election, held on Tuesday, November 7, 1876. It was one of the most contentious and controversial presidential elections in American history. The results of the election remain among the most disputed ever, although it is not disputed that Samuel J. Tilden of New York outpolled Ohio's Rutherford B. Hayes in the popular vote. After a first count of votes, Tilden won 184 electoral votes to Hayes's 165, with 20 votes unresolved. These 20 electoral votes were in dispute in four states. In the case of Florida, Louisiana, and South Carolina, each party reported its candidate had won the state, while in Oregon one elector was replaced after being declared illegal for being an "elected or appointed official". The question of who should have been awarded these electoral votes is the source of the continued controversy concerning the results of this election.

While Hayes was probably a better president than he has been given credit for, certainly if he is to be judged by the caliber of his cabinet, the Old Guard was distinctly disappointed. In 1880 all the forces were gathered for a return to power, and their chosen candidate was U.S. Grant. The anti-third term cry was raised, and the claim that the bar did not apply where a term had intervened, went unheeded. In 1880 Missouri's delegation was pledged to Grant, but we held a convention of delegates from many states in St. Louis, who resolved that they would not support Grant if he was nominated. Among our members were several delegates to the National Convention from other states. They voted with us, but when I watched their course in the National Convention they did not appear to be so sure of their position. I attended that convention for an entire week, until the nomination for candidates was made. It was an experience that I cherished as one of my thrilling memories. For that period the hall was unusually large, and it was packed to the guards. The convention was seated on the ground floor, and delegates spoke and could be fairly well heard from that point. Megaphones, loud speakers and cameras had not yet been introduced to contribute to confusion and discord. In some respects a political convention still had something of the character of a deliberative body. Senator Hoar of Massachusetts was the chairman, which in itself was some guaranty of orderly proceedings. The New York delegation sat near the front to the left of the chairman; farther down the Ohio delegation, and still farther back the Maine delegation, both on the same side of the aisle. Illinois was on the other side near the center, and behind that Indiana. These were the delegations of which the chairmen were particularly prominent figures. Experienced politicians have a way of giving the convention time to get settled, and then entering, for such approval as the assembled populace may have in store for them. The result is sometimes disappointing. Senator Logan of Illinois of course received generous recognition in the City of Chicago. Harrison of Indiana had some applause, which was also true of Senators Hale[a] and Fry[b] of Maine. When Senator Conkling[c] of New York walked down the aisle like a conquering hero, amid wild acclamations of the people present, there could be no question of his significance. In bearing he had something of the ancient knight in armor. Garfield came very quietly from the side, taking a seat almost under the gallery, and had a hand clap from a few in his immediate vicinity. By chance I had obtained a reserved seat for the entire convention in the third row from the front of the platform. I

a Eugene Hale (June 9, 1836 – October 27, 1918) was a Republican United States Senator from Maine.
b William Pierce Frye (September 2, 1830 – August 8, 1911) was an American politician from the state of Maine. Frye, a member of the Republican Party, spent most of his political career as a legislator, serving in the Maine House of Representatives and then U.S. House of Representatives, before being elected to the U.S. Senate, where he served for 30 years; dying in office. Frye was a member of the Frye political family, and was the grandfather of Wallace H. White, Jr. and the son of John March Frye. He was also a prominent member of the Peucinian Society tradition.
c Roscoe Conkling (October 30, 1829–April 18, 1888) was a politician from New York who served both as a member of the United States House of Representatives and the United States Senate. He was the leader of the Stalwart faction of the Republican Party, the first Republican senator from New York to be elected for three terms, and the last person to turn down a U.S. Supreme Court appointment after he had already been confirmed to the post by the U.S. Senate. While in the House, Representative Conkling served as body guard for Representative Thaddeus Stevens, a sharp-tongued anti slavery representative, and fully supported the Republican War effort. Conkling, who was temperate and detested tobacco, was known for being a body builder through regularly exercising and boxing. Conkling was elected to the Senate in 1867 as a leading Radical, who supported the rights of African Americans during Reconstruction.

could hear every word; and for some years I could substantially repeat some of the speeches. I generally sat next to Joseph Medill[a], the editor of the Chicago Tribune, the most effective newspaper opponent of the third term. Grant and Blaine[b] were the two active and intensely antagonistic candidates; Conkling with Logan's support, in charge of the former's cause; and Hale and Fry of the latter's. During the early more formal proceedings Conkling and Hale had something of an exchange of words which, however, served as a mere intimation of the coming encounter. The first real demonstration of the feeling came about the second or third day. It was known that Grant needed only a comparatively few votes. It was as well known that the great majority of the others were irreconcilably opposed to him. The final result depended upon the decision of the credential committees upon a few disputed delegations. But it was also understood that some delegates would not support Grant even if he received the nomination. At these Conkling directed his first attack, no doubt to give early proof of his power. He offered a reso-

a   Joseph Medill (April 6, 1823–March 16, 1899) was a Canadian-American newspaper editor, publisher, and Republican party politician. He was co-owner and managing editor of the Chicago Tribune, and was Mayor of Chicago after the great fire of 1871.
b   James Gillespie Blaine (January 31, 1830 – January 27, 1893) was an American statesman and Republican politician who represented Maine in the U.S. House of Representatives from 1863 to 1876, serving as Speaker of the U.S. House of Representatives from 1869 to 1875, and then in the United States Senate from 1876 to 1881. Blaine twice served as Secretary of State (1881, 1889–1892), one of only two persons to hold the position under three separate presidents (the other being Daniel Webster), and unsuccessfully sought the Republican nomination for President in 1876 and 1880 before being nominated in 1884. In the general election, he was narrowly defeated by Democrat Grover Cleveland. Blaine was one of the late 19th century's leading Republicans and champion of the moderate reformist faction of the party known as the "Half-Breeds."

lution that every delegate be pledged to support the nominee of the convention. This Garfield, who had not said anything, opposed with a few admonishing words, and closing with "I advise the gentlemen from New York to withdraw that resolution." Conkling, with a gesture and words of derision, insisted upon his resolution, and a vote was taken by delegations. The overwhelming majority voted in the affirmative, among them a few members of our anti-third term convention, probably in the belief that Grant would fail in any event. But a few delegations recorded protesting votes. The resolution having carried, Conkling then moved that those delegates who had voted not be excluded from the convention. Garfield rose again, this time with calls that he stand on his chair so that he might be seen and better heard. He renewed his advice, and added that this was not the first time when such action had been tried, and that on one such occasion his distinguished predecessor in Congress, Mr. Giddings, had taken his hat and walked out of the convention. But Conkling could not be moved. At that stage the chairman of the West Virginia delegation rose to say that he had voted for the resolution, but the one vote against it had been cast by the man who was probably the most distinguished Republican of his state, the man who had published the first Republican newspaper and introduced the first negro speaker in West Virginia. The great audience assumed an expectant attitude; and with that this delegate rose to his feet and spoke about as follows: "Mr. Chairman, I carry my independence under my own hat (at this the crowd broke out in the greatest storm of approval so far). The gentleman from New York and I are not strangers. We have sat together as delegates in other conventions. In 1876 both favored a candidate who failed. Rutherford B. Hayes was nominated; and we were equally disappointed. The gentleman from New York returned to his state and

Fig. 50: The Chair of John Stuart Mill - currently in the editor's custody

sulked in his tent. I returned to mine and made one hundred speeches for Rutherford B. Hayes." Public admiration could not have a more signal illustration. The whole crowd cheered with wildest demonstration. How that resolution was disposed of I never quite understood, but it was dead. Garfield had caught the attention of the whole convention, which was now keyed to the highest pitch.

A convention has much more or less perfunctory business to attend to. Platform framers are busy, and individual members have their own irons in the fire. After all, the real issue rested with the credential committee. This committee made reports from time to time confirmatory of expected decisions; but no word came about the one question whether a congressional district had the right by a majority vote to name the delegates to a National Convention, or whether subdivisions of the district could name their own delegates. If the first position was approved, Grant was victor; if the second, his case was hopeless. While we were waiting for this decision, the convention would at times adjourn and at other times give volunteer orators a chance to disport themselves before us. One night, I think it was Friday, expectation ran high because it was assumed that adjournment would come with the end of the week. There had been speakers, most of whom even then excelled in verbosity rather than clarity of convictions. Hour followed hour until we approached two o'clock in the morning. General Sheridan[a], in full uniform, walked across the stage and was heartily cheered as the friend of Grant. He was followed by a Chicago lawyer, Storrs, noted for his eloquence. He soon proved that there could be no question of his power over a crowd. He made an extended speech, wisely dwelling more upon Grant's military record than his civil reputation. He wound up with a withering criticism of the renegade enemies of the Republican party, and how in the campaign in the fall they would be hanging about the tents of the loyal defenders, longing to warm their feet at the camp fire, etc. His success was complete. The spontaneity with which the crowd rose to shout its approval seemed to remove the last doubt of the result. When the excitement ceased the unexpected happened; both unaccountable and effective in its consequences. About two seats behind me a man rose and stood on his chair. He wore a long linen duster. With his left hand he rolled up the right sleeve to his elbow, and taking his

a   Philip Henry Sheridan (March 6, 1831–August 5, 1888) was a career United States Army officer and a Union general in the American Civil War. Both as a soldier and private citizen, he was instrumental in the development and protection of Yellowstone National Park. In 1883, Sheridan was appointed general-in-chief of the U.S. Army, and in 1888 he was promoted to the rank of General of the Army during the term of President Grover Cleveland.

straw hat in his hand he sailed it into the air, far above the delegates, and in a voice that reached every corner of the hall he said these simple words: "And now, three cheers for James G. Blaine." That was all of him; but the uproar came with such a shock that I involuntarily looked to see whether the roof was still there. I have never seen another such political demonstration. Coats and hats and open umbrellas were waived, and I think the pandemonium must have lasted for fifteen minutes. I have wondered, in view of those conflicting exhibitions, what that crowd would have done with a direct primary. At last the noise subsided, and as if in response to an awaited signal the credential committee filed in and made a majority report in favor of the right of subdivisions to name their own delegates and that report was at once adopted by the worn out convention. The belated contests came from Cook and St. Clair counties in Illinois, and Conkling and Logan entered upon the second stage of their final defeat. Logan accepted the result with manly dignity; and after adjournment I saw Conkling out in the open, his famous lock of hair floating in the breezes, still receiving the ovations of his admirers—chiefly ladies.

Of the next day, Saturday, I recall nothing but that it was agreed to make the nominating speeches that night. These I was anxious to hear. I had a telegram calling me home on account of illness, but sat in my place as long as I dared, without hearing any of them. As I went out from a side door I saw within two entrances from me the figure of a man. His back was toward me but at once I recognized Garfield. He was gazing at the heavens as though he were studying the stars; and I left for my train wondering whether all the prophets had lived in the past. The next morning I visited a friend who was ill—Mr. Finkelnburg, one of our first lawyers, and as fair and gentle a man as I ever knew. He had served in Congress with Blaine, and wanted to know whether he had any chance. I told him none. He asked me who would be nominated, and I answered Garfield. But, came the protest, "he has not been placed in nomination." That, I said, will make no difference. Grant has three hundred and three votes and can not get another. Blaine destroyed him, and with that defeated himself. In a convention of so much feeling as this has shown, Sherman is impossible, and as for Garfield, you could not buy a paper collar in Chicago until you declare for him.

I have been tempted to write this account without consulting any record, relying simply upon my memory of incidents in a convention that left an impression as few experiences have.

For the first time I felt that I had been an active participant in a real struggle about an important political issue, and we had won. Even that was largely sentimental; there was no particular act to point to. I had written a few screeds for rather obscure papers, and had sent one letter to the Chicago Tribune. In it I cited Chancellor Kent's comments upon the third term doctrine in his introduction to his commentaries. To my surprise it was published prominently. The Chicago Tribune was reaching out for support wherever it could be found. There were those of course who sought to minimize the victory by criticizing Garfield's career, but with little effect upon me. A school teacher once, he had become a general; and when he and others had left the field as lost, it was he alone who at the sound of battle returned to join General Thomas at Chicamaugua. I argued, and I think with truth, that while our candidate had no doubt made political concessions in incidental questions, he had been essentially right from the start upon every paramount problem of his time. He was probably the only man who at one and the same time was a member of Congress, just elected to the Senate and now the victorious candidate for the presidency. Above all, it was he who by his wise but uncompromising guidance had saved us from a third term. No other issue of such far-reaching consequence could I felt arise in my time. I could not have hoped to live to see the present political turmoil.

During the next ten or fifteen years my interest in national politics was less keen. Party supremacy and personal ambition were stressed more and more at the expense of principle. More or less active, I voted the party ticket without enthusiasm and often with misgiving. But to state and local politics I gave considerable attention. I felt that the source of our danger was at the bottom and not at the top. Only through the successful administration of local affairs could the national system be conserved; and in the last analysis salvation rested with the integrity and self-respect of the citizenship itself. I took an interest in the selection of candidates for the judiciary, and while for many years I had openly supported more Democratic than Republican candidates for election, I did succeed in having a few outstanding candidates nominated, and in some instances took charge of their entire campaigns. I wrote screeds, arranged for meetings, made speeches, and finally learnt to smoke, which is one of the surviving convictions of that period.

Of the ten years following 1880 I find it difficult to speak. My wife's illness, contracted before we married in 1876, had not yielded to treatment, and our happiness was at all times clouded by apprehension. We lived with my parents, and she brought to our home an influence that we had no doubt felt, but never found the way to express. Her feeling for literature and art was part of her being; and her love and understanding for music was very unusual. We now had two pianos in our home, and she and three associates for a number of years gave concerts in our home, that were attended by our friends and others whom we scarcely knew. Chopin, Mozart, Schumann and other masters were given to us in a manner to let us feel as it were that we might cross the threshold. Father particularly was completely won. My participation in affairs was a source of interest and gratification to her, as it was to me. At the election of 1880 I was sent to the House of the Missouri Legislature, and attended the regular and the extra sessions. As a member of the Committee of Constitutional Amendments I was instrumental in defeating a proposed prohibition amendment. As usual many arguments were bandied about—pro and con—good and bad; but as has been the case since then, statistics were freely used, largely by those who knew least about them. In one instance, a proposition advanced on our side seemed so doubtful that I invited confidence by puncturing it. A friend, the best parliamentarian in the House, submitting a vast array of figures, contended that the saloon could not be the source of crime, because the large cities had a smaller percentage of convicts in the penitentiary than the country districts. I answered regretfully that perhaps the cities achieved their percentage because their administrations were too rotten to bring their criminals to justice. I won the fight; but my suspicion of statistics has never been quite removed. On the floor of the House I helped to defeat a bill to place benevolent societies under the supervision of the State Insurance Department. I introduced a bill to prohibit betting on races away from the race track. It was never reported; but I was editorially reprimanded for my disregard of my city's interests. Finally, I cast one vote which I should probably not repeat now, in opposing a measure to

Fig. 51: Anders Zorn's Portrait of William Howard Taft

prohibit industries from making agreements with their employees to buy supplies at the company stores. The law was enacted and declared unconstitutional by the State Supreme Court. That is a long time ago, and much water has gone over the dam since then. I had no doubt that in some cases such contracts would be abused by the proprietors, and that in others would serve to protect the employees. A desire to save the under dog was of course uppermost; but the determination to preserve the independence and self-respect of the individual man prevailed. Perhaps I read Herbert Spencer[a] and John Stuart Mill[b] with too much sympathy then; but even now I can not resist the feeling that a more general reading of those authors would be wholesome. Perhaps earlier reading of the Iliad might have better prepared me for looking for help to some god or goddess.

Very soon after I was nominated for the State Supreme Court. Candidates had to be sought because there was no prospect of success. I accepted the empty honor. When a third party, which advocated some vagaries that have since then become more or less popular, offered to put me upon its ticket, I fortunately was in a position to decline upon the ground that I could not run upon conflicting platforms. Perhaps this would cause some amusement

a Herbert Spencer (27 April 1820 – 8 December 1903) was an English philosopher, biologist, anthropologist, sociologist, and prominent classical liberal political theorist of the Victorian era. Spencer developed an all-embracing conception of evolution as the progressive development of the physical world, biological organisms, the human mind, and human culture and societies.
b John Stuart Mill (20 May 1806 – 8 May 1873) was an English philosopher, political economist and civil servant. One of the most influential thinkers in the history of liberalism, he contributed widely to social theory, political theory and political economy. Dubbed "the most influential English-speaking philosopher of the nineteenth century",[5] Mill's conception of liberty justified the freedom of the individual in opposition to unlimited state and social control.
Coincidentally, John Stuart Mill was a friend and influencer of Sir William Randall Cremer who founded the International Arbitration League of which the editor is currently acting chairman. The John Stuart Mill chair is currently in our possession.

now; but to put principle before men was at least not misunderstood then. The returns of the votes showed that my acceptance of the second nomination would have elected me. The escape was as welcome as it was narrow. I was always persuaded that the bench was no place for me. In later years I had opportunities for judicial preferment by election or appointment, but avoided both.

Early that year I was made a member of the board of Washington University's Art School. The director was Halsey C. Ives[a], who was afterwards director of the Art Departments of the Columbia Exposition in Chicago and the Louisiana Purchase Exposition in St. Louis. The association with him and members of the faculty proved to be most interesting, and within my small resources I bought quite a number of their pictures, some of which are still in my family's homes. At the Chicago Exposition Ives and I bought quite a number of foreign paintings and some statues, which now form an important part of the university art collection. There I first met Anders Zorn[b], the Swedish artist. I admired his etchings from the first and bought a number of them, adding to them since then as opportunity offered. We became friends, and two family portraits by him are among our treasured possessions[c]. There I also

a Halsey Cooley Ives (27 October 1847–5 May 1911) was the founder of the Saint Louis School and Museum of Fine Arts. The institution later became two distinct bodies; the Saint Louis Art Museum, and the Washington University School of Art which includes the Mildred Lane Kemper Art Museum. Ives was also a landscape painter, but is best remembered for the organization, administration, and popularization of art in Saint Louis, Missouri.
b Anders Leonard Zorn (18 February 1860–22 August 1920) was one of Sweden's foremost artists. He obtained international success as a painter, sculptor, and etcher.
c The drawing of Mrs Nagel made in 1897 was recently auctioned. It can be viewed at: https://s-media-cache-ak0.pinimg.com/originals/75/f9/5a/75f95acf2086bffaedb2060341174b9d.jpg

saw Sorolla's painting "Another Marguerite"; perhaps the first example of his art in this country. I was then a member of our City Council at an annual salary of Three Hundred Dollars. Multiplying this by a four year term, and estimating what I might receive while officiating as Acting Mayor, I realized the cost of the painting, bought it, gave it to the University, and rid myself of municipal money for good.

About the same time I was elected a member of the Board of Trustees of Washington University, of which I am now in point of service the oldest member, and in which I have served as vice-president, acting president, and for a time as president.

In 1895 Dr. Hammond, Dean of our Law School, appointed me as a member of a committee of three to pass upon the theses of the graduating class. Each one of us read every thesis. When we met for conference the other two agreed upon a particular one, and I had chosen another. I could not understand them, and said that in my opinion no student could have written the one I had chosen. We set aside three days to pursue the inquiry. Consulting Maine's Ancient Law I found that one student had made rather free use of the author's wisdom; but there was no trace of my particular candidate. Finally I turned to Holmes' Common Law. I had read Kent's Commentaries in Holmes' edition with his notes. Later on a Boston friend had given me his Common Law, which I had read, confessing some difficulty in grasping its accredited merit. But here I found that my choice among the theses was a literal copy of one of Holmes' chapters. I joined the other two in their selection; my candidate was denied his diploma, in spite of an appeal to both faculty and Board of Trustees; and there the chapter seemed to end, with the exception of the disturbing disclosure that the unhappy student was the son of one of the most respected members of the bar. Within a month Dean Hammond, who was a real scholar, appeared in my office and addressed me about as follows: "I am delighted to find a young lawyer west of the Mississippi river who has read Holmes' Common Law with sufficient understanding to recognize the text when he comes upon it in unexpected places."

Without giving me time to protest, he continued by inviting me to join his faculty. I accepted with the usual reservations, and served in that capacity for twenty-four years; until President Taft's invitation to become a member of his cabinet necessitated my retirement. During that period my subjects were Agency, Partnership, Corporations, Contracts and, finally, Constitutional Law. For a few years I taught Medical Jurisprudence at the Medical School, of which I was also legal adviser at the time. As always, I was well aware that I was not well grounded in a technical sense; my lectures were informal, without manuscript notes or text book in the class room. Much of the time was taken up with discussions, growing out of such questions and answers as the subject suggested. That method was favored by the fact that the classes rarely exceeded twenty-five. A new dean, who no doubt suspected that my method might be unduly liberal, at one time asked me whether I felt that I was successful in impressing the students with the precise conclusions of the Supreme Court. I parried at first by saying that this might be unsafe because the court had been known to shift its position. However, to meet his point I concluded that I was not sure in my own mind, but I could say with some confidence that no student had ever entered my class who did not go out with more respect for our institutions than he had come with. We left it at that.

During the years 1889-90 our only son, my wife, my father and my mother died, leaving me with one little girl, who would run through the rooms waving her arms like a bird's wings and saying "All gone, all gone." By that time I was professionally fairly busy, so that with my lectures and memberships in several boards there was little time for more; but I sought refuge in anything that came my way.

About that time I had made an address upon local government, in which I contended that a solution of the problem depended upon an entire withdrawal from the control of national party organization. The general aims and the immediate problems are so distinct that they can not be successfully met by a common system which is bound to deteriorate into a scheme for the perpetuation of mere office holding. I was asked whether I would be willing to make a contest upon such a plan, and agreed. A full ticket was nominated, and popular approval was shown by a surprising support of volunteers. The result showed that I had been successful in defeating my own party and in triumphantly electing the Democratic ticket. Upon reflection I found that all the gentlemen who had invited me were Democrats. I made no question that they had voted for me to a man, but I never heard of another Democrat who did. Two years later the second section of the city government had to be elected, including the Mayor and the President of the City Council. I was asked to run for the Council, but declined. After the full Republican ticket had been named, it was decided that the candidate for President of the Council would have to withdraw. An appeal to have me take his place came not only from politicians, but also from influential supporters of my earlier candidacy, and reluctantly I accepted. During this campaign I stressed, as I had two years before, playgrounds and improved police courts. Perhaps this was the reason why Joseph Lee[a], now president of the National Recreation Association, entrusted me in 1903 with the fund to make it possible to have an exhibit of a playground at the Louisiana Purchase Exposition. The response was a surprise. While newspapers took little notice of my platform, ward politicians told me that the idea had caught the public. The meetings were large, and although women had no vote, they attended in large numbers. I ran three thousand votes ahead of my ticket, and was elected. For four years I presided at every meeting, barring two. In 1895 I had married again, and was away on a brief wedding trip. I was Acting Mayor at frequent intervals, sometimes for periods of weeks. I spent hours to successfully save a lad from the horrible House of Refuge[b], by proving that the police officer who had made the arrest was mistaken in his charge and report. That impulse has never left me, and has furnished many a chance to intercede in time. After all, first aid should not be the prerogative of doctors and Boy Scouts alone. When the customary list for releases from the equally horrible Workhouse[c] was submitted to me, because the place was

a Joseph Lee (1862–1937) was a wealthy Bostonian, who trained as a lawyer but never practiced law, and is considered the "founder of the playground movement."
b Most homes for dependent children in St. Louis between 1850 and 1870 were church affiliated. The notable exception to this was the House of Refuge, chartered by the State of Missouri in 1851. In theory the House of Refuge was a progressive social reform intended to preserve society's juvenile offenders from the influence of hardened criminals. In brief, it was a reform school. In practice, the House of Refuge became a residence for indigent and orphaned as well as delinquent boys and girls in St. Louis.
(http://www.visheritage.net/page6.php).
c Besides the city jail, criminals in 1875 were also sent to the St. Louis Workhouse at Broadway and Meramec streets. The workhouse's main function was supplying crushed limestone for city streets. All day long, inmates toiled "making little stones out of big ones."

overcrowded, I discovered by personal investigation that the practice was to release the professional offenders, and to retain those who had not yet been broken in. I reversed the method, and called for inmates who were not on the list and thought they had a good case. The result gave me perhaps as much satisfaction as it did the beneficiaries of the new rule. I well remember two—a splendid Irishman, a horse shoer, and a bewildered German, a shoemaker. Neither had ever been arrested before; both seemed to be victims of overzealous neighbors. The Irishman was grateful; but the German could not understand how I guessed his trade, although the poorly clad fellow was wearing handmade boots. When those who were released and those who were held assembled in opposing lines, I saw a fine picture of comradeship, as those who were free threw all their little treasures, like tobacco, etc., back to those who had to stay.

As presiding officer of the Board of Health I got a clear impression of the deplorable condition of our eleemosynary institutions. Those who despair of improvement in local conditions need only look at those institutions now, however inadequate they may still be. But in our time little enough was accomplished. At the next election my name was proposed as candidate for Mayor. It is perhaps true that I would have been sure of election. The Republican organization was, however, doubly strong, largely because of our conduct. I was ingloriously defeated, to my great relief. I now felt that I was through with office holding and could devote myself to my profession and incidental interests, chief of which was always the political condition.

> Women were sentenced to the workhouse right beside men, and in 1875 alone more than 1,100 women picked up their hammers and headed to the rock yards.
> (http://www.historyhappenshere.org/node/7698).

In 1900 we had one of the most serious street car strikes. The official representatives were disposed to play politics. We persuaded the sheriff to avow the cause of law and order, as he did. Violence of every conceivable kind was indulged in. Dynamite explosions were of daily occurrence; women were ejected from cars and, actually stripped of their clothing, left to find refuge where they could. I sent my family away and organized a company of seventy-five men (one of several) as deputy sheriffs. This was my second experience as deputy sheriff. They called me Captain; I was in truth moderator. For twenty-one days and nights we were kept on duty. The crowds jeered and threatened, but there were few actual collisions — barring a few arrests, and as I am glad to say, convictions. In the end the strike was lost in the sand; and we seemed to be assured of a period of normal conditions. Our state had been consistently Democratic ever since the defeat of Schurz for re-election in the seventies, and at last we saw hope in the candidacy of Theodore Roosevelt for President in 1904. I could not agree with him on many points, but I regarded him as a crusader for cleaning house. That was our platform, and the Republicans organized as never before. The personality of Roosevelt carried far beyond mere party politics, and at last we won the state. I got to know Mr. Roosevelt fairly well. He consulted me at times about judicial appointments. He disregarded some of my suggestions in a manner bordering on contempt, and I thought my informant might not be far from the truth when he said that the President had called me a parlor politician. I have every right to say that he would have been glad to give me a judgeship; but that was very far from respecting me as a political adviser.

I was an original supporter of Howard Taft in 1908; was elected as the Missouri member of the National Committee for that campaign; was appointed on the Executive Committee, and was practically in charge of Chicago headquarters. My appointment to the cabinet was perhaps the greatest surprise of my political experience, and I had had many of considerable variety.

Those four years were rich in associations not to be forgotten. There were times of high hope and even confidence, and in the end of sore disappointment. I supported Mr. Taft actively for re-election, and believe today that in him the finest purpose was destroyed by the machinations of cheapest politics and inordinate ambition. But this is another story.

I was permitted to retire without scandal, had helped organize the present Chamber of Commerce of the United States; had presided over the Commission of four nations that finally put an end to the seal controversy by agreeing upon a treaty that settled all questions, past, present and future; and came away with my feeling against centralized government well confirmed.

Personally I retired, not only without regret, but with a distinct sense of relief. I have never felt ambition for any office, and I trust my feeling for public interest may never die. Accordingly I served as opportunity offered, many interests of the most varied kind, commercial, charitable or educational; consistency there was none; unless it be the comforting notion that good will might serve as a substitute for training. I never accepted compensation for speeches and for articles in only one instance; neither political expense money nor passes. I felt something of a dread of the implied committal. Every article or address was my own, with this proviso. Since my marriage in 1895, I made few, if any, important decisions without a conference with my wife. Indeed, in many cases it would be difficult even for me to say who made the suggestion or the decision. Perhaps that accounts for her lack of interest in woman's suffrage. We were blest with rare family harmony, which embraced every member, and now includes a number of grandchildren, all of whom provide the family circle, whose sympathetic approval is after all the most treasured reward.

At the age of forty-five I learnt in a way to sail a catboat which may account for my escape since then from seasickness; and more especially I took to tennis, which by the tolerance of a thoughtful family and a wise doctor, I am still permitted to play.

I was getting along in years. What I remember most vividly is new to listeners. Any further consideration of me for office was in any event cut short by the Great War. I could not make a secret of my convictions. I questioned the charge of "sole guilt," warned that the ultimate economic and social consequences of a protracted war might prove more serious than the war itself; was regarded as an enemy of democracy and self-determination, and paid the usual penalty. There were three wars in my time, and I was never right at the right time. I was distressed at the intense feeling against the German element in our country, and was equally surprised to find that intelligent people actually looked upon the so-called protocols of the elders of Zion with apprehension. Evidently the negro did not stand alone in his need for sympathy amid tragic conditions. I am grateful now to have been permitted to live long enough to have some of my views of that time justified by better judges than I profess to be, and to be in a sense re-established in old time circles. It is true I lost friends, whose loyalty had seemed to me to be beyond question. That I can not forget. But there is great compensation in the knowledge that many others have come forward to assure an old man that he may go out without remorse. But I must not continue. That is quite another story.

Alphabetical Index

1848	33, 53, 65, 81, 115, 198
Abolitionist	216
Adler, Dr. Felix	388
Adorante	400
Alexander Hamilton	367
Alligator	23, 41pp., 45, 47, 55, 60, 164p., 167pp., 221, 240
Americanization	60, 124, 152, 204, 230
Amslin	49, 66, 85, 215
Anders Zorn	430
Another Marguerite	396, 431
Aristotle	406
Arkansas	102, 188, 206
Arndt	104
Atlantic Coast	64
Aunt Marie	343, 350
Austin County	47, 51
Bad Man's Out	282
Baden-Powell	185
Baltic	51
Baltimore	297, 306, 383
Barbarossa	137
Barton Street	299
Baseball	118, 121, 176, 310, 364
Bastille	60
Bastrop	229
Bayard Taylor	343
Becker, Dr.	95p., 244
Beef	43, 89, 91, 165p., 217, 347, 405
Bellville	7, 59p., 83, 195, 210, 220
Ben DeBar	375
Berlin	22, 67, 71, 76pp., 95, 101, 117, 198p., 295, 299, 334, 384, 392, 394, 397p., 400
Betende Knabe	400
Bierstadt	149
Bijou Museum	399

Biscuit	275
Bismarck	79, 115, 383, 390pp.
Black jack oak	19, 51
Black Man's Out	121
Black oak	142
Blackbirds	249
Blackstone	97, 368
Blaine	277, 420, 424p.
Bleecker Miller	385
Blind Man's Buff	153
Bloody Ninth	378
Bluecher	295p.
Board of Health	435
Boarding	75, 106, 293, 298p., 319, 322, 328, 331
Bohemian	66, 89, 99, 108, 123, 125, 205, 207, 231, 246
Booth	18, 375
Boston	214, 367, 431
Brandeis, Justice Louis D.	103
Brandenburg	69, 71
Braunschweig	355
Brazos	47, 167
Bread	89, 91, 165, 167, 170, 220, 293
Bremen	62, 71, 342p., 357, 383
Breslau	53, 115
Bristol	367
British Eloquence	105, 117, 366p.
Broadway	326
Brooks	297p., 308, 323
Brougham	367
Brown sugar	91
Brownsville	166, 240p., 275
Buckeye	309p.
Buckle's "History of Civilization,"	105
Buckle's History of Civilization	367
Buffalo	167
Bulwer	105
Burke	367
Burns	366
Busch	192, 407

Butter	86p., 89, 91, 97, 170, 275, 293, 310, 315
California	346
Cardinal	323, 400
Cardinal Gibbons	323
Carl Schurz	416
Carrots	91, 127
Carter	309, 311, 315, 326, 385
Carter, James	385
Catfish	23, 45, 164, 166
Catholic	70, 264, 391
Catspring	48, 59, 83, 120
Central High School	330
Chamber of Commerce	437
Chamber of Horrors	345
Champion	65, 77, 309
Charlie	307, 312, 314, 368
Cherries	92
Chicago	116, 275, 419p., 423, 425, 430, 437
Chicago Tribune	420, 425
Chicamaugua	425
Chickens	28p., 46, 52, 134, 149, 151, 312
Chief Justice Marshall	121
Childs	333
Choate, Joseph	406
Cholera	313p., 363
Chopin	427
Christ	264, 313, 323
Christmas	88, 157pp., 162, 256, 258, 263, 267, 305, 326, 397
Christmas Eve	88, 157pp., 162, 397
Cincinnati	297, 300
City Council	392, 431, 433
City Council of Berlin	392
Civil War	1, 4, 16p., 19, 33, 56, 60, 63, 67, 117, 130, 157, 175, 211, 229, 232, 245, 251, 335, 340, 374, 411, 415
Clara	88, 95p., 130, 162, 213, 235p., 305, 313, 374
Clergyman	70, 72, 106, 322, 357, 406, 413
Cleveland	247, 327
Clown	156
Colorado County	19, 60

Colorado County, Texas	19
Colorado river	47, 168
Columbus	60, 151, 237
Confederate	130, 175, 211, 240, 243, 251, 287, 293, 300, 303, 328, 361
Congress	247, 391, 393, 421, 425p.
Conkling	276p., 419pp., 424
Conscription	225p., 233
Constant	26, 49, 56, 74, 83, 96, 128, 221, 267, 322
Constant Creek	159
Constantinople	393
Constitution	38, 119, 347, 381, 427p., 432
Constitutional Amendments	427
Convention Hall	31, 275
Copperhead	27, 178
Cornbread	89, 220
Correggio	344
Cortinas	272
Cotton	19p., 58, 86, 88, 109, 124, 128p., 175, 178, 213, 237, 271, 273, 282
Cowboy	125, 140p.
Crown Prince Frederick Williama	394
Crown Princess Victoriab	394
Curran	367
D'Arcy	380, 405p., 408
Dante	366
Davidson	333, 365
Davidson, Thomas	365
Dead Man's Creek	55p.
Deborah	375
Deer	25, 83, 122, 171, 184, 187, 211, 364
Degener	245pp.
Deiler, J. Hanno	64
Denton J. Snider	333
Diaz	149
Dickens	105, 359, 366
Disraeli	66
Dittmar	51, 56, 66
Dogwood	49, 176

Doherty	163
Dom	264, 347, 350, 355
Don Quixote	306, 341, 414
Dr. Felix Adler	388
Dr. Hammond	431
Dr. Herz	250
Dresden	343p., 349p.
Drooping moss	49
Drought	43, 146, 249
Dryden	366
Ducks	20, 23, 48, 240
Duerer	345
Dühring	386p.
Durer	30
Dynamite	436
Eagle Pass	248
Education	33, 101, 109, 119, 130, 339pp., 345, 350, 361, 411, 437
Egmont	396
Ehrenbreitstein	347
Eickhoff	72
Eighteenth Amendment	113
Elephant	150, 155p.
Ella	301, 307, 311p.
Elly	32, 305
Emerson	262, 367
Emperor Maximilian	263
Engelking	4, 53, 109, 111, 205pp., 215
Episcopal	264, 322
Ethical movement	322
Eucken	118p., 323
Eucken, Prof Rudolph	118
Faust	396, 411
Federal army	341
Firearms	145, 278
Fischel	335, 340, 343, 352, 354, 363, 366, 375, 383pp.
Florida	290p.
Folterkammer	345
Forty-eighters	199

Fox	91, 96, 367
Franklin Avenue	299, 363, 367
Fred Wislizenus	403
Frederick the Great	392, 399p.
Freeman, Historian	364
Friedericka	235
Frithjofssage	102p.
Fundamentalism	86
Galveston	62pp., 84, 226
Gambrinus	297
Garfield	278, 419, 421p., 424p.
Garfieldc	276
Geese	20, 23, 48, 241, 273p.
General Bee	240
General Davis	275p.
General Moltke	393
General Price	328
General Thomas	425
George Eliot	390

German   8, 17, 30p., 45, 51, 57pp., 64pp., 79, 97, 101p., 104, 107, 111, 114, 118, 123, 130, 132, 136, 152p., 157p., 213, 226pp., 241, 243, 246, 250, 253, 268, 277, 282, 299, 302, 331, 333, 335, 337, 340, 342, 358, 367, 376, 380, 383, 390p., 393, 395, 405, 407, 411, 414, 416, 435, 438

German Empire	391
German school	376
Germania	411, 415
Germania Club	415
Gerstaecker	102, 188
Gladstone	406
Glaeser	299
Glover	368p., 371p., 374, 403
Glover & Shepley	368p., 403
Goethe	105, 343, 396
Goodrich	105, 117, 367
Goodrich's "British Eloquence."	105
Grant	275p., 309, 321, 370, 404, 416pp., 420p., 423, 425
Grattan	367
Great War	17, 117, 192, 226, 326, 337, 397, 438

Green Tree Hotela	298
Gretchen	375, 396, 411
Grimm	400
Gulf	19, 58, 62, 146, 151, 242, 289
Gulf of Mexico	19, 58, 242, 289
Hagemann	56p., 83, 177
Halberstadt	71, 264, 343, 349p., 355p.
Halle	37, 47, 55, 75, 77p., 83, 140, 175, 278
Halsey C. Ives	430
Hamlet	18, 375, 412
Hammond	431p.
Hans Sachs	345
Harz	71, 264, 343, 346, 350, 357
Hawthorne	366
Hayes	417p., 421p.
Hays, explorer	364
Hazlitt	366
Hazlitt's	367
Hecuba	368
Hegel	367, 384
Hegel's Philosophy of History	367
Heine	343, 366
Helene	32, 46, 88, 157
Henry Hitchcock	380, 406
Henry I. D'Arcy	380, 405
Herbert Spencera	429
Herder	104
Hermann	69, 79p., 87, 129p., 137pp., 144p., 159, 205, 235, 304, 314
Hermann Vahl	87, 129, 205
Hickory	31, 33, 40, 49, 61, 88pp., 92, 99, 134, 176, 287, 306
High School	101, 330p., 334, 339, 368
Hilboldt	56
Hildegard	103
Himly	51
Himmelsleiter	397
Holbein	344
Holmes' Common Law	431p.
Home Guards	329

Horace H. Morgan	333
Horse meat	384
Houston	34, 51, 59p., 62, 65, 83p., 90, 117p., 151, 206, 213, 226
Illinois	418p., 424
Indiana	418p.
Indianola	242
Indians	25, 55, 97p., 144, 170, 251, 255p., 333
Innes	149
Interlaken	345
Irish	75, 91, 127, 283, 302, 404p.
Jack rabbit	249
Jackson Street	299, 315pp.
James Carter	385
Janauschek	375
Jena	118
Jewish cemetery	354
Johann Strauss	352
John R. Shepley	369
John Stuart Mill	429
John William Burgess	388
Johnson, John G.	406
Joseph Lee	434
Joseph Medill	420
Jule	307, 310pp.
Jungfrau	345
Junker	66, 199pp.
Justice of the peace	54, 195, 302, 404p.
Kardinal	28, 172
Karl Georg Bruns	389
Kent's Commentaries	431
Keppler	414
Kingfish	291
Kinkel	399
Kirby	408
Kleberg	54, 195p.
Kleist	104
Klopstock	104
Kloss	51

Kluever	58, 236p.
Koelner Dom	347
Koemer	104
Koenig	299, 304
Kornblume	127
Kriminalzeitung	101
Krueger	355
Kruse, Max	117
Kuehl	192
Kugler	400
Kugler's History of Art	400
Kummer	414
LaGrange	229
Langhammer	55, 237
Lark	77, 109, 147, 172, 176
Lasker	391, 393p.
Lasso	23, 98, 140pp., 144, 165, 218
Law School	119, 328, 334, 368, 379p., 390, 403, 405, 408, 431
Lee	246, 309, 321, 434
Lenbach	386
Lessing	104
Lincoln	31, 152, 326, 361, 367, 376
Lithography	101
Litzman, Louis	51, 66, 69p., 272
Litzmann	66, 305
Logan	419p., 424
Logand	276
Louisiana	434
Louisiana Purchase Exposition	434
Lowell	403
Lucca	398
Lucerne	345
Lutheran	70, 100, 102, 203, 264
Lynx	187, 208
M. Cooley	381
Macaulay	367
Maerker	199p.
Maetze, Ernst Gustav	52p., 109, 115, 157, 206p., 247
Maeusethurm	347

Maine	418p., 431
Mark Brandenburg	69
Masquerade balls	412
Massachusetts	418
Matamoras	251, 268, 271p., 279p., 283
Matterhorn	345
Max Kruse	117
Mayor	431, 433pp.
Measles	302
Medical Jurisprudence	388, 432
Medical School	363, 375, 432
Meissner	221p., 225, 234, 237, 242
Mephistopheles	411
Mexican	35, 121, 138, 142p., 177, 219, 227, 250, 254p., 263, 269p.
Mexicans	97p., 143p., 243, 251, 256, 262, 280p.
Mexico	19, 33, 58, 60, 63, 65, 153, 186, 234, 237, 242, 244pp., 256, 268, 271p., 274, 280, 289, 293, 313, 319, 327, 333, 359, 361
Micawber	366
Michael Angelo	400
Mill Creek	56p., 128, 168, 195, 220
Millheim	7, 47, 51, 53, 81, 83p., 88, 96, 109, 304
Mississippi	298, 321, 432
Missouri	68, 96, 275, 309, 321, 327, 346, 415p., 418, 427, 436
Moccasin	27, 159, 167, 170
Molasses	91
Moliere's "Tartuffe."	335
Mommsen	386
Montague	211, 404
Monterey	250p., 257p., 261, 279
Morgan Street	334
Morrison	411
Mozart	427
Muenchen	345
Mules	90, 127, 149, 154, 248pp., 253pp.
Mullanphy Street	334
Murf	26, 35pp., 41, 45pp., 171
Mustang grape	92, 171

Myers	368p., 374, 400, 403, 405, 414
Nagel, Fanny (Brandeis)	103
Nagel, Hermann	69, 79
Nagel's Band	60
Nathaniel Myers	368, 400
National Convention	418, 422
National Recreation Association	434
Naturalization	37, 232
Neu Braunfels	64, 229
Neu Ulm	64, 229
Neue Museum	399
New England	70, 85
New Orleans	62, 84, 89
New Ulm	53
New York	63, 101, 151, 153, 192, 290, 293, 296p., 300, 313p., 359, 385, 411, 414, 418p., 421
Newcomes	366
Niemann	398
North Carolina	64
North German Lloyd steamer "Ohio"	383
Norther	84, 107, 143, 146p., 238, 270
Nuernberg	345
Oak	19, 31, 42, 49, 51, 60, 92, 109, 134, 142, 153, 171
Ohio	297, 309, 383, 418
Olive Street	301, 322
Opossum	26, 92, 176p.
Orden	102
Oscar Wilde	414
Panther	24, 170
Parepa	375
Parepa and Parepa Rose	375
Paul	32p., 46, 63p., 85, 95p., 130, 136, 173, 180, 182, 186, 235p., 243p., 248, 304p., 313, 355
Paul Krueger	355
Peaches	92, 108, 127, 303
Pecan	49, 89, 213
Pendennis	366
Pennsylvania	64
Phil	303pp., 309pp., 315, 323, 326, 329pp.

Philadelphia	306
Pickwick Papers	366
Piedras Negras	250
Piedras Negrasa	248
Piloty	345
Pinne	75
Pitt	367
Plattdeutsch	57
Plums	92
Police	68, 77p., 324, 364, 404, 433p.
Policeman	68, 324, 364
Pope	366, 400
Pork	91
Potato	43, 75, 91, 127, 165p.
Prader	352
Prairie chicken	27, 146
Prayer	164p., 259
Presbyterian	322
President Taft	432
Pritzwalk	69pp., 356
Prof. Wagner	386
Prussia	69, 79, 95, 115, 351
Public Library	335, 363p.
Pulitzer, Joseph	411p., 416
Punishment	75, 112, 114, 148, 164
Puritan	107
Quinine	38, 247
Rabbis	354
Rabbit	19, 26, 30, 52, 172pp., 179p., 236, 249
Radishes	47, 91, 127
Railroad	71, 151, 297p., 300, 310, 415
Raphael	344
Rattlesnake	27
Rauch	392, 399
Razorback hogs	19
Reichardt	51, 66, 236
Reichart	84
Religious	63, 105, 118, 203, 257, 264, 313, 323, 330, 350, 354
Republican	275, 327p., 369, 378, 416p., 421, 423, 426, 433, 435

Republican Conventionb	275
Republicans	327, 415p., 436
Reuter, Fritz	57, 70
Rhine	56, 346
Rhine wine	56
Richelieu	375
Rieckchen	235, 314
Rigi	345
Rio Grande	151, 166, 240, 249pp., 273, 278, 280
Ristori	375
Robert	173pp.
Roman Law	389
Romantic Period	104, 343
Romeo and Juliet	404, 411
Roosevelt	436
Rosenfeld	204
Rossa	137, 139p., 142p., 218p., 223, 236, 245
Rostock	51, 162
Rothe Schloss	384
Rousseau	150
Rowing club	363
Rozier	204
Rubens	345
Rudolph Gneist	390
Rueckert	104
Russian	358p., 400
Saddle Mountain	261
Saint Bernardo	19p., 35, 43p., 48, 68, 83, 85, 109
Sam Houston	34, 59p., 226
San Antonio	205, 226, 233, 242pp., 248, 359
San Antonio River	245
San Felipe	60, 83, 154, 157, 218pp.
Sancho	414
Sans Souci	399
Santa Anna	65
Satan	400
Schaefer	333
Schiller	102p.
Schlegel	102, 104

Schleiermacher	70, 104
Schlueter	399
Schmidt	282p., 287
Schneider	56p.
School	7, 29, 37, 45p., 53, 60, 73, 75pp., 89, 95, 99, 101, 104, 106, 109pp., 119pp., 123, 125, 130, 133pp., 138, 143, 154, 157, 161p., 164, 173, 184pp., 192, 215, 229, 234pp., 243, 245, 299, 301p., 304, 307p., 319pp., 328, 330pp., 339p., 343p., 355p., 363p., 367p., 375p., 379p., 387, 390, 403, 405, 408, 415, 425, 430pp.
School board	415
School-house	111
Schopenhauer	120, 355p.
Schulenburg	64
Schumann	427
Scott	222, 366
Sealfield	227
Sealsfield, Charles	66
Seebach	375, 396
Senator Hoar	276, 418
Senators Halea and Fryb of Maine	419
Shakespeare	102, 357, 365p., 396
Shepley	368pp., 372, 374p., 403
Sheriff	436
Shreyer	21
Singing society	192, 376
Sittlichkeit	203
Smoke house	89
Snakes	23, 27, 36, 47, 56, 159, 168, 176pp., 182, 185
Soder	49, 59, 237, 239
Sorolla	187, 396, 431
Sorrel	136, 140
South Germany	57
Southampton	358
Southern Hotel	403
Southern sympathizer	326
Spanish oak	49, 60, 171
Spremberg	73
Squirrel	19, 26, 171

St Louis	248
St. Antonio	304
St. Bernardo	243
St. Louis	63, 116, 130, 152p., 192, 205, 247, 293, 297p., 300, 313, 321, 328, 359, 367p., 403p., 414, 417p., 430
Stars and Stripes	211, 321, 326, 335
State Supreme Court	428p.
Store	16, 49, 53, 56, 59, 76, 85, 99p., 110p., 137p., 157, 164, 179, 191, 193p., 196p., 206, 215, 220, 222, 237, 243, 250, 256, 263, 299, 363, 367, 370, 428
Storekeeper	164
Strawberries	91
Struwwelpeter	153
Sugar cane	216
Sugar corn	36, 40, 91p.
Swanson	246
Swearengen	58p., 117, 123, 125, 207, 211p., 236, 300
Sweet peas	91p.
Sweet potato	91, 127
Switzerland	66, 345p.
Sword fish	290
Symphony Orchestra	376
Synagogue	323, 355
Taft	432, 436p.
Tegner	102
Ten Commandments	106
Ten pin alley	191
Thackeray	105, 366
Thayer, Ellen	103
The Deluge	400
The Federalist	367
The Messenger of Marathon	117
The system	74pp., 78, 197, 385
Theodore Roosevelt	436
Thirty Year War	103
Tieck	104
Titian	344
Tobacco	92, 349, 435
Topsy	413

Trenckmann	54
Trollope	366
Turner	149
Turnips	91, 127
Ulrich	173
Uncle Carl	343, 350, 352
Uncle Wilhelm	73, 340
Unconstitutional	428
Union army	233, 279, 321
Unitarian	322, 406
University of Berlin	22, 76, 79, 198p., 299, 334
Unter den Linden	199, 392
Urban	243p., 247p., 250, 268, 359
Vanity Fair	366
Veal	74, 91
Venison	91, 281
Virchow	385, 392
Von Roeder	53, 66
Wagner	295, 386, 397pp.
Walnut Street	298
Washington	58, 247, 300, 323, 364, 367, 430p.
Washington Cathedral	323
Washington E. Fischel	340
Washington University	364, 430p.
Washington University Art School	430
Watermelon	92p., 99, 134, 168, 170
Westminster Abbey	323
Wien	352, 354
Wild turkey	19, 23, 27, 147, 171, 183p., 186
William T. Harris	344
Willoughby	104
Wislizenus	403
World War	79, 117, 211
World's Fair in Chicago	116
Wurzburg	78, 198
Zachary Taylor	262
Zeughaus	399
Zorn	187, 430
Zukunftsmusik	295, 398

Picture References

Fig. 1: Charles Nagel

Taken from collection.

Fig. 2: Razor Back Hog (Feral Pig)

CSIRO (https://commons.wikimedia.org/wiki/File:CSIRO_ScienceImage_1515_Feral_pig.jpg), „CSIRO ScienceImage 1515 Feral pig", https://creativecommons.org/licenses/by/3.0/legalcode

Fig. 3: Wild Turkey(Meleagris gallopavo)

By Riki7 - Own work, Public Domain, https://commons.wikimedia.org/w/index.php?curid=6957499

Fig. 4: Male Pantanal Jaguar

Charlesjsharp (https://commons.wikimedia.org/wiki/File:Jaguar_(Panthera_onca_palustris)_male_Rio_Negro_2.JPG), https://creativecommons.org/licenses/by-sa/4.0/legalcode

Fig. 5: Florida Water Moccasin Agkistrodon piscivorus conanti

By Ltshears - Own work, CC BY-SA 3.0, https://commons.wikimedia.org/w/index.php?curid=6675843

Fig. 6: Western diamondback rattlesnake (Crotalus atrox)

Clinton & Charles Robertson from Del Rio, Texas & San Marcos, TX, USA (https://commons.wikimedia.org/wiki/File:Crotalus_atrox_(2).jpg), „Crotalus atrox (2)", https://creativecommons.org/licenses/by/2.0/legalcode

Fig. 7: Young Hare" (German: Feldhase) Albrecht Dürer 1502

By Albrecht Dürer - NgGmZAZW17zfhw at Google Cultural Institute maximum zoom level, Public Domain, https://commons.wikimedia.org/w/index.php?curid=21792126

Fig. 8: Sam Houston, circa 1850

By unidentified - George Eastman House, Public Domain, https://commons.wikimedia.org/w/index.php?curid=40885474

Fig. 9: American Alligator (A. mississippiensis)

By Me - Own work, Public Domain, https://commons.wikimedia.org/w/index.php?curid=6575846

Fig. 10: Pink variety flower clusters on a Dogwood Tree

By Famartin - Own work, CC BY-SA 3.0, https://commons.wikimedia.org/w/index.php?curid=28041080.

Fig. 11: The Nagel House Today

Photo by courtesy of Jamie Elick.

Fig. 12: Unter den Linden, around 1900

Von Unbekannt - Original image: Photochrom print (color photo lithograph) Reproduction number: LC-DIG-ppmsca-00344 from Library of Congress, Prints and Photographs Division, Photochrom Prints CollectionDieses Bild ist unter der digitalen ID ppmsca.00344 in der Abteilung für Drucke und Fotografien der US-amerikanischen Library of Congress abrufbar. Reproduction by Photoglob AG, Zürich, Switzerland or Detroit Publishing Company, Detroit, Michigan, Gemeinfrei, https://commons.wikimedia.org/w/index.php?curid=442840

Fig. 13: Berlin University in 1850

By A. Carse - Berlin und seine Kunstschätze, Payne Leipzig und Dresden, ca. 1850, Public Domain, https://commons.wikimedia.org/w/index.php?curid=501528

Fig. 14: Robert Gould Shaw Memorial, Boston

By Carptrash at the English language Wikipedia, CC BY-SA 3.0, https://commons.wikimedia.org/w/index.php?curid=27154774.

Fig. 15: Charles Sealsfield 1864

By Unknown - Gero von Wilpert: Deutsche Literatur in Bildern. Alfred Kröner, Stuttgart 1957, S. 255., Public Domain, https://commons.wikimedia.org/w/index.php?curid=4804130.

Fig. 16: Cerro de la Silla (Saddle Mountain) near Monterey today

By Nathaniel C. Sheetz, CC BY-SA 3.0, https://commons.wikimedia.org/w/index.php?curid=83960.

Fig. 17: Emperor Maximiliano around 1864

By François Aubert (Lyon, 1829 - Condrieu, 1906) - http://www.metmuseum.org/collections/search-the-collections/190039124#fullscreen, Public Domain, https://commons.wikimedia.org/w/index.php?curid=12765560

Fig. 18: Zachary Taylor

Zachary_Taylor_half_plate_daguerreotype_c1843-45.png: unknown, possibly Maguire of New Orleansderivative work: Beao - Zachary_Taylor_half_plate_daguerreotype_c1843-45.png, Public Domain, https://commons.wikimedia.org/w/index.php?curid=15194058.

Fig. 19: Edmund J. Davis (1827-1883)

By Unknown - crop of Image courtesy of the Texas State Library and Archives Commission, Public Domain, https://commons.wikimedia.org/w/index.php?curid=1348999.

Fig. 20: Ulysses S. Grant

By Brady-Handy Photograph Collection (Library of Congress) - This image is available from the United States Library of Congress's Prints and Photographs division under the digital ID cwpbh.03890. Public Domain, https://commons.wikimedia.org/w/index.php?curid=33527

Fig. 21: The Blücher Memorial in Berlin, Unter den Linden

By James Steakley - Own work, CC BY-SA 3.0, https://commons.wikimedia.org/w/index.php?curid=22818877

Fig. 22: Swordfish (Xiphias gladius)

By Werner - Histoire naturelle des poissons, Public Domain, https://commons.wikimedia.org/w/index.php?curid=15306191.

Fig. 23: Menticirrhus americanus (Kingfish)

By Cláudio D. Timm - http://www.flickr.com/photos/32674493@N04/3148513145/in/set-72157610328039849/, CC BY 2.0, https://commons.wikimedia.org/w/index.php?curid=6022304.

Fig. 24: A statue of Gambrinus with a goat at the Falstaff brewery in New Orleans

By FalstaffBreweryNOLAStatueHowieluvzus.jpg: Flickr photographer Howie Luvzusderivative work: Skitof (talk) - FalstaffBreweryNOLAStatueHowieluvzus.jpg, CC BY 2.0, https://commons.wikimedia.org/w/index.php?curid=6700874.

Fig. 25: Tartuffe

Public Domain, https://commons.wikimedia.org/w/index.php?curid=349642.

Fig. 26: Bayard Taylor

Public Domain, https://commons.wikimedia.org/w/index.php?curid=1714867.

Fig. 27: Unfinished cathedral, 1856 with 15th-century crane on south tower.

By Johann Franz Michiels - Uta Grefe: Köln in frühen Photographien 1847-1914, Schirmer/Mosel Verlag, München, 1988, ISBN 3-88814-294-6Scan by Raimond Spekking, Public Domain, https://commons.wikimedia.org/w/index.php?curid=2237940.

Fig. 28: Photograph of Johann Strauss II by Fritz Luckhardt

y Fritz Luckhardt (1843-1894) - PhotographerAdam Cuerden - Restoration - This image is available from Gallica Digital Library under the digital ID btv1b8453822q, Public Domain, https://commons.wikimedia.org/w/index.php?

curid=46539095.

Fig. 29: Thousands of gravestones are crammed into the Old Jewish Cemetery in Prague.

By Postdlf from w, CC BY-SA 3.0, https://commons.wikimedia.org/w/index.php?curid=10983863.

Fig. 30: The Old New Synagogue in Prague

By Øyvind Holmstad - Own work, CC BY-SA 3.0, https://commons.wikimedia.org/w/index.php?curid=33016366.

Fig. 31: Gardekürassier etwa 1830

Von Heinrich Ambros Eckert - Kunstbibliothek Berlin, Gemeinfrei, https://commons.wikimedia.org/w/index.php?curid=3715581.

Fig. 32: Polish uhlans from the Army of the Duchy of Warsaw 1807–1815 January Suchodolski painting

By January Suchodolski , Public Domain, https://commons.wikimedia.org/w/index.php?curid=1309240.

Fig. 33: Isaac I. Hayes portrait by Mathew B. Brady, circa 1860-1875

By Mathew B. Brady - http://hdl.loc.gov/loc.pnp/cwpbh.00491, Public Domain, https://commons.wikimedia.org/w/index.php?curid=4251487.

Fig. 34: Euphrosyne Parepa-Rosa

By Unknown - NYPL Digital Gallery (Muller Collection), http://digitalgallery.nypl.org/nypldigital/id?1541175, Public Domain, https://commons.wikimedia.org/w/index.php?curid=58389849.

Fig. 35: Ben DeBar as Falstaff

By J.H. Fitzgibbon - Missouri History Museum (http://collections.mohistory.org/resource/147947.html), CC0, https://commons.wikimedia.org/w/index.php?curid=50277665.

Fig. 36: Henry Hitchcock

By Unknown - Bar Association of St. Louis, Memorial. Henry Hitchcock, 1829-1902, 1902, frontispiece, Public Domain, https://commons.wikimedia.org/w/index.php?curid=7879507.

Fig. 37: Thomas McIntyre Cooley

Public Domain, https://commons.wikimedia.org/w/index.php?curid=4817595.

Fig. 38: Rudolf Virchow

By James S. King - George Alfred Miller (1909) "James Coolidge Carter. 1827-1905." in W. D. Lewis, ed. Great American Lawyers, VIII, between pages 2 and 3., Public Domain, https://commons.wikimedia.org/w/index.php?curid=25011179.

Fig. 39: Franz von Lenbach Self-portrait (1903)

By Unknown - http://ihm.nlm.nih.gov/images/B25666, Public Domain, https://commons.wikimedia.org/w/index.php?curid=19353800.

Fig. 40: Adolph Wagner

By Unknown (Loescher & Petsch) - http://www.gettyimages.co.uk/detail/news-photo/wagner-adolph-economist-finance-scientist-germany25-03-news-photo/545336503, Public Domain, https://commons.wikimedia.org/w/index.php?curid=44053216.

Fig. 41: James Coolidge Carter

By Onbekende schilder - op [1], Public Domain, https://commons.wikimedia.org/w/index.php?curid=3796811.

Fig. 42: Frederick III, German Emperor

By John Phillip - http://www.royalcollection.org.uk/collection/406819/the-marriage-of-victoria-princess-royal-25-january-1858, Public Domain, https://commons.wikimedia.org/w/index.php?

curid=32200437.

Fig. 43: The Marriage of Victoria, Princess Royal and Prince Frederick William of Prussia, 25 January 1858, by John Phillip.

By Napoleon Sarony - Metropolitan Museum of Art, Public Domain, https://commons.wikimedia.org/w/index.php?curid=30638597.

Fig. 44: Albert Niemann

By Fritz Luckhardt - Dieses Bild der ist Teil der Porträtsammlung Friedrich Nicolas Manskopf der Universitätsbibliothek der Johann Wolfgang Goethe-Universität Frankfurt am Main. Signatur: 5467374. Public Domain, https://commons.wikimedia.org/w/index.php?curid=2993499

Fig. 45: Oscar Wilde - Photograph taken in 1882 by Napoleon Sarony

By Ehrhart, S. D. (Samuel D.), ca. 1862-ca. 1920, artist. (from Dalrymple, Louis, 1866-1905, artist.) - This image is available from the United States Library of Congress's Prints and Photographs division under the digital ID cph.3g06550. Public Domain, https://commons.wikimedia.org/w/index.php?curid=5625656

Fig. 46: Self portrait by Keppler

By Joseph Ferdinand Keppler - Keppler, Joseph (1893) A Selection of Cartoons from Puck, New York: Keppler & Schwarzmann, Public Domain, https://commons.wikimedia.org/w/index.php?curid=5659765.

Fig. 47: Carl Schurz is Don Quixote in this cartoon by Thomas Nast from Harper's Weekly of April 6, 1872

By Thomas Nast - Harper's Weekly, April 6, 1872, p. 272; Boston Public Library, Public Domain, https://commons.wikimedia.org/w/index.php?curid=5152802.

Fig. 48: Rutherford B. Hayes

By Brady-Handy Photograph Collection (Library of Congress) - This image is available from the United States Library of Congress's Prints and Photographs division under the digital ID cwpbh.04352. Public Domain, https://commons.wikimedia.org/w/index.php?curid=12643087

Fig. 49: Columbia wearing a warship bearing the words "World Power" as her "Easter bonnet", cover of Puck (April 6, 1901)

By Ehrhart, S. D. (Samuel D.), ca. 1862-ca. 1920, artist. (from Dalrymple, Louis, 1866-1905, artist.) - This image is available from the United States Library of Congress's Prints and Photographs division under the digital ID cph.3g06550. Public Domain, https://commons.wikimedia.org/w/index.php?curid=5625656

Fig. 50: The Chair of John Stuart Mill - currently in the editor's custody

By courtesy of the International Arbitration League

Fig. 51: Anders Zorn's Portrait of William Howard Taft

By Anders Zorn - White House Historical Association, Public Domain, https://commons.wikimedia.org/w/index.php?curid=1756350.

Further Reading

The Engelking Letters: A Collection of Letters Written by or Pertaining to Ferdinand Friedrich Engelking 1810-1885 by Flora von Roeder (translator) and Stephen Engelking (editor) ISBN: 978-1481059992.

These Are the Generations: A Biography of the von Roeder Family and its Role in Texas History (Volume 1) by Flora von Roeder ISBN: 978-1484096833.

These Are the Generations: A Biography of the von Roeder Family and its Role in Texas History (Volume 2) by Flora von Roeder ISBN: 978-1497599345.

The History of Austin County, Texas: Edited and published in 1899 as a supplement to the Bellville Wochenblatt by William Trenkmann (Author), Stephen A. Engelking MBA (Editor), William, Else, and Clara Trenkmann (Translator) ISBN: 978-1511991605.

Experiences and Observations: an autobiography of a German Texan newspaperman by William Andreas Trenckmann (Author), James Woodrick (Introduction) ISBN: 978-1514335758.

Journey to Texas, 1833 by Detlef Dunt (Author), James C. Kearney (Editor), Geir Bentzen (Editor), Anders Saustrup (Translator) ISBN:978-0292740211.

The Material Culture of German Texans by Kenneth Hafertepe (Author) ISBN: 978-1623493820.

Settlement in the Forks of Mill Creek: Settlement in the

Forks of Mill Creek by James V. Woodrick ISBN: 978-1469956558.

Austin County: Colonial Capital of Texas by James V. Woodrick ISBN: 978-1466476509.